M*A*S*K*

MASK is the codename for one of the most sensitive, long-term sources ever run by any British intelligence organisation. It concealed the existence of a radio interception programme operated by the Government Code and Cipher School (GC&CS) which succeeded in monitoring, and reading, large quantities of encrypted wireless traffic exchanged between the headquarters of the Comintern in Moscow, and numerous Comintern representatives abroad, in countries as far apart as China, Austria and the United States. The content of these secret messages were of immense use to the very limited group of people who had access to it, but of greatest interest to MI5 and Stanley Baldwin's Cabinet was the material passing to and from the Communist Party of Great Britain (CPGB), which was monitored from a covert intercept station located on Denmark Hill, south London. Its principal target was the daily wireless traffic of a clandestine transmitter based in Wimbledon and operated by a member of the CPGB's underground cell, controlled by a Scot, Bob Stewart.

MASK is the first detailed account of MI5's penetration of the CPGB and the Burgess, Maclean, Philby, Blunt and Cairncross network. It also reveals the role of a hitherto unknown spymaster, Bob Stewart, who controlled the Cambridge Five.

Nigel West is a military historian specialising in security and intelligence topics. He lectures at the Centre for Counterintelligence and Security Studies in Washington DC and is the European editor of the *World Intelligence Review*. In 1989 he was elected 'the Experts' Expert' by the *Observer* and in 2003 he was the recipient of the US Association of Former Intelligence Officers' Lifetime Literature Achievement Award.

MASK

MI5's Penetration of the Communist Party of Great Britain

Nigel West

Routledge
Taylor & Francis Group

LONDON AND NEW YORK

First published 2005
by Routledge
2 Park Square, Milton Park, Abingdon, Oxon OX14 4RN

Simultaneously published in the USA and Canada
by Routledge
711 Third Avenue, New York, NY 10017

Routledge is an imprint of the Taylor & Francis Group, an informa business

First issued in paperback 2012

© 2005 Westintel

Typeset in Bembo by BC Typesetting Ltd, Bristol

British Library Cataloguing in Publication Data
A catalogue record for this book is available from the British Library

Library of Congress Cataloging in Publication Data
A catalog record for this book has been requested

ISBN 978 0 4156 4992 6

One found it very difficult to believe in Moscow gold
or sinister subversive plots directed from abroad.
The Reverend Michael Scott in *A Time To Speak*

Every little act of a real Communist is a blow to
imperialism and the imperialist knows it; therefore,
if the Communist does not act secretly he must pass
his life in prison.
M.N. Roy, in the Assembly Letter, September 1928

CONTENTS

ACKNOWLEDGMENTS

My thanks are due to the many intelligence professionals who made this book possible. I owe particular gratitude to those who assisted my research, among them Hayden Peake, Dan Mulvenna, Gary Kern, Herbert Romerstein, and the staff of the National Archives at Kew.

ABBREVIATIONS

BN-FMRA	British Non-Ferrous Metals Research Association
CID	Committee of Imperial Defence
CPGB	Communist Party of Great Britain
CPI	Communist Party of Italy
CPUSA	Communist Party of the United States of America
CWR	Civilian Wireless Reserve
FBI	US Federal Bureau of Investigation
FCD	KGB First Chief Directorate
FPA	Federated Press of America
GC&CS	Government Code & Cipher School
GRU	Soviet Military Intelligence Service
INO	Foreign Intelligence Department of the OGPU
IPI	Indian Political Intelligence
KPD	Communist Party of Germany
KGB	Soviet Intelligence Service
MI5	British Security Service
MI6	British Secret Intelligence Service
NKVD	Soviet Intelligence Service
NUWM	National Unemployed Workers Movement
OGPU	Soviet Intelligence Service
PCF	French Communist Party
PNG	Persona non grata
RAE	Royal Aircraft Establishment, Farnborough
RCMP	Royal Canadian Mounted Police
SIS	British Secret Intelligence Service
SOE	Special Operations Executive
YCL	Young Communist League

GLOSSARY OF MASK TERMINOLOGY

CC   Central Committee
Cominform   Communist International
CP   Communist Party
ECCI   Executive Committee, Communist International
ECYCI   Executive Committee Young Communist International
ILP   Independent Labour Party
INO   Foreign Directorate of the NKVD
INPRECORR   *International Press Correspondent*
KIM   Kommunisti Internationale Molodoi
MOPR   International Labour Defence of the Communist
              International
OMS   International Liaison Department of the Comintern
PB   Politburo
PC   Political Commission
Profinform   Red Trade Unions International
RILU   Red International of Labour Unions
SD   Social Democrats
YCI   Young Communist International
YCL   Young Communist League

GLOSSARY OF MASK PERSONALITIES

ABRAHAM	Abramoff, alias of Jakob Mirov
ALEXANDER	A.E. Abramovich, Comintern Sercetariat, former secretary in the Soviet embassies in Tallinn and Vienna
ALLISON	George Allison, editor of the *Daily Worker*
ARNOT	Robin Page Arnot
BELL	Tom Bell
BERNAL	Professor J.D. Bernal
BOB	Bob Stewart
BRADLEY	Benjamin Bradley
BROCKWAY	Archibald Brockway MP
CACHIN	Marcel Cachin, leader of the PCF
COHEN	Sam Cohen
CRIPPS	Sir Stafford Cripps MP
DISRAELI	
DMITROV	Georgi Dmitrov
DUTT	Rajani Palme Dutt, Vice Chairman, CPGB
EDWARDS	Bob Edwards of the ILP's National Administrative Council
ERCOLI	Afredo Ercoli, alias of Palmiro Togliatti, General-Secretary of the CPI
FOX	Ralph Fox
FRED	Stephen Wheeton
GALLACHER	Willie Gallacher MP
GORDON	Rajani Palme Dutt
HARDY	George Hardy, Seaman's Union activist
HARDY's wife	Paddy Ayriss
HARRY	Harry Pollitt
HOLMES	Walter Holmes
HORNER	Arthur Horner, leader of South Wales miners
KENYATTA	Jomo Kenyatta
KERRIGAN	Peter Kerrigan, Scottish District Secretary
KREBS	Felix Wolf

KUN	Bela Kun, leader of Hungarian Communist Party
LANSBURY	George Lansbury MP
LOSOVSKY	Solomon Losovsky, Soviet Deputy Foreign Minister
MCILHONE	Robert McIlhone
MANN	Tom Mann, member of the Executive Committee of the Profintern
MANUILSKI	Dmitri Manuilsky, Soviet Central Committee member
MARKET	
MARTY	André Marty, Commander, International Brigades in Spain
MICHAEL	
MUNZENBURG	Willi Munzenburg
NEUMANN	Heinz Neumann of the KPD
NORMAN	
PIATIZSKY	Osip Piatnitsky
POLLIT	Harry Pollitt
ROBERTS	Jack 'Russia' Roberts
ROBINSON	Trevor Robinson, District Organiser in Manchester
ROBSON	Robert Robson, London District Organiser
ROY	Manandranath N. Roy
RUST	William Rust, editor of the *Daily Worker*
SHIELDS	Jimmie Shields
SPENCE	William Spence
THALMAN	Ernst Thaelmann, KPD leader
VARGAS	President Vargas of Brazil
WINCOTT	Len Wincott, Invergordon navy mutineer.

INTRODUCTION

MASK is the codename for one of the most sensitive, long-term sources ever run by any British intelligence organisation. It concealed the existence of a radio interception programme operated by the Government Code and Cipher School (GC&CS) which succeeded in monitoring, and reading, 14,000 messages of encrypted wireless traffic exchanged between the imposing headquarters of the Communist International in Moscow, at 36 Mokovaia Street, directly opposite the Kremlin, and numerous Comintern representatives abroad, in countries as far apart as China, Austria and the United States. The source was so secret that its existence was not revealed to the Americans until 1946 when copies of the traffic were given to Cecil Phillips of the US Signals Security Agency when he was posted to GCHQ's postwar headquarters at Eastcote.

The Third Communist International, so-called because the 'First', Karl Marx's International Working Men's Association, founded in London in 1864, had lasted only nine years, and the 'Second', created in Paris in 1889, had been the Labour International (but this had been condemned by Lenin as having sold out to social democrats), had come into being in March 1919 to promote the Bolshevik objective of world revolution. Initially headed by Grigori Zinoviev, until he was replaced in 1926 by Nikolai Bukharin, the Comintern was run from July 1935 by a Bulgarian Communist, Georgi Dmitrov, until its announced dissolution in the spring of 1943. Although intended to support, coordinate and direct individual national Communist movements, the Comintern actively engaged in espionage and its International Directorate communicated in codes to trusted members of the organisation across the globe. These agents, usually vetted by the leadership in their own countries, often had attended the Lenin School in Moscow for up to two years, taking overt classes in political ideology while also attending parallel courses in tradecraft and clandestine communications. Created in October 1926, with up to a thousand students in residence, the 'International Lenin University' acted as an espionage finishing academy for candidates drawn from mainly English-speaking countries (chiefly Britain, Ireland, India, Canada and the United States), mixed with smaller groups from Spain, France, Germany

1

and China. All returned to their countries of origin as indoctrinated organisers and propagandists, if not fully-fledged professional spies.

Although nowadays the KGB (previously the OGPU and NKVD) and the GRU (often referred to as the Fourth Department of the Red Army's General Staff) are well recognised as the major Soviet intelligence agencies, there was a third, far less well-known, which was concealed under the initials OMS, the Russian acronym for the Comintern's Foreign Liaison Department. This book concerns the operations of the OMS, its relationship with its two rivals, the overlap that occurred in their separate networks, and the enciphered communications that were exchanged between Moscow and its spy-rings in Britain. Because the OMS had full confidence in its cipher system, and never learned that its integrity had been compromised, the messages were quite informal, if not indiscreet, with only some of the correspondents taking the trouble to adopt covernames to conceal their true identities. Even when they did so, their security procedures were appallingly lax by modern standards, thereby allowing the cryptanalysts to exercise their arcane skills.

The contents of these secret messages were of immense use to the very limited group of people in London who gained covert access to it, but of greatest interest to MI5 and Stanley Baldwin's Cabinet was the material passing to and from the Communist Party of Great Britain (CPGB), which was monitored from an unmarked intercept station located in south London, and its principal target was the daily wireless traffic of a clandestine transmitter based in Wimbledon.

In historical terms, the traffic was of the greatest significance for two reasons. First, it proved that the Soviet government's pretence that the Comintern was an independent organisation outside of its control was nothing more than an artificial sham, and that it was really a covert instrument of the country's undeclared foreign policy. While that was no great surprise to those who had always assumed this to be the case, and only the very politically naïve had swallowed the lie, MASK provides the copper-bottomed proof. Second, it showed that the Comintern concealed the existence of a clandestine network that extended its activities beyond semi-legitimate political agitation and the dissemination of propaganda, into the field of espionage and the collection of military and political information that would be of use to an enemy. The extent to which ostensibly loyal Britons were willing to adhere to a foreign power, take direction from a potential adversary and conspire to undermine Parliamentary democracy struck to the heart of conventional understanding of the concepts and norms of loyalty to the Crown, if not to the actual government of the day. The issues raised were so alien to accepted political orthodoxy that the idea of treasonous contact with sworn enemies of the state was both novel and dangerous. While committed socialists were perfectly entitled to combine as the Communist Party, field candidates at elections and campaign for or against particular policies, the idea that a legitimate political party with a significant following in the electorate, while apparently engaging in

Westminster democracy and electing MPs to the Commons, could also plot to steal secrets and pass them abroad, seemed quite extraordinary. However, MASK was the daily proof that such a conspiracy existed, even if the authorities would have to wait more than sixty years before learning the true scale of the connivance.

Looking at such events through the prism of history can lead to a disproportionate concentration on a particular issue overlooking, for example, the social conditions of the day. At the time of the MASK traffic Britain was experiencing high unemployment and hunger marches, and witnessing the rise of fascism in Germany, Italy and Spain. Thousands of well-intentioned activists were drawn into the political maelstrom of the period, but only a few chose to throw in their lot with Stalin and participate in espionage. It is arguable that those who did take the treason path have achieved extraordinary, doubtless justified notoriety, but these pages are intended to demonstrate that the scale of the conspiracy was far wider, and much more complex, than has been appreciated hitherto by the scholars, historiographers and journalists who have attempted to delve into this most intriguing area of research. What motivated Britain's most infamous traitors to betray their country? Who recruited them, and how large was the conspiracy? What emerges is a gigantic, three-dimensional puzzle in which many of the key participants were connected to each other, and MASK is revealed as the secret ingredient which helped the counter-intelligence analysts to reconstruct the links, put together the missing pieces and develop a comprehensive picture of the events that were to shape much of the rest of the twentieth century, influence Anglo-Soviet relations and set the foundations of the Cold War. Whereas the public became all too familiar with the ideological struggle between east and west, the very existence of some of the agencies on the front line, such as the Government Code and Cipher School, was a closely-guarded secret, even among those who wielded political power.

GC&CS was one of the most secret branches of Whitehall, under the control of the Secret Intelligence Service (SIS), and for years had supplied the Prime Minister and a handful of Cabinet ministers with summaries of decrypted foreign communications. The cryptographers of the Naval Intelligence Division's famous Room 40 had scored numerous successes during the Great War, including solving the code used in the Zimmerman Telegram (the notorious German diplomatic message which had helped bring the United States into the conflict in 1917) and GC&CS, created in January 1919 in the old Marconi headquarters at Watergate House, Adelphi, had continued its pioneering work in the field of signals intelligence into the peace. The staff of twenty-five, supported by forty-six juniors, achieved undisclosed success in breaking numerous foreign military and diplomatic ciphers, and in particular was able to read significant amounts of Soviet messages.

This was achieved largely through the dedication of two émigré Russian cryptographers, Ernst and Felix Fetterlein, who exploited the fact that the

Bolsheviks had inherited many of the *ancien regime*'s ciphers, which Felix himself had helped devise. When these decrypts were circulated in Whitehall they caused consternation because they proved that Lenin's government was intent on fomenting subversion in the Middle East and undermining British power in India, and was funding political agitation in England, including a hefty subsidy to the *Daily Herald*. Lloyd George's Cabinet decided in August 1920 that the best way to put a stop to this intolerable and dangerous mischief was to publish the evidence, thereby influencing public opinion at home and embarrassing the Kremlin, without disclosing the actual source. However, the resulting news report in *The Times* was prefaced with the unambiguous statement that 'the following wireless messages have been intercepted by the British Government' which only served to confirm to the Soviets that the integrity of their codes had been compromised, thereby causing them to introduce an entirely new system, based on supposedly unbreakable book ciphers. Without physical possession of the chosen book, maybe a novel or an obscure travel guide, the messages would remain meaningless gibberish. While Moscow was confronted publicly about its plans to destabilise the Empire, the cryptanalysts at GC&CS soon found that the previously steady flow of solvable wireless traffic exchanged between the Trade Delegation in Chesham Place and Moscow had dried up entirely. Although work was to continue on this material for the next two decades, the only significant breakthrough occurred a dozen years later when a mysterious channel, subsequently codenamed MASK, was the subject of sustained attack.

The encrypted signals were exchanged from January 1934 between Stephen J. Wheeton, a veteran member of the Communist Party of Great Britain, and Moscow, and the resulting transcriptions were circulated by GC&CS on a very limited basis to the Security Service (MI5), the head of one SIS section, and senior members of the Cabinet. For more than two years, MASK represented a unique window into the most secret decisions and deliberations of the CPGB, and eloquently demonstrated that, far from being independent, the Party was nothing more than a very pliant instrument of the Communist International, directed by the Kremlin, and that the CPGB's long-serving General-Secretary, Harry Pollitt, received his instructions direct from Moscow. According to MASK, Pollitt sought Moscow's guidance on virtually all policy issues, and even the most trivial aspects of administering the Party. In a more sinister vein, the CPGB acted as a recruitment centre for trainees to undergo indoctrination and espionage courses at the Lenin and Wilson Schools, and vetted candidates nominated by the shadowy Soviet contacts who disguised their identities behind codenames.

GC&CS's monitoring station at Grove Park, Camberwell, headed by Commander Kenworthy, first began intercepting Wheeton's signals in February 1934, and he continued to transmit until April 1935 when he fell ill with tuberculosis, and was replaced by another veteran Communist, William Morrison. The cipher used, and revealed by an MI5 mole, was studied by a veteran code-breaker, Leslie Lambert, and together with a seasoned colleague, Brigadier John Tiltman, he succeeded in reading the traffic until January 1937. Through the use of direction-finding equipment located at the army intercept station at Fort Bridgewoods, outside Chatham, at the Air Ministry W/T Section at Waddington, headed by Wing-Commander Lywood, and the Royal Navy's receiver at Flowerdown, near Winchester, GC&CS's technicians were able to show that Moscow was also communicating with a Comintern station in Vienna using the call-sign 3PD, and others in Shanghai, Paris, Athens, 3OS and 9RP in Prague, Spain, Basle, Zurich, Copenhagen and the United States. Altogether 938 messages from Moscow were read, and 633 from London, making a total of 1,571 decrypts altogether. The length of the individual messages varied from a couple of lines to several paragraphs, but they revealed the scale of the subsidies paid by the Kremlin to the CPGB and to the *Daily Worker*, disclosed the tradecraft employed by the Party's secret cadres and also identified by name clandestine couriers, and the Comintern's secret policies concerning the 1936 general election and the civil war in Spain.

MASK was but one vital component of MI5's scrutiny of the CPGB, and everyone connected with the channel was placed under surveillance. Once the address from which the illicit transmitter had been operating, 401 Durnsford Road, had been ascertained, the sole occupier was watched, and his identity established as Stephen Wheeton. MI5's B3 watchers, led by Harry Hunter, noted that he regularly met Alice Holland, another CPGB member who was also placed under surveillance. Neither realised that their mail and telephones were being intercepted, nor that they were followed wherever they went. Anyone they met was also watched, and over a period of months MI5 was able to build a comprehensive picture of the CPGB's underground network, an apparatus that existed *sub rosa* and in parallel to the overt Party, but one that also used the Party's headquarters at 16 King Street, Covent Garden. The evidence suggested that while not all the CPGB's leadership were aware of the covert *apparat*, some most certainly were, and if they did not actually participate in the underground network, they acquiesced whenever their co-operation was required. MI5's task was to infiltrate the clandestine organisation, identify its membership, monitor its activities and assess the degree to which it was engaged in sedition or espionage. The undertaking was one of enormous sensitivity because several senior members of the Labour Party were implicated, among them the Members of Parliament John Strachey, Archibald Brockway, Wilfred Vernon and Denis Pritt QC. In addition, two CPGB national organisers, Percy Glading and Douglas Springhall, would be imprisoned for running spy-rings that were successfully penetrated by MI5 informants, and a third, Bob Stewart, would be identified as the Party's spymaster. The picture that was to emerge of the CPGB was not of a bona fide political party in the Westminster tradition of Parliamentary opposition, but rather a gigantic, foreign-directed conspiracy engaged in espionage on a massive scale. Nor was this some insignificant minority group with ludicrous political ambitions. The Party counted on the overt support of manual labourers, skilled workers, intellectuals, academics, journalists and people of influence, as well as on a cadre of fellow-travellers and hardened crypto-Communists who belonged to undeclared underground cells, with an unknown number of non-card-carrying members in regular touch with Soviet intelligence professionals. Furthermore, these networks succeeded in penetrating Special Branch, MI5, GC&CS and the Secret Intelligence Service. Although some of these moles are now well-known, such as Anthony Blunt and Kim Philby, there were others, including Ray Milne in SIS and Celia Luke in MI5, whose identities have not been exposed previously.

When Stephen Wheeton handed on the task of communicating with Moscow to William Morrison, working from his home at 215 Earlsfield Road, London SW18, his activities were also monitored. Indeed, his MI5 personal file reveals his entire extraordinary story, and discloses that after the war he supplied the Security Service with some very valuable intelligence. It confirms that Morrison also had transmitted from a site at Hersham, near Walton-on-Thames in Surrey, and then from Buckhurst Hill in Essex where Sally Friedman, one of his former pupils at the Lenin School, had run the station.

Morrison had never read any of the traffic, which had been handed to him encrypted in five-figure groups by Alice Holland, but his story, as recounted to MI5's Max Knight at the end of August 1939, was remarkable. Something of an adventurer, Morrison explained to his interrogator that he had joined the Royal Navy at the age of sixteen at Chatham and had been trained as a tele-graphist, but had deserted from the light cruiser HMS *Constance* in Mobile, Alabama in 1926, having been under somewhat of a cloud after he had been disciplined for drunkenness. Thereafter he had become involved in smuggling bootleg Canadian whiskey into California but had been arrested and deported in early 1928. After a further spell as a seaman on a Swedish ship, the SS *Heron*, in Hong Kong and Australia, he had returned to Edinburgh but, having failed to find any work, in 1931 had settled in North Shields and had been recruited into the CPGB by a well-known activist, William Spence, and then persuaded by Alec Robson to participate in the Seaman's Minority Movement. As secretary of the Party's local branch in Tyneside he was also introduced to George Aitken and took over responsibility for the Party's anti-militarist campaign in the north of England. It was in that role that he had distributed seditious litera-ture at Catterick Camp, an act that had resulted in the prosecution of a soldier there who had been found in possession of it.

Early in 1932 Morrison had been invited to London where he was inter-viewed by a senior CPGB figure, Bob Stewart, who was in charge of the Party's clandestine activities and invited him to undertake a secret mission to Moscow. A Scot from Dundee who had been imprisoned during the First World War and ran the Socialist Prohibition Fellowship, Stewart instructed Morrison to travel to Berlin where he was to go to a back-street tobacconist who would exchange his own passport for one identifying him as an Australian named

Ernest Bell. Morrison then went on to Moscow where, for the next three years, he had worked under the alias 'Walter Campbell' as a radio instructor at two special schools, one in the suburb of Metischev, and the other, located at Podlipki and known as the Wilson School, which had opened in 1926. Altogether, while in Moscow, he trained more than fifty British and American operators, and later identified several of them by their true names to MI5. Even though all had worked under Party aliases as a security precaution, many of the volunteers had been accommodated together at the Hotel Lux and had found it hard to conceal their true names and backgrounds. MI5 was later to estimate that between 1927 and 1933 the CPGB had sent 167 operators to Moscow for training.

Upon William Morrison's return to England via Stockholm in May 1935 he had taken over the Wimbledon transmitter from Wheeton, who then had travelled to the Soviet Union for treatment for his chronic tuberculosis, an illness he subsequently died of. Meanwhile, Morrison married Mia Exell, a Lyons waitress who lived in Earlsfield, and continued to work as the CPGB's principal operator, using *Treasure Island* as a codebook, until October 1937 when he was asked to join the XVth International Brigade fighting in the Spanish Civil War, and the MASK traffic appeared to come to an end.

Under instructions, and accompanied by five other volunteers, Morrison went to Paris and then made his way to Figuras where he was assigned to Teruel as a wireless operator. After just six months in Spain Morrison deserted from the 2nd British Battalion and returned to Gravesend on 23 April 1938 where he was interviewed by an inquisitive Metropolitan Police Special Branch detective, Sergeant J. Blomfield, who passed his brief report on to MI5. Under Blomfield's questioning Morrison had admitted that, disenchanted with the disorganisation, muddle and petty jealousies, he had deserted on the Aragon-Belchite front and had made for Barcelona where he had stowed away aboard the *Canford Chine*, a British freighter bound for Algiers and Rotterdam. There he had joined the *Batavier 111* and had completed his voyage to England.

It was at this point that Morrison had abandoned the CPGB, although his wife had continued to draw her separation allowance, the grant given to the Party's volunteers in Spain, and he had found a job as a radio tester at Peto-Scott Limited, a firm manufacturing equipment for the Air Ministry. He had also enrolled in the Civilian Wireless Reserve. Both developments were recorded in his MI5 file, and had brought him to the attention of Max Knight, MI5's legendary case officer. Highly eccentric, and later the presenter of natural history programmes for children on BBC radio, Knight believed in investing long-term in sources, waiting patiently for one to worm their way, perhaps over many years, into a position of access. His technique was to recruit youngsters and encourage them to join certain target organisations, guiding them through the ranks to positions where they could supply useful information. While this strategy sometimes took a long time to develop, and start paying dividends, Knight believed that infiltration was more effective than external observation, the more conventional, orthodox approach to counter-espionage. By February 1934, when MASK first came on stream, MI5 had accumulated very little knowledge of Soviet espionage in Britain, and had experience of only a single case, dating back to 1927 when a CPGB member, Wilfred Macartney, had been imprisoned for passing classified information to his Soviet contact, a twenty-four-year-old German student who used the alias Georg Hansen. MI5 had been tipped off to Macartney's activities by a member of the Lloyd's insurance market, George Monckland, who had reported his interest in consignments of weapons shipped to Finland. Under MI5's guidance, Monckland had helped Macartney, and when he had expressed an interest in the RAF, Monckland had procured for him an obsolete training manual. This had been seen to be passed by Macartney to a member of the Soviet Trade Delegation in Moorgate, and had been used as the pretext for a huge police raid on the building in May 1927. The subsequent search, conducted over three days by Scotland Yard detectives, failed to recover the RAF document, but did reveal a wealth of other material which the government published in a White Paper. Macartney was arrested at a Marble Arch café five months later, in November 1927, when he met Georg Hansen who claimed to be a journalist attending a language school. It was not until the defector Walter Krivitsky was debriefed in February 1940 that MI5 received confirmation that Hansen had been an important Soviet spy who, as well as collecting information from Macartney, had been on a mission for the Soviet Red Army's military intelligence branch, to see how Krivitsky's subordinate, Max Unschlicht, could be established in London. While Macartney admitted to having been a member of the CPGB's Paddington branch, there was no evidence to suggest the Party had any other involvement, or that the Soviets had been directly linked to its King Street headquarters. When MASK became available, this evidence was to emerge in abundance. Apparently impressed and dismayed by the speed with which the British authorities had caught Georg Hansen, the Soviets had decided to adopt a more sophisticated strategy, one that would take many years of study by counter-intelligence experts and historians to understand and unravel.

1

THE RED MENACE

MI5's understanding of Soviet espionage in Britain following the Bolshevik revolution in Russia was surprisingly limited and, according to MI5's own internal history, it had suspicions, but no proof, that between 1921 and 1929 there was a secret organisation in London headed by Jakob Kirchenstein,[1] an American passport-holder of Lettish background who was a regular visitor at the offices of the Russian Trade Delegation. Surveillance on Kirchenstein had linked him to a pair of cipher clerks who worked in the building, and to various left-wing figures in the trade union movement. Certainly the Trade Delegation had been of interest to MI5 for years, and suspicions had been aroused at a very early stage when Nicolas Klishco had arrived as a senior official in 1920. Previously, he had landed in England as a Bolshevik refugee in 1907 and had been employed as a technical translator for Vickers, but he had been deported in 1918 as an undesirable. His brief reappearance in London, had made him a target for MI5 surveillance although no conclusive evidence was found to link him to espionage before he returned to Moscow in 1923, ostensibly to join the Foreign Trade Secretariat.

Concern about the CPGB's covert activities culminated in October 1925 in a massive, simultaneous police raid on King Street, and the headquarters of the Young Communist League and National Minority Movement at 38 Great Ormond Street. Thousands of letters, books, files and pamphlets were removed, and the CPGB's Executive Committee and two other members, making a total of twelve, were tried at the Old Bailey the following month. All were convicted of offences under the 1797 Incitement to Mutiny Act and imprisoned, but only because they refused to be bound over. Albert Inkpen (the CPGB secretary), Harry Pollitt, Willie Gallacher (later the Communist MP for West Fife), Wal Hannington and William Rust (YCL Secretary), who all had previous convictions, received twelve months, while Arthur MacManus, Tom Bell, Jack Murphy (a delegate to the 1924 Congress in Moscow), Johnny Campbell (editor of *Workers' Weekly*), Robin Page Arnot (the director of Labour Research), Tom Wintringham (the founder of the *Left Review*) and Ernest Cant (the London Organiser) received six months. Although the raid had given Special Branch the opportunity to scrutinise the CPGB's affairs, and focus attention on a mysterious profit of £14,000 from a bookshop, virtually no evidence was found of any sinister links to Moscow or secret funding from the Kremlin. Probably the most significant item seized was a letter from G.W. Middleton, Glasgow's District Organiser, seeking the Party's guidance on members wishing to join the police. He had been advised that 'half a dozen good Party members in the police force in the bigger towns like Glasgow would certainly be very useful'.

Thus, after six years of surveillance, the raid and trial had merely served to keep the CPGB's leadership out of circulation temporarily, and impress upon the Party the need to maintain good security. In retrospect, it may be noted that among the many documents recovered during the raid were a few referring to the activities of a pair of students at Oxford who, on the CPGB's instructions, had attended the *Majlis*, a regular social and political gathering for Indian students. Their objective had been to spread Communist propaganda, talent-spot suitable candidates for cultivation, and obtain speaking invitations for Shapurji Saklatvala, the Communist MP for Battersea. Working with Rajani's brother Clemens Palme Dutt, Saklatvala had attempted to indoctrinate susceptible students who attended these discussion groups, and encourage them to seek appointments in the Indian government where they could be of greater use to the cause. At the time little attention was paid to these activities as the majority of Indians at Oxford were wealthy young men whose families generously supported many of the more innocuous organisations, such as the Bengali Literary Society, that the CPGB targeted for special attention. Much later it would become clearer that the CPGB's university branches had provided the Soviets with a pool of potential recruits for the opportunity to 'work for peace', a euphemism for helping the Comintern, which might result in a career in espionage.

MI5's original information implicating Kirchenstein had come from a letter found on Robert Koling, a Soviet courier, which indicated that he had been active in Britain as a spy, and had first entered the country in 1922, posing as an American citizen and using the All-Russian Cooperative Society Limited, Arcos, as a convenient commercial cover. Officially he was registered as an official of the Arcos Steamship Company but MI5 received information from two low-level informants who worked in the Arcos offices and had reported on some of the personalities in the building. Most of them were Russian, but quite a few were British Communists and among them was Tom Wintringham, listed as an editor in the Arcos Publishing Department, and Andrew Rothstein, manager of the Arcos Information Department. Both of MI5's sources had been prompted to volunteer their knowledge because they were aggrieved. One, a former Vickers employee, had lost his job when he was replaced by Koling, the other feared he would be edged out by Soviets. However, MI5's most significant source was Major Aubrey Morris who reported that he was acquainted with a former Czarist cavalry officer, a Captain Dembritzky, late of the 4th Imperial Hussars, a refugee from the revolution who had decided in December 1922 that he wanted to return to his home in Kursk. In an effort to ingratiate himself with the new regime, Dembritzky had offered to work for the Trade Delegation, and reportedly had been recruited into the Soviet intelligence service. According to his friend Major Morris, Arcos was a nest of spies, and another office, at 28 New Bond Street, concentrated on the collection of military information. Later, evidence would emerge that the Soviets had exploited similar businesses, including the Amtorg Trading Corporation and Prodexco in New York, Yuzhamtorg in Buenos Aires and the Handelsvertung in Berlin in much the same way, as a useful means of concealing espionage, subversion and other clandestine activities. The Handelsvertung offices in Berlin's Lindenstrasse were to be raided twice by the police, in 1924 and again in July 1927. When the French police raided the Trade Delegation offices in Paris they found a printing press set up to counterfeit the banknotes of several countries, and a raid on Yuzhamtorg in Buenos Aires resulted in more than 160 arrests. The last of these uncoordinated police operations took place at the end of August 1931, when the Communist Party of Canada's headquarters, in Church Street, Toronto, was occupied by the RCMP.

Running parallel to the investigation of Kirchenstein was an MI5 operation, prompted by the City businessman George Monckland, which had identified a CPGB member and former British military intelligence officer, Wilfred Macartney, as an intermediary anxious to acquire information about the shipment of munitions to Finland. Monckland was an insurance underwriter at Lloyd's, where Macartney also worked, and he had seen no harm in supplying the information requested. However, when he received an unsolicited payment, and was asked if he could answer a questionnaire about the RAF, Monckland had approached his acquaintance, the Member of Parliament and former Director of Naval Intelligence, Admiral Sir Reginald Hall, who in turn had alerted MI5. Macartney then received from Monckland a classified but obsolete RAF handbook for onward delivery to his contacts, and was watched in March 1927 as it was passed to a man identified as a Soviet Trade Delegation employee who had taken it straight back to his office at 49 Moorgate, which shared premises with Arcos. This sequence of events had been enough for the authorities to obtain a search warrant, and on the afternoon of 12 May fifty Special Branch detectives entered the offices, accompanied by a hundred City of London police officers, and seized control of the entire building. In the basement they found two Soviets, a member of the Trade Delegation, Igor Khudiakov, and the chief cipher clerk, Anton Miller, feeding documents into a furnace, and they were also able to arrest a courier, Robert Koling, who had carried messages between Arcos and the Soviet diplomatic mission at Chesham House in Belgravia.

Koling had come to Britain first in 1908 from Riga as a shoemaker and during the First World War he had been interned in Germany. After his return to England in November 1918 he married an Englishwoman in Blyth and opened a boarding house for seamen, but also while there worked for

Kirchenstein, according to his MI5 dossier. He was found in the Photostat Department, carrying incriminating letters, when Arcos was raided, and his personnel file showed he had been recommended for employment by the 'Secret Department' in 1925 by Kirchenstein, Karl Bahn of the Russian–Norwegian Shipping Company, S.K. Melnechuk and J. Jilinsky. The Special Branch analysts Hugh Miller and Guy Liddell referred to Jilinsky, who had left London a few days before the raid as 'the principle Soviet combined espionage and secret propaganda agent for Europe' (Robert Koling, personal file). Koling's main role had been that of courier, moving messages between Hamburg, Antwerp and London, and together with Jim Messer, Jack Tanner and Jack Walker, he had copied Macartney's documents before passing them along the route to Moscow. Soon after the raid Koling worked his passage to Canada where he later became a naturalised citizen, and settled in Ontario with his wife and five children. He abandoned Communism and atheism, and converted to Christianity, or so the RCMP reported to MI5.

Although the missing RAF manual was never found in the search that lasted four days, delayed by the need to break into several heavily reinforced strong-rooms, hundreds of other documents were recovered and examined by Foreign Office interpreters. MI5 concluded that the papers proved the existence of 'a secret organisation in which the prime mover was Piatnitsky, the head of the Finance Department of the Third International'.[1] A selection were later pub-lished, at the end of the month, as part of a government White Paper released by the Prime Minister, Stanley Baldwin, to justify the immediate suspension of diplomatic relations with Moscow, a rupture that was to last two years. The Soviet Chargé d'Affaires, Ivan Maisky, and his staff were given ten days in which to leave the country, and they departed from Victoria Station on 3 June 1927. According to the Director of GC&CS, Commander Alastair Den-niston, who recalled this episode in a memorandum he wrote in 1944, 'HMG found it necessary to compromise our work beyond any question. From that time the Soviet government introduced unbreakable one-time pads for their diplomatic and commercial traffic to all capitals where they had diplomatic representatives'.[2]

This severance of official Soviet representation in London, which lasted until a Labour government was elected in 1929, had the effect of forcing Moscow to abandon any hope of establishing a legal *rezidentura* in London, and to rely on an illegal apparatus. Even if the diplomatic links had remained, one of the lessons of the episode was that Arcos had not enjoyed the same legal status as the Soviet Trade Delegation under the Anglo-Soviet Trade Agreement of March 1921 negotiated by Ramsay MacDonald's government that had granted it immunity. The police had been authorised to search Arcos, but because the two organisations shared the same premises, it had been impossible to distin-guish between the two. This had been a hard lesson for the Soviets to learn, although an intercepted telegram dated 18 May had assured Moscow that 'there was none of our ciphers or very secret material at the trade delegation'.

Nevertheless, in the aftermath it was clear that the British had read some of the Russian wireless traffic and had maintained a watch on suspect personnel, and even if formal relations between the two countries had not been cut, Moscow would have had to have placed greater reliance on an illegal *apparat* to maintain contact with its networks in England.

The government's White Paper was, in intelligence terms, counter-productive because it referred to telegrams intercepted and read by the Foreign Office, a disclosure that proved the vulnerability of Moscow's cipher system, which was quickly changed, thereby eliminating a useful source for GC&CS's cryptographers. Nevertheless, the material retrieved during the raid showed Anton Miller, and possibly his brother Peter, to have been Jakob Kirchenstein's assistant, and suggested that the pair were answerable to an Osip Piatnitsky, then head of the Finance Department of the Third International, an organisa-tion clearly dedicated to covert propaganda, industrial sabotage and espionage across the Baltic and northern Europe. Although largely unknown outside Moscow, Piatnitsky was one of Lenin's closest confidantes, and in the early part of the century had been entrusted with taking Lenin's illegal paper *Iskra* from Switzerland to Russia. When the Comintern had been formed, Piatnitsky had been Lenin's personal choice for this powerful post, and he survived until he succumbed to a purge in October 1939. His assistant was Jakob Mirov, alias Abramoff, formerly the press attaché at the Soviet embassy in Berlin and an experienced undercover operator.

As well as implicating the senior leadership of the Comintern, the docu-ments recovered also proved the complicity of Soviet officials at Chesham House who evidently had known very well that Miller and Kirchenstein were using Arcos as a cover for their clandestine activities. Miller had been in London for the past three years, having arrived originally in 1921, and although he was questioned and released during the raid, Kirchenstein was never detained, with MI5 learning later that he had fled to the United States, a country that he had never previously visited. There he had been supplied with a new identity, that of 'Frank Kleges' by Nicholas Dozenberg, a veteran GRU agent. Of Latvian origin, and a member of the CPUSA's Central Com-mittee, Dozenberg was to be recalled to Moscow in 1929 by the GRU Chief Jan Berzin and assigned to Bucharest where he ran the American-Rumanian Film Corporation. Later he would undertake a mission to China, but in early 1932 returned to the United States where he served a year's imprisonment in 1939 for passport offences. Although implicated in a massive plot to swamp Latin America with counterfeit dollar bills, Dozenberg was never indicted and quietly left the Party in 1937, eventually retiring with his wife Frances to Florida where he was later interviewed by the FBI. Meanwhile, Kirchenstein adopted his new identity, opened a bank account with the Irving Trust Company in New York and eventually moved to France where he worked for two GRU front companies, the Far East Fur Trading Company, and Impor-tation de Legumes Sec SA, both controlled by a German firm Ostwag, later to be identified to MI5 by Walter Krivitsky as the GRU's principal commercial cover in Europe.

Although Kirchenstein successfully slipped from MI5's grasp, only to reappear a decade later as Frank Kleges, the documents recovered from the Moorgate offices served to implicate several of his British contacts, including J.T. Murphy, Jack Tanner (later General-Secretary of the Amalgamated Engineering Union), David Ramsay, James Messer, all CPGB members, and Dick and Charles Beech of the Seamen's Union. Ramsay and Murphy had been leaders of the Shop Stewards Movement and founders of the Party, and their connection with Kirchenstein represented the first tenuous evidence of a direct link between the CPGB and Moscow's espionage.

Very little is known of this early period of the CPGB's clandestine activities, but it is clear that the organisation was under some scrutiny from at least three British intelligence agencies, all anxious to determine the precise link between the Party and the Kremlin. Individual members of the Party, including such well-known figures as Willie Gallacher and Harry Pollitt, were the subject of mail intercepts and their letters routinely were photographed and filed. Their dossiers show that all of their correspondents were logged meticulously, and where necessary new personal files were opened on potential suspects. Regular summaries on the Party's activities and personalities were prepared by the Home Office Directorate of Intelligence, a specialist unit led by Sir Basil Thomson at Scotland Yard which employed several ex-army officers, among them Guy Liddell, Nigel Watson and Hugh Miller, as civilian analysts. In addition, detectives of the Metropolitan Police Special Branch, headed by the Assistant Commissioner (Crime), Sir Wyndham Childs, attended all political gatherings, and succeeded in recruiting at least one informant, codenamed ALLEN, on the CPGB's Executive Committee. This was Arthur Lakey, a detective sergeant until his dismissal from Scotland Yard in August 1919 during the police strike. Formerly a Royal Navy rating for eleven years, Lakey had joined the Metropolitan Police in November 1911. Later, as we shall see, he was to be employed by the Vigilant Detective Agency, which was run by other former police strikers, and he would become involved in espionage.

The existence of this source inside the Party's Executive Committee emerged during the aftermath of the scandal which became known as 'the Zinoviev Letter' in October 1924, a highly controversial, three-page document published in the *Daily Mail* just four days before the general election. Purporting to be a directive from Grigori Zinoviev, Lenin's President of the Comintern, urging the CPGB to create agitation in the armed forces, it proved to be political dynamite, helping ensure the defeat of Ramsay MacDonald's Labour administration, and a landslide victory for Stanley Baldwin.

The question that few had time to answer before the poll was whether the document was genuine, and upon closer investigation, over many decades, it emerged that it had been fabricated by a group of skilful White Russian forgers who often had peddled counterfeit Soviet documents to embarrass the regime. In this particular case the letter, typed in Russian and dated 25 September 1924, had been sold to the SIS station commander in Riga, Colonel Ronald Meiklejohn DSO, who had arranged for it to be translated, and the new English version sent by courier to London. At SIS's headquarters the politically explosive directive was circulated by SIS's Head of Production, Major Desmond Morton, to MI5, Scotland Yard, the Naval Intelligence Division and the Foreign Office, and within days news of its existence had reached Conservative Central Office and the *Daily Mail*. By the time the *Daily Mail* published it, the content had been authenticated by the SIS Chief, Admiral Sir Hugh Sinclair, who had been advised by Morton that the letter must be genuine because it had been discussed a few days earlier at a meeting of the CPGB's Central Committee. But how had Morton learned this?

Later, in 1940, Morton was to be appointed Winston Churchill's intelligence adviser, but in 1924 he had been in SIS for five years. An Etonian who had served on the staff at GHQ in France during the war, Morton was a Freemason and well connected to the powerful. In 1930 he was to be seconded from SIS to run an offshoot, the Industrial Intelligence Centre, which was created to analyse foreign economic data and advise the Air Targets Sub-Committee of the Committee of Imperial Defence.

Much to MI5's irritation, it subsequently emerged that Morton's agent inside the CPGB, codenamed ALLEN, had been reporting to MI5 until 1922, when he had left the Security Service to work for Sir George Makgill, a baronet who ran a commercial security organisation for private businesses, the Industrial Intelligence Board (IIB). Although the IIB was sponsored by the Federation of British Industries, and sounded official, it was entirely private and acted as a link between business and contacts within Whitehall's intelligence community, depending on Makgill's dining club, known as the Monday Club, to exchange information. The relationship between Makgill and Morton was a close one, and they attended the same Masonic lodge, but Morton was to lose confidence in the reliability of his agent when, in 1925, Morton spotted him using material for one of his reports which he recognised had been copied, without attribution, from a book he had read recently. However, on 17 October the previous year Morton had not experienced any qualms about hearing from his agent that the CPGB Central Committee had met to discuss Grigori Zinoviev's directive. It should be added that whilst Morton may not have harboured any doubts about his agent in October 1924, MI5 certainly did, and claimed that their sources inside the CPGB had denied any such meeting had ever taken place.

The debate over the letter's authenticity, and the extent of its impact on the electorate, would rage for many years, but it was undeniable that even if the actual document was a forgery, the contents accurately reflected the

Comintern's true intentions. Communists were dedicated to undermining the established order, and dissension in the ranks was but one strategy that had been adopted by the Party. But whereas the Zinoviev Letter demonstrated the Comintern's wish to subvert the armed forces, none of this amounted to anything more than the suggestion of a clandestine intelligence-gathering network, until an advertisement appeared in the *Daily Herald* on 24 November 1924:

> Secret Service: A Labour group carrying out investigations would be glad to receive information and details from anyone who has ever had any association with or been brought into touch with any Secret Service Departments or operations. Write to the following address: Post Box 573, Daily Herald.

By following up this entry in the classified columns MI5 found a man who called himself 'VX' and who was later identified as a journalist, William Ewer, a veteran CPGB member and former diplomatic correspondent of the *Daily Herald*. An MI5 agent was planted near him but Ewer soon became suspicious and broke off contact. However, by the time the meetings terminated, the Security Service had noticed that Ewer and the MI5 agent had been kept under observation by other watchers, and in turn had started a counter-surveillance operation which revealed a man and a woman, who were seen to visit Chesham House, then the Soviet Trade Delegation headquarters in London. The woman was identified as Rosa Edwards,[3] the daughter of a former policeman, now employed as a secretary by the Federated Press of America (FPA), a press agency with offices at 50 Outer Temple and managed by Ewer. When Edwards was followed from Chesham House to a post office, where she paid a telephone bill on behalf of the FPA, MI5 had sufficient evidence to link the FPA to the Soviets, and obtain Home Office letter and telephone intercept warrants. By reading his mail MI5 established that Ewer received letters from Paris addressed to 'Kenneth Milton' containing secret French diplomatic correspondence and reports on the economic and political situation in France, as well as messages from Indian Communists for onward transmission to the CPGB.

In the middle of September 1925 MI5 identified the author of the mail from France as George Solcombe, the *Daily Herald*'s Paris correspondent and also the manager of the FPA's Paris branch. Evidently Ewer periodically sent money to Solcombe to pay for the services of officials in the French Ministry for Foreign Affairs, and at the end of the year MI5 discovered a proposal from Solcombe to send his material directly to Moscow, thereby by-passing London, a suggestion prompted by the arrival in Paris of what was described as 'a very capable man who had previously received this material'. This development, noted MI5, coincided with the transfer to Paris of the Soviet Chargé d'Affaires in London, Christian G. Rakovsky.

Further investigations in London led to the identification of several other people connected with Ewer, including the CPGB members Walter M. Holmes, Albert Aller and Walter Dale, all former Scotland Yard detectives who had been sacked following the 1919 police strike, as well as a private detective, Joe Paul. Dale was the man who had followed the MI5 agent planted on Ewer, and it was established that, with the help of private investigators employed by the Vigilant Detective Agency, Dale had also kept watch on foreign embassies in London. All this, of course, was duly reported to MI5 by their key source, Arthur Lakey, codenamed ALLEN.

After the raid on Arcos, the activities of the Federated Press of America gradually diminished and in March 1928 it closed down altogether, but not without first making a redundancy payment to MI5's agent, Arthur Lakey. Nevertheless, MI5 maintained its interest and in August 1928 established contact with Albert Aller, who was short of money, and he confirmed that Christian Rakovsky had received material from Ewer and had financed his organisation. He claimed that Ewer had remained in contact with him after he had gone to Paris, and he also disclosed that Ewer had two sources in Scotland Yard who had supplied him with weekly reports of the kind useful to the Soviets and the CPGB, and with lists of people on whom MI5 kept a watch. MI5 turned its attention on Ewer and he was observed meeting Holmes and Dale at the Fitherston Typewriting Bureau, where Rosa Edwards worked. Intensive surveillance of all three revealed separate meetings of Dale with two people who afterwards returned to Scotland Yard, and turned out to be Detective Inspector Hubert Ginhoven and Detective Sergeant Jane, both of the Special Branch. Ginhoven had been in the Branch since 1910 and, known to his colleagues as 'Gin', had been seconded for special duties in the Great War, during which he had undertaken numerous secret missions behind enemy lines in Germany, Turkey and Austria. Once described as 'a brilliant linguist and the master of disguise', Ginhoven was Dutch in origin, speaking eleven languages and was much admired.

On 11 April 1929, Dale, Ginhoven and Jane were arrested during a meeting, but in order to avoid a scandal the two serving officers were summoned to appear in private before a Disciplinary Board of Inquiry headed by the Deputy Commissioner, Admiral Sir Charles Royds, and were sacked from the police without a pension. A search of Dale's flat turned up his diary which showed that he had routinely kept watch on various SIS and MI5 buildings and certain Russians living in London, and had conducted counter-surveillance operations for Ewer's group. In addition, Dale had received lists of political and public figures on whom the Soviets wanted information, and other data traced to Scotland Yard. From this evidence MI5 drew the conclusion that during the preceding ten years Ewer's organisation had received every scrap of information on the operations of Scotland Yard's supposedly elite Special Branch. The Yard had been completely compromised, and this episode had been enough to undermine what trust there had been between Special Branch and Vernon Kell's Security Service, with the result that in 1931 the Branch's civilian staff, led by Guy Liddell, transferred permanently to MI5.

Soon after the arrest of Dale and the two police officers, the typewriting bureau was closed down and Ewer disappeared to Poland. When he finally returned to England, in September 1929, MI5 had insufficient resources to keep a permanent watch on his movements, but decided that his organisation had been inactive since 1925. It would be many years before MI5 realised the scale of the Soviet espionage organisation that had existed in Britain, or discovered that extensive efforts were underway to rebuild the network using a combination of local political sympathisers, all members of the Party, and professionals based on the Continent who acted as couriers and controllers.

The person who had sparked off this extraordinary chain of events, prompting the raid on Arcos and the disruption of the Soviet *apparat* in London was, of course, the hapless Wilfred Macartney who, understandably, had taken fright and warned George Monckland to lie low. However, as there was nothing recovered in the Arcos raid to incriminate Macartney, MI5 continued to watch him and encouraged Monckland to re-establish contact with him, in the hope of meeting Macartney's contact, a certain 'Mr Johnson'. Finally, in November 1927, Monckland met the mysterious Johnson at the Marble Arch cinema café and agreed to supply him with shipping manifests and other information from Lloyd's the following day. However, at the arranged rendezvous Special Branch detectives arrested Macartney and 'Johnson', and identified the latter as Georg Hansen, a twenty-four-year-old German language student. At their subsequent trial, both men received ten years' imprisonment, but neither made any significant admissions. Macartney's two other sources, apparently soldiers named Barton and Davis, were never prosecuted, and the means by which he had acquired an authentic British passport in a false name, which he had used to travel on the Continent and was recovered from his home, remained a mystery despite a lengthy investigation at the Passport Office. Although the passport had been found at Macartney's home, there was no record at Petty France of any application for it, indicating collusion and a serious breach of security. While Macartney returned to journalism upon his release, Hansen disappeared in Europe, only to be named by the defector Walter Krivitsky in 1940 as a German Communist who had been despatched to London on a mission to prepare for the arrival of a more senior figure, Max Unschlicht. However, with Hansen's arrest, and the possibility that Unschlicht's intended mission had been compromised, the plan had been abandoned.

With the imprisonment of Macartney and Hansen the trail of Soviet espionage effectively went cold. There were still plenty of pieces of the jigsaw for MI5 to fit together, but the connecting threads were absent. The investigation and trial had failed to clarify Hansen's precise role and, although the suspicion remained that the Soviet Embassy or the CPGB had been involved, no firm evidence had emerged apart from the obvious shift in Macartney's interest from the export of munitions to the Baltic, in which the Kremlin could arguably have a legitimate interest, and information about the Royal Air Force, which was indefensible. The one cause for continuing anxiety was the assertion, made by Macartney, that he and others had been warned several days in advance of the raid that Arcos was to be searched by the police. But how had that news leaked out?

2

THE PERSONALITIES

The MASK traffic took place at a critical moment in Britain's history, with the country divided in its attitude towards the growth of Fascism in Europe, and the threat of Communism from Moscow. While there was an overt dimension to this political polarisation, with the CPGB enjoying widespread electoral support and a membership of over 50,000, and Sir Oswald Mosley's Blackshirts leading massive demonstrations, rallies and marches, there was also a very extensive covert side to both organisations, and they were the subject of surveillance and penetration by the Security Service.

Prior to MASK, MI5's knowledge of the CPGB came from three principal sources: reports of political meetings submitted by Special Branch detectives who took notes at all public rallies (and at a few private gatherings, when they could gain access); technical surveillance by means of a microphone concealed in the CPGB's headquarters at 16 King Street, Covent Garden, and intercept warrants on the telephones of selected members; and finally, physical penetration, using informants and directed agents. Naturally, the existence of a clandestine or underground cadre was a closely-guarded secret which was never discussed within the hearing of police eavesdroppers or on vulnerable telephone lines, so the first hint that the CPGB harboured a more sinister group came from the initial MASK messages.

It was as a consequence of the MASK traffic that MI5 decided to step up its coverage of the Party, and some of this task fell to Olga Gray, an MI5 agent codenamed M-12 and recruited in 1931 for the sole purpose of cultivating the CPGB's National Organiser, Percy Glading, who had just returned from Moscow where he had attended a course at the Lenin School using the alias 'James Browlie'. Previously, Glading had worked at Woolwich Arsenal as a grinder during the First World War, and then from June 1925 as an examiner in the Arsenal's Navy Department, but he had been dismissed in 1928 when he was identified as a Communist who had been an agitator in India three years earlier.

The daughter of a *Daily Mail* journalist who had been killed in the trenches during the First World War, and calling herself Ann, Gray was recruited by MI5 at a Conservative Party garden fete at Edgbaston and paid £2.50 a week. Over seven years of operational work, initially at the Anglo-Soviet Friendship Society and then at King Street as John Strachey's secretary, she proved to be an exceptionally talented agent and after she had gained Glading's trust, even to the point that he used her as a courier to deliver secret information to Party contacts in India, she was to report to MI5 on the long-suspected overlap between the CPGB and Soviet espionage. Most importantly, she revealed to Max Knight the existence of Harry Pollitt's covert link with Moscow, and explained how the cipher system was based on a book, information which enabled the GC&CS cryptographers to break the traffic codenamed MASK.

Prolonged surveillance, and information from Olga, showed that Glading had renewed contact with some of his old colleagues at the Woolwich Arsenal and was copying blueprints supplied by them of armaments manufactured at the plant. Also implicated was Paddy Ayriss, the wife of George Hardy, a CPGB activist in the seamen's unions, based in London but originally from Merseyside. Both Hardy and his wife would appear in the MASK traffic, but although she was suspected of having acted as a courier, moving between Glading, the illegal 'Paul Hardt' and the Soviet embassy, there was never any evidence to justify her arrest. Accordingly, she was one of the members of the spy-ring who escaped any criminal charge when the police rounded up the network in January 1938.

Although Glading was suspected of being the ringleader, evidence later emerged to suggest that Albert Williams, a thirty-nine-year-old carpenter employed at the Arsenal, in whose home at 24 Albion Road the police found a photographic studio and dark-room, was the real mastermind. Williams had been considered 'a very dangerous Communist' since he first came to the attention of Special Branch in September 1927. Born in 1899, Williams had enlisted in the Royal Field Artillery in June 1915 and had served with the British Expeditionary Force in France and Flanders as a gunner, and with the North Russian Expeditionary Force. Demobilised in June 1919, he had joined Woolwich Arsenal as a labourer and had been promoted to a gun examiner. He was also elected secretary of the local branch of the CPGB and gained a reputation as an uncompromising revolutionary. It was only after his conviction, when regular reports were submitted about him to MI5 by a stool-pigeon named Parkinson at Parkhurst prison on the Isle of Wight, that it emerged that he, not Percy Glading, had really directed the spy-ring. Of particular interest to MI5 was an overheard conversation with another convict, George Whomack, in which Williams had mentioned that an important, senior Foreign Office official was being paid £15,000 a year for his espionage. He had also boasted that he had been very lucky, for if MI5 had acted a week earlier, or a week later, he would have been in possession of some very incriminating material that would have earned him a much longer sentence. MI5 paid close attention to Williams, and his wife Nellie, and noted that he considered Glading, incarcerated separately at Maidstone, to be the weakest link. Even in prison he kept up his links with the CPGB, apparently through the owner of the Victoria Tea Shop in Cowes High Street which Nellie visited on her trips to Parkhurst, and Frank Munday, another visitor whose brother also had been convicted. Williams was released in November 1940 and, unrepentant about his conviction, found work as a carpenter with a corn merchant. When he attended a government-sponsored training scheme in Croydon, to learn engineering, MI5 had intervened discreetly to ensure that, as an ex-convict, he was not offered a government job, and instead he had spent the remainder of the war working for a building contractor repairing bomb-damaged property in south London.

Although MI5 had been aware since 1927 that Williams had been an active Communist, there had not been any complaints about his work at the Arsenal, and he had not been connected by MI5 with Percy Glading, who had been the principal focus of the original investigation, which had been conducted by Max Knight with the help of Olga Gray. Born in 1906, Olga had been recruited by MI5's star agent-runner to work as a typist in the Anglo-Soviet Friendship Society, where she had been talent-spotted by the CPGB as a potential courier. Her first mission, to Paris in June 1934, carrying a wad of sterling notes concealed in a sanitary towel, led to her voyage to India to deliver cash to an address in Bombay. This was considered an important mission by Knight because it had demonstrated that she had succeeded in gaining the trust of the CPGB leadership, was being initiated into the Party's clandestine organisation, and was likely to increase MI5's knowledge of subversion in India where the Communist Party of India (CPI) had been outlawed. Olga's visit to Bombay had been an opportunity to assess the damage sustained by the CPI, assist the local security apparatus, the highly efficient Indian Political Intelligence (IPI), and gauge the strength of the CPI's links to the outside world, if not the Comintern.

Because Colonel Cecil Kaye's Central Intelligence Bureau was believed to have made it almost impossible for the CPI to function in India, the Comintern had transferred its headquarters to Berlin where it operated as the *Westbureau* under the leadership of a Meerut defendant, Manandranath Nath Roy, from the Fuhrer Verlag bookshop at Wilhelmstrasse 131–132. Formerly the Comintern's representative in China, Roy was well-known to MI5 as an Indian subversive, and his wife, Louisa Schoeller, was later to be identified by Walter Krivitsky as a GRU agent.

Naturally, the bookshop became a target for British surveillance which was conducted by SIS's local representative, located conveniently close by at the Passport Control Office in Tiergartenstrasse. Unexpectedly in 1933, the SIS station commander, Frank Foley, received a 'walk-in', a disaffected German Communist who had been court-martialled for leading a mutiny on the battleship *Westfalen*. Sentenced to death, but freed in an uprising before the sentence could be carried out, Johan deGraff had become a KPD member and had been sent for training to the Lenin School, and then the Frunze Military Academy. Of particular interest to SIS was his account of two visits he had made to London, in 1931 and 1933, to the CPGB on behalf of the Comintern.

Having decided to defect when his wife was purged from the Party for political deviation, deGraff was persuaded by Foley to remain active for the Comintern, but to maintain contact with SIS and keep Foley, and his superior, Colonel Valentine Vivian of SIS's counter-intelligence section, informed of developments. Thus 'Jonny X', as he became known within SIS, acted as a mole within the Comintern while undertaking clandestine missions to Shanghai, Austria, Czechoslovakia, France, Rumania and Argentina.

In 1940 his double life came to an end after he was sent to supervise an insurrection in Brazil, and ensured its failure. Using the alias 'Paul Gruber', deGraff had been one of several German agents, including Arthur Ewert and Olga Benario, who had been assigned the task of giving military advice to the plotters from the Brazilian Communist Party. Almost compromised by the collapse of the uprising, suppressed in November 1935 with bloody efficiency by President Getulio Vargas, to place Moscow's nominee, Luis Carlos Prestes, in control of the country, deGraff went underground in Rio de Janeiro while Moscow tried to work out what had gone wrong. Surprisingly, deGraff had been cleared of the betrayal, and had been briefed for a new mission, this time to Japan, when the war broke out and the decision was made to leave him in Brazil. However, he was eventually captured in January 1940, and as soon as SIS learned of his arrest urgent representations were made in London to prevent his return to Germany, where he was wanted by the Gestapo as a senior KPD functionary. SIS succeeded in obtaining his release, and he was resettled in Canada where he became an adviser to the Royal Canadian Mounted Police on German espionage, and in 1943 participated in a double agent operation with a captured Abwehr agent, Waldemar von Janowsky, codenamed WATCHDOG. After the war, deGraff remained in Canada to assist the RCMP, and in his retirement ran the Horningtoft guesthouse in Brockville, Ontario, where he died in 1980, aged eighty-six. His fellow conspirators, Olga Benario and Arthur Ewert, fared rather less well. Benario had fallen in love with Prestes and was expecting his child when they were both arrested in Rio in March 1936.

Benario had been a KPD activist in Munich from the age of sixteen, and had travelled to Moscow in 1931 after evading arrest on a charge of treason and possession of forged documents. In Moscow she had been elected a member of the Executive Committee of the Young Communist International (ECYCI) and later the same year sent on a mission to France. While there she had been persuaded to visit London, where she was arrested during a demonstration in Hyde Park. Once released, and safely back in Moscow, Benario had taken a course at the Zhukovsky Military Academy, and then had been introduced to Luis Prestes who had arrived the previous November to attend the fourteenth anniversary of the Bolshevik November revolution. Soon they were planning the coup in Brazil, and the Comintern had sponsored their circuitous return, posing as a wealthy pair of Portuguese newly-weds on their honeymoon, to Rio via Paris, New York, Miami, Santiago and Buenos Aires.

Fearing her deportation to certain execution in Nazi Germany after her arrest in Rio, the MASK traffic shows that the Comintern attempted to mobilise efforts to obtain her release from *La Coruna*, the liner on which she was transported under escort back to Hamburg. However, the German captain cancelled the ship's scheduled stops at other European ports, where a rescue might have been attempted, and she was delivered to the Gestapo. Upon arrival she was escorted to Berlin, and gave birth to a daughter, Anita, in November in Berlin's Barnimstrasse prison. Soon after her confinement she was transferred to Lichtenburg concentration camp, and when her daughter was fourteen months old she was released to her paternal grandmother and taken to Mexico. Olga was then moved to Ravensbruck where she died in February 1942. Luis Carlos Prestes was released from prison in 1945, left the Communist Party in 1980, and died in Rio de Janeiro ten years later.

Arthur Ewert, who had been arrested in Rio in December 1935, was a seasoned revolutionary with a German background who had emigrated from East Prussia before the First World War to Detroit, where he had found work in a leather factory and become an active trade unionist. In 1917 he and Elise Saborowski had moved to Toronto, only to be arrested by the RCMP and deported for attempting to organise a branch of the banned Communist Party. Undeterred, Ewert had worked for the CPUSA, and was invited to Moscow by the Comintern. He attended the Fifth Congress of the CPUSA in New York in August 1927 as Stalin's personal representative, and upon his return to Moscow was elected to the Executive Committee of the Third International, and also to the Reichstag as a KPD deputy.

In 1931 Ewert was sent on a mission to Yuzhamtorg in Montevideo, the Comintern's Latin American cover organisation, and when this had been completed successfully he was posted with Elise to Shanghai, the Comintern's Far East headquarters, carrying false American passports in the names of Harry Berger and Machla Lenzychi. They remained in China until July 1934, when they were recalled to Moscow and prepared for a new assignment, to accompany Luis Prestes to Brazil and participate in the military coup that would establish a Soviet-style government.

Although sentenced to ten years' imprisonment, Ewert was amnestied in May 1945 but, upon his return to Germany in 1947, was found to have been driven insane by the torture he had endured in captivity. He died in 1959. His wife Elise, deported to Germany with Olga in 1938, was last seen alive at Lichtenburg in 1941.

★　★　★

In the spring of 1935 Olga Gray suffered a nervous breakdown and cut her ties to both the CPGB and MI5. However, in February 1937 she reported to Max Knight that Glading was back in touch with her, and had asked her to rent a safe-house in Holland Road, Kensington, and having accepted the task she began a second period as an MI5 agent, which was to culminate in the arrest of Glading and his accomplices. During this second period she reported to MI5 on the installation of photographic equipment in the safe-house, and her introduction to two Soviet illegals, 'Dr Peters' (Theodore Mally) and Willy Brandes (Mikhail Borovoy), who had supervised an espionage network in London.

Gray was so trusted by Glading and Bob Stewart that at the end of March 1936 she was selected, under cover of attending the Lenin School in Moscow, to act as a courier again, taking secret messages to and from the Soviet Union. Indeed, on this occasion she was chosen to carry vital documents in preference to the two other CPGB members who accompanied her on the journey.

Information from Gray implicated Glading in a large spy-ring that removed documents from his former workplace, the Woolwich Arsenal, and passed them on to Soviet spies. Glading effectively acted as an intermediary, supervising his sources inside the Arsenal, photographing their material, and then relaying it to Gray's mysterious European visitors, whom MI5 would not be able to identify positively until 1940. Although Glading, Williams and Whomack pleaded guilty to the charges against them, and received prison sentences, none of their contacts were ever caught. In particular, 'Mr and Mrs Stephens', who had been living at Wallace Court, a block of flats in the Marylebone Road, had long since departed. Records showed that 'Paul and Lydia Hardt' had first entered the country in December 1935, and had rented accommodation at 6 Lansdowne Place in Bloomsbury. There they had remained until January 1937 when the couple moved to Wallace Court in Marylebone for their last five months in England, until June when Mally was suddenly recalled to Moscow. Olga Gray had only met 'Mr Peters' once, in late April 1937, but a chance remark by Glading, describing him as having been an Austrian who had served in the Russian cavalry, had been sufficient for MI5 eventually to identify him, with Walter Krivitsky's help, as Theodore Mally, the illegal who, the defector said, had played an important role in running John King, a fact confirmed to MI5 by Henri Pieck in 1950 who had known Mally well. According to Anthony Blunt, who never met him, Mally had been in contact with both Kim Philby and Guy Burgess, and had earned the deep respect of both. Indeed, Philby had later remarked to Blunt that his admiration for Mally had hugely increased when he discovered that Mally had willingly answered his summons to Moscow, even when he knew it was likely to be his death warrant. Certainly Mally had been under no illusions about the probable fate awaiting him. Ignace Reiss's widow, Elisabeth Poretsky, who spent many hours with him in Paris in June 1937 following his withdrawal from London, and his final journey to the Soviet Union the next month, recalled that 'he knew terror even better than we did'. Mally knew all about the purges underway, but was resigned to his duty.

According to Walter Krivitsky's interviews two years later with MI5, 'Peters' was the alias adopted by the illegal *rezident* in London, Theodore Mally, who had also been engaged in two other cases. One involved someone with information from the Committee of Imperial Defence, and the other was a journalist of good family whom the OGPU considered at one point as a potential prospect to assassinate General Franco. At the time there were no obvious candidates for these descriptions, but years later they were interpreted as clues pointing to two of the Cambridge spies, John Cairncross and Kim Philby.

Nothing more was heard of Mally, and in fact he was recalled to Moscow to perish in the purges. Similarly, Mikhail Borovoy, alias Willy Brandes, also disappeared, and his true identity did not emerge until the KGB's archives were opened and he was revealed as a member of the OGPU's new Scientific and Technical Section who had visited the United States under the alias Abraham Hoffman and during September and October 1936 had acquired naturalisation papers and obtained a marriage certificate in Montreal to apply for authentic Canadian passports in the name of Willy and Mary Brandes. Once back-stopped with this documentation, Borovoy had taken up residence in Fonset Court, posing as the representative of a New York cosmetics company.

Olga had also been introduced by Glading at the Holland Road safe-house in October 1937 to 'Mr and Mrs Stephens', the couple who had taken over from 'Mr Peters' and they were traced to Fonset House where they were registered as tenants in the name of Brandes. Although Krivitsky recalled having met him in Moscow, he was unaware of his true identity, or his ultimate fate.

The degree to which the OGPU exercised *konspiratsia*, or the security discipline required to separate operations into compartments to avoid cross-contamination, is evident when considering the number of Soviet clandestine operations being conducted in London during the period that GC&CS was intercepting and reading the MASK traffic. Several illegals were active and John King was haemorrhaging Foreign Office secrets to Pieck and Mally. The Woolwich Arsenal ring was fully operational, a network had been established in the Royal Aircraft establishment at Farnborough, Kim Philby had been in contact since June 1934 and Donald Maclean was becoming a diplomat under the supervision of the illegal *rezident* Ignaty Reif. When viewed in retrospect, with the references to Glading and Bob Stewart, and the visits to England of Johan deGraff, Leopold Trepper and Ernst Baumann (of whom more will be heard later), London had become a veritable centre of Soviet espionage, teeming with spies, with clues to the identities of some buried deep in the Comintern's secret communications.

It was the evidence of William Morrison in August 1939 that proved so helpful in identifying some of the personalities mentioned in the MASK traffic. Seven were radio operators he had trained in Moscow, although he said that Bill Savage and George Ives were 'never any good'. One of his best pupils was Sally Friedman, who may have been the 'Sol Freeman' mentioned in MASK as having sailed on the *Rykow* to Leningrad in November 1934.

Apart from Morrison, Krivitsky and deGraff, there was another significant source from inside the Comintern who, on becoming disillusioned with Soviet Marxism, decided to abandon the Party and reveal knowledge that was helpful to building MI5's understanding of its adversary. Richard Krebs was a German whose father, an officer in the Kaiser's navy, had mutinied in 1919 but had been killed in the bitter street-fighting in Bremen during the uprising. Also a seaman, Krebs had gravitated towards the KPD and undertaken several clandestine missions across Europe, including two to Britain to liaise with the CPGB and organise the seamen's unions, and a couple to the United States. He made a brief visit in 1921, but in 1925 he was convicted of assault with a deadly weapon in Los Angeles, when he had been instructed to kill a supposed traitor, Maurice Goodstein, and sentenced to between one and ten years' imprisonment. Upon his release from San Quentin in December 1929 he had been deported back to Germany.

On his first visit to London Krebs had been arrested and deported, and his second resulted in his detention at Newcastle as he tried to enter the country. In November 1933 he had been arrested by the Gestapo in Hamburg and was only released in May 1937 when he agreed to act as a spy for them in Copenhagen where the KPD's leadership had taken refuge. Intent on deceiving the Gestapo, but anxious about the fate of his wife and child held hostage in Germany, Krebs declared his precarious position to the Comintern but was abducted and held in a cottage in Denmark while his case was reviewed in Moscow. Aware of what his fate was likely to be if he was sent back to the Soviet Union he escaped to Esjberg and joined a ship bound for France, where he again eluded the OGPU. As the Communist newspapers identified him as a traitor and a Gestapo spy Krebs went back to sea, jumping ship in Baltimore. Illegally in the United States, he had worked as a handyman at Yashive College, and in 1940 published an account of his underground work for the Comintern in *Out of the Night* using the pseudonym Jan Valtin. His fame enabled him to become a legal immigrant and he went on to write four more books before he moved to Chestertown, Maryland, where he died of pneumonia in 1952, aged forty-eight.

Krebs' autobiography proved to be a detailed account of his underground work for the KPD, for whom he had collected shipping information for a secret *apparat* headed by Felix Neumann which included a maritime section heavily dependent on the seamen's unions. The book also included the first published description of a covert mission undertaken by a Comintern agent. According to Krebs, the Comintern had been deeply impressed by the strike of the Royal Navy's Home Fleet at Invergordon in September 1931, although the CPGB had played absolutely no part in it. Certainly three of the mutineers, Fred Copeman, Len Wincott and Jimmie Shields, subsequently joined the Party, but the episode had been spontaneous, sparked by the Admiralty's announcement of a cut in pay for all naval personnel. For the most junior ratings, this meant a reduction of a quarter of their meagre income, which none could afford, and the unrest manifested itself in a very good-natured strike lasting just thirty-six hours, during which the lower decks refused to allow their ships to put to sea on exercises, thereby paralysing the fleet. The government had backed down and twenty-four men considered to be the ring-leaders were quietly discharged, their papers marked only 'services no longer required'. The fact that the mighty Royal Navy, easily the world's most power-ful maritime force, had been rendered impotent by a relative handful of agitators had impressed Moscow and increased representation in Britain's ports became a priority.

Krebs' tasks had been to revive the shipping paper, the *Seafarer*, undertake a tour of the principal ports, reorganise the Communist-dominated trade unions and, having delivered June and July subsidy for the *Daily Worker*, which had been paid by Moscow since the paper's creation in 1930, conduct an audit of the accounts. To do this he entered the country on a Dutch passport, posing as a wholesale fish merchant from Rotterdam, used a Norwegian passport to identify himself to the CPGB, and kept an American passport in reserve in case escape became necessary. Krebs flew to Croydon from Hamburg and began his inspection with the help of an Irish OGPU man, Pat Murphy, and a German secretary who had worked at Arcos. What he found, he claimed, was waste, extravagance and corruption, and 'expenses' that included 'fairly luxurious apartments, maintenance of mistresses, vacation trips to the south coast, and fur coats and automobiles for the wives of prominent British Stalinists'. Krebs reported to Moscow that the 'anti-communist terror was a kindergarten affair when compared to the hardships encountered by our comrades in most European and Asiatic countries'.

The Krebs inspection had two other objectives, but he failed to accomplish either. One was to take control of the West Indian Association (WIA), an organisation based in Cardiff and dedicated to the improvement and protection of black workers in the Caribbean. Krebs' strategy had been to offer a hand-some subsidy from Willi Münzenburg's Secretariat for the Friends of the Soviet Union, or to replace O'Connell, the WIA's non-Communist leader. O'Connell had declined the bribe, and had resisted when Krebs' alternative candidate, a graduate of the Lenin School named Jones, had been foisted on the WIA. Krebs claimed this rebuff had been because Jones had been recruited by Special Branch, and acting on a tip O'Connell had packed the meeting at which he was to be deposed, sending the Cardiff police on a hunt for 'the Russian with an American accent'. Krebs' other failure, during a second trip to England via Grimsby in August, had been to persuade the East Indian Seamen's Union to acquiesce to Moscow's demands and move their head-quarters from London's East End to Calcutta, where most of its membership was. Mystified by the union's stubborn refusal, Krebs used some strong-arm tactics on the Hindu who headed the union, and learned that he had resisted Moscow because he had developed a lucrative drug-running operation. When Krebs threatened him with exposure, it was Krebs who found himself arrested by Special Branch detectives and escorted back to Grimsby. A further attempt to enter the country, through Newcastle, resulted in his expulsion after a night in jail at the port. Following this experience, Krebs had observed that 'to the Comintern, Great Britain has always been one of the least dangerous yet one of the most difficult terrains'.

Many of the very candid disclosures made by Krebs dovetailed neatly with what MI5 had already learned from MASK, an example being the cases of Ernst Thälmann, the KPD leader, and his blood-thirsty subordinate Heinz Neumann who had long advocated a terrorist campaign against the Nazis. Neumann, who was Willi Münzenberg's brother-in-law, had helped create the 'Red Marines' who organised ambushes of Nazi supporters and the murder of individual blackshirts and stormtroopers, but he fled to Moscow as the Gestapo retaliated in kind. He was later followed by Thälmann who ordered Neumann back to Germany on what amounted to a suicide mission. Neumann appeared to consent, but only reached Switzerland and refused orders to return to Moscow. According to Krebs, the OGPU then denounced Neumann to the Swiss police for possession of forged documents and in 1934 offered to deport him to either Germany or the Soviet Union. Neumann chose Moscow and survived, but not for long. Having begged the forgiveness of Stalin and the Central Control Commission he was despatched to Madrid but, at the height of the purges, was recalled to Moscow, arrested in April 1937 and executed seven months later. According to MASK, the CPGB orchestrated a campaign, drawing in two Labour MPs, Sir Stafford Cripps and George Lansbury, to apply pressure on the Swiss government to either release Neumann or deport him to the Soviet Union. As for Thälmann, he was to perish in a Nazi concentration camp, his name having been given to the XIth International Brigade.

The knowledge Krebs demonstrated of personalities who had appeared in the MASK traffic was highly relevant to MI5 because the Comintern's regional headquarters for northern and western Europe was located in Berlin and largely staffed by KPD members who were known to him. Moscow had decided to establish the *Westbureau* in Berlin, rather than Paris, because of its geographical convenience, the lack of interference from the local security apparatus and, in contrast to the often difficult relations with the PCF, a relatively compliant KDP. When the Nazis eventually made the *Westbureau's* continued existence in Berlin impossible, it was moved to Copenhagen.

One area of possible confusion, concerning MASK messages sent from Moscow and signed KREBS, was later to be cleared up by Elisabeth Poretsky, who broke with the Party after her husband, Ignace Reiss, had been murdered in Lausanne in September 1937. Like Krebs, Poretsky knew many of the Comintern leadership, and she explained that KREBS was the codename of Felix Wolf, a senior KPD functionary who had run the Party's intelligence branch for the GRU. In 1917 Wolf had sided with the Bolsheviks and had made his reputation spreading propaganda among German troops in the Ukraine. At the end of the First World War 'General Wolf' had returned to Germany but after his arrest and imprisonment he had worked undercover as 'Nikolai Rakov' and had been appointed a military attaché at the Soviet embassy in Vienna under the name Inkov, an invention he had created from his Russian wife's name, Inka. However, Wolf's Comintern codename was KREBS, and this was how his name appeared in the MASK traffic.

After her husband's murder Poretsky had moved to the United States, and later wrote her memoirs, *Our Own People*, in which she described what she knew of the NKVD's role in his death. Although she was to be interviewed several times by the FBI, sometimes at MI5's request, she never knew of the huge investigation that had been conducted in Switzerland and Britain into the murder. One of the suspected assassins, a man named Rossi, had been traced to his hotel in Lausanne, where there was evidence that he had also used the name Roland Abbiate, and had visited London where he had bought some of his clothes. This trail was pursued by MI5 and Special Branch and led to proof that Abbiate had visited Britain using both identities, and also had been associated with 'Paul Hardt' and his assistant, Dr Joseph Lappit. Although MI5 continued to follow up leads until at least 1956, the scent was cold and the inquiries really centred on scanty prewar immigration records which showed that a Special Branch detective had interviewed Lappit at his rented home in Chelsea in 1936 when he had been posing as a Czech journalist learning English. On that occasion no suspicion had attached to Lappit and he had been allowed to remain in England for a further twelve months.

3

THE GREAT GAME

The fate of India was a constant preoccupation both for the Comintern plotters in Moscow, Berlin and London, and for their adversaries in Whitehall and Delhi. Several of the senior figures in the British intelligence establishment had cut their teeth in countering subversion in India, including Sir David Petrie, the Director of the Intelligence Bureau from 1924 to 1931, and the author of a secret report, *Communism in India 1924–1927*, who was later to be appointed Director-General of MI5 from 1940 to 1946. One of his subordinates, Felix Cowgill, updated the document in 1935 for Petrie's successor, Sir Horace Williamson, and later was posted back to England to SIS's counter-intelligence branch, Section V, then headed by Valentine Vivian, who himself had retired from the Indian Police in 1925 after nineteen years of experience. Another influential figure in the British intelligence community in London was Sir Philip Vickery, another Indian intelligence chief, demonstrating that the intelligence establishment was staffed in large measure by professionals who had acquired ample experience resisting Soviet-inspired political subversion which had been infiltrated into the jewel in Britain's crown from Persia, China and Afghanistan. Nor had the IPI operated in isolation. The long-serving Deputy Director-General of the Security Service, Eric Holt-Wilson, who had been appointed in 1912 and had remained in the post for twenty-eight years, took great pride in what he regarded as his greatest accomplishment, the creation and coordination of an Imperial Security Intelligence Service which had extended across the globe and had included 260 chiefs of police in more that fifty overseas territories. Excluded from Holt-Wilson's overall supervision was the IPI which had developed its own ethos and methodology, and was considered highly effective, running well-informed agents in all the bazaars and keeping the Comintern at bay.

Much of what MI5, SIS and the IPI knew of their Soviet adversary in those early days came from defectors, with two in particular providing crucial inside information. The first, who appeared in April 1928, was a twenty-seven-year-old Russian, Boris Bajanov who, prior to his escape to Persia with a companion the previous January, had served as Stalin's secretary and latterly as a functionary in the Politburo's secretariat. Bajanov and his companion were escorted to

Simla where he was interviewed by a group of British intelligence officers, among them Frederick Isemonger, the Inspector-General of Police in the North-West Frontier province, who was also acting director of the Intelligence Bureau during Petrie's temporary absence, an IPI interpreter, Edmund Rowlandson, and the Deputy Director of Military Intelligence, Brigadier Macan Saunders, who previously had served as an intelligence officer on General Dunsterville's staff in the Caucasus in 1918 and later had been the military attaché in Tehran.

Bajanov and his friend, Arkadi Maximov, who turned out to have been his OGPU guard, were questioned for over three months, and their account of the Soviet intelligence structure was compelling and obviously well-informed. In the summer of 1923 Bajanov had been appointed Stalin's assistant, and in January the following year had worked as the Politburo's secretary. However, at the end of 1923 he had fallen foul of the OGPU and had been transferred to the post of Vice President of the Economic Bureau. The following year he was moved to the editorial board of the *Financial Gazette*, only to be demoted to the rank of economic adviser in the Ministry of Finance. In October 1927 he had narrowly escaped death during an ideological purge but, because of his relationship with Stalin, had merely suffered exile to Turkestan with an OGPU guard.

Bajanov's account of the OGPU's development followed the unexpected but natural death of its founder, Feliks Dzerzhinsky, in July 1926, which had allowed Genrikh Yagoda, then the administrative chief of the Cheka's Special Department, to succeed him. An ambitious, thirty-five-year-old Polish Jew and a leading Chekist since 1919, Yagoda had effectively displaced Dzerzhinsky's deputy, V.R. Menzhinsky, who had been in failing health. Most importantly, Bajanov revealed the existence of a highly secret foreign intelligence department, the *Inostrannyi Otdel* (INO), which had been headed successively by Iakov Davtian, later the Soviet ambassador in Warsaw, Solomon Mogilevsky and finally Mikhail Trilliser, who had been appointed in August 1921. Five years later Trilliser was to be promoted to the OGPU's Second Deputy Chaiman, subordinate only to Menzhinsky and Yagoda, a reflection of the enhanced standing of the INO, which was administered by Trilisser's Estonian deputy, V.A. Styrne.

The fact that India was considered a vital prize by the Kremlin was confirmed in 1930 by the defection of Georgi Agabekov, an Armenian who had joined the Cheka from the Red Army at the age of twenty-four in 1920. Over the next decade Agabekov had received several promotions, and in June 1926 was recalled to Moscow to be selected by the OGPU Chief, Mikhail Trilliser, to be his *rezident*-designate in Tehran with the task of developing networks in India. However, before he took up his post he was briefed by Osip Piatnitsky of the Comintern, and M.N. Roy, who was then staying at the Lux Hotel. Agabekov, who was posted to the Soviet consulate in Tehran under diplomatic cover, later described Roy as 'extremely homesick, and also timid', and did not trust him. Agabekov ran the OGPU's operations in southern Persia until September 1929 when he was given a new mission, to Bombay. He was instructed to travel there via Berlin and Egypt, but at the last moment he was appointed the OGPU's illegal *rezident* in Turkey.

In October 1929 Agabekov arrived in Constantinople operating under commercial cover as a business importing bicycles and typewriters. However, upon his arrival he advertised for an English teacher, and engaged Isabel Streater, the twenty-year-old daughter of an expatriate Briton who worked for a local shipping company. By Christmas they were in love, and when in January 1931 Agabekov received a summons to return to Moscow for routine consultations he decided to confide his true identity and mission to Isabel who worked part-time as a typist at the British embassy. Hopelessly entranced by Agabekov, Isabel had been undeterred by such details of his past as the OGPU man had disclosed, and he had agreed to defect, offering his services to the embassy. He received no reply and Isabel's family, appalled at her relationship with a foreigner fourteen years older than herself, had taken her to Paris. Agabekov had followed, and again approached the French and the British Consul-General with an offer of collaboration, information about the OGPU and a copy of his recently completed memoirs. Acting on a complaint from Isabel's outraged parents, who escorted her back to Turkey, the French authorities expelled Agabekov who took up residence in Belgium. Finally, after many dramas and the intervention of the SIS station in Brussels, Agabekov was reunited with Isabel, and they were married in early 1931, an event followed quickly by the publication of *OGPU: The Russian Secret Terror* in which the author recalled his career in Trilliser's service, and the Comintern's interest in India. In particular, from the safety of political asylum in Belgium, he described the relationship between the Comintern and the Kremlin:

> The Bolshevik press, both of Russia and outside was forever printing the assertions of Chicherin and Litvinov to the effect that the Soviet Government had nothing in common with the Third International and that the Comintern, while enjoying Soviet hospitality, retained complete independence and full responsibility for its acts. It is surprising that even today there are large numbers of people who refuse to admit the least identity between the Soviet Government and the Third International. But let these people consider the following: The President of the Comintern (he is now called Secretary General, but it's the same office) has always been at the same time a member of the Politburo (Political bureau of the Central Committee) which, in effect, controls the political system and makes the laws of the USSR. The President of the Comintern is bound to conform his political policy and acts to those of the Government. He goes no further than to execute decisions made by that Government. The first President of the Comintern, Zinoviev, was also one of the most active

chiefs of the Politburo; not only was his successor, Bukharin, a member of the Politburo, but he was also the official exponent of Communist theory in Russia. Right now the new President of the Comintern, Molotov, is not only a member of the Politburo, but also Stalin's right arm.

Agabekov explained that the aims of the OGPU and the Comintern were identical.

Until 1926 the relations between OGPU and the Third international were very intimate, because of the friendship between Abram Trilliser, Chief of the Foreign Section of OGPU, and Piatnitsky, Chief of the International Relations of the Comintern (Executive Committee of the Third International). Indeed, such relations were natural, in view of the struggle being waged by OGPU against anti-Communists of every feather, from Socialists of the Second International to Fascists. OGPU is in duty bound to put all its information at the service of Comintern. You see, no end of *agents provocateurs* are at work in the very midst of the Communist Party, in the orient, everywhere; and it is OGPU's function to unmask them. One should expect the two institutions to work in closest concert. It isn't, however, the fact that they always do. Certain methods employed by the OGPU *rezidents* here and there abroad (especially in Persia, Turkey and England) are of peculiar interest. As the danger involved in the use of Russian agents seemed excessive, use was made of the machinery and personnel of the native Communist parties. They were called on to furnish the goods. It cost less; and perhaps more valuable information was obtained.

When originally assigned to Tehran by Trilliser, Agabekov had accompanied his chief to see Piatnitsky for a briefing at which various methods of infiltrating agents into India had been discussed, including a suggestion that M.N. Roy 'procure an American passport and sail from the United States to an Indian port'. While in Tehran Agabekov was given a budget of $5,000 a month 'for pushing work in India and Iraq' and his experience, having been Chief of the OGPU's Oriental Section, made him an invaluable source for the British when he defected. Although he never came to London, he was interviewed extensively in Brussels and over the next three years worked intermittently for SIS, undertaking missions to Berlin and proposing some extravagant schemes to turn some of his old contacts in Kurdistan. Nothing came of these ideas, but he was placed on SIS's payroll at a modest salary and was able to identify individual OGPU agents across the Near and Middle East, compromise a successful intercept operation that had gained access to British diplomatic circulars, and explain the relationship between the Comintern, the OGPU and the Red Army's intelligence branch, the GRU. Undoubtedly the Kremlin and Agabekov's former colleagues were outraged by his defection, for he was lured to France in January 1937, on the pretext of participating in the disposal of art treasures looted during the Spanish Civil War, and he disappeared in the Pyrenees, probably abducted and murdered by republicans acting on Moscow's orders.

Another useful source of information about the Comintern's activities in the region was a collection of documents seized in Shanghai a week after the arrest in Singapore in April 1931 of Joseph Ducroux, a French businessman previously linked to M.N. Roy in Marseilles in 1926. According to the Ducroux material, the Communist movements in Burma, Siam, Malaya and the Dutch East Indies were controlled from Singapore, whereas a Far East Bureau operated in Shanghai, in parallel with the Pan-Pacific Trades-Union Secretariat, directing Comintern and Profinform activities in China, Japan, Indonesia and the Philippines. Ducroux was sentenced to eighteen months' imprisonment.

The father of Indian Communism was Manandranath Nath Roy, who left India in 1915 while on bail facing charges of terrorism. After a long tour of the Far East he turned up in San Francisco where he was indicted on conspiracy charges, and fled across the Mexican border. In 1920 he visited Europe and Russia, where he was enrolled into the Comintern, and later sent on two missions, to Afghanistan in 1920 and then to China in 1926. Usually accompanied by his American wife, Evelyn Trent, he established a propaganda school in Tashkent, lived in Germany until he fled to Paris in 1923, and was expelled from France in early 1925. Wherever he went, he left a trail of anti-British agitation and plots, and in February 1924 was named as a defendant in the Cawnpore conspiracy trial in which 168 Indian Communists were charged with conspiring to remove the King Emperor of the sovereignty of British India. In the end only four defendants were convicted, and Roy responded by formally establishing an Indian Communist Party, and despatching Percy Glading, alias Robert Cochrane of the National Minority Movement, to report on its progress. Glading took a poor view of the ICP's efforts, and more CPGB leaders, including George Allison, alias Donald Campbell, arrived in Bombay in April 1926 for the second time, ostensibly to organise an Indian Trades Union Congress. Seven months later Allison was arrested on a charge of forging a Foreign Office seal on his British passport and served eighteen months' imprisonment. Shortly before he had completed his sentence he was placed aboard a ship at sea and deported back to England, where in November 1931 he was sentenced to three years' imprisonment for attempting to incite a mutiny in the Royal Navy. Allison had been replaced by Philip Spratt, ostensibly in Calcutta to open a Labour Publishing House, and in September 1927 he was joined by Ben Bradley, a London-born engineer who had helped found the Communist-led Workers' and Peasants' Party. Finally, in September 1928, Hugh Hutchinson reached Bombay where he fell for Mrs Suhasini Nambiar, the sister of Virendra Nath Chattopadhyaya, Roy's rival in founding the Indian Communist Party.

The Meerut trial in 1929 had led to the conviction on conspiracy charges of a dozen Cawnpore trade unionist agitators, among them Ben Bradley and Lester Hutchinson. Through his association with the Workers' and Peasants' Party, Bradley had been a key figure in organising the wave of strikes that had swept across India in 1928. As one of the thirty-one defendants, Bradley was eventually convicted in January 1933 and received ten years' imprisonment. Another CPGB activist, the Cambridge educated Philip Spratt, was sentenced to twelve years.

Roy himself did not return to India until March 1931 but news of his appearances in Bombay and Karachi reached the IPI and he was eventually arrested in Bombay and sentenced, in January 1932, on the original 1924 Cawnpore conspiracy charges, to twelve years' transportation, later reduced on appeal to six years' rigorous imprisonment.

British knowledge of the relationship between the Workers' and Peasants' Party and its parent, the Indian Communist Party, stemmed from a document, later known as the Assembly letter, so-called because it had been read out during a debate in the Legislative Assembly in September 1928. Written by M.N. Roy and sent via Clemens Palme Dutt (Rajani's brother) in London it was addressed to the 'Central Committee C.P. and Workers' and Peasants' Party' and, while dealing with mainly financial and organisational issues, revealed that both parties were really under the same control. Roy, who exercised considerable influence through the distribution of his Moscow-sponsored newspaper *Masses of India*, advocated making the relationship between the two less transparent and suggested that the WPP should liaise with the Comintern in Paris and Berlin, and not be affiliated with the CPGB's Colonial Bureau apart from an affiliation with the League Against Imperialism. When the Party met in Bombay in March 1929 to discuss Roy's proposals almost all the membership was arrested, thus neutralising the leadership.

Ever since the Indian Communist Party had been founded in 1924 by Satya Bhakta, the local security apparatus had monitored its activities, placed informants inside the organisation and made mass arrests whenever the opportunity had arisen. In December 1925 much of the leadership had been detained at the Cawnpore Conference, and in March 1929 thirty-one leaders, including Spratt and Bradley, had been charged with being revolutionaries acting on the Comintern's instructions. Finally, in January 1933, all but four of the defendants were convicted, and the judgment covered seven hundred foolscap pages, amounting to a highly detailed account of the scale of the Communist-inspired conspiracy in India and implicating several plotters who were not present, including M.N. Roy, George Allison and Clemens Palme Dutt. These individuals, of course, became the subject of surveillance, and some of their correspondence was intercepted. This revealed that the principal CPGB emissaries all had code names, with Allison being DAVID, Spratt was DESMOND, Bradley was FRED and C.P. Dutt was DOUGLAS, and they used a cipher based on Palgrave's *Golden Treasury*. MI5 and the IPI were also interested in the Party's finances, and noted that Spratt was supported by remittances of more than £1,000 during his mission to India, which had lasted eighteen months until his departure in June 1928. During that period he received payments from the City bankers Samuel Montagu & Company via Olive and Douglas Parsons. Parsons was general manager of the *Sunday Worker*, and his wife Olive's father was a director of Samuel Montagu. This particular route exposed another covert CPGB link, although the participants were unaware that their activities had come under scrutiny. The Comintern also used an American channel to pass money to the Party, and in early 1930 an American antiquarian, William Kweit, accompanied by his wife Helen Bowlen arrived in Bombay to be joined in July by a third US passport holder, Harry Somers, who claimed to represent a cellulose company. All three were arrested and deported under the Foreigners Act in September 1930. Similarly, Henry G. Lynd, who arrived in Bombay in February 1931 under commercial cover purporting to be an importer of skins with a business in New York, and attended several of the Party's Executive Committee meetings in Bombay, was also arrested and deported.

Although the ICP leadership, such as the Chairman Doc Adhikari and the General-Secretary P.C. Joshi, were Indians, there was a strong covert European cadre organised by the Bishop of Bombay's chaplain, the Reverend Michael Scott and Michael Carritt, an Oxford graduate and until 1938 an Under-Secretary in the Government of India's Political Department. Later a philosophy lecturer at Oxford, Carritt had access to IPI material addressed to Sir John Anderson, then the Governor of Bengal, and was able to leak intelligence reports from the Police Commissioner, Leslie Colson, to the Party, thereby neutralising some of its effectiveness. Fortunately for MI5's mole, Olga Gray, her true identity and details of her mission had been held tightly in London, and not imparted to the IPI, thereby enabling her mission to Bombay to be completed without arousing any suspicions on the part of Harry Pollitt or Percy Glading. Although there are no references to Olga's voyage to India in the MASK traffic, Michael Scott is referred to as 'the priest', and after two years in Bombay he went on to Calcutta, but joined the RAF in 1940. Invalided out of the service in 1941 he returned to South Africa, where as a student he had attended St Paul's College Grahamtown, and was active among the tribes of South-West Africa. The son of an Anglican vicar, he was appointed to the Diocese of Chichester in 1950, and two years later had helped found the Africa Bureau. Later he was to write *Shadow Over Africa* and *African Episode*, but in his 1958 autobiography, *A Time To Speak*, he gave an account of the clandestine role he had played for the CPGB, recalling that he had 'told the Communists I would be prepared to do anything I could to help their cause there, provided it did not positively conflict with my conscience'. Scott had been given a 'very crude form of code to be used for anything that might be thought confidential' and £100 for delivery to addresses in India and Japan 'to help towards the travelling expenses of delegates to the Seventh World

Congress of the Communist International in Moscow'. Scott also tried to make a delivery to a contact in Singapore, but 'found that he had already been apprehended by the police and returned to India'.

> The thought of being involved in this conspiracy gave me some pleasurable excitement. I derived some satisfaction from devising ways of escaping detection, of establishing contact and maintaining it without betraying my own or other people's identity. I knew enough to realise that, not only were the forces of law and order extremely efficient, but the Communists themselves could become very vindictive and suspicious in the event of failure to fulfil any commission they had given – though I really had no conception of the ramifications of all that I was becoming involved in and for which I was accepting moral responsibility.
>
> (Scott 1958: 65)

In September 1932 another source of funds, John Magnus Clark and William Bennett, were taken into custody, both claiming to be travelling to Moscow from Canada, having arrived in Bombay a year earlier. Secret correspondence suggested they were Profinform couriers who had delivered large sums of money to the Indian Communist Party, and they both opted to leave the country voluntarily rather than face prosecution under a special statute, passed by the Governor General in Council at Simla on 10 September 1932. Using a reserve power under the Sea Customs Act 1878, a ban was placed on any document emanating from the Communist International, or any organisation controlled by it or affiliated to it, and on any person holding office in such organisations. Thus it became an offence to attempt to enter India as a Comintern agent, or to import Comintern literature. This draconian, wide-ranging law proved to be a powerful instrument in the IPI's hands.

The IPI's successful intervention in these cases strongly suggested a breach in the internal security of either the Comintern or the local Party, and in 1934 Ben Bradley went to Moscow to discuss a resumption of the CPGB channels that had served so well prior to 1929, a visit disclosed in the MASK traffic. Fortunately both Moscow and the CPGB concluded that the Party was an obvious target for penetration by hostile agents, and leaks were an occupational hazard. Georgi Agabekov had disclosed in 1930 that three years earlier there had been an attempt to maintain some separation between the Party and its illegal *apparats*, and had attributed this to the embarrassment caused by the Zinoviev Letter affair in 1924, as though the letter had been authentic. In any event, it was inevitable that Moscow would want to exploit the opportunities offered by Communist sympathisers. Accordingly, the CPGB took measures to tighten its internal security and protect against MI5 informants, but remained vulnerable through its communications because nobody ever suspected the existence of a super-secret source codenamed MASK.

4

THE MASK TRAFFIC

The traffic exchanged between Moscow and London during the period February 1934 to January 1937 was transmitted in cipher, and the fact that the parties involved used such surreptitious means for their communications, instead of the ordinary, commercial cables, indicates that the messages were never intended to be read by anyone else, and therefore is something of a guarantee that the content would be of interest to MI5. According to William Morrison, the wireless operator who underwent a lengthy debriefing by Max Knight and John Archer, even he was not allowed to encipher the clear text, and he only handled ciphered messages. The secrecy surrounding the channel is highlighted by the fact that Krivitsky had no knowledge of its existence (and MI5 did not enlighten him). Indeed, the wireless was not used exclusively, as the messages show that some innocuous texts were sent by wire, thereby emphasising the clandestine nature of the channel. Of course, it could be argued that the CPGB's General-Secretary, Harry Pollitt, was perfectly entitled to consult with Moscow and other Parties overseas over issues of policy, and other confidential matters, but the correspondence shows his deep complicity in the covert side of the Party's activities, the fact that he personally was receiving expenses from Moscow, and that he sought and received political direction from the OLD MAN. He is also directly implicated in the despatch and delivery by trusted couriers of suitcases, mainly via Paris, which seem to have contained contraband of some description, perhaps money or documents, and certainly numbered letters written in cipher. It is also possible that the suitcases themselves may have been of some importance, for when Glading was arrested in January 1938 he was found to be in possession of a suitcase with a false bottom that had been used to smuggle plans and blueprints out of the Woolwich Arsenal. Doubtless MI5's knowledge of this route was increased by Olga Gray who was also used as a courier to Moscow, although she was probably never told exactly what she was carrying or where the material was concealed. Since it usually took about a week for GC&CS to decrypt the messages, there seems to have been little opportunity for Special Branch or Customs officers at the ports to have opened and illicitly copied whatever the couriers were carrying.

The practice of concealing identities through the use of codenames is standard tradecraft or, as the Soviets call it, *konspiratsia*, and can cause confusion, even to those involved; occasionally the object of the exercise is defeated when an individual's true name is requested, as happened when Moscow asked who JOHN was, and he was revealed as GORDON. Apart from Pollitt, who used his own surname to sign messages, and also his first name, the messages from London were signed by WEST and the radio operator appears to have been FRED. Their replies were signed mainly by ABRAHAM, ALEXANDER and MICHAEL, and their stilted use of English suggests they were Russians. Most likely, ABRAHAM was Abramoff, the alias of Jacob Mirov, then the head of the OGPU's communications who, according to Krivitsky, was arrested in 1936 in the purges and was executed the following year. A graduate of universities in Germany, Abramoff had been selected to be the OMS representative in Berlin, operating under embassy cover, until he was recalled to Moscow in 1930 to be Piatnitsky's assistant. In 1935 he was transferred to the Foreign Ministry, but was arrested during the purge in 1937, and is thought to have perished.

Another frequent correspondent was ALEXANDER, the codename for A.E. Abramovich, one of the original Russian Bolsheviks who had met Lenin in Switzerland in 1911. After the First World War he worked in Berlin and Munich, but was arrested in Nice in January 1921 under the alias Zalewski. Upon his release he was appointed secretary of the Soviet embassy in Tallinn, and in 1924 transferred to the embassy in Vienna. Thereafter, he was based in Moscow, supervising some of the Comintern's operations in western Europe.

MI5 was, of course, intensely interested in the names that cropped up in the traffic, but the task of sorting out the real names from the codenames was far from easy. For example, one text is clear that MARY, who refers to his wife, must be a man, yet there is another in which MARY is referred to as 'she', suggesting there may have been one person with the codename, and another with the real name, which is not entirely surprising given that it is such a common name. What makes the puzzle more interesting is that Litzi Philby's codename was MARY, and it may be that she was using this channel for some of her messages to Moscow. If MI5 had succeeded in linking MARY to Litzi Friedman, and then connecting her to Kim Philby, his subsequent career might have taken a rather different course.

Similarly, the identity of FRED is not certain, but his use of the international Morse 'Q' code for reporting interference and acknowledging reception in December 1934 suggests he was a conventional radio operator, and most likely was Stephen Wheeton. SPENCE was probably William Spence, a senior CPGB veteran who seems to have had responsibility for the Young Communist League (YCL), and clearly ARNOT was Robin Page Arnot who signed several of the messages from Moscow in 1936.

As regards the numbering of the MASK texts, each in its original form bears a GC&CS date and serial number, but these are for the organisation's internal reference only, and therefore have been omitted from the reproduction of messages here, which seem to run in sequence from 1 to 100 before beginning again, although the operators in Moscow were occasionally quite careless and sometimes duplicated a serial number, or even omitted it entirely.

The actual content of the messages is interesting, ranging from banal, with policy instructions from the Comintern (Communist International), KIM (Young Communist International) and the Profinform (Red Trade Unions International), to requests for information about the trustworthiness of individual students attending the Wilson or Lenin Schools in Moscow, and their travel arrangements.

First, the messages from London to Moscow:

10 March 1934. No. 111
For Political Commission
Political Bureau with exception RUST endorsed Secretariat proposals I.L.P. after Easter conference which we have sent to MCILHONE. RUST's position after conference (2 groups) bring I.L.P. supporters directly into Communist Party.
POLLIT

17 March 1934. Nos. 74, 75
For C.C.
Instruct editors for Editorial Conference to prepare report following questions. Organise editorship and collaboration with party. Source of information, construction of worker correspondence movement and collaboration. Popularization resolutions ECCI and Soviet power. Fight against Social Democracy, connection with red trades union opposition and trades union functions. Fight against fascism work among town and country middle class, unmasking Imperialist foreign and armament policy. Propagation peace policy USSR. Fight against war CHINA and Soviet CHINA, unmasking pacifist and Social democracy, work in army. Fight against anti-Soviet campaign. Popularization USSR. Wire name editor delegate. Acknowledge receipt.
KUN

17 March 1934. No. 77
MOPR invites ALLISON and wife Soviet Union English comrades responsible fare to Soviet border.
HELEN

21 March 1934. No. 119
For KUN
Shields will arrive Editorial Conference on March 24th.

21 March 1934. No. 120
For Political Commission
We have information from BRIDGEMAN that Gerald HAMILTON is taking up press work in MANCHURIA, and will also interest himself in munitions traffic.
WEST

22 March 1934. No. 122
For ABRAMOV
Glad inform you visit of messenger Little Bob's country entirely successful. You will have full report very soon.

22 April 1934. No. 140
For WEST
Relief Committee want Dmitrov Queen's Hall demonstration May 17th. Urge him wire agreement.

22 April 1934. No. 141
FRED not sending until completion larger set. Will notify when ready; received numbers 4, 5, 6 and 7.

23 April 1934. No. 142
For MCILHONE
Pennifold with workers delegation has material for you. Arrange meet him; received number 8 and 9.
B

24 April 1934. No. 144
U.M.S. executive meets week-end imperative reply regarding attitude PIATNISKY's attack.
Failing immediate reply Secretariat will publish repudiation Daily Worker.

24 April 1934. No. 145
For WEST
PHYLIS anxious to know date of TOM's return. Can you find out.
B

11 May 1934. No. 155
For ABRAMOV
HART informs me he could not make contact in PARIS. Handed material to American comrade with whom he was travelling.
From WEST

11 May 1934. No. 155
For MAZUT
Assure you in telegram to country included every point especially about amalgamation. It was stupid error part (?) Daily not to have published resolution (?) in full. This is being corrected.

Also from LANCASHIRE the important points sent to necessary papers and trades unions. We get very little news from the country, can you help a little. From POLLIT

11 May 1934. No. 158
For ABRAMOV
Meet WINCOTT at Leningrad steamer Smolny. He has important material for you.
From POLLIT

16 May 1934. No. 160
For ABRAMOV
Please note FRED will not be able to receive messages May 19th, 20th, 21st.
POLLIT

16 May 1934. No. 161
For Little BOB
Messenger fixed but shipping company warns you this wrong time travel. If messenger were to travel now may rouse suspicion, therefore we have fixed to sail two weeks time.
WEST

17 May 1934. No. 162
For MCILHONE
Absolutely essential EDWARDS returns May 24th enable him attend I.L.P. Conference Lancashire.
POLLIT

30 May 1934. No. 169
Essential EDWARDS WHALLEY return for campaign I.L.P. also essential BEN return. All messages correct up to 47. 161 re-despatched.
BURNS

2 June 1934. No. 170
Little BOB
Wood can be used for money. Sailing June 21st. First messenger sailing June 10th.
Received nothing 0100 GMT. June 2nd from FRED.
Repeat all messages from No. 47.
GLADING

5 June 1934. No. 174
We recommend an Indian student for 6 repeat 6 months study in Moscow. July December period. Can then return home.
GLADING

6 June 1934. No. 175

For ABRAMOV

Trying hard to get students you require. BOB has this in hand; the messages correct up to number 51. Don't repeat.

From POLLIT

6 June 1934. No. 176

For ABRAMOV

Re Seamen: HAMBURG man is German and has contact. ROTTERDAM seaman has already made (?) contact SITPAUL who was in charge communications in HAMBURG. BORDEAUX man without contact. Will carry out any suggestions you offer. The tried and trusted men. Weekly mailings.

WEST

12 June 1934. No. 180

For ABRAMOV

Comrade DOCKER Australian leaves LONDON for LENINGRAD June 9th. Arrange meet him he has important material for you. Travelling steamer 'DZHEZINSKY'.

POLLIT

12 June 1934. No. 180

For KIM

Report joint meeting sent. Scottish Unity Conference 17th. National Committee League 23rd (1 group) ENGLAND 24th.

MEINHART

13 June 1934. No. 183

For YUSOPVITCH

This repeats FRED's message number 10. Comrades do not consider COHEN should come for work among seamen in your ports.

POLLIT

14 June 1934. No. 188

Political Commission

Received your instructions date of World Congress. Will you inform us how many delegates we are invited to send, and what instructions you have about their election.

POLLIT

16 June 1934. No. 188

MCILHONE

Understand DMITROV willing attend anti-war Youth Congress. Necessary apply visa in MOSCOW. Let us know immediately if he will do this so we can give publicity. We will organise big campaign round (?) this soon you reply.

POLLIT

19 June 1934. No. 189
ABRAHAM
What FRED wanted cancelled was request for repeat. All messages up to 65.
WEST

20 June 1934. No. 190
For the Old Man
Very important you give serious consideration to urgent message TOM BELL will give you.
POLLIT

20 June 1934. No. 191
ABRAMOV
Have you any news of Mrs. MORRIS.
WEST

23 June 1934. No. 194
KIM
LE-HARDT requires new brochures (4 groups). Your instructions re women anti-war conference received.
SPENCE

26 June 1934. No. 197
MCILHONE
Imperative replies I.L.P. should arrive here; we are in favour BELL taking charge school section.
POLLIT

26 June 1934. No. 198
ABRAMOV
HART states not suitable, was given to hand over to me.
RENNA

27 June 1934. No. 199
MCILHONE
Invitation attend Anti-War Congress sent DMITROV. Essential he applies visa and lets us know he accepts invitation.
POLLIT

27 June 1934. No. 200
ABRAMOV
Excuse delay in answering your wire re BOB WILSON. Absolutely favourable your using him. He is one of our best. You can rely on him with confidence.

9 July 1934. No. 5
MCILHONE

Received information about number of delegates world (?) congress, but what method of selection has to be adopted?

POLLIT

9 July 1934. No. 7
For Little BOB

What decision about Student (?) Khan whose particulars we sent. He write in 'HINDUSTANI' under the name JAISAINGH. Reply immediately.

WEST

9 July 1934. No. 9
For MCILHONE

Essential doctor's certificate GRIFFITHS death be went (?) enable family get insurance money.

POLLIT

9 July 1934. No. 10
For DMITROV

Essential you attend SHEFFIELD anti-war congress. Have you applied for visa? Let us know so that big campaign can be organised.

POLLIT

12 July 1934. No. 13
For ABRAMOV

Fred bitterly complains your man does not play the game. Fred must have time to send the messages as well as receive yours. Fred says your man wastes a lot of time. Will you see into this at once.

POLLIT

12 July 1934. No. 14
ABRAHAM

BICKERTON says he knows nothing of FRANCIS of TORIO and believes letter a frame up. BICKERTON was released on bail and absconded. Will interview him and let you know.

WEST

13 July 1934. No. 15
MCILHONE

Two letters have been sent inviting DMITROV to attend SHEFFIELD but (?) no reply from your end. Get a move on and let us know if DMITROV has applied.

POLLIT

13 July 1934. No. 16

ABRAHAM

Thanks for congratulations. No revision of trial possible (?). But it cost 400 repeat 400 pounds. What about that side of it (?) Would you like to see me arrested for debt.

WEST

14 July 1934. No. 17

Inform Political Commission directives August last received. The messages up to number 88 received correct.

WEST

2 August 1934. No. 21

Railway Unions meeting separately 8th August our slogans united meeting three unions delegate bodies and joint action enforce (?) return cuts. Also urging joint action each depot and resolutions the branches to 8th August meetings.

WEST and MAHON

8 August 1934. No. 33

ABRAHAM

Little Bob's messenger's mission successful in every way. Report follows. Recommend this messenger for other work similar kind; cuttings from PARIS received August 6th.

WEST

9 August 1934. No. 34

ABRAHAM

From August 10th to 18th please call FRED as usual but send no messages his way until August 27th. Apparatus being overhauled.

WEST

10 August 1934. No. 36

LOSOVSKY

TOM MANN leaves London on Wednesday August 15th steamer RYKOV for LENINGRAD.

3 September 1934. No. 46

MCILHONE

You have now full list Congress delegation it might still include DUTT (?) Is it (1 group).

POLLIT

3 September 1934. No. 47

ABRAHAM

Courier brought opposite information about Congress delegates for Little BOB.

WEST

3 September 1934. No. 48
ABRAHAM
Sent you full report from BICKERTON. Did you receive it?
WEST

5 September 1934. No. 50
MCILHONE
There has been criminal delay in I.L.P. pamphlet it is on press and ought to be out this week. EDWARDS and WHALLEY practically dropped out of doing anything.
POLLIT

6 September 1934. No. 51
ABRAHAM
Congress delegate DURAN of Colombia leaves LONDON September 5th on steamer DZERZHINSKY. Delegate SIMS leaves LONDON September 8th.
WEST

7 September 1934. No. 53
ABRAHAM
No contact with SOUTH AFRICA to inform them method election Congress delegates: once more we inform you BICKERTON has sent report. Have you received it?
WEST

10 September 1934. No. 55
ABRAHAM
Four Mexican Congress delegates left LONDON September 8th on steamer RYKOV. They should be met at LENINGRAD.
POLLIT

12 September 1934. No. 56
ABRAHAM
FREDA fixed up will arrive PARIS September 18th.
POLLIT

12 September 1934. No. 58
ABRAHAM
Re: WILSON's School so far despite special efforts failed get students – negotiations still going on. Will carry out instructions for SMITH's mother.
WEST

12 September 1934. No. 61
MAZUT
Everything courier brought back given to ROCK.
WEST

14 September 1934. No. 62

ABRAHAM

Received wire postponing Congress nine p.m. September 8th. Too late prevent Mexican New Zealand delegates leaving. Have informed HATCH and GORDON. Australian on way LONDON. What do we advise them?

POLLIT

15 September 1934. No. 66

ABRAHAM

Not our FRED but FREDA repeat FREDA going to PARIS, will (1 group) you further information from BICKERTON soon as possible, trying get insurance things; not yet got students youth (?) school.

WEST

16 September 1934. No. 67

ABRAHAM

Two Australian delegates here, what has to be done? ROBERT SMITH's family been interviewed nothing has arrived there. General impression formed family (1 group) talkative.

17 September 1934. No. 68

ABRAHAM

FRED you ask about is FREDA LEVINE.

WEST

18 September 1934. No. 66

MCILHONE

MITCHELL will travel September 29th to LENINGRAD from LONDON. Hope everything ready for him.

POLLIT

18 September 1934. No. 70

ABRAHAM

Heard nothing GERHARDT.

EMILE BURNS address no good.

If not too late ask him make contact Doctor DUNSTAN, 84 Boyson Road, CLERKENWELL, LONDON repeat LONDON 84 Boyson Road, CLERKENWELL.

WEST

18 September 1934. No. 71

ABRAHAM

BICKERTON just had letter dated July 8th, that comrade charge communications JAPAN been arrested. Sending you full report first opportunity.

POLLIT

19 September 1934. No. 72

For MICHAEL

Last December decision made that League should have regular monthly allocations. This has not been received for months, and what we asked you to send is fulfilment decision made with old man and WEST.

POLLIT

20 September 1934. No. 74

MCILHONE

POLLIT will arrive October 3rd via LENINGRAD. MITCHELL travelling with POLLIT, necessary arrangements be made reception MITCHELL immediately arrive in MOSCOW.

POLLIT

24 September 1934. No. 77

ABRAHAM

Your code letter addressed to DON repeat DON is impossible to decipher here.

WEST

24 September 1934. No. 78

MCILHONE

GALLACHER already been IRELAND before receiving your wire. Our comrades were in bad position. We gave them directives in general same as what sent by P.C. Will have comrades present at Congress.

POLLIT

26 September 1934. No. 79

ABRAHAM

Hope to send two students Wilson's school next week.

WEST

26 September 1934. No. 80

ABRAHAM

We have three students ready Wilson's School. Shall we send them direct LENINGRAD or STOCKHOLM?

WEST

27 September 1934. No. 81

ABRAHAM

POLLIT arrive LENINGRAD via Steamer DZERZHINSKY October 5th with important material make arrangements get through. On same boat two Australian delegates MOREY and MARSH. Inform MCILHONE that MITCHELL travelling with POLLIT.

WEST

1 October 1934. No. 75
ABRAHAM from Codist
FRED is having difficulties with R transmission. Until you hear from us send messages via STOCKHOLM.

2 October 1934. No. 84
POLLIT from WEST
Man you saw with EMILE has offer go KOREA. Can leave LONDON November via INDIA where he can stay two three weeks. Wire whether should accept.

5 October 1934. No. 86
For Brigadier
Passport question Orland repeat Orland enquiries show impossibility arrange LONDON. Necessary return before expires.
BILL

10 October 1934. No. 88
ABRAHAM
STEPHENS and IVES left for WILSONS SCHOOL on steamer SEBIR to LENIN-GRAD today. Make necessary arrangements.

11 October 1934. No. 89
POLLIT
Can you do anything regarding THW repeat THW proposition raised in December (4 groups).
WEST

16 October 1934. No. 91
ABRAHAM
HILL repeat HILL left for WILSON's by steamer 'SMOLNY' to LENINGRAD October 13th.
WEST

17 October 1934. No. 92
POLLIT
MUNZENBURG utilizing MARLEY independent of all without consulting Committee or Party. MARLEY (?hoping) that no Communists be allowed or proposed Commission to help SAAR workers. Stop this (one group) writing.
WEST

21 October 1934. No. 94
ABRAHAM
Australian delegates MILES left LONDON for LENINGRAD by steamer RUDZUTAK 20th October. MILES carries very important letters and port-manteau for you. Arrange meet him.
WEST

22 October 1934. No. 96
Political Commission
Advise you examine possibilities of using (?mass) movement amongst church people in GERMANY for developing the fight against HITLER. An examination British press proves that the result of churches is really tremendous. We ought to ensure WEST party takes advantage of this. Letter follows.
POLLIT

25 October 1934. No. 97
ABRAHAM
Canadian called NAWIZOSKI left LONDON for MOSCOW via NEGORILOGE October 24th.
POLLIT

26 October 1934. No. 98
Political Commission
We propose organisation international demonstration on November 13th in place second International meetings with speakers from FRANCE, GERMANY, AUSTRIA, BRITAIN and ITALY, Austrian communist and social democratic. We are organising such a meeting in LONDON.
From POLLIT

26 October 1934. No. 99
VASILIEV from WEST
KEEBLE cannot go Soviet Union, but his wife who is well acquainted with every phase Esperantist position and shares KEEBLE's views could come. Wire your decision.

26 October 1934. No. 100
For LENIN School
Propose ROBINSON of MANCHESTER as organisation instructor.
From POLLIT

27 October 1934. No. 1
ABRAHAM
Comrade FREEMAN on steamer RYKOV leaves LONDON for LENINGRAD October 28th. He carries very special portmanteau and letters for you. Arrange meet him.
From POLLIT

27 October 1934. No. 5
Clear that journalist HEWER undoubtedly is a police agent. Take this into consideration. The business with him must be broken; send responsible member CC to PARIS for registration with ERCOLI as representative.

30 October 1934. No. 3

ABRAHAM

Inform JOHN MURRAY that his girl friend will be coming as student. Do you accept IRIS HARDY? Inform us when you receive material from FREEMAN.

POLLIT

31 October 1934. No. 4

ARNOT, HENRI

Regret MURRAY's wife now refuses to go out to WILSON's School owing domestic difficulties. Will try find substitute.

POLLIT

31 October 1934. No. 5

ABRAHAM

Please repeat name of journalist who is dangerous; Inform P.C. Spanish directive No. 10 received. Correct up to eleven.

WEST

2 November 1934. No. 5

ABRAHAM

Inform P.C. that Spanish directives numbers twelve, thirteen and fourteen received.

WEST

4 November 1934. No. 7

ABRAHAM

The girl students will leave for Wilson's school on November 7th. Can send you two more men students if you require them.

POLLIT

4 November 1934. No. 8

MCILHONE

Hurry up STASSOVA regarding costs SWANSEA trial.

POLLIT

5 November 1934. No. 9

ABRAHAM

I mentioned name BARBARA ARCHER to you. Have now found out she worked for Austrian comrades under name HERTHA TARNAY and HERTHA HOLLERING. She is known to comrade FEDIN now working on German Moscow Daily News. Let us know if you want to use her. Would make good courier.

WEST

6 November 1934. No. 10

ABRAHAM

Our wire stated that SOL FREEMAN is leader of British Worker's delegation travelling on RYKOV and carrying special portmanteau and letters for you.

WEST

6 November 1934. No. 11

ABRAHAM

Received your wire re woman and PARIS. It will be attended to on November 8th.

POLLIT

7 November 1934. No. 12

ABRAHAM

Three pounds sent ABERCROMBIE November 6th. Why give me a dog's life about girl students? Sending you two by steamer this week do you want all the women we have? Begin suspect you personally keep harem.

WEST

7 November 1934. No. 13

ALEXANDER

Thanks for suggestions. They agree with line already given.

POLLIT

7 November 1934. No. 14

ABRAHAM

MARY has arrived safely and she asks you to take special care of her artist friend who you will meet and who is a very valuable person.

HARRY

7 November 1934. No. 15

ABRAHAM

Received order S.F. 41000 and DG 11000.

8 November 1934. No. 16

ABRAHAM

Two girl students for WILSON's school left LONDON November 7th on DZERZHINSKY for LENINGRAD. Arrange meet them.

HARRY

13 November 1934. No. 23

P.C.

Received telegram going to PARIS on November 12th at 4.30. Made arrangements go PARIS then heard on telephone from HUMANITE that no demonstration taking place.

POLLIT

14 November 1934. No. 24

KIM

Manifesto issued 50,000 copies copyright twenty pounds. Our representative will be KLINE or LEES.

SPENCE

16 November 1934. No. 17

P.C.

Strongly urge manifesto on SPAIN should be issued by E.C.C.I. and not simply by four parties. Importance Spanish events demands whole authority of E.C.C.I. behind any statement issued.

POLLIT

16 November 1934. No. 18

P.C. and LIM

Given careful consideration your proposals ILP Guild Conference. Believe they are incorrect and if carried through would give rise to main issue becoming who are the splitters. This would be political mistake with serious consequences future development United Front activity all Sections Youth organisations.

16 November 1934. No. 19

We consider our proposals correct line. BROCKWAY informed POLLIT this week NAC would make electoral pact with CP if CP could refrain carrying on activity in ILP and guild. If your proposals carried out bound have serious reaction in present involving relations of CP and ILP.

Party and ICL Secretary

17 November 1934. No. 25

MCILHONE

Have received today full bill of costs all proceeds POLLIT MANN case. Amount 577 repeat 577 pounds. You must ask OLD MAN to fulfil promise about getting native from MOHR. Position desperate for me. Must have help.

POLLIT

17 November 1934. Nos. 26, 27

ABRAHAM

Received from PARIS two portmanteaux. Small one contains material only for SIEGFRIED repeat SIEGFRIED obviously not for me. Have sent material back to PARIS. The other large portmanteau contained materials agreed on by CHARLES and myself, and also little gadget which contained letters numbered 4011–1, 02043, 02044, 02081, 0—, number 02116. Will arrange speedy departure messenger GORDON's country review.

HARRY

19 November 1934. No. 28

IM

Return from LONDON November 22nd. Inform MICHAEL.

MEINHARDT

21 November 1934. No. 29

P.C.

Strongly protest against line of UN's article on results of PARIS Conference of Second International. Consider whole line wrong and harmful. Letter follows: your directives numbers 34 and 35 received. We await number 23 and 24 also 32, 33 and 36.

POLLIT

23 November 1934. No. 30

KIM

KLINE left LONDON November 22nd by boat.

SPENCE

24 November 1934. No. 31

MCILHONE

On steamer SIBIER which left LONDON for LENINGRAD November 23rd are COHEN your referment and KLINE for KIM. Arrange meet them.

POLLIT

24 November 1934. No. 32

P.C.

GORDON will publish article Congress Specialists in INPRECORR. Messenger will leave for Little BOB's country immediately.

WEST

27 November 1934. No. 33.

ABRAHAM

Cannot understand what you mean by 'Send the available KAVKAS' repeat KAVKAS in your telegram No. 40.

HARRY

28 November 1934. No. 43

Surprised your information that you did not receive our Nos. 23, 24, 32, 33 and 36. We received acknowledgment radio telegraphist that he received these numbers. We sent repetition November 25th. Clarify and wire.

29 November 1934. No. 31

ABRAHAM

Mistake our part making repeat numbers 23 and 24. Other numbers deciphered after our telegram sent. Telegrams correct up to 46.

WEST

29 November 1934. No. 34

WASSILIEF

IEBEL not possible come over because his employment. British ESPERANTO organisation very small but we have our members working here. Not advisable invite anybody else. Necessary information and material re this organisation sent over recently.

MARY

30 November 1934. No. 35

MCILHONE

Absolutely imperative MARTHA PETTIGREW returns home immediately. Reply when she leaves.

POLLIT

4 December 1934. No. 37

ABRAHAM

Article signed by BRADLEY appearing current issue INPRECORR. GORDON states addresses he has are not reliable enough for contact with C.C.Y.

HARRY

5 December 1934. No. 39

MICHAEL

Who is JOHN. You ask us pay salary to you, received order YN 39000.

WEST

5 December 1934. No. 40

ABRAHAM

Tell BRANDT to stop troubling my wife with thousand rouble bills for not used rest home KUNCEVO. Where from would she take the money from anyhow? Have you arranged my family allowance?

MARY

6 December 1934. No. 41

ABRAHAM

My transmitter hundred watts and O.K. Trouble is your end. Suggest you find frequency clear of QRM and wire me same. Don't say QRV until you can read my sign. Here also QRM but I invariably get your message.

FRED

7 December 1934. No. 42

ABRAHAM

Student named ROCHE for WILSON's School is on steamer RYKOV for LENIN-GRAD. Meet him he carries important portmanteau and material.

WEST

8 December 1934. No. 43
PIATIZSKY
The Labour Chairman of Glasgow Municipal Housing Committee is anxious for invitation from Moscow Soviet to Glasgow Town Council to visit Moscow Soviet Housing Scheme. Recommend you consider this may be means of getting useful contacts.
POLLIT

8 December 1934. No. 46
Did you get the material from ROCHE?
HARRY

10 December 1934. No. 36
ABRAHAM
DON repeat DON unable to decipher message 4011–1.

10 December 1934. No. 38
NORMAN
What has happened TOM MANN's materials in PARIS nothing for him MAHON says.
POLLIT

11 December 1934. No. 44
ABRAHAM
The messages received up to number 58. Inform P.C. Spanish directives received.
WEST

11 December 1934. No. 45
ABRAHAM
Let me know your decision re BERTHA TARNAY. As personal favour would you inform FELIX who once worked for you his mother in FINLAND is ill and would like to hear from him.
POLLIT

14 December 1934. Nos. 48, 49
P.C.
Our part faction international students conference BRUSSELS December 29th express opinion political line proposed PARIS faction for conference is too much party line and prejudices prospect effective broad united front among students. It is certain British delegation which is very broad will not agree on present political line and approach that is being proposed. We ask you investigate position.
POLLIT

14 December 1934. No. 50
NORMAN
TOM MANN never informed me he had received 70. He told me you owed him 30 which I had to pay him.
HARRY

17 December 1934. No. 51
ABRAHAM
On steamer SIBIER is Comrade NICHOLLS last student for WILSON's School. He has letters and portmanteau.
WEST

17 December 1934. No. 52
ABRAHAM
Cannot yet recommend COHEN's wife.
WEST

17 December 1934. No. 53
ABRAHAM
Accept your proposal SMITH as organisation teacher ROBINSON impossible just now.
HARRY

17 December 1934. No. 54
ABRAHAM
Your last message of 34 groups completely indecipherable.
WEST

18 December 1934. No. 55
ABRAHAM
ROCHE left LONDON December 7th on steamer RYKOV for LENINGRAD certain.
WEST

23 December 1934. No. 58
ABRAHAM
ROCHE was strongly recommended by BIRMINGHAM organiser and by STEWART. We sent you best we have.
WEST

24 December 1934. No. 59
MCILHONE
Has date World Congress been changed? Must let me know because of fixing arrangements. View our party congress February, is it necessary I come for any discussion, if so you must wire immediately as I would have to be back here by January 23rd.
POLLIT

24 December 1934. No. 60

Regret cannot report any success stopping coal for SPAIN. Questions taken up in detailed directives with all party organisations leading mining comrades. Daily Worker January 22nd indicates far as campaign has gone. We have sent out further urgent call for action.

POLLIT

10 December 1934. No. 59

JOHN is GORDON. You wire you received order 39,000 repeat 39,000 Swiss francs. Please always acknowledge receipt of money.

25 December 1934. No. 56

ABRAHAM

Your message of 34 groups completely indecipherable. Please revise and repeat. All other messages correct to 75. Thanks for informing FELIX.

WEST

27 December 1934. No. 57

VAFLIEV

Esperantist KEEBLE now available for discussion if required.

POLLIT

24 December 1934. No. 61

ABRAHAM

Thanks for Parisian portmanteau received all right. MICHAEL. Received part order December D.G. 13,000 and S.F. 6,000.

29 December 1934. No. 62

ABRAHAM

Please ask OLD MAN what is his direction on PRAVDA correspondent that I wrote him about. CONDON is still writing for PRAVDA see issue December 25th.

HARRY

2 January 1935. Nos. 1, 2

December 31st sent back NICHOLS as he declared that he must without fail quickly return to his lonely mother. Our indication on possible non return to ENGLAND after finishing school were unacceptable for NICHOLS. My remark that such answer was not answer of a party member had no effect on him. He answered only by worrying about his mother. He has not been in school and does not know anybody. He gave his signature not to tell anybody why he came to us. He will speak only to WEST or BOB.

ABRAHAM

3 January 1935. No. 65
NORMAN
TOM MANN requests you send pamphlets (?) soon as possible.
POLLIT

3 January 1935. No. 66
ABRAHAM
Only received message about going to PARIS today January 3rd. Will send immediately.
HARRY

3 January 1935. No. 67
P.C.
Directives about NEIMANN received.
LANSBURY has promised interview Swiss Legation on behalf of NEIMANN.
POLLIT

3 January 1935. No. 68
MCILHONE
Concerning your directive numbers 71, 72, 73 on Party Congress 'while refraining from putting forward slogan support Third Labour Government' etc. Consider you don't face issue squarely. Please give definite decision on formulation as in Congress resolution.
POLLIT

5 January 1935. No. 64
ABRAHAM
Student NICHOLS is for WILSON's School and the two letters are for there also.
WEST

7 January 1935. No. 71
ALEXANDER
Will send MACGREE soon as possible. He is doing best job any comrade yet done.
POLLIT

8 January 1935. No. 72
ABRAHAM
Received PARIS case containing 02173, 0222, 0224, 02263, 02465, 02494, 02495, 02496, 02497 and one letter to be mailed NEW ZEALAND.
WEST

9 January 1935. No. 73
MCILHONE
Thanks for all your letters. Very helpful you are now forgiven.
HARRY

9 January 1935. Nos. 74, 75
P.C.

Please treat this information absolutely confidential. LANDBURG interviewed Swiss Embassy formed impression that NEUMANN will be allowed to go country of his own choosing but this not absolutely certain. Difficulty is Swiss Government if definite murder charge against NEUMANN by HITLER. Swiss Government being bombarded by protests against deportation (?) GERMANY. LANSBURY also written GRIMM as result action save NEUMANN.
POLLIT

9 January 1935. No. 76
ABRAHAM

Extremely inadvisable MARY stay for Party Congress which is in MAN-CHESTER. MARY will leave for STOCKHOLM end January await your instructions there. Will be easy MARY return later.
WEST

9 January 1935. Nos. 21–25
C.C.

Necessary to repulse anti-Soviet campaign in connection shooting of counter revolutionary Terrorists to give a more militant and aggressive character. Explain masses that reformist and other protest resolutions against shooting of Terrorists really represents an open action together with anti-Soviet front of bourgeoisie for defence of White Guards and worst enemies of working class and proletariat state and solidarity with them.

Explain that force is used against White Terrorists in interest of defence of millions of working people against cruel class enemy and represents an act of real humanity. At same time widely utilize telegram material which was sent to newspapers on January 5th. In order to bring confusion in masses, French reformists speak about execution of 100 workers.

Necessary resolutely refute this insolent lie. Those who are shot are (? Participants) in murder of KIROV as well as other White Guard terrorists, who from abroad penetrated in USSR (27 groups indecipherable). Necessary develop protest wave of basic organisations of Socialist parties reformist and other Trade Unions against attitude of leadership these organisations. For this widely utilize local organisation League of Friends of USSR. Arrange that telegrams of consent resolutions delegations of reformist and revolutionary organisations meetings committees factory workers etc. be sent to Soviet representatives. Necessary wider information regarding facts of wide terror which is monstrously growing in many countries with direct participation of friends of those who protest against shooting of White Guardists.

Acknowledge receipt.
P.C.

11 January 1935. No. 28
After we became acquainted with your proposal to I.L.P. published Daily Worker November 21st to discuss line United Front we would like to know what were your reasons for such proposal. Please wire immediate reply in order to enable us to discuss matter with MCILHONE before his departure.

20 January 1935. No. 40
For Codist

We deciphered your number 69 afterwards. You ciphered it with cutting which was used already 3 days before for telegram number 68. Is it possible that you don't burn cutting and all first copies immediately after finish work? This is inadvisable from point of view of risk and discipline. Request to improve this matter.

23 January 1935. No. 42
Pay from your sums to 9 LENIN School student families assistance for December 1934 total forty repeat 40 pound. This sum will be returned on first occasion.
MICHAEL

23 January 1935. No. 1
Answering telegram from WEST inform you that in our opinion participation of (Welsh) Communists in SAAR Committee is inexpedient.

29 January 1935. No. 95
P.C.

Urgently request two hundred pounds for Party Congress expenses. MCILHONE arrived safely.
WEST

8 February 1935. No. 98
ABRAHAM

Religious adviser to GORDON and CANADIAN has departed with first directives, but last directives arrived too late. He will do a (1 group) job.
HARRY

8 February 1935. No. 99
ABRAHAM

Messenger last sent to Little BOB's country returned having delivered material and accomplished splendid success.
WEST

8 February 1935. No. 100
P.C.

Best Congress since formation CPGB urgently request you grant three hundred pounds for Party Congress expenses. Its success should soften your hearts and help us. Will lead to splendid results.
POLLIT

9 February 1935. No. 2

P.C.

Relief Committee has already proposed to Labour Party to make common collections victims Spanish Fascism.

POLLIT

14 February 1935. No. 8

ABRAHAM

Received 18000 repeat 18000 Dutch Gulden.

WEST

15 February 1935. No. 5

ABRAHAM

Received two letters dated January 27th on February 8th. Inform RENSHAW her child is well sends love.

Will let her have official (?) letter (?) and belongings within ten days.

WEST

22 February 1935. No. 12

MASSIE

YCL financial position serious.

Forwarding arrears of allocation also payment for second issue 'Challenge' and agreed sum for Youth PLENUM.

WEST

28 February 1935. No. 14

ABRAHAM

WEST's message number 10 stated that girl comrades were told keep clothing given them, as keeping and sending them plus expenses of altering to fit somebody else made return not worth while.

All messages up to number 111 received.

WEST

4 March 1935. No. 16

ABRAHAM

Devine demands his be sent BASEL (?) immediately (?) HARRY arrives via POLAND March 9th.

WEST

10 March 1935. No. 127

Send O'NEILL IRELAND immediately as referent.

BOB

11 March 1935. No. 20
POLLIT

Seek (?) (1 group) new approach Second International on basis of armaments increases and new developments our situation.

Please inform P.C. directives (?) re Profinform letter received.

WEST

14 March 1935. No. 27
ABRAHAM

BAILEY never reported here but on receipt of your telegram we located and got message that he connected BERLIN but not elsewhere.

Portfolio in our hands wire instructions regarding it.

WEST

14 March 1935. No. 23
ABRAHAM

SMITH travelling today. Will give further details BAILEY.

WEST

13 March 1935. No. 24
KIM

Budget exhausted. Fifty pounds required to complete quarter. Necessary send record quarter immediately.

MASSIE

15 March 1935. No. 25
ABRAHAM

Interviewed SLAVINAS at address given. All correct.

WEST

18 March 1935. No. 27
ABRAHAM for HARRY

Priest completes first job. Receipt received.

WEST

10 March 1935. Nos. 28–31
ABRAHAM for CHARLIE

Re your question about two comrades who left my country for your place I received letter from SINGAPORE at beginning of this month.

Letter was from one of leading comrades not signed by him but by name I know. He said they were very short of funds and gave address for communication with him but no indication as to how to get financial assistance to him even if I had any to send.

He also asked if there was a party group or contact in SINGAPORE. I enquired at Centre but they had no information about SINGAPORE and could not assist.

I replied to comrades letter immediately by next air mail informing him I knew no one at SINGAPORE and that he (had?) not said where financial assistance should be directed.

I told him to make every effort and use any means to get through but if possible to let me know how and where I could assist him. Have heard nothing further.
GORDON

19 March 1935. No. 32
ABRAHAM
Until further notice please send telegrams via STOCKHOLM as FRED is ill.
WEST

20 March 1935. No. 33
BAILEY reported here. Propose help him unless you instruct otherwise.
WEST

21 March 1935. No. 34
HARRY
According ordinary Press complete absence any manifestation against BERLIN air provocation.
Is this fault Party leadership or failure news service?
Try arrange regular news from BERLIN.
BILL

23 March 1935. No. 35
ABRAHAM
FRED recommences work Monday March 25th.
WEST

23 March 1935. No. 36
ABRAHAM for HARRY
Still waiting information re supplied from STOCKHOLM. Scandalous delay serious handicap.
WEST

25 March 1935. No. 37
ABRAHAM
HARRY arrived quite safe.
WEST

26 March 1935. No. 38
KIM
SUEZ transport March essential you send assistance. Position critical.
'Challenge' last publication after next issue.
MEINHARDT
(Note: This message is very corrupt)

28 March 1935. No. 41
STASOVA
Canadian delegate for MOHR named REBECCA EWAN arrives MOSCOW March 31st via POLAND.
POLLIT

30 March 1935. No. 44
ABRAHAM
HEARN reported here with letter case which we sent you via SMITH. HEARN will now remain here.
POLLIT

30 March 1935. No. 45
ABRAHAM
We don't keep copies messages for fortnight.
Please send list legible words in our number 12.
We will endeavour to reconstruct.
WEST

2 April 1935. No. 47
ABRAHAM
Can find two good reliable women messengers one Party one non Party. Both however have your country's visa on their passports. Non Party messenger is relation LANSBURY. I recommend her hundred per cent. Send me your decision.
HARRY
(Note: This message is very corrupt)

8 April 1935. Nos. 67, 58
Old Man
Our number 46 stated that the best contact that CANADIAN had in that country had gone insane and we can no longer use this person. The Priest was instructed to get in touch with this contact but also given a second one if necessary, but it is not too clear whether the second one is not connected with Opposition fraction. We have no means communicating with Priest about this latest development, and sent you to appreciate the position.
WEST

8 April 1935. No. 59
Brigadier
Political Commission take full responsibility for WATSON and BIRMINGHAM comrade returning with other students expiration school course.
POLLIT

10 April 1935. No. 62
ABRAHAM
Names proposed messengers ROSA SHAR and IRENE HAVERSON; by personal message sending details about SPRATT.
WEST

10 April 1935. No. 63

ABRAHAM

Essential train another comrade deputise for FRED who is ill and may have to go into hospital for treatment for consumption.

HARRY

13 April 1935. No. 65

ABRAHAM for KING

Inform BYRON that YCL have appointed OLIVER BELL for Colonial work. Wire your acceptance as (?) we can arrange date of departure.

WEST

16 April 1935. No. 67

ABRAHAM

FRED very ill. Please send messages via STOCKHOLM.

WEST

19 April 1935. No. 68

ABRAHAM

Arrange meet ROBINSON arriving LENINGRAD on 'SMOLNY' leaving LONDON April 20th. He carries important personal message.

HARRY

19 April 1935. No. 69

ABRAHAM

First woman passenger we place your disposal leaves April 27th for LENINGRAD. ROSA SHAR is name please arrange meet her fix everything all right. You can rely upon her hundred per cent.

HARRY

20 April 1935. No. 72

ABRAHAM

ROBINSON not travelling on 'SMOLNY' but steamer 'CO-OPERATZIA' leaving LONDON 20th April.

Cancel previous message.

WEST

20 April 1935. No. 73

MEHRING

COHEN's wife allowance paid.

HARRY

24 April 1935. No. 74

ABRAHAM

Have just heard that MIRAJKAR been arrested SINGAPORE and taken back own country.

The comrades who lately left centre for GORDON's country arrived safely but not been heard of since.
WEST

24 April 1935. No. 75
ABRAHAM
Have sent money to NEW ZEALAND.
All messages correct to No. 194.
WEST

30 April 1935. No. 77
KREPS
Strongly urge facilitate visa for Geoffrey TREASE and wife.
POLLIT

1 May 1935. No. 78
ABRAHAM
ROSA SHAR travelling in name YORK repeat YORK leaves LONDON for LENINGRAD May 4th.
Arrange meet her.
HARRY

1 May 1935. No. 79
ABRAHAM
Excellent idea send WALLY in FRED's place. FRED will be sick six months. Will consult him about coming to you.
WEST

2 May 1935. No. 83
MEHRING
Policy Trades Council is to continue to resist but be prepared for manoeuvre to avoid formation of new Trades Councils and prevent isolation from main body.
HARRY

2 May 1935. No. 84
ABRAHAM
In four weeks absolutely reliable seaman will leave for YOKOHAMA. Have you anything to send? I recommend this comrade as very trustworthy.
WEST

6 May 1935. No. 85
Old Man
KITCHENER repeat KITCHENER has agreed when he returns LONDON country to assist production printed material in his house.
WEST

8 May 1935. No. 86
BELA KUN
Send your BREST-LITOVSK book.
Can arrange publication.
POLLIT

10 May 1935. No. 88
ABRAHAM
On your instructions SLAVINAS leaves LONDON by steamer 'CO-OPERATZIA' for LENINGRAD 11 May. You must arrange meet him as he has material for you and only has ticket to LENINGRAD.
POLLIT

10 May 1935. No. 89
ABRAHAM
On steamer 'CO-OPERATZIA' are KERRIGAN and wife coming as Party representative ECCI.
KERRIGAN has important material for you and leaves LONDON 11th May.
WEST

10 May 1935. No. 90
ABRAHAM
On June 1st I am coming to see you and will travel via LENINGRAD with two very reliable women messengers.
WEST

16 May 1935. No. 92
KREPS
Strongly protest your treatment author TREASE. He is held up in LONDON waiting for visa. Why don't you give permission?
ABRAHAM
All messages received to 215 except 213.
POLLIT

16 May 1935. Nos. 221, 222
WEST
Draw your attention to meeting Peoples Court appointed (?) by World Committee for beginning or middle of June and organised by International committees with aim of public tribunal against HITLER fascist (?) GESTAPO murders, abduction of people and imprisonment of TAILMAN. Consider important yours and C.C. support, closest assistance and indications to corresponding English mass organisations for organising and carrying out meeting of Peoples Court.
Acknowledge receipt.
KUN

17 May 1935. Nos. 93, 94

P.C.

Have interviewed Labour Members of Parliament on question of NAZI Terror. Obtained promises put down questions. Arrangements made for Poster parade outside German (?) Travel Bureau and Consulates. Trying to obtain opinions representative people on Terror. Special instructions given Party for campaign.

ABRAHAM

Number 216 last message received but still (?) await 215.

POLLIT

10 May 1935. Nos. 95, 96

ABRAHAM

Just learned HARDY's wife since September 1934 been helping comrade called ALEX from COPENHAGEN establish WILSON apparatus here for special purposes. Private cover address for the correspondence been visited by police who informed comrade that a man was arrested in COPENHAGEN on charge of espionage and then had asked (?) for HARDY's wife by her former name. Consider matter very serious and suggest (?) you call her to see you.

Why can such questions be carried on without my knowledge?

WEST

18 May 1935. No. 97

P.C.

Look 'Daily Herald' May 9th results of my interview Labour Members of Parliament on NAZI Terror.

POLLIT

21 May 1935. No. 99

ABRAHAM

WALLY arrived. All right.

I leave LONDON for LENINGRAD June 1st, bring with me two very reliable messengers for your work. Arrange meet us.

HARRY

21 May 1935. No. 100

KIM

Agree you see OLIVER BELL for colonial work.

ABRAHAM

All messages received up to 227.

POLLIT

23 May 1935. No. 1

NORMAN

Are you aware that when ROBERTS goes on journeys he sends postcards to friends in BIRMINGHAM from various capitals?

ABRAHAM
All messages correct to 229.
WEST

24 May 1935. No. 2
ABRAHAM
Have interviewed COHEN and his wife again and both are willing come and
work for WILSON fully understanding all involved. Recommend you accept
them. Send instructions so I can settle before I leave.
Number 230 re time of Congress received.
HARRY

26 May 1935. No. 3
KIM
GOLLAN says transfer WINSTONE to the YCL of Soviet Union.
POLLIT

26 May 1935. No. 4
ABRAHAM
Don't forget I leave with messengers for LENINGRAD by steamer leaving
LONDON June 1st.
Arrange meet us.
HARRY

31 May 1935. No. 8
ABRAHAM
Making enquiries about documents for DICK.
WEST

17 June 1935. No. 12
ABRAHAM
KEELING repeat KEELING sailed for LENINGRAD by 'JANRUD (-) UBAK' with
message for N.
WEST

17 June 1935. No. 12
KERRIGAN
BURNS can only arrive July 9th provided guarantee return, arriving LONDON
August 7th. Please confirm.
WEST

26 June 1935. No. 18
MIFF
MAMUD repeat MAMUD here lingering because of passport difficulties.
DON

27 June 1935. No. 16
ABRAHAM

Have notified DEVINE as you instructed. Have you any instructions regarding FREDA? All messages correct to 272.

WEST

2 July 1935. No. 22
ABRAHAM for POLLIT

LEO wants answer to question of two Germans which you promised to handle.

WEST

5 July 1935. No. 23
POLLIT

EVA and PARSANS suggest BICKERTON and COLLETS instead of HARDY.

WEST

5 July 1935. No. 26
ABRAHAM

Seventeen English delegates one Irish and one Australian leave by steamer 'RUDZOTAK' 6th July 1935.

5 July 1935. No. 27
ABRAHAM

53 repeat 53 pounds sent to NEW ZEALAND as you instructed.

WEST

7 July 1935. No. 28
ABRAHAM

British Consul General HAMBURG wires that sailor RICHARDSON was released yesterday and is on way home.

All messages correct up to 283.

POLLIT

11 July 1935. No. 31
ROBERTS from WEST

Cancel (1 group) No. 465 arrangement (3 groups missed) for sick delegation. (2 groups) serious setback. Propose reconsideration.

(Note: Many groups missed in this message)

13 July 1935. Nos. 32–34
Sailor RICHARDSON reports following comrades arrested in HAMBURG (1 group) KUHLER, WALTER SWEINHARDT, ARTHUR VEISEVOL alias SCHULTZ, HEINZ KOK and two sailors, one known as FRET (1 group), the other name unknown, all charged with high treason; WALTER LYRITE and other sailor also charged with carrying material to Far East; (2 groups) believed now released. Necessary you notify HOLLAND party that German comrade

PAUL WANKTE, labourer as (?miller) in AMSTERDAM and registered as of Swiss nationality is known to be there by Fascist police, who have his address.
(Last part of this message has not been received)

15 July 1935. No. 37
ABRAHAM
FRED still ill, now anxious accept invitation. Make arrangements to meet him LENINGRAD. As soon as we receive your radio message will notify date of sailing.
WEST

17 July 1935. No. 39
KERRIGAN
Why no reply sick delegation.
GALLACHER

17 July 1935. No. 40
HARRY
When arrived everything O.K.
Send instructions.
BUTCH

19 July 1935. No. 41
ABRAHAM
GOLLAN and POVEY leave tonight via NEGORELYA for KIM.
WEST

21 July 1935. No. 42
ABRAHAM for T. ROBERTS
M C DONALD sick delegate leaves by SIBIAR on Saturday, July 20th.
WEST

22 July 1935. No. 43
ABRAHAM for POLLIT and BRADLEY
Desperately urgent SANBAG given permit to return. Can we advance fare?
WEST

22 July 1935. No. 44
ABRAHAM
Inform ORDJONIKITZE that G KNOTT has been given permit accept position Institute Molecular Chemistry LENINGRAD X Ray Department. He vouched for by BERNAL. Is reliable party member.
WEST

26 July 1935. No. 47
ABRAHAM for POLLIT
Know sick delegation cancelled. Want to know why it was. F.S.U. branch for breaking up account arbitrary calling off without slightest explanation.
WEST

26 July 1935. No. 48
ABRAHAM for POLLIT
'MANCHESTER GUARDIAN' reports POLLIT's PRAVDA article thus 'Party will work for return Labour majority Government after return such Government Party will fight for carrying out United Front programme'.
Wire exact formulation.
WEST

27 July 1935. No. 49
ABRAHAM for POLLIT
Wired SELBY on Tuesday, not arrived nor sent explanation delay.
WEST

27 July 1935. No. 50
ABRAHAM for POLLIT
We still wait instructions regarding WENN reply immediately.
WEST

5 July 1935. No. 52
POLLIT
W.G. thinks AKERMAN's speech as reported here weak. No mention United Front Petit Bourgeoisie nor of opportunities provided by religious fight for street demonstrations.
WEST

1 August 1935. No. 53
ABRAHAM
KNATT (? KNOTT) recommended by BEMAN who is known to you. Reliable Party comrade who will be released for KAGANOWITCH.
Wire when he must travel.
WEST

1 August 1935. No. 54
POLLIT
SELBY leaves today travelling over land.
WEST

19 August 1935. No. 59
POLLIT
Cancel number 52 repeat 52; Letter and tickets received from ROCK. Will attend all points but still weak from sickness.
STEWARD

19 August 1935. No. 60
POLLIT

Tell ABRAHAM August not yet here. July received 1,000 repeat 1,000 D.G. equal to 2,037 pounds 16 shillings and 9 pence.

BOS suffering from food poisoning hence delay.

WEST

19 August 1935. No. 53
KIM

KIM delegation including student ERIC HUNT leave for LENINGRAD 21st August.

WEST

19 August 1935. No. 53
POLLIT

MASANI Secretary Indian Congress Socialists arrives Moscow 23rd August. Important he talks with you and BEN.

19 August 1935. No. 63
POLLIT

BURNS (1 group) Canadian left 17th for LENINGRAD by steamer 'DZERZHINSKY' before your message came.

WEST

20 August 1935. No. 64
POLLIT

Good C.C. meeting accepted line unanimously insists on speedy return POLLIT.

WEST

(Note: The rest of this message, Nos. 65 and 66, cannot be deciphered)

23 August 1935. No. 69
POLLIT

TUI and RENSHAW have had nothing July and August so paper cannot appear. GEORGE asks you arrange send for four months.

WEST

24 August 1935. No. 69
POLLIT or KERRIGAN

Why was visa refused to WILLIAMS who was to lead Teachers delegation which travelled without him. If anything against him we must be informed.

WEST

27 August 1935. No. 70
POLLIT

Police man leaves end September.

BURNS

27 August 1935. No. 71
ABRAHAM
COX and SHIELDS arrived.
All messages received up to 328.
WEST

29 August 1935. No. 72
KERRIGAN
DEGROS CLARKE and Secretary sail on 31st August arrange that all possible is
done to put them under care of Health Commission (?). POLLIT already raising
matter here.
WEST

31 August 1935. No. 75
KERRIGAN
BRAD——, THOMAS and THOMPSON students left by steamer 'SIBIER' for
LENINGRAD August 31st also DEGROS CLARKE.
WEST

2 September 1935. No. 74
KERRIGAN
Cancel cutting number 509.
GEORGE is RENSHAW in charge of paper 'Trades-union Information' for which
four months allocation (1 group) is due.
WEST

2 September 1935. No. 76
ABRAHAM
The last (?) receipt sent by me was for July. I have now received for August
21,000 repeat 21,000 D.G. and have received from SELBY 3,000 repeat 3,000 D.G.
WEST

3 September 1935. No. 77
ABRAHAM
Received from MOFFAT six thousand Swiss francs. M. organ five thousand
Swedish kroner.
WEST

3 September 1935. No. 34
MASSIE
Meeting of Youth organisation went O.K. Report follows.
COLLAN

5 September 1935. Nos. 79–82
DMITROV (?)
Fraternal telegram of Russian Trades-unions created very favourable impres-
sion among delegates and leading circles General Council. CITRINE has been

given leave of absence visit Soviet Union in private capacity (?) and leaves London September 14th.

In General Council CITRINE stated he received an invitation from MAISKY a year ago and is anxious to explore things. Every advantage must be taken of his visit in spite of his slanderous attacks on Communist International at MARGATE.

Other members General Council have approached me and expressed opinion that if Russian Unions invited General Council to send official delegate to MOSCOW it would be accepted.

WOLSTEN CROFT of Amalgamated Society of Wood Carvers told me his (?) union will send a delegation any time to visit Russian wood workers.

Have appointment with EDWARDS secretary Miners Federation and confident will get him to agree visit Soviet Union.

POLLIT

6 September 1935. No. 83

Secretariat

Accept your proposal HOLMES. Leaves immediately.

POLLIT

8 September 1935. No. 84

Secretariat

In conversations on closer relations with Russian trades-unions (?) RICHARD COPPOCK Secretary National Federation Building trade Operatives and CHARLES DUKES Secretary National Union General and Municipal Workers would accept invitation visit Soviet Union.

POLLIT

(Note: This message is very corrupt)

7 September 1935. No. 85

KIM for MASSIE

COLLAN arrives MOSCOW air port evening 11th September.

WEST

7 September 1935. No. 86

KERRIGAN

BARKEK and SMALLBONE students left today for LENINGRAD by steamer 'DZERZINSKY' with material for you.

WEST

7 September 1935. No. 87

ABRAHAM

The husband of Comrade THOMPSON is visiting Soviet Union on Intourist tour. Hope you have no objection to him seeing his wife.

He will bring important material from me. Will wire you date of his arrival.

WEST

7 September 1935. No. 88

ABRAHAM

All comrades returned safely.

Can get you two splendid women passengers but one worked (?) in your institution here some time ago the other still works here. Both just the type you want.

HARRY

7 September 1935. No. 89

CHARLIE JOHNSON

The contact who is prepared to have a duplicator in his house is GORDON's lad leaves LONDON at end of September. Wire any instructions.

HARRY

7 September 1935. No. 90

KERRIGAN

What is decision about two German seamen?

They have cost us eighty pounds to date and it is impossible to continue.

You must insist upon (?) a decision.

POLLIT

10 September 1935. No. 92

ERCOLI

Agree with proposed answer to BROCKWAY, but strongly emphasise disorganising role of Unity Bureau in fight to achieve national and international unity of action.

POLLIT

10 September 1935. No. 74

In view of the fact that British miners now campaigning for wage increase which might lead to strike recommend you seriously consider this.

(Note: This might be the second part of a message which cannot be deciphered)

10 September 1935. No. 95

ABRAHAM

Ask SHULLER or KOEPLINIY if they will confirm my recommendation of BARBARA TARNAY as messenger for your department.

WEST

10 September 1935. No. 96

ABRAHAM

Cancel cutting 532.

Regret state of Mrs. HOLMES makes it impossible her undertaking long journeys.

WEST

11 September 1935. No. 97
Secretariat
Cancel cutting 533
Do you not think ECCI should issue statement on Abyssinian situation or alternatively that statement be made by number of European parties?
WEST

11 September 1935. Nos. 88, 89
Secretariat
In view of response of General Council leaders to ROTHSTEIN's interviews on the significance of the Russian Trades-unions to Trades-union Congress, please consider advisability of Russian Central Council making direct appeal to IFTU for negotiations with International Trades-union Unity. Especially in view of the situation in ABYSSINIA, which it is clear is causing trades-unionists to be apprehensive of new World War.
POLLIT

11 September 1935. No. 100
KERRIGAN
Syllabus for study circles on 7th Congress decisions urgently wanted. Speed up comrades at School on this.
HARRY

12 September 1935. No. 1
ABRAHAM
Received 23,000 repeat 23,000 D.G. for September.
WEST

12 September 1935. Nos. 2–4
KERRIGAN and KREPPS

DMITROV Report	50,000 at two pence, also cloth edition 2,500.
Reply	1,000 one penny
Concluding remarks	3,000, one penny
PIECK Report	2,000, three pence
MANUILSKY Report	3,000, two pence
MOSCOW Actives	5,000, two pence
ENGELS	5,000, two pence
ERCOLI Report	10,000, two pence
KUUSINEN	3,000, two pence
WANG Min	3,000, two pence
Resolutions	5,000, two pence
Complete Edition	3,000, one shilling

These first (?) prints, holding type for reprints.
Don't want Abridged DMITROV.
POLLIT

12 September 1935. No. 5

Using Party balance (?) (1 group) mass throw away for advertising. Cost of lot about 850 repeat 850 pounds. Loss about 350 repeat 350 pounds excluding propaganda.

Rush remaining manuscripts.

13 September 1935. No. 7

ABRAHAM

JIM states it will take one month to construct reserve station.

IRIS should not come by steamer from LENINGRAD.

WEST

13 September 1935. No. 8

ABRAHAM

Husband of THOMPSON leaves LONDON on steamer 'SMOLNY' with important material for you. His name is BRANSON. Make him welcome.

HARRY

14 September 1935. No. 9

ABRAHAM

BRANSON leaves LONDON September 14th on steamer 'SMOLNY' with important portmanteau and letters for you. Arrange to meet him.

HARRY

19 September 1935. No. 10

KERRIGAN

C.C. aware of facts regarding CAERAU.

HARRY

19 September 1935. No. 16

CHARLIE JOHNSON

The letter to comrade in GORDON's country on new line for United Front including programme urgently required.

All messages correct to 376.

WEST

21 September 1935. Nos. 17, 18

KERRIGAN

P.C. considers proposal for liquidation of Y.C.L. incorrect and dangerous. We favour adoption of all measures for broadening out whole basis of Y.C.L. especially in connection with Labour League of Youth.

We propose Y.C.L. come out as champions for one Socialist Youth organisation and invite discussion and collaboration with League of Youth and Guild of Youth. Also to make this the chief issue before National congress Y.C.L.

POLLIT

21 September 1935. No. 19
KERRIGAN
We insist aspirants fulfil their pledge to provide syllabus for Study Circles on World Congress decisions.
POLLIT

21 September 1935. No. 20
MICHAEL
Received order D.G. 11,000 repeat 11,000 from DUTT.
WEST

25 September 1935. No. 22
ABRAHAM
Your (?) messenger BAKER has arrived after successfully completing mission, but it is clear police have been suspicious at most places where she had to change.
In my opinion it would be unwise to use her again only for journeys in EUROPE.
Do you want her to come and report to you.
HARRY

25 September 1935. No. 23
ABRAHAM
Our South Wales organiser thinks STEVENS girl is not yet fit (1 group) to come out for your work.
I am prepared to accept this opinion.
WEST

25 September 1935. No. 24
KERRIGAN
What about syllabus on 7th Congress.
It is scandalous it is not ready.
POLLIT

25 September 1935. No. 25
ABRAHAM
The portmanteaux with clothes are for comrade THOMPSON.
BRANSON can stay for four weeks after that must return.
HARRY

25 September 1935. No. 26
KERRIGAN
Just got your letter and COLLAN's September 15th.
My personal opinion is support COLLAN's proposal.
POLLIT

26 September 1935. No. 27
ABRAHAM

Practically impossible to read your signals on your present wave length due to heavy interference WIF. Please try to increase frequency sufficient to clear W I F. WEST, Telegraphist

28 September 1935. No. 28
ABRAHAM

Irish students MORRISON and MOHAHAN left September 25th by 'RUDEUTAK'. Meet at LENINGRAD.
WEST

23 September 1935. No. 21
ABRAHAM

Irish student MC GREGOR left LONDON September 21st on steamer 'SIBIER'. Arrange to meet him.
All messages correct to 383.
POLLIT

2 September 1935. No. 74
ABRAHAM

On steamer 'DZERZINSKY' leaving LONDON for LENINGRAD September 26th is JANE ARBUS student for Lenin School.
She carries important letter for you and KERRIGAN. Arrange to meet her.
HARRY

28 September 1935. Nos. 30, 31
KERRIGAN

Explain to Secretariat that I sent our letter to Labour Party suggesting they call International Conference two hours before receiving appeal of C.I. to Second International.
Went to PARIS on 25th but came back today as passport arranged up to now. Will go (?) again when arrangements definitely fixed.
Labour Party Conference next week and also important I attend.
POLLIT

30 September 1935. No. 33
KERRIGAN

GOLLAN will not return. Impossible for him to spend all the time travelling backward and forward.
MASSIE must return here and help carry out new tactics inside Y.C.L.

3 October 1935. Nos. 35–37
Secretariat

Regret unable to make any progress at Brighton Labour Conference so far, as leaders concerned with immediate meeting of two Internationals. Interviewed ADLER as to when he thought DMITROV's letter would be considered and

ADLER stated he couldn't do anything without consent of his Executive Committee.

I was informed that Executive of Second International is having a meeting between October 5th and 12th. At this meeting there might also be a joint session with International Federation of Trades-unions.

Hope delegates will demand Labour Conference agree to DMITROV's proposal in one of the sessions today but no influential leader will promise to be publicly identified with it.

POLLIT

3 October 1935. No. 38
ABRAHAM

Will forward BAKER's report as soon as possible.

Cancel cutting 575.

All messages correct up to 397.

WEST

3 October 1935. No. 38
ABRAHAM

Received from STOCKHOLM 15,000 repeat 15,000 Dutch guilders.

WEST

3 October 1935. No. 39
ABRAHAM

JIM says progress being made (1 group) reserve station but also he has instructions from you to leave here on October 14th. It is impossible for him to leave unless we have substitute ready to carry on. Send him new instructions.

HARRY

3 October 1935. No. 40
ABRAHAM

Inform JOHNSON already gone to prepare students for GORDON. Also person has gone who will deliver all Congress material, but it is a scandal that he couldn't take letter you so surely promised.

We keep our promises, why are they not kept your end.

POLLIT

4 October 1935. No. 41
KREPS

Publishing House strongly complain that they have not yet received following Congress reports:-

ERCOLI	Report
MANUILSKY	Report
MOSCOW	Active

WAN MING on Colonial Struggle.

Please expedite despatch.

POLLIT

4 October 1935. No. 42
ABRAHAM
After investigation personally recommend MURIEL THOMPSON for limited journeys.
POLLIT

7 October 1935. No. 45
ABRAHAM
Received portmanteau from PARIS
Astonished to find contained only letters written last April, May and June chiefly.
What a speedy delivery.
HARRY

8 October 1935. No. 46
MASSIE
SETZ arrived.
Insist GOLLAN's (?) speech and Congress documents be (?) sent here forthwith. Position impossible without these. Delegates must come back immediately Congress closes. Party P.B. insist MASSIE return here after holiday. All here endorse P.B. decision.
GOLLAN

9 October 1935. No. 50
ABRAHAM
FRED is now out of hospital and ready to travel to one of your sanatoriums. Please send word when he shall come. Make it soon.
HARRY

9 October 1935. No. 51
ABRAHAM for KERRIGAN
MILLER is willing to radio position.
Will we send him immediately.
WEST

10 October 1935. No. 55
ABRAHAM
ANDREWS of NEW ZEALAND arrived here safely.
HARRY

10 October 1935. No. 54
KERRIGAN, MASSIE
Secretariat have no objections to immediate return of DUNCAN alias BURNS. Must be made clear that no Party employment is available. Believe he has acted so as now to justify further confidence.

11 October 1935. Nos. 55, 56

Secretariat

Everything points to General Election end of November. National government in very strong position. Our general line support Labour. GALLACHER and POLLIT only two candidates the Party proposes to put forward. We want to organise biggest unity campaign ever undertaken with eight page 'Daily Worker' for four weeks. Posters, leaflets, pamphlets and General Election literature as well.

Request you make a grant of two thousand pounds for assistance of Party in this fight.

POLLIT

11 October 1935. No. 67

ABRAHAM

Advise you not to use JANE ARBUS as messenger. Just learned from a close relation she is subject to fainting fits and has had four such fits in last ten months.

WEST

14 October 1935. Nos. 58–63

DMITROV and MANUILSKY

Confidentially FIMMEN informed me in BRUSSELS that in I.F.T.U. Conference JOUHAIX reported that the LOSOVSKY telegram to I.F.T.U. was really a message received from POST offhand who stated they had been asked by MOSCOW to cancel LOSOVSKY telegram. When this was reported great sigh of relief as it avoided I.F.T.U. have to make any decision. Understand certain jokes made in I.F.T.U. that CITRINE gave instructions to cancel telegram. FIMMEN also stated general opinion among all leading Trades Union leaders was that instead of appointing MONMOUSEAU the Russian Trades Union leaders should come themselves. I.F.T.U. leaders opposed to talking to foreign comrades . . . (several groups missing) contact.

(Next part No. 31 missing) . . . he would do more good in two days than all the letters and telegrams. FIMMEN also of the opinion that opportunity afforded Russian transport unions get in touch with International Transport Workers Federation view present crisis. Our impression from conversations that FIMMEN would like to visit Soviet Union again.

POLLIT

14 October 1935. No. 64

ABRAHAM

Comrade JEEOP leave here tonight by steamer 'NEGARELYE' for MOSCOW. Bringing material for you.

WEST

14 October 1935. No. 65

ABRAHAM

ANDREWS of NEW ZEALAND wants balance of wife's maintenance paid in by him to be forwarded immediately.

WEST

15 October 1935. No. 66

ABRAHAM

MARIAN JESSOER leaves tonight for MOSCOW via NEGORCLYE with material for you.

Arrange meet her MOSCOW without fail.

WEST

18 October 1935. No. 67

ABRAHAM

Regarding payment of three pounds ten shillings to ROBINSON SHEFFIELD. You don't say whether this is monthly or weekly. Please inform us at once.

WEST

16 October 1935. No. 70

ABRAHAM

We paid ANDREWS the amount allocated immediately he called here.

WEST

19 October 1935. No. 71

ABRAHAM

FRED leaves by steamer 'DZERZINSKY' today October 19th. As he is too ill to walk please meet with car at LENINGRAD. In event of mishap he will go to October Hotel and wait.

WEST

21 October 1935. No. 72

ABRAHAM

Thanks for messages of October 8th.

I would trust you anywhere with my friends, if I could see you.

Having difficulty in getting suitable messengers but still trying. What I mean by relief for messengers is to pay dependants allowances for them.

HARRY

21 October 1935. No. 73

ABRAHAM

Tell us how many students you definitely want for WILSON School and when they should come. We can send you some when you say ready.

POLLIT

21 October 1935. No. 74
Secretariat

Urgently request you grant assistance we asked for in connection with the General Election.

I am borrowing money to carry on with but must know where we stand.

WEST

21 October 1935. No. 75
KERRIGAN

Hope School quota will be filled on time.

Districts have rotten attitude whole question.

21 October 1935. No. 76
ABRAHAM

Our Number 67

We asked if three pounds ten shillings is to be for a month or a week in case of student ROBINSON family.

WEST

23 October 1935. No. 78
ABRAHAM

Your number 440 of 47 groups badly mutilated. Repeat. Number 439 not received.

Sending all our messages from number 72 via Stockholm as JIM is ill. Please do likewise until further notice.

WEST

27 October 1935. No. 79
Secretariat

Surprised at your suggestion regarding HORNER which is quite impossible now. This matter discussed from all angles and decision to run POLLIT considered best in all circumstances.

WEST

27 October 1935. No. 80
ABRAHAM

HAWKINS student sailing for LENINGRAD today by steamer 'SMOLNY'. He has BAKER's case and clothes for you. Arrange to meet boat.

WEST

28 October 1935. No. 81
ABRAHAM

Message re courier to PARIS received tonight.

Some one will travel at once and will call our usual place AUGUSTINE.

JIM ready with reserve but at present he is rather sick.

WEST

30 October 1935. Nos. 83–85
ABRAHAM

Received STOCKHOLM January to September total 185,000 D.G., 9,300 S.F., and 6,350 S.K. as follows:-

January	D.G. 18,000
February	S.F. 3,000
February and March	S.F. 2,000 and D.G. 41,000
April and May	D.G. 40,000
June	S.F. 2,300. S.K. 6,350 and D.G. 21,000
July	D.G. 21,000
August	D.G. 21,000
September	D.G. 23,000
Total	185,000 D.G., 9,300 S.F. and 8,350 S.K.

Have received instructions in part only for October and November. Please send full instructions. Orders in hand so far are:-

D.G. 15,000, D.G. 1,000 (per R.P. Dutt), S.F. 6,000, D.G. 3,000, S.K. 3,000 and A.D. 2,781 per POLLIT.

WEST

2 November 1935. No. 90
Secretariat

Election campaign: Thanks for thousand books, but let us have them soon, we are very eager to read them. Not necessary KERRIGAN return. All Party mobilised. Don't understand your protest about our open telegrams to DMITROV. We beg you in all seriousness to insist upon message GALLACHER and myself success in elections. Speaking for RHONDDA EAST I am putting every ounce of energy into fight and going to win. If you will insist DMITROV sends message. Have already stated DMITROV urges electors vote for me. Beg you insist CHACHIN and THOREZ come over last days Election Campaign.

Please consider further permanent materials for 'DAILY WORKER'. Will be a tragedy if we have to return to four page.

POLLIT

2 November 1935. No. 90
ABRAHAM

Received portmanteau this morning. Will destroy.

WEST

2 November 1935. No. 90
ABRAHAM

KERRIGAN detained as Consul refuses (?) grant Soviet visa until he consults MOSCOW. This new regulation serious handicap as it means long delay in case of comrade travelling on Party business.

Can you effect change so that our endorsement is sufficient.

WEST

4 November 1935. No. 91

ABRAHAM

Messenger went to PARIS and collected case. ANDREWS left NEW ZEALAND October 17th. JIM's work going fine (?).

When shall we send WILSON students?

Next time you see me I will be Member of Parliament.

WEST

4 November 1935. No. 92

ABRAHAM

Have encountered great difficulties about courier. Please let me (1 group) finish with elections. Regret Mrs. HOLMES ill and unfit for long journey.

HARRY

4 November 1935. No. 94

ABRAHAM

Your signals absolutely unreadable after 1930 G.M.T. Please work at 1800 G.M.T. and give me a call sign with which to call you. Present method impossible for me communicate with you except in reply call from you. This does not allow for any emergency.

JIM

15 November 1935. Nos. 99–101

ABRAHAM

All messages up to number 474 received.

Delayed telegram number 453 dated November 2nd received only today.

If you have not yet received numbers 72 to 78 and 88 and 89 then something wrong at STOCKHOLM. Apply there for them. One of these notified you of JIM's illness and requested you send by STOCKHOLM until further notice. Numbers 88 and 89 partly out of date. HARRY will deal with this on his return. Would be helpful if you acknowledged messages received more systematically. JIM now better.

WEST

18 November 1935. No. 2

ABRAHAM

BYRON arrived and making contact with JIM.

WEST

19 November 1935. No. 3

NORMAN

M.M. CARTER. T.U.I. October November due urgent.

WEST

20 November 1935. No. 6
Secretariat
Do you require me for discussion election results Election and next steps?
POLLIT

21 November 1935. No. 7
BRUNO
Received F.F. 30,000. BERTRAND notified. Will transmit at earliest possible moment.
PARSONS

22 November 1935. No. 8
Secretariat
KERRIGAN will arrive November 29th.
POLLIT

23 November 1935. No. 9
ABRAHAM
BAKER was instructed by me to keep the money to help her to live until she got a job.
All BAKER's clothes have been sent to you with LEN HAWKINS a student in the LENIN School.
Will be seeing you very soon and (2 groups) all questions.
WEST

20 November 1935. No. 16
ABRAHAM
KERRIGAN leaves LONDON on steamer 'DZERZHINSKY' 30th November for LENINGRAD. Arrange for him to be met.
HARRY

30 November 1935. Nos. 18, 19
MARKET
Have taken responsibility in consultation with KERRIGAN of coming over for important discussions with Secretariat arising out of General Election experiences. This will be my last chance of some months ahead of being able to come and see you.
Will be ready report immediately on arrival and could be away within six days. Hope arrive MOSCOW 6th or 7th December.
POLLIT

6 November 1935. No. 21
POLLIT
PEDAR has paid BUTCH.
ABRAHAM
All messages received up to 505.
WEST

10 November 1935. No. 23
POLLIT or KERRIGAN
RENSHAW has had nothing for twelve months. Take this matter up and rectify.
WEST

14 December 1935. No. 25
POLLIT
Visas still (?) being detained lack of instructions from your end. Protest vigor-
ously. Having to pay those waiting who have given up work.
WEST

17 December 1935. No. 27
POLLIT
JIM very reluctant to meet SYLVIA no place yet ready for reserve to work, also
SYLVIA very well known here which adds to risk. Am perpetually insisting JIM
meet SYLVIA who arrived today.
WEST

19 December 1935. No. 28
KERRIGAN
ESTHER URQUHART leaves here by train via NEGORELYE on December 19th.
Arrange to meet her.
WEST

20 December 1935. No. 29
KERRIGAN
Arrange to meet CLARA DEANER who leaves tonight via NIEGORELYE.
WEST

21 December 1935. No. 35
ABRAHAM
Don't send any messages on December 24th, 25th, 26th. Arrived home safely.
POLLIT

24 December 1935. No. 31
KERRIGAN
Send BOLSOVER home immediately for work on 'DAILY WORKER'.
HARRY

24 December 1935. No. 32
Brigadier
On basis of last year's work political bureau together with Tyneside district
committee endorse ARTHUR THOMPSON as student for Lenin School.
POLLIT

24 December 1935. No. 33
DOCTOR
Sixty-five repeat sixty-five members of Parliament of all parties have signed

demand for the release of THALMANN, appointed representative delegation to BERLIN.
POLLIT

24 December 1935. No. 34
FOX is unsuitable for kind of work we discussed with IVAN will look round for another comrade

24 December 1935. No. 35
GEORGE HARDY gone to PARIS to interview Market re South Africa.
POLLIT

27 December 1935. No. 36
Secretariat.
GEORGE HARDY has interviewed MARKET in PARIS who advises him to go to you for further conversations on situation south AFRICA. Please give permission visa immediately GEORGE HARDY, British passport.
POLLIT

27 December 1935. No. 37
ABRAHAM
Remittance sent to VIENNA as requested.
HARRY

27 December 1935. No. 38
Secretariat
We proposed offer (?) ARNOT as Party representative. Reply is acceptable.
POLLIT

30 December 1935. No. 40
CHARLIE JOHNSON
Pan-Asiatic Labour Congress being organised initiative International Labour Office with JOSHI Indian trades-union leader taking leading part.
Will send further information.
POLLIT

30 December 1935. No. 41
DISRAELI
Reliably informed on financial grounds BROCKWAY resigning secretaryship I.L.P.
HARRY

30 December 1935. No. 42
Secretariat
Been approached by intermediary from PADMORE who states PADMORE would come to MOSCOW to discuss his differences. Stated I was not interested. Sending this for your information.
POLLIT

30 December 1935. Nos. 43, 44
Secretariat
Very reliable information that BEDAUX inventor of the BEDAUX system of speed-up is applying through VOX and his connections with American Ambassador in PARIS for visa to Soviet Union for personal enquiry into STAKHANOV Movement. Hopes use experience for speed-up drive capitalist factories.
POLLIT

30 December 1935. No. 45
Secretariat
Political Bureau strongly urge visa be given JOHN PATRICK CONWAY to come as (1 group) LENIN School. Strongly urge visa be granted ERNEST WOOLEY and EMMA WOOLEY. All three British subjects.
POLLIT

30 December 1935. No. 46
Secretariat
Arrangements being made delegation visit Frau CLAUS and family. Will let you know prospects (?) delegation to BRAZIL within few days.
HARRY

31 December 1935. No. 48
ABRAHAM
Please inform OKANA to cancel proposed visit PARIS. Our contact is very dangerously ill and will not be well for many weeks. Later it may be necessary get him Soviet Union for medical treatment.
HARRY

1 January 1936. No. 50
ABRAHAM
Your code letter re sending supply of cuttings received.
CODIST

1 January 1936. No. 51
ABRAHAM
Ernest and Emma WOOLLEY arrive MOSCOW via NEGOLILYE January 4th. Arrange to meet them. Ernest is 'DAILY WORKER' correspondent, Emma is for you.
HARRY

1 January 1936. No. 53
KIM
Election fifty received. Very useful but urgently require hundred due to end year.
GOLLAN

4 January 1936. No. 55
DISRAELI
GEORGE HARDY will come (?) immediately MARKET arranges his visa.
POLLIT

7 January 1936. No. 58
Secretariat
Central Committee unanimously co-opted ARNOT as member Central Committee and appointed ARNOT British representative YCCI. Request you arrange visas immediately for ROBIN PAGE ARNOT and his wife OLIVE BUDDEN both British subjects.
POLLIT

7 January 1936. No. 60
WATERLOO
Party sympathiser named BERTRAM arrives MOSCOW January 10th en route PEKING. BERTRAM stays in MOSCOW three days before proceeding PEKING where for one year he completes studies. BRADLEY recommends you interview BERTRAM for possible contact.
POLLIT

7 January 1936. No. 61
ABRAHAM
Visas wanted for WILSON students SAMSON SYDNEY FINK, JEAN HYMAN, comrade SMITH and comrade SCHOFIELD. All British subjects and passports and all for WILSON school.
HARRY

7 January 1936. No. 62
ABRAHAM
Visa wanted for JOHN GIBBONS British subject and passport, who is to work radio centre for FRUMKIN.
WEST

7 January 1936. No. 63
ABRAHAM
Visa wanted for JOHN PATRICK CONWAY British subject and passport. Student for LENIN School.
POLLIT

10 January 1936. Nos. 65–67
ABRAHAM
TERENCE STEVENS left by steamer 'LAFAYETTE' January 8th for CANADA via NEW YORK which was most suitable French ship available. He has transit visa across UNITED STATES. If he has not made contact with your friends by January 20th he will in his own name be staying at:-

Prince George Hotel repeat Prince George Hotel, 91 repeat 91 York repeat York Street, TORONTO.

Or if that one is full at:-

Royal York Hotel repeat Royal York Hotel, Front West Street repeat Front West Street, TORONTO where you must send to him. Whoever calls on him must use password 'We have a mutual friend Mr. JACKSON' repeat 'We have a mutual friend Mr. JACKSON'.

WEST

13 January 1936. Nos. 70, 71

WATERLOO

For delegation to BRAZIL propose Viscountess HASTINGS and Lady MURIEL CAMPBELL who speaks Spanish. Also well known author RALPH BATES who speaks Spanish and been in BRAZIL before. We propose as secretary reliable Party member FREEMAN. Must have your final decision and directives.

POLLIT

13 January 1936. No. 72

ABRAHAM

Please arrange visas for SAMSON HENRY COHEN and his wife WINIFRED ISABELLA McKEIG, British subjects and passports. Going as instructor and student to WILSON school.

WEST

14 January 1936. No. 74

ABRAHAM

MILLER is suitable and prepared to take up radio announcing (?) as requested by you through KERRIGAN. Confirm appointment immediately and expedite visa.

WEST

16 January 1936. No. 81

Secretariat

Strongly request you expedite visa for George HARDY delay causing great inconvenience. MANU demanded I act quickly. I fulfilled promise and HARDY waiting three weeks for visa. It is intolerable.

HARRY

16 January 1936. No. 83

ABRAHAM

Leave Emma WOOLLEY and cipher work open question for seven days as might have a better suggestion.

HARRY

16 January 1936. No. 84

ABRAHAM

You promised me decision my account. What about it.

POLLIT

16 January 1936. No. 85

ABRAHAM

Re your number 9.

Who is GINA KURTIS and what is the comrade supposed to do.

HARRY

17 January 1936. No. 87

ABRAHAM

GIBBONS for work for FRUMKINA arrives MOSCOW January 19th via POLAND.

Meet him, has material for you.

HARRY

20 January 1936. No. 88

International Control Commission

Stirringly recommend you give immediate facilities for comrade DUNCAN known to you as ROBERT BURNS to return to England. There is employment secured for him that we would like him to undertake.

POLLIT and MASSIE

21 January 1936. No. 89

Secretariat

On January 31st I have an interview with NEHRU. Have you any special points you want me to discuss.

POLLIT

21 January 1936. No. 90

MUNRO

Strongly protest against delay in decision delegation to BRAZIL. People here think I have made fools of them. Give me definite decision one way or other.

HARRY

23 January 1936. No. 91

ABRAHAM

Unexpected difficulties have arisen connection reserve station. SYLVIA's ankle prevented getting going but things now arranged and JIM will be back end of February. All messages up to number 31 received except 23 and 27.

WEST

23 January 1936. No. 92

ABRAHAM

Agree with your proposal EMMA WOOLLEY for cipher work. Do you require any more women messengers.

HARRY

24 January 1936. No. 93

ABRAHAM

Cable for BRADLEY only arrived here on twenty third. He cannot be in PARIS

until Monday twenty seventh. He will stay at HOTEL MODERNE, Place Republic. Tell friend to call there from twenty seventh onward.
WEST

24 January 1936. No. 94
ABRAHAM
EDWARD SMITH arrives MOSCOW January 26th. JEAN HYMAN and SYDNEY FINK arrive MOSCOW January 28th. All for WILSON school. Please meet them.
WEST

27 January 1936. Nos. 95, 96
DISRAELI
Immediately after 7th Congress a decision was taken to increase allocation to IRELAND to bring the sum to twenty pounds. This has never been done and Irish comrades are in consequence facing desperate situation regarding 'Workers Voice'. MINGULIN (1 group) POLLIT and MURRAY all participated in discussing this matter and were unanimous that the figure stated was the absolute minimum necessary. Please send addition amount plus arrears from September.
WEST

27 January 1936. No. 97
ABRAHAM
Please send details how sums sent were to be allocated in November and December. When do we collect new supply coding material.
WEST

29 January 1936. No. 98
ABRAHAM
McCARTNEY arrived safely. Strongly advise you not to use MARY SHELLEY as messenger.
HARRY

29 January 1936. No. 99
ABRAHAM
Please give GOLLAN visa to attend KIM. British subject and passport.
WEST

29 January 1936. No. 100
ABRAHAM
When will you settle my account.
HARRY

30 January 1936. No. 101

ABRAHAM

Have reliable (1 group) for you. Give visa to EVELYN MARY TAYLOR British subject and passport.

HARRY

30 January 1936. No. 102

ABRAHAM

Give visa for ALBERT McCONOCHIE, ROBERT KIDDIE, WILLIAM GIBSON all students for LENIN school. British subjects and passport.

POLLIT

3 February 1936. No. 106

ABRAHAM

Give visa immediately for CLARA DIENER return Soviet Union. Last message received was number 42 but numbers 33, 34, 35 and 36 not received.

HARRY

3 February 1936. No. 107

ABRAHAM (?)

Received instructions for Professor.

Sending report.

WEST

3 February 1936. No. 109

ABRAHAM

ARNOT will report on conversations with Professor. Have arranged PALME DUTT meet professor 15th February. Let me have further proposals on basis ARNOT's report on time.

HARRY

3 February 1936. No. 110

ABRAHAM

Expedite visa for JOHN GOLLAN and also for CLARA DIENER.

Both extremely urgent.

WEST

4 February 1936. No. 110

ABRAHAM

Expedite visa for ISADORE GALVIN student from South African Party for LENIN School. Very urgent.

Your messages received up to number 48.

WEST

5 February 1936. No. 112

MARKET

Soviet Consul LONDON not yet received visa for HARDY. It is a scandal all this delay beg you enquire.

POLLIT

10 February 1936. No. 115

ABRAHAM

Thank you for settling my account. Directives from Secretariat re BRAZIL and YUGOSLAVIA received.

WEST

12 February 1936. No. 117

MARKET

Unless Consulate give HARDY visa immediately we shall give him other work. The delay has been simply disgusting. We want to help you but to wait from December till February is the (1 group) limit.

HARRY

12 February 1936. No. 118

MONROE

Delegation left with splendid credentials and introductions. Special attention will be given EWART confident good results.

POLLIT

3 February 1936. No. 106

KIM

MASSIE and GOLLAN arrive February 18th to report on Conference. DOUGHY remains in LONDON till GOLLAN returns.

GOLLAN

14 February 1936. No. 121

ABRAHAM

Don't use MARY SHELLEY repeat SHELLEY for messenger work under any circumstances. Sending you special letter. Cipher material safely received.

WEST

17 February 1936. No. 124

DISRAELI

DUTT is aware my conversations with Professor and have sent you your three points.

WEST

17 February 1936. No. 125

ABRAHAM

Give instructions your Consul LONDON grant visa to FRANK LEE repeat

FRANK LEE, NEW ZEALAND subject to C.P.N.Z. Coming as student LENIN School.
WEST

17 February 1936. No. 126
ABRAHAM
Please instruct your Consul give visa to Alexander MASSIE returning to KIM. Also visa for Evelyn Mary TAYLOR CPGB British subject and passport coming work for ABRAHAM
POLLIT

17 February 1936. No. 127
ABRAHAM
Please instruct your Consul give visa to ISABEL BROWN repeat BROWN member CPGB. British subject and passport. Instructed come Soviet Union by WILLY connection with THALMAN.
POLLIT

20 February 1936. No. 131
ABRAHAM
Expedite visa for PERCIVAL BEAK repeat BEAK known as WILLIAMS (?) of NEW ZEALAND student for Lenin School.
WEST

20 February 1936. No. 132
ABRAHAM
Still waiting for visas for MOCONOCHIE, KIDDIE, GIBSON, GRAY, GALVIN, LEE and TAYLOR.

24 February 1936. No. 133
Secretariat
On April 15th Tom MANN is eighty years of age. Propose ECCI issue greetings in same way as for PIECK.

POLLIT
29 February 1936. No. 134
ABRAHAM
EVELYN TAYLOR arrives MOSCOW via POLAND February 29th. Arrange to meet her.
POLLIT

25 February 1936. No. 135
ABRAHAM
Please arrange visa for ANN GRAY student for WILSON SCHOOL British subject and passport.
WEST

25 February 1936. No. 137

ABRAHAM

Please arrange visas for following students for LENIN school:-

Albert MACONOCHIE, William GIBSON, William MORRIS and Robert KIDDIE. All British subjects and passports. All endorsed by Political Bureau.

POLLIT

26 February 1936. No. 139

ARNOT

SARAH arrived our office February 24th. Will start work immediately. What about BEATTIE MARKS for SARAH's place your Secretariat? She cannot do shorthand.

HARRY

26 February 1936. Nos. 141, 142

Secretariat

We have severely censured comrades on 'DAILY WORKER' for inadmissible treatment of foreign news and their enquiries in MOSCOW. COX and SPENCE given responsibility supervise more carefully in future. Same time Editorial Board state that in November 1935 they received letter from RUNA MOSCOW stating that they should always approach RUNA for any foreign information that is required.

POLLIT

(Note: This message was very corrupt)

28 February 1936. Nos. 143, 144

MARKET

The two NEW ZEALAND students are LEWIS WILLIAMS whose proper name is PERCIVAL BEAK. He is a miner and was born in ENGLAND and is vouched for by NEW ZEALAND Communist Party on credentials signed by LEO known to you as ANDREWS. FRANK LEE is also vouched for by LEO. He is an undergraduate and general labourer from PALMERSTON North NEW ZEALAND. Both have been active Party members for three years.

Please understand British Party cannot accept responsibility for foreign students neither can we maintain them indefinitely.

POLLIT

28 February 1936. No. 145

ARNOT

Please arrange visa for John J. VICKERS Lenin School Student British Party subject and passport. Full name of Lenin student from SOUTH AFRICA is ISADORE GALVIN. He has been waiting here for four weeks.

HARRY

29 February 1936. No. 148

ABRAHAM

COHEN and MC KEIG (?) instructor and student for WILSON school arrive MOSCOW March 3rd. Please meet them.

POLLIT

29 February 1936. No. 149

ABRAHAM

COHEN arrives MOSCOW March 3rd. Has important material. Please acknowledge receipt.

2 March 1936. No. 150

ARNOT

Received letter number 00320 all right points noted. CITRINE is having book published by ROUTLEDGE understand it is lousy, will send you copy. Propose CITRINE's translator writes pamphlet on CITRINE's visit, any use of his material by us will only create suspicion.

HARRY

2 March 1936. No. 150

MARKET

Received letter number 00362 and will give PETER hell.

POLLIT

2 March 1936. No. 152

ARNOT

Arrange visa for STEPHEN GEORGE EDWARD PURDEY. 31 years old, shipping clerk. Four and a half years in COMNIIE AUSTRALIA, member of Central Committee. On instructions Political Bureau going to work in (1 group) American Secretariat.

POLLIT

4 March 1936. No. 154

ARNOT

Arrange visa for VICTORIA MAY HARVEY and her child MARGARET INESSA GIBBONS wife and daughter of John GIBBONS now working for FRUMKINA and SLOAN. We understand GIBBONS has arranged for visa to be given but you confirm this.

HARRY

4 March 1936. Nos. 155, 156

ABRAHAM

John MURRAY went into forces on Party instructions. So far as we know he never was in cavalry but only as telephone operator. We know he served on North West Frontier as telephonist. MURRAY is given to boasting but we

know of no instructions ever given to him in way he describes. But if he was instructed to carry out certain orders he would have been compelled to do so.
HARRY

4 March 1936. No. 157
ARNOT
We request HOLMES be brought back immediately for taking over charge foreign page 'DAILY WORKER'. This is urgently required.
POLLIT

6 March 1936. No. 158
ARNOT
ISADORE GALVIN, JOHANNESBURG vouched for by secretary South African Party JOHN MARKS and MAPUTSINANA member of Secretariat. Left South Africa for I.L.S. on specific instruction from Party and has been waiting here since February 2nd for visa.
POLLIT

12 March 1936. No. 160
ARNOT
GALLACHER is making tour CANADA August. Do you require some comrade specially for May-day TORONTO.
POLLIT

2 March 1936. Nos. 161, 162
DISRAELI
Following measures taken for PRESTES.
Delegation visiting Brazilian Embassy, questions will be asked Parliament, letters sent 'MANCHESTER GUARDIAN', 'NEWS CHRONICLE' etc. Telegrams sent Brazilian government and will try really big campaign.
Our delegation to BRAZIL was prevented from landing on arrival, measures taken here since try and allow them land understand they were successful but delegation has not been able to carry out aims intended. We are waiting further report and will let you know.
POLLIT

15 March 1936. No. 165
Secretariat
23 members Parliament signed telegrams protest to Brazilian Government on arrest PRESTES. Question on order paper Parliament next week. Brazilian Ambassador refuses see delegation. All Press and BBC notified protest.
POLLIT

15 March 1936. No. 166
Secretariat
We understand Lady HASTINGS now OK.

We kept silent avoid any possibility delegation not being allowed to land at all. We suggest best course let delegation tell own story to get best Press publicity.
HARRY

15 March 1936. No. 167
Secretariat
Have got good comrade who can investigate position BRAZIL. Send all instructions how make contact and further directives.
POLLIT

18 March 1936. No. 174
ABRAHAM
GRAY, LEE and PURDIE arrive Moscow March 22nd. GRAY and PURDIE had material for you.
POLLIT

19 March 1936. No. 176
KIM
Expedite visa for John Bruce URQUHART known in Party as Johnny DOUGHY. Coming represent British YCL in KIM.
POLLIT

20 March 1936. No. 177
ARNOT
Arrange visa for POLLIT and GALLACHER. POLLIT will leave LONDON April 2nd.
HARRY

21 March 1936. No. 178
DISRAELI
Will arrive by aeroplane on March 24th.
POLLIT

25 March 1936. No. 179
ABRAHAM
Comrade BEAK student from NEW ZEALAND to I.L.S. arrives MOSCOW March 26th.
POLLIT

5 April 1936. No. 183
ABRAHAM
STEWART declares that ANN GRAY has a suitcase containing important material.
POLLIT

8 April 1936. No. 188
Charlie JOHNSON
Messenger returned from GORDON's country with mission successful and (?) good (?) material.
WEST

11 April 1936. No. 190
ARNOT
IRELAND protests scandalous delay issuing (?) decisions allocation.
POLLIT

13 April 1936. No. 191
ARNOT
Take up with KIM financial position of YCL here. Heavily indebted. Paper endangered. Only three hundred received from KIM this year.
GOLLAN

15 April 1936. No. 192
ABRAHAM
Understand engineer BAILEY works Soviet institutions LONDON and has good attitude. Is Party member.
POLLIT

15 April 1936. No. 193
ABRAHAM
STEWART informs me books will be sent later.
WEST

15 April 1936. No. 183
ARNOT
What is decision about BICKERTON? He can travel in (? four) weeks.
HARRY

16 April 1936. No. 195
ARNOT
Strongly recommend ESTHER (?) YOUNG first class shorthand typist and political worker for your secretariat. Former worker C.I. (1 group) ten years member YCL and CPGB. Consult Brigadier and arrange visa. Knows Russian, German and French.
POLLIT

18 April 1936. No. 196
ABRAHAM
Comrade URQHART representative of YCL will arrive Moscow April 21st. Meet him and collect case and important materials WILSON school.
POLLIT

19 April 1936. No. 197
ABRAHAM

Please arrange visa JANE MEADE who I recommend as messenger for you all confidential work. All messages received up to 177 except 176.
WEST

21 April 1936. No. 198
CADRE Commission

We propose SHIELDS member Political Bureau as our representative on CADRE Commission. Are you prepared to find accommodation SHIELDS his wife and child.
POLLIT

21 April 1936. No. 199
ARNOT

Elizabeth HOUMAN arrived from South AFRICA with letter from Secretariat asking us to facilitate journey to MOSCOW for study. According your instructions we have advised her return to South AFRICA, Wire confirmation.
POLLIT

21 April 1936. No. 200
MONROE

We have a reliable comrade ready to go to BRAZIL for confidential investigation into Party questions. What is your definite decision.
POLLIT

23 April 1936. No. 201
ABRAHAM

On steamer 'DZERZHINSKY' leaving LONDON for LENINGRAD is comrade MASHEDER he carries very important material for you and Wilson's student. Please arrange meet him.
POLLIT

24 April 1936. No. 204
ABRAHAM

We understand about reserve station and will carry out your instructions.
POLLIT

26 April 1936. No. 205
EPOCH

Your directives to INPKIN arrived after he had left for MOSCOW
POLLIT

26 April 1936. No. 206
DISRAELI

Promise you immediate attention to THAELMAN question. I saw WILLY in PARIS and got all information.
HARRY

26 April 1936. No. 207
DISRAELI

At great inconvenience went to PARIS to speak in election campaign. Kept sitting two days and comrades refused allow me speak. Such treatment as I received in PARIS is a scandal.

POLLIT

29 April 1936. No. 208
DISRAELI

During conversations with person close to LLOYD GEORGE on question of THAELMAN was informed on last visit RIBBENTROP he interviewed LLOYD GEORGE and gave him (? personal) invitation from HITLER to visit GERMANY. Treat this as confidential.

POLLIT

29 April 1936. No. 209
DISRAELI

Having difficulties on THAELMAN question get statesmen make public declarations but got promises they will speak privately German officials in LONDON.

POLLIT

1 May 1936. No. 210
ARNOT

Permission for visa for Mrs. GIBBONS and child not yet here.

POLLIT

1 May 1936. No. 212
ABRAHAM

On steamer 'RYKOV' is UNA JACKSON worker for ARNOT's apparatus who carries important material for you. 'RYKOV' leaves LONDON May 2nd for LENINGRAD arrange meet comrade.

POLLIT

14 May 1936. No. 221
ARNOT

Must have immediate decision on Esther YOUNG. Impossible play about with comrades like this.

HARRY

14 May 1936. No. 222
MOSAIC

Please send budget materials for League against Imperialism. Nothing received since November and I have accepted heavy personal responsibility.

WEST

17 May 1936. No. 228

ARNOT

Enquire where HOLMES is. Last we heard stranded at JIBUTI.

POLLIT

20 May 1936. No. (?234)

ABRAHAM

Necessary we close down station used up to present owing to Post Office enquiries in neighbourhood regarding interference. Have we your permission operate reserve meantime? Please reply immediately.

WEST

24 May 1936. Nos. 231, 232

MASON

DOBROVSKYS had letter of clearance as good Australian party members going to Soviet Union. No provision made for visas before leaving so they are stranded here. Facilitate entry if you consider advisable and also instruct responsible Australian comrades not to give letters or encouragement in future unless they have permission from you regarding entry.

POLLIT

24 May 1936. No. 233

ARNOT

MAC MAKIN recommended by SEAN MURRAY and SHIELDS has previously worked in MOSCOW. Regarding MILLER we have repeatedly sent you information upon which you can come to decision to employ him.

POLLIT

30 May 1936. No. 237

ABRAHAM

On steamer 'Co-operatsia' leaving LONDON for LENINGRAD May 30th is MAURICE BROWN who carries very important material for you. Arrange meet him and acknowledge receipt material.

POLLIT

3 June 1936. No. 241

DISRAELI

Request DEVINE be withdrawn from IRELAND for work in British Party.

POLLIT

4 June 1936. Nos. 242, 243

ABRAHAM

SYLVIA's foot requires another operation and we recommend you call in order that doctor who is (1 group) with her case should perform operation.

To facilitate working reserve station we recommend you send a different wave length (widened) (?) and later in the evening. Suggest twenty GMT.

What is position of FRED?

Is JIM to stop here permanently?

If SYLVIA comes to you for operation JIM will then work reserve.

WEST

(Note: The first part of this message was very corrupt)

9 June 1936. No. 245

ARNOT

(6 groups missing) YOUNG without delay.

POLLIT

10 June 1936

DISRAELI

Serious situation in Irish Party. Strongly recommend you call DEVINE and MURRAY over for immediate discussion.

POLLIT

12 June 1936. No. 249

Secretariat

Suggest no separate August 1st anti-war day, but continuous campaign through-out August for World Peace Congress with special effort on August 2nd which is Sunday Socialists usually have demonstrations on.

POLLIT

12 June 1936. No. 250

Secretariat

Essential we have name of German steamer on which travel EWERT, his wife BENARIO and all letters and wires to VARGAS from influential friends here are returned marked refused admission (?) censor.

POLLIT

13 June 1936. No. 251

DISRAELI

Beg you ensure (?) that all materials (?) owing to Party and 'DAILY WORKER' for last six months should be sent immediately. I cannot raise more credit and my friends are demanding I fulfil pledges to repay. I am placed in impossible situation.

WEST

13 June 1936. Nos. 252, 253

DISRAELI

Understand proposal has come from PARIS that International Writers Conference should be postponed account of GORKI's illness. This impossible carry out as most influential group English writers ever brought together has been organised. Hope you insist French writers attend as we are going on with the conference.

WEST

13 June 1936. No. 254

MOSAIC

Please forward materials for League Against Imperialism. Nothing this year and I have borrowed to enable League function.

WEST

14 June 1936. Nos. 255, 256

ABRAHAM

Ethel STOKER Party member and Olive DAVIES not Party member to my knowledge, applied your consulate LONDON for visas to come SOVIET UNION. They are wife and future wife of reliable Party members Richard STOKER and Richard STOKER junior. These comrades work in MOSCOW district, one manager collective farm the son technician factory. Hope you help get visas. All messages received up to number 260.

WEST

15 June 1936. No. 257

ABRAHAM

On steamer 'Co-operatsia' leaving LONDON for LENINGRAD June 13th is Kathleen MEASURE who has very important material for you. Arrange meet her.

HARRY

21 June 1936. No. 262

ABRAHAM

PHILLIPS leaving LONDON for LENINGRAD by steamer 'SIBIER' with large map for you. REULLEN by same steamer brings very important material for you. Meet both comrades LENINGRAD.

WEST

23 June 1936. No. 265

MARKET

Serious complication (3 groups missing) over sick Australian comrade. Consider very grave mistake let her leave Moscow. Now going (2 groups missing) LONDON.

POLLIT

26 June 1936. No. 270

MARKET

Irish comrades trying equip own printing press. They need 100 repeat 100 English pounds obtain linotype machine. We opened appeal but poor response.

HARRY

26 June 1936. No. 271

MARKET

We shall recall DEVINE for work in ENGLAND. (1 group missing) reference to MURRAY not clear. We have asked comrades prepare Irish report.

WEST

26 June 1936. No. 272

ARNOT

POLLIT and FERGUSON coming on date fixed. Expedite visas. GALLACHER impossible account CANADA tour.

WEST

26 June 1936. No. 273

ARNOT

Reply urgently required school project otherwise cancellation of premises (1 group).

WEST

1 July 1936. No. 276

DISRAELI

GALLACHER cannot come account CANADA tour. POLLIT, SHIELDS arrive July 20th. BRADLEY coming soon as you give visas. Secretariat consider these 3 sufficient deal all problems.

HARRY

1 July 1936. No. 277

ARNOT

Urge you help Dick STOKER's wife and son's intended wife obtain visas. (? Full) particulars (? sent) weeks ago.

2 July 1936. No. 278

ABRAHAM

On steamer 'SIBIER' leaving LONDON July 4th is Esther YOUNG worker for Comintern. Please meet her on arrival LENINGRAD.

WEST

5 July 1936. No. 280

KIM

URBAN has arrived safely.

GOLLAN

9 July 1936. No. 283

ARNOT

Pat SLOAN recommends Walter KNOX for (? radio) appointment. Qualifications satisfactory wire decision.

POLLIT

16 July 1936. No. 289

ARNOT

SHIELDS leaving today coming by NIEGORELYE.

POLLIT

21 July 1936. No. 290

POLLIT

HELEN and brother leave by steamer RYKOFF for LENINGRAD with letters and report as arranged.

WEST

26 July 1936. No. 292

Secretariat

Winifred PALMER left LONDON on 22nd July to join ship leaving LISBON for LOURENCO MARQUES.

WEST

28 July 1936. No. 294

ARNOT

Find out why visa for F.C. MOORE of BIRKENHEAD refused. He applied through INTOURIST to sail on 1st August. He is ten years party member, active in Educational Workers' Union. Was in USSR 1926, 1930 and 1931. Refusal inexplicable. Try to get reversed.

POLLIT

5 August 1936. No. 298

DISRAELI

Major ATTLEE travels on steamer 'RYKOV' visit Soviet union personal capacity. Advise you see him he is anxious private conversations Russian leaders.

POLLIT

6 August 1936. No. 299

ARNOT

Expedite visa for PHILIP ABRAHAMS.

POLLIT

6 August 1936. No. 300

DISRAELI

Have been trying to get Red Cross send volunteers to SPAIN. Understand Lady Muriel PAGET, Secretary British Red Cross, is in Moscow. Consider wife of diplomat could help support our idea. Your directives on Peace Congress received.

WEST

9 August 1936. No. 301

ARNOT

ERNEST WALTER TRORY sails today in 'CO-OPERATSIA' for LENINGRAD with important material.

POLLIT

11 August 1936. No. 303

ABRAHAM

TIM BUCK repeat BUCK of CANADA waiting here for visa. If not already here expedite speedily.

POLLIT

12 August 1936. Nos. 305, 306

DISRAELI

From absolute reliable information British Government circles believe Spanish Government will win. Every British Consul in SPAIN has informed LONDON that victory for Spanish Government certain. Spanish fascists desperate (?) clamouring for armed assistance and promising ITALY and GERMAN big concessions if this intervention is given.

WEST

13 August 1936. No. 307

DISRAELI

On highest authority learn HITLER informed British Cabinet his intention land troops in BARCELONA. British Government exerted strongest pressure warned HITLER of consequences. This caused later German declaration no intervention.

WEST

13 August 1936. No. 309

ARNOT

Ask DOUGLAS what arrangements have been made for Phyllis PEDDAR and Hubert COLLINS for a rest home in CRIMEA.

HARRY

14 August 1936. No. 311 and 312

DISRAELI

MUNZENBERG and SMERAL urgently requested me ask you inform them on following questions, as answers essential success BRUSSELS Congress:

1. Who will represent and speak for Comintern?
2. Should there be another speaker besides SVERNIK?
3. Send copy SVERNIK's speech soon as possible.
4. Who is Soviet delegation?
5. Help needed for Far East delegation.
6. Essential international fraction meet August 31st (?)

HARRY

20 August 1936. No. 318

ABRAHAM

Waiting anxiously PHILIP ABRAHAM's visa.

POLLIT

23 August 1936. No. 322
(This is the third part of a message of which the other parts cannot be deciphered)
DISRAELI from WEST
... but MUSSOLINI (1 group) strong and is (1 group) in SPAIN, if FRANCE gave ITALY 24 hours' time-limit end intervention SPAIN and Italy refused then BRITAIN would certainly not interfere if FRANCE supplied Spanish Government with all it needed. End of conversation.
I immediately sent STRACHEY to PARIS. Is to interview BLUM, BELBOS and COT. Treat this very confidential

22 August 1936. No. 325
(This is the second part of the message. First part as yet indecipherable)
Will go PARIS personally August 26th. Impossible leave LONDON before owing to special conference of National Council of Labour which we have fixed for August 24th. Suggestion regarding ultimatum to BALDWIN by Labour Council being carried out.

23 August 1936. No. 326
ARNOT
Inform us if KNOX is acceptable to radio and expedite visa.
POLLIT

28 August 1936. No. 332
ARNOT
PATRICK FORKIN repeat FORKIN CANADA waiting here for visa. Consult CANADA representative and expedite forthwith.
POLLIT

30 August 1936. No. 333
ARNOT
ANNIE STEWART has now received new British passport and is ready to return. Best arrangement will be for you to instruct PARIS to grant visa. She will reach PARIS September 20th. Advise me forthwith if suggestion satisfactory.
WEST

8 October 1936. No. 2
Secretary
(5 groups missing). Arrange him give you (1 group) BRADLEY also waits give you report.
POLLIT

9 October 1936. No. 3
ABRAHAM
Absolutely inadvisable work station 1 repeat 1 in (?) present location due new short wave station with aerial parallel (1 group) 25 repeat 25 feet working full time.

Have 3 repeat 3 books please state if I use same book (?) as station 2 repeat 2. Wire if we must set up new location.
WEST

14 October 1936. No. 4
PITT
Policy our SHEFFIELD Conference already having effect. CRIPPS asked for meeting with me. MORRISON asked meet me.
WEST

17 October 1936. No. 6
Secretary
Please give immediately visa George HARDY also BRADLY because INDIA information cannot remain LONDON much longer.
WEST

21 October 1936. No. 5
BERTHA
Necessary you send 3 (1 group) certificates for (?) OREDS wife. OREDS family making (?) difficulties.

23 October 1936. No. 8
ARNOT
Please arrange Harry ADAMS receives invitation November celebrations.
POLLIT

23 October 1936. No. 9
Secretary
CLARA DEANER only (?) received visa October 20th. CLARA has now left LONDON.

24 October 1936. No. 10
— S
Reliably informed BARCELONA will be (?) bombarded November 3rd to 4th. At MAJORCA lay 112 aeroplanes. Ships transported troops MAJORCA to CATALAN coast being chartered MARSEILLES.
HARRY

26 October 1936. No. 14
Secretary
Propose party delegation of POLLIT, BOTT, CAMPBELL (?), HORNER, KERRI-GAN, HILL – ER arrive MOSCOW December 23rd. Arrange visas (3 groups and signature missing).

20 October 1936. No. (?16)
MULLER
On steamer DZERZINSKY leaving LONDON October 27th for LENINGRAD is

PETER KELLE. He carries important portmanteau for (2 groups missing) receive it at LENINGRAD.
POLLIT

31 October 1936. No. 17

MULLER

On steamer SIBIER (?) leaving LONDON for LENINGRAD October 31st is BEN FRANCIS carrying important portmanteau for you. Arrange to meet him.
POLLIT

8 November 1936. No. 19

Secretary

On steamboat Co-operatsia leaving LONDON 9th November is TOM BELL. Meet BELL at LENINGRAD.
POLLIT

14 November 1936. No. 20

ABRAHAM

There is VY (very much) QRM (interference), on wave length you now work. Would you work XTER (transmitter) 1 when I ask for QRY (are you ready) longer.
WEST

14 November 1936. No. 21

ABRAHAM

Not advisable allow South African LAZABACK return on his present passport. Destroy his passport.
WEST

17 November 1936. No. 22

ABRAHAM (?)

Please give visa to (? TAMARA RUST) want her as messenger for urgent report.
POLLIT

17 November 1936. No. 23

ARNOT

Draw your attention very bad news service from your end on such questions as arrest Nazi Saboteurs. Our paper will not print anything about USSR that does not come from you but we are placed in an impossible position as a daily paper.
POLLIT

23 November 1936. No. 24

ARNOT

Soviet Film Office (4 groups missing) Spanish news reel material for English French American (1 group). Important represent ROOSEVELT refused this material for Spanish Government publicity in AMERICA.
POLLIT

3 December 1936. No. 29
RICHARD
NELLY arrived today. Five members DICKENS family sent to SWITZERLAND. One ambulance already warned. Field kitchen and food being sent. 100 pamphlets sent by (3 groups missing) all in our power to help but great legal difficulties.
ROSE

11 December 1936. No. 30
PITT
Political Bureau unanimous that situation (1 group) and SPAIN makes proposed visit Party delegation in December impossible. POLLIT arrives December 24th for consultation. Wire confirmation.

15 December 1936. No. 32
RICHARD
Send SHIELDS LONDON immediately to work Editorial Board 'DAILY WORKER'. Our staff seriously depleted through comrades going to SPAIN (?). SHIELDS must be in LONDON December 27th.
POLLIT

15 December 1936. No. 33
Send no more telegrams after December 20th. POLLIT will arrive MOSCOW via WARSAW December 24th arrange meet him.

22 December 1936. No. 34
RICHARD
450 pamphlets sent ANDRE, Impossible send DICKENS until financial question settled. DICKENS (1 group) lose their pensions.
NELLY (?)

22 December 1936. No. 35
MANU (?)
(3 groups missing) finding (?) surgeons. Will arrive December 29th.

In reply, the traffic from Moscow read:

16 February 1934. No. 37
Send immediately all copies of CALCUTTA paper Statesman of September, October, November and December. Urgent.

16 February 1934. No. 39
PARSONS complain of not receiving money. In our number 3 of January 2 we give order about money for publishing. Wire when and how much transmit.

16 February 1934. No. 40

Your wire about money MEERUT Committee and indebtedness BREDAN not quite clear please report in other vocabulary (?). But BREDAN is at your place. Impossible join with him.

16 February 1934. No. 41

Informed through Daily it will be proposed to congratulate elect deputation present Parliament hunger march demands. If this unavoidable then necessary support demand of deputation by organizing demonstration London and province.

From L.S.

16 February 1934. Nos. 42–47

Part I

C.C. most important task is to give correct explanation of meaning and importance armed revolt Austrian proletariat. This revolt signifies collapse ideology and policy Social Democrats ( ) that S.D. masses are making sharp turn towards proletarian revolution and proletarian dictatorship.

Part II

This is the beginning of an enormous wave of civil war in EUROPE . Bourgeoisie are going way of war, proletariat the way of revolution. Working class revolted against Austrian bourgeoisie which tried to follow the footsteps of HITLER, at a time when owing to systematical treachery of Austrian social democrats bourgeoisie managed to strengthen its position and to weaken position proletariat. Heroic significance revolt Austrian proletariat is all the greater.

Part III

Workers don't wish to be slaves any longer, they wish to be free citizens, construct socialism, for this purpose take power. In AUSTRIA fight is developing either for socialism or capitalism, for proletariat dictatorship; proletariat is fighting for Soviet power. Fight of Austrian proletariat is business of whole world proletariat. Austrian revolt is together with general strike in FRANCE turning point which signifies that workers in several countries are starting counter-offensive against bourgeoisie.

Part IV

Therefore required from C.P. of all countries more actual and decisive action against own bourgeoisie, as the most efficient means for support Austrian proletariat. Necessary call masses to strike demonstrations with slogan 'Soviet Power'. Austrian revolt together with general strike in FRANCE opens a new page in development united fighting front and below lessons which must be realised in your country through united action with social democratic workers.

Part V

General strike and armed revolt are the only way to power. Difficulties of Austrian proletariat are great, but heroism of workers is greater still. Those who during struggle count on inevitable defeat are enemies of working class, counter revolutionaries. The longer struggle will go on, the more social democrats and opportunists of every kind will retire and begin to act against. . . .

Part VI
Necessary only pitilessly unmask all renegades who don't wish to understand meaning and importance of great struggle in AUSTRIA. Press must mobilise workers of all countries for support Austrian proletariat. It must inform broad masses about continuation struggle and heroism Austrian workers. It must explain international political significance struggle Austrian proletariat. Acknowledge receipt.
P.C.

16 February 1934, No. 53
POLLIT
KENYATA was in Schooling and sent to LONDON. No promise was given about (?) money (?) for journey to KENYA. After his removal from leadership KIKU on rejoin, tries to appear as a left one is connected with PADAN who excluded from party. Propose him choose himself how (?) to go to his country; BRADLY (?) must come middle March.

16 February 1934. No. 55
While confirming work in helping (?) League against Fascism Party must act independently organising meetings and demonstrations throughout (?) country especially DUBLIN as only force seriously leading fight against Fascism. Work for broad representative conference League against Fascism from unions (?) and lower republican organisations. Continue.
L.S.

20 February 1934. No. 49
Pamphlet 'Into Action' party proposal National (?) congress while generally correct lack criticism of labour and trades union leaders sabotage of workers struggle against national government and new employment bill.
Necessary correct this shortcoming before congress in party manifesto criticising (?) activity reformists attempting show parliamentary gesture as real fight against bill.
Acknowledge receipt and deciphering.
MCILHONE

20 February 1934. No. 93
Our opinion is that they should have publicly stated demands they would put forward to Socialist Party and then met them. This would have had great international significance in present situation.
Secretariat

21 February 1934. Nos. 51, 52

For C.C.

In order mobilise worker and working masses against growing reaction in SPAIN, support AUSTRIA workers and as a token of solidarity with demonstration and strike proletarian. C.P. red trades union and youth declare general strike February 19th.

They called Socialist Party reformist and anarchist syndicalist trades union joint declaration strike.

Socialist anarchist syndicalist refused, by this way disrupted strike and actually acted in capacity of helper and agent of LEROUX, ROBLES, DOLLFUSS of reaction and fascism. In struggle against social democracy of your country necessary wide utilization treason Spanish socialists and anarchists.

Acknowledge receipt.

P.C.

23 February 1934. No. 53

Sent you copies plenary material five items you reprint separate pamphlets. Acknowledge receipt.

From KREBS

26 February 1934. No. 14

Organise in Societies – it campaigns against unification Austria Workers Cooperative.

Demand return seized property and establishments release arrest. Propagate collection for victims struggle likewise and case children in co-operative children homes.

Co-operative Department.

27 February 1934. No. 99

When BRAINLEY left Little BOB's country he handed 200 repeat 200 pounds to our comrades for Party work. This money belongs MEERUT Committee who demand it be produced, or there will be public scandal. We beg you attend to this.

WEST

27 February 1934. No. 101

For ABRAHAM

My arrest creates grave difficulties. Beg you return cost messengers and business for ROCK's council immediately.

POLLIT

27 February 1934. No. 102

For ABRAHAM

FRED (?) hopes to transmit to you after April 1st.

WEST

27 February 1934. No. 55

C.C.

March 28th editors conference will be held.

Representative your paper must be here March 26th. Agenda: First editorial report second fight against war, fascism, SD, for SU, third circulation periodical press. Arranged preparation report editorial work against fascism, SD and for SU also attitude press connection with VIENNA revolt and Parisian general strike. If possible send chief editor or actual leader of paper. Acknowledge receipt.

P.C.

28 February 1934. No. 54

For C.C.

In connection campaign against terror GERMANY develop strong campaign against Fascist terror AUSTRIA. In all mass organisations create committees for carrying out protest meetings and demonstrations. Arrange money and food collection and start special press campaign against terror AUSTRIA. Organise patronage for children killed workers. Send worker delegation to AUSTRIA. Acknowledge receipt.

Political Commission

28 February 1934. No. 57

For C.P.

Utilise liberation DMITROV for strengthening campaign meetings and demonstrations for liberation TAILMAN. Utilise persecutions and tortures prisoners for mobilisation publicity. Strengthen agitation in factories and trade unions. Send telegrams to BERLIN demanding liberation TAILMAN. Acknowledge receipt.

Political Commission

3 March 1934

Impossible BRADLEY leave before March 24th. Inform political Commission all messages up to 58 received correct except 48 and 49.

Repeat these.

POLLIT

4 March 1934. Nos. 59–61

For C.C.

Part I

In Germany terror growing. Fascists taken course for physical destruction party activists. Necessary by all means strengthen campaign against German and Austrian Fascists and terror. Daily elucidate in Press any facts of torture revolutionary workers, intellectuals, condition prisons and concentration camps, terror in factories. Murders of most important party workers pass almost unnoticed in international Press, this is inadmissible.

Part II

Necessary on occasion each murder and death sentence and arrest every important worker mobilise mass organise meetings demonstrations demand liberation
all arrested workers, Communists and S.D. Keep German and Austrian
Embassies and Consulates in constant trouble and menace. Concentrate special
attention campaign for liberation TAILMAN. Mobilise for this purpose all our
organisation and those standing near to us.

Part III

. . . resolution for liberation TAILMAN, . . . in parliament, organise public
opinion, intellectuals – liberty prisoners depends on strength world proletariat.
Our campaign must attain liberty TAILMAN and other prisoners. In interest
working class movements every country and C.I. in general demand such
campaign. Acknowledge receipt.
P.C.

9 March 1934. No. 66

You will receive from STOCKHOLM 30,000 repeat 30,000 Swiss francs and
1100 repeat 1100 gulden. Distribution following: C.P. IRELAND, C.C. advance
on account March 12188 repeat 12188 Swiss francs, for paper 7441 repeat 7441
Swiss francs and 11000 repeat 11000 gulden.

C.P. IRELAND advance for March 664 repeat 664 Swiss francs. Youth England
advance for first quarter 399 repeat 399 Swiss francs, English edition advance
on account February and March 9308 repeat 9308 Swiss francs. Acknowledge
deciphering and receipt.
MICHAEL

15 March 1934. No. 69

Inform MUIR he invited come over discuss party questions and attend RILU
meeting beginning May. For American tour must send somebody else.
From MEHRING

15 March 1934. No. 72

If sympathetic delegates because lack finance not in position attend conference
you should assist them. Cachin refused permit to enter Britain trying to get
Marty to come.

1 April 1934. No. 88

For SPENCE C.C. Youth
Choose verified comrade for colonial work here.
Y.C.I.

1 April 1934. No. 89

For MAHON
For ninth session PROFINFORM four delegates ALLISON or ALLAN,
HANNINGTON, HORNER, TOM MANN.
ALEXANDER

4 April 1934. No. 90

C.C.

In spite great importance there was no response from you to wide campaign developed by MOPR around LUZK trial. Put question widely in your press. Report this campaign by all means (?)

P.C.

9 April 1934. No. 96

POLLIT should come Moscow for several days immediately following trial. We will discuss with him also question of delegation our I.L.P. supporters. Possibility of delegation coming here end of April.

P.C.

11 May 1934. No. 25

POLLIT

By all means intensify solidarity campaign Indian textile workers strike. Wire if you arranged messengers BOB's country.

11 May 1934. No. 26

POLLIT

Soviet office seamen international disposed to take as instructors two fellows recommended by you. Send them.

ALEXANDER

11 May 1934. No. 27

MAHON

Sent to PARIS for you April May 12082 repeat 12082 francs. Send on address which I gave to HARRY.

NORMAN

13 May 1934. No. 26

C.C.

World Congress starts protest action against German law of peoples tribunal (?) which is intended also for preparation THALMAN trial. Support campaign according to instructions world committee.

P.C.

14 May 1934. No. 28

WEST

HART behaved well in PARIS.

On occasion let him return last bought coat and suit which he apparently forgot to hand over to us.

15 May 1934. No. 32

POLLIT

Lend Youth England through Massie 33 repeat 33 pounds for negotiation with Youth Guilds. We will (?) return this amount.

MICHAEL

18 May 1934. Nos. 34–36

C.C.

Sending decision Political Commission on TALMAN campaign.

First: Propose start widest campaign against Peoples Court Law drawing in broadest strata of petty Bourgeois for defence liberation TALMAN German anti-fascist fighters —ly emphasize retroactive power of law.

Second: C.C. C.P. and central leading red trades union must address themselves to leading places of Social Democratic parties and Reformist Trades Union with proposal to organise joint mass meetings and demonstration, etc., against new terror law, and on day of announcement begin from trial protest demonstration before German Embassies.

Third: Slogans and campaign:

A. Against TALMAN trial before special court, free defence, safe conduct of witnesses, admission representatives public opinion.
B. Abolition retroactive power all decisions of law.
C. Public pleadings of cause.

Fourth: In campaign to show by facts that NAZI attacked workers, that workers were in defence against sudden attacks of NAZI. NAZI victims were results of defensive struggle of workers. Arms in hands of Communists were means of defence against threat and sudden attacks of armed NAZI. You receive list of NAZI murders.

Political Commission

9 June 1934. No. 52

WEST

Do you agree appointment TOM BELL LONDON manager English Section Lenin School? Wire positive or negative reply LUX.

BOB

7 June 1934. No. 54

Youth MASSIE

Is joint meeting of N.C.C. the Y.C.L. delegations June 9th or July 9th? Wire answer immediately.

8 June 1934. No. 56

SPENCE

Immediately fulfil your promise to ANDREW.

KIM

8 June 1934. No. 57

WEST

Regard student you recommend for study send detailed letter description who where from who known and recommends.

From Little BOB

8 June 1934. No. 53

MAHON

Decided from July 1st issue INGEN twice monthly 8 page each issue. Assigned 16 pound for edition 8 and technical assistance altogether 24 pounds monthly.

11 June 1934. No. 59

C.C. ENGLAND, IRELAND

Inform delegates 7th Congress they must be in RUSSIA between 20th and 25th September. Date secret not for publication.

P.C.

15 June 1934. No. 63

WEST

Intend sending BOB WILSON for very responsible work outside ENGLAND. Your opinion? Urgent.

ANDREW

15 June 1934. No. 64

WEST

Inform on fulfilment P.C. decision and agreement LEO and JOHN about participation International Conference oppositional branches of Transport Unions affiliated to I.F.T. Take measures basis COPENHAGEN appeal for support these branches to Oppositional initiative committee I.F.T.

21 June 1934. No. 66

C.P.

Consider (one group) your passivity in preparation women anti-war conference. Expecting now definite (?) change beginning campaign Daily Worker creation committees, election delegates.

P.C.

29 June 1934. No. 73

Don't quite understand your No. 185 we have given order for May and June. Why don't you acknowledge receipt. About what reminder for April and May do you wire?

11 July 1934. No. 84

WEST

Sincerely to congratulate to result of trial. Will there not be review of the (1 group).

ABRAHAM

21 August 1934. Nos. 41, 42

Part I

For G.C. and D.W.

German party developing campaign against joining SAAR division (?) to HITLER GERMANY. People's vote this question January 13th. According

VERSAILLES Treaty three possibilities joining to GERMANY or FRANCE or Status Quo. Our Slogan: Hinder HITLER's victory through voting for Status Quo. Turn down HITLER at SA but we help Herman proletariat release itself from yoke of butchers through Empire.

Part II

Greater defeat of HITLER at SAAR sooner possibility joining SAAR to free GERMANY. Support this campaign actively through articles in press, demonstration, constant explanation adversary argument. Organise resolutions to SAAR population also organise letters of SAAR people to their country mobilize (?) demonstration intellectuals against joining to third Empire. Acknowledge receipt.
P.C.

21 August 1934. No. 43

Wire immediately what courier reported regarding delegates coming to congress from Bob's country.

22 August 1934. No. 44

For Youth ENGLAND, IRELAND, INDIA, SOUTH AFRICA

After congress of adults will take place your congress. Inform us immediately name nationality and code book of delegates for receiving entrance visa in time will inform later date of arrival, Number of delegates decided: England 4 repeat 4 Ireland one repeat 1 India one repeat 1 South Africa one 1.
KIM

21 August 1934. Nos. 45–47

For C.C.

Part I

Continuing campaign meetings demonstrations against war provocation JAPAN in FAR EAST; organise together with ILP anti-War Committee. Under L.P. organisations, protest actions against arms and munition transport to JAPAN. Mobilize good agitators for speaking at meetings L.P.

Part II

Propose mutual measures for struggle of anti-fascist, trades union congress. Address yourself through Railway vigilance movement with leaflets and treatise to railwaymen of lines leading to big commercial ports: LONDON, PORTSMOUTH, SHIELDS, LIVERPOOL in order that the producing and transport of war material will be signalled.

Part III

In ports win over port workers through Port Workers Unity Movement with aim of active vigilance over every effort of chartering arms and munition and hindering their transport. One C.C. member must be responsible for organisation and control of whole work. Acknowledge receipt.
P.C.

29 August 1934. No 16, 17, 18

C.C.

Conclusion united front against YCL BELGIUM and TROTSKY Youth Group and Socialist Youth published in number 35 DRAPEAU ROUGE of August 18th, and HUMANITE same date, according which Socialist Youth has right to always put last speaker in mutual demonstrations, itself defend TROTSKY, represents complete capitulation YCLB before counter revolutionary TROTS-KYISM and unprincipled blockade. Agreement facilitates Social democrat with support of TROTSKYISM to calumniate against CPSU and CI. It means practically deliver YCL to reformism. ECCI takes opportunity draw attention party to fact, terrible under the circumstances, is against united front with TROTSKYIST as well as with the other red groups, when there is no mass basis behind them.

Belgian mistake must be utilised in campaign against TROTSKYISM. Follow up HUMANITE Rundschau Inprecor, utilise their articles directed against such capitulation before SD and TROTSKYISM, but same time continue energetically (4 groups) capitulation, also from above. Acknowledge receipt.

P.C.

3 September 1934. No. 37

HARRY

Up to present nobody arrived for School BOB WILSON. You promised to send to September 1st. P.C. allowed you five places. Conditions are known to you. P.C. insists these are sent also girls. Wire when students will be sent and if they come with their own passports.

ABRAHAM

7 September 1934. No. 39

WEST

Prepare immediately good messenger for BOB's country. Stuff and message will be sent as soon as preparation will be ready. We have not yet received a single copy Indian Forum Norman report. Gordon's activity and plan of work. We have also not received report from returning messenger.

KARDON

7 September 1934. No. 40

Please inform ROBERT SMITH's mother that he was arrested in PRAGUE. He is already released and in good health. If his mother receives letters or money from PRAGUE please take this from her and send to us.

About everything delivered to you wire us.

7 September 1934. No. 46

JOHN BOB WILSON's friend asks to take his things and books from his father and send them here. Please arrange this and send by first steamer to LENIN-GRAD. When will BOB WILSON leave for school.

15 September 1934. No. 51

Our directive should have been understood as follows: Indian delegates to come at expense of Indian party, English at expense of British party.

15 September 1934. No. 55

C.C.

Propose largest utilization of disclosures Washington Senate (Committee about International armament) Capital. Combine campaign with anti-Fascist movement. Point on VICKERS. Underline what disclosures in WASHINGTON about VICKERS are confirmation of the Soviet disclosures at that time on VICKERS espionage. Enquire, reveal carefully on foundation WASHINGTON materials, completed by own enquiries.

Part II

All connection between English armament and (1 group) capital especially with JAPAN GERMANY. Organise most energetic campaign among gang of VICKERS factories. Combine economic demands with WASHINGTON unmasking special profit from shifting arms. Spread in Navy pamphlets about disclosures especially about shifting with submarines. Put this question in trades union of workers in metals.

KUN

16 September 1934. No. 57

Delegates about whom your telegram 62 be sent here, wire names and place where to send visas.

17 September 1934. No. 59

Agree your proposal regarding visit HAW. Prepare report on united front and anti-fascism struggle organisation and situation party. When are you coming.

From DICK

18 September 1934. No. 58

POLLIT

Yours from September 11th communicate how much is needed and for what money is spent.

MICHAEL

22 September 1934. No. 67

GERHARDT's coming postponed.

BOB

22 September 1934. No. 68

Campaign for election November delegation to be carried out under sign of United Front. Ensure 75% Labour party workers are working when main industries leaders mass struggle.

Special attention to be given delegation South Wales.

Acknowledge receipt.

P.C.

23 September 1934. No. 69

WEST

Speed up preparation messenger for BOB's country.

GORDON

22 September 1934. No. 70

POLLIT

Necessary if not already done suggest call MANCHESTER rate-payers to protest against 1,000 repeat 1,000 pounds for BELLEVUE and utilize this in other similar programs.

BOB

23 September 1934. No. 74

Your number 73. Don't insist on sending girls too, but this is desirable. Demand minimum general education, even don't insist on serious technical knowledge, send only trustworthy candidates.

ABRAHAM

26 September 1934. No. 76

SPENCE and MASSIE

We object to liquidation of Young Worker. You forgot our directives. Propose paper be published regularly. Inform us what help is necessary.

KIM

2 October 1934. No. 77

We instructed Sweden to hand out 45480 repeat 45480 Swiss francs and 315 repeat 315 Holland gulden. From this give for October CC CP, ENGLAND 11850 repeat 11850 Swiss francs, CP ENGLAND for newspaper 30980 repeat 30980 Swiss francs, CP IRELAND 315 repeat 315 H G, for 4 quarter YOUTH ENGLAND 2650 repeat 2650 Swiss francs. Total 45480 repeat 45480 Swiss francs and 315 repeat 315 Holland gulden.

From MICHAEL

3 October 1934. No. 78

For WILSON SCHOOL better to send direct LENINGRAD. Try with other books, but this should not delay departure.

10 October 1934. No. 94

For YOUTH MASSIE

Immediately go to PARIS and make connection with RAYMOND.

KIM

10 October 1934. No. 53

C.C. ENGLAND and IRELAND

Necessary that legal semi-legal illegal party and trades union press give sufficient attention Spanish event in general and statement ECCI to second international and its answer in particular.

Those CC and local parliament and trades union organisations which haven't daily or weekly paper must issue leaflet or appeal.
From P.S.

14 October 1934. No. 96
PARSONS
Urgent hold up circulation and binding STALIN's book October Revolution. Receive instructions POLLIT letter following. From political aspect distribution possible if on second page you print: 'First published by Cooperative Publishing Society of Foreign Workers in USSR.' This also refers to letters to KUGELMANN and others.
KREPS

17 October 1934. No. 55
You will receive from Stockholm for League for six months including October 4090 repeat 4090 HOLLAND gulden.
MICHAEL

19 October 1934. No. 97
Did WEST arrive well? 19th arrived 2 for WILSON School, thanks. Instantly request to send quick remaining. Course beginning; instruct all those coming for WILSON School that they should speak about aim their journey and (1 group) here only with ABRAHAM.

20 October 1934. No. 98
Where is Australian delegate MILES, why doesn't he come over?
From BOB

22 October 1934. No. 100
Suitcase HOLMES sent October 18th with TOM MANN by steamer RYKOV. Cancel our No. 80

23 October 1934. No. 2
Youth C.C. SPENCE.
Anti-war movement must not be turned into narrow organisation with membership cards and dues. Details letter.
Y.C.L.

26 October 1934. No. 3
You will receive in STOCKHOLM for November 43000 repeat 43000 Swiss francs and 315 repeat 315 Dutch gulden. From this amount for C.P. ENGLAND. C.C. 18850 repeat 18850 Swiss francs and paper 31150 repeat 31150 Swiss francs. C.P. IRELAND 315 repeat 315 Dutch gulden.
MICHAEL

26 October 1934. No. 4
WEST from ABRAHAM
Came to find understanding with JOHN that he remains with us although he

intended to go to factory. Urgently send his wife and belongings from Father. Awaiting telegraphic reply. October 26th MILES delivered letters and suitcase.

31 October 1934. No. 7
Canadian (?NAWIS) delivered two letters. Girl proposed by you at the last moment accepted with reciprocal enthusiasm.

31 October 1934. No. 8
Request immediately select five or six negro comrades for school, members of Negro Welfare Association who have not lost contact with their countries. Send short biographical data for final approval here. Possible send non-party comrades with condition that they are recommended by Party faction.
BOB

31 October 1934. Nos. 12, 13
CC ENGLAND IRELAND of YOUTH
In spite of indication ECCI your campaign support Spanish proletariat extremely inefficient. In SPAIN especially in ASTURIA terror highest (?) and hundreds of workers being shot without trial already fallen victim of it. Non execution for the present of sentences of martial court is only vile manoeuvre of Spanish fascist Government in order to turn away attention of mass shooting without trial. In addition to meetings and demonstrations necessary organise sending to SPAIN delegations, beside Spanish Consulates with protest demonstrations, raise scientists writers and radical bourgeois politicians. Send correspondents of party papers to SPAIN in order to collect material. Acknowledge receipt.
P.C.

31 October 1934. No. 20
CC ENGLAND and IRELAND
Necessary raise campaign in whole international Communist press against leaders of Spanish anarchists as vile agents of fascism who through their treason doomed to mass destruction by fascist reaction Spanish proletariat among them also many anarchist workers who participated in struggle. Acknowledge receipt.

1 November 1934. No. 14
C.C. ENGLAND IRELAND
Refusal Second International to accept proposal C.I., immediate organisation mutual mass action defence Spanish proletariat insufficiently utilised by you in your press in order to raise discontent Socialist workers and organisations against attitude Second International. Necessary carry on intensive daily campaign of condemnation Second International by Socialists themselves obtaining publications of Socialist organisation and meeting. Acknowledge receipt.
P.C.

2 November 1934. No. 15

Who is FREEMAN who arrives on RYKOW? Please in future always inform us in your telegrams to whom comrades are coming. This is absolutely necessary.

2 November 1934. No. 16

November 8th send a woman repeat a woman to PARIS to fetch suitcase for BOMBAY and tube for you. Wire when received and when you will send suitcase to BOMBAY.

3 November 1934. No. 20

WEST

Send by mail from address of a non Communist 3 repeat 3 pound to following address: DAVID ABERCROMBIE, c/o ARCHER's Book Shop, PARTON Street, KINGSWAY, W.C.1 LONDON repeat DAVID ABERCROMBIE, c/o ARCHER's BOOK SHOP, PARTON Street, KINGSWAY, W.C.1 LONDON. Shall return money. Wire when sent.

ABRAHAM

3 November 1934. No. 21

In spite of Irish and MURRAY's girl I insist on your sending two more girls for school. This is very important for school. I won't allow that one or other student arrives later on, it will be difficult for them to make up for lost time. I repeat again, PC pays much attention to presence of women in school.

ABRAHAM

3 November 1934. No. 22

C.C. SPENCE.

Immediately print and distribute not less than 100,000 copies of our letter to ECYCI. We pay the expenses. Cable fulfilment.

Y.C.I.

5 November 1934. No. 23

SPENCE.

8th MITCHELL will be there with our answer on the Guild. MASSIE must meet him in LONDON.

KIM

5 November 1934. No. 24

Your question telegram number 5. It is the same journalist for whom you asked money to be given, His name is HEWER.

November 1934. No.

Consider inadvisable to put ANDREW's work in editorial board Daily Worker. From BOB

9 November 1934. No.

SPENCE

Organise actions of YCL organisation with demand to immediately call plenum of ECYCI discussing proposal of YCI on defence of Spanish youth.

ECYCI

11 November 1934. No. 25

We will not issue call to guild. Inform us name of your representative.

Y.C.I.

12 November 1934. No. 27

Agree two more come here for WILSON School on condition they are absolutely reliable and suitable. Wire when you think they will be able to leave. Desire one more girl.

14 November 1934. No. 28

SPENCE

Immediately organise mass campaign in defence of RASADO secretary of C.C. YCL of SPAIN and KEIRANA secretary of MADRID. They are in danger of death sentence.

KIM

14 November 1934. Nos. 29, 30

Action Leadership of Committee against War and Fascism ENGLAND. Faction Leadership World Committee against War and Fascism requests not to send faction letters to address of World Committee. For all letters of COM faction use following address. RENE repeat RENE LECLERC repeat LECLERC. INGENIER, one Rue Charles Cross repeat one Rue Charles Cross, PARIS twenty repeat PARIS twenty. Inside envelope 'Pour Jean'. Urgently send to this address report on activities your committee in connection effect World Bureau meeting and S.U. joining League of Nations, as well as plan of work.

KIM

19 November 1934. Nos. 32–35

C.P.

Estimation decision 2nd International following. Decision for (?International) common action for SPAIN signifies refusal to organise support Spanish workers and blow against Spanish united front. Repeal of prohibition united front agreement on national scale is first modest success of united front struggle. Refusal of prohibition, on one hand necessity to yield to pressure of social democrat workers of those parties which signed United Front on other hand means (?confirming) sabotage of united front also on national scale by socialist parties of HOLLAND, SCANDINAVIA, CZECHOSLOVAKIA, ENGLAND. Through this decision pretext of sabotage of National Parties referring to prohibition Second International was resolved. Decision shows incapacity second International for International common action. Special declaration of seven parties is serious only when confirmed by deeds. Every discussion concerning possibility relation MENSHEVIKS signifies attempt of splitting. Emphasise energetically culmination of struggle for United Front on national scale for Spanish proletariat joint lower organisations of parties and trades union. Press must continually utilise results executive decision and its treatment in social democratic press. Through world committee and Red aid organise delegations of well-known persons of social democratic and communist workers to SPAIN especially through reformist trades union. Support youth campaign in this direction. (1 group) ist campaign against Russian MENSHEVIKS and their support by social democrats. Further proposals following. Acknowledge receipt. P.C.

19 November 1934. No. 36
C.C.
International Red Aid organises from 10th to 16th December International Solidarity week for victims of terror in SPAIN. In view importance this campaign necessary support by Party forces.
P.C.

20 November 1934. No. 37
Decision PC regarding ILD. Send llo.
BOB

21 November 1934. No. 39
BRADLEY
Wire whether you agree article sent by us on anti-imperialist struggle in INDIA 'Re National Congress' and sent name INPRECORR for publication. Send report re your activity.

21 November 1934. No. 40
POLLIT, BRADLEY
Send us immediately all reliable Indian YAVKAS. Messenger from BOB's country must start out at once. Instruct messenger notify leading comrades that as (?) immediate 'Resolution Eighth Session Profintern' task Indian trade union movement published Indian forum number 3 differs Comintern Profinform latest decisions to immediate tasks present repeat present situation in INDIA.

23 November 1934. No. 41
Pay out of your money YOUTH ENGLAND for publication leaflet letter Socialist Youth International twenty repeat twenty pounds and fare for journey to us representative CC youth eighteen repeat eighteen pounds. – total 38 repeat 38 pounds. This sum will be returned by us when we will send December money.
MICHAEL

27 November 1934. No. 42
In view of agitation against embassies and trade representatives of the USSR in capitalist countries, E.C.C.I. propose to forbid categorically members of your party who work in embassy or trade representation of USSR to build initial party organisation at Soviet institutions in foreign countries and to use premises of those institutions for party purposes.
C.P.

28 November 1934. No. 44
GORDON
Wire, whether you signed and sent IMPRECORR article re National Congress. Send immediately by safest channels couple most reliable contacts (addresses) with Indian party Central Committee.

28 November 1934. Nos. 45, 46
POLLIT
Approve line NUWM resolution concentrating struggle against part second Unemployment Act for mobilisation trades union branches support local united front committees. Propose NUWM issue United Front appeal TUC for joint action NUWM employed associations and trade unions with simultaneous appeal NUWM branches to Unemployed Association. Concentrate attention municipalities with Labour majorities organising trades union investigation committees of camps as in LONDON GLASGOW mobilising working class organisations to demand closing camps. Official party propose ILP include struggle against TUC circular in united front agreement.
ALEXANDER

1 December 1934. No. 48
Our number 40 we asked you to send us immediately all reliable Indian addresses for correction.

1 December 1934. No. 49
SPENCE
Governments of BOLIVIA and PARAGUAY are mobilising students studying in FRANCE and ENGLAND for front. Propose in connection with this carrying out of anti-war campaign among students, exposing interests of Imperialist group in CHACO conflict, explaining LENINIST slogan of turning Imperialist war into civil war.
KIM

2 December 1934. No. 51
Journey representative YOUTH 38 repeat 38 pounds or 575 repeat 575 Swiss francs. POLLIT for Student School according to his statement of October 8th. 355 repeat 355 pounds or 5085 repeat 5085 Swiss francs. CC CP ENGLAND in return for amount (1 group) by MASSIE for journey 20 repeat 20 or 300 repeat 300 Swiss francs. (Remainder of message indecipherable)

8 December 1934. No. 58
Please send us one copy of CALCUTTA paper New Statesman No. 19020. Paper must be given to ABRAHAM. Your No. 32. JOHN about whom you ask is DON.

10 December 1934. Nos. 53, 54, 55, etc.
C.C.

In connection decision Spanish Government to break resistance miners of ASTURIA through starving them and closure of mines and to order in mean-time coal from ENGLAND, necessary party should take urgent measures for hindering coal transports to SPAIN. Propose following measure: party issues popular appeal to Labour Party trade unions Cooperative party utilising decision Labour Conference about sympathy with Spanish worker. Widely spread in lower organisations proposition of hindering coal transports. Issue directives through party faction to mobilise railway vigilance movement, take resolutions trades union units, district committees, with proposal to executive to undertake necessary action. Take measures mobilise dockers and seamen utilise the connection to transports trade unions. Party factions should induce miner organisations to send letters to transport and railwaymen trades union organisations with appeals for support. Party groups in ports have to address themselves to Labour Party trade unions party factions in trade unions in ports raise question through Trades Union Council for united front campaign. (Remainder of message not yet deciphered)

11 December 1934. No. 60
WEST

TOM MANN before departure received 70 pounds for two and half months.
NORMAN

11 December 1934. No. 61
MEHRING to remain until after Party Congress.
P.C.

13 December 1934. No. 62
WEST

Wire immediately your opinion on COHEN. Have you found out who is his wife, what kind of person is she. Does she suit work in our secret place. Can she work in town or in school. Please reply immediately, as during last days conduct of JOHN MURRAY very strange.

13 December 1934. No. 63
Pay from your money assistance to 9 families of LENIN School students. Total 183 repeat 183 dollars. This sum will be returned by us on first occasion.
MICHAEL

13 December 1934. No. 64

Proposal after return ENGLAND SOUTH TYNESIDE January return here study for work an organisation instructor LENIN School. This addition to proposal regarding ROBINSON. Wire me affirmative negative.
BOB

17 December 1934.

November 29th with our No. 47 enquired you where was worker and where works that comrade who made aeroplane proposition, today is December 17th but no answer from you. Please hurry up. FELIX about his mother informed.

17 December 1934. No. 73

Your telegram No. 49 re British delegation first four groups mutilated. Repeat.

17 December 1934. No. 67

HARRY GORDON
Japanese comrade NISHIOONO arrested in VANCOUVER for deportation JAPAN. Launch immediate wide mass campaign against deportation and demand immediate release NISHIOONO. For particulars wire American and Canadian Parties.

18 December 1934. Nos. 68–71

C.C.
We are sending for your information copy of telegram on SAAR questions sent by us to C.C. HOLLAND: on decision of council League of Nations Dutch Government sends troops to SAAR region. In our opinion your line must be following: 1st In Parliament and press meetings you must declare that Communists are against militarism and BOURGEOIS army and the real defence of SAAR people can be guaranteed only by arming working class. 2nd. As German Communist are for status quo and as at same time short time stay of League of Nations troops in SAAR can also mean certain safeguard against HITLER riot and attack of Fascist gangs during voting time, Dutch Communists declare their neutrality on this question. 3rd. At same time resolutely demand that these troops be used only against Fascist terror and attack of Fascist gangs and must on no account interfere in internal life of SAAR people. 4th Absolutely protest against sending of volunteer troops by Dutch Government as this means sending of reactionary elements. 5th. Expose TROTSKYIST demagogy which represents attack against Soviet Union and support of HITLER 6th. When discussion takes place in Parliament demand decision this line if rejected then abstain from voting. Acknowledge deciphering this telegram.

19 December 1934. No. 74

ROCHE arrived on 19th with material. Thanks for same. Send former Communists. Do you expressly recommend ROCHE.
ABRAHAM

19 December 1934. No. 75
C.C.
Wire immediately what has been done to help Asturian miners and prevention of coal transport to SPAIN in conformity with our telegram of December 7th, especially what steps have been taken drawing in reformist trades union in this campaign. In press nothing is to be seen. We expect detailed current information.
P.C.

21 December 1934. No. 76
Directive concerning platform Students Conference already given. Send immediately your written objections to AIS fractions.
P.C.

21 December 1934. No. 77
Hasten fulfilment instructions re sending six Negro students from LONDON selecting same from Negro Welfare Association. Send characterisation of comrades.
BOB

23 December 1934. No. 78
Don't need aeroplane comrade here since he is not thorough specialist but amateur.

23 December 1934. Nos. 78, 80, 81
Following your pre-Congress discussion great interest, recommend place centre discussion, broadcasting United Front against National Government, against capitalist offensive, for increased wages improved working conditions, Fascism war development mass work in trades union. Problem party building, wider discussion programme action contrasting programme reformists. Municipal electoral tactics in general defines approach general elections. Striving head mass discontent National Government, sparing no efforts develop United Front struggle, party should systematically patiently explain Labour Party workers that Labour Government will not repulse Fascism and war. While refraining from putting forward slogan support third Labour Government or issuing general call unconditional support Labour candidates begin, immediately extend United Front agreements with local Labour Party's Labour candidates being guided by October decision of E.C.C.I.
L.S.

23 December 1934. No. 82.
Send for important portmanteau in PARIS.
ABRAHAM

26 December 1934. No. 84
Cannot choose for you definitive frequency for whole time, as interfering stations are changing. You must make QSY every time on our indication.

27 December 1934. No. 85

NICOLS here with two letters, present for WILSON School.

28 December 1934. No. 86

Agree your proposal establish broad committee prominent people and trade unionists even if necessary to leave out Communists for campaign against Indian White Paper. Consider advisable that committee should get into contact with left congress elements League against Imperialism India and Congress Socialist party and trade unions. British League should give full support without jeopardising committee while continuing independent campaign.
P.C.

28 December 1934. Nos. 87, 88

C.C.

German Government on December 23rd put action for extradition of NEUMANN. Aim of NAZIS is immediate trial for accusation of criminal offence and execution in order to create atmosphere for THALMAN trial and his sentence. Request POLLIT immediately take up connections with LANSBURY CRIPPS and other persons from Labour Party with the aim of intervention to be at leaders Swiss social democracy REINHARD, GRIMM and Swiss Government for immediate release of NEUMANN and permission to stay in country. Develop immediately press campaign and connect it with struggle against extradition, increase action for release of THALMAN. Utilise increase of penal servitude sentences last time against German Communists as well as new wave of NAZI terror against anti-fascists. Acknowledge receipt.

29 December 1934. No. 89

On January 2nd sent one comrade to PARIS to receive there two things with very urgent material. Acknowledge receipt.

31 December 1934. No. 89

POLLIT

Confirming and approving general line your article and Congress resolutions, necessary bring forward first place Congress question United Front against capitalist offensive wage increases intensify mass work trade unions. Necessary make key note Congress discussions building Communist Party.
B.S.

31 December 1934. Nos. 90, 91

You will receive in STOCKHOLM 43,000 Swiss francs and 325 gulden. From this pay: C.C. ENGLAND remainder for December 5,850 repeat 5,850 SF and on account January 5,790 repeat 5,790 total 11,640 repeat 11,640 SFs. For paper remainder for December 16,150 repeat 16,150 and on account January 15,150 repeat 15,150 total 31,300 repeat 31,300 SF. C.P Ireland remainder for December 165 repeat 165 Dutch gulden and account January 160 repeat 160 total 325 repeat 325 gulden. POLLIT 560 repeat 560 SF to cover amount of

183 repeat 183 dollars paid by him for families LENIN School. Total amount to pay: 43,500 repeat 43,500 SF and 525 repeat 525 Dutch gulden.
MICHAEL

2 January 1935. No. 8
POLLIT
Send immediately LEO MACGREY discuss question of work among seamen ENGLAND.
ALEXANDER

2 January 1935. No. 9
From beginning new year numeration of telegrams and R communications has to be transformed into one joint numeration. Differences between telegram and R cipher remain.

3 January 1935. No. 10
Do you recommend JANETTE JACKSON? Her husband works in DAILY NEWS. She is one of the three previous MANCHESTER girls.

3 January 1935. No. 83
Would be very valuable for you write article on United Front. We request however you send article for our consideration prior to its publication in ENGLAND.
P.C.

4 January 1935. No. 11
WEST
No necessity seen here discussion meantime if you have important questions no objection your coming.
BOB

7 January 1935. No. 17
SARAH FRIEDMAN asks to pay two or two and a half pounds monthly support for her mother. ROCHE asks to pay his wife thirty shillings weekly. Please find out if this is really necessary and pay out if needed.
ABRAHAM

8 January 1935. No. 18
We sent you to PARIS 100 repeat 100 pounds M.M. January pay TOM 26 repeat 26 pounds for 1934. We will return to you.
NORMAN

9 January 1935. No. 19
WEST personally.
Wire if you recommend NENNI STEWART, daughter of BOB for journeys as well as for money.
ABRAHAM

15 January 1935. No. 81
EMILE BURNS
Inform your friend KOREAN position very important and he should accept. Will speak to him before he goes.
WEST

25 January 1935. Nos. 43, 44
Steamers COOPERATIA repeat COOPERATIA, LADOGA, repeat LADOGA, KR. PROFINTERN, repeat KR. PROFINTERN, KISTA repeat KISTA, KARL LIEB-KNECHT repeat KARL LIEBKNECHT, VISHERA repeat VISHERA, MANITCH repeat MANITCH, VANZETTA repeat VANZETTA, KYKOV repeat KYKOV, KOLA repeat KOLA, BAIKAL repeat BAIKAL, and USSURI repeat USSURI must not be used for sending illegal people. Legal people can be sent with these steamers.

25 January 1935. No. 45
POLLIT
TAMARA delivered one letter.

27 January 1935. No. 46
January 27th (?MC) GREE delivered letters and suitcase with books for MURRAY. In post 26 biographies. SARAH delivered two parcels. We shall make arrangements for her.

28 January 1935. No. 47
Stop all advertising and sale writings MAGYAR and SAFAROV.
Acknowledge receipt.
KREPS

29 January 1935. No. 50
We understand by your telegram no. 91 that comrade going to BOMBAY is the Priest. If this not so wire immediately.

29 January 1935. Nos. 53–60
POLLIT
Give the priest who is going to Far East on our account 100 pound sterling for delivery to party in GORDON's country. Priest must insist upon immediate arrival two or three delegates to C.I. Congress. Our advice delegates should apply for passports for journey to CHINA or INDO-CHINA and should go from there to FRANCE then come to us. For this they must go to C.C. C.P. FRANCE or to an editorial office of Humanite. Connection in BOMBAY or CALCUTTA you must take from GORDON. Tell him to ask Indian comrades to inform GORDON what Socialist Congress Party represents, what adherents of ROY are doing and whether possible to apply United Front tactics with them and on what questions.
Elaborate with BICKERTON (desirable to call him the Canadian in corres-pondence) plan for priest's connection with adherents C.C. and Opposition of

Japanese party but we advise not to connect priest directly to BICKERTON, in order that you could send him couriers if necessary. Make arrangement with priest regards cipher, give him good LONDON addresses and give him strict instruction not to make notes of any Indian or Japanese addresses open writing, not to keep them with him and not to send them anywhere unciphered. Give priest on our account 100 pound sterling for delivery to C.C. JAPAN party for immediate arrival of delegates verified and known to comrades OKANA and TANAKA from CC and opposition to PARIS where they can go to editorial office of Humanite. Priest must insist that C.C. should give half of this sum to Opposition for arrival of delegates and inform them that this money is given BICKERTON. Priest must inform Japanese comrades that we insist upon immediate liquidation of factional subscription and gathering of party on basis of OKANO's article.

We recommend Party and all adherents of class trades union movement immediately transfer centre of gravity of whole work inside reformist unions and to conduct resolute struggle for trades union unity on basis class struggle and trades union democracy. Illegal revolutionist trades union which are united in ZENKYO must immediately take resolute course for entrance in left Radical unions HIOGIKSI and carries this actual merging in such manner that neither police nor treacherous trades union bureaucrats will know about this, in order that Left legal trades union will not lose legal existence.

Adherents of class trades union movement must maintain resolute struggle for political strengthening and organisational widening of HIOGIKSI through systematic carrying out wide supported front of Left reformist unions; also send GORDON statement of work of workers Youth unions. Are they connected with party, which opinion on how they should develop in future and where help is necessary from us. Necessary workers Youth unions should choose delegation so YCI Congress. Couldn't you connect GORDON with worker Youth unions?

4 February 1935. No. 73
We accept ROBERTS as representative. Cable when he is leaving.
ALEXANDER

4 February 1935. No. 73
WEST
In answer POLLIT to MAXTON on Congress and in project of resolution (in retrospective part) concerning unification C.P. and IZA there was nothing said at all on what basis this unification can take place. Therefore P.C. recommends to say in retrospective place of resolution concerning unification – unification of these two parties can only take place mainly on basis of programme Communist International.
P.C.

4 February 1935. Nos. 74–76
POLLIT

You will receive STOCKHOLM 20300 repeat 20300 Swiss francs and 160 repeat 160 Gulden.

From this pay second time advance on account January CC IRELAND 5800 repeat 5800 Swiss francs and paper 13230 repeat 13230 Swiss francs.

CC IRELAND 160 repeat 160 Gulden. Salary JONES from December 16th to February 1st 360 repeat 360 Swiss francs.

POLLIT in return for money given by him to Youth IRELAND for Conference Labour Youth 20 repeat 20 pounds or 300 repeat 300 Swiss francs and account given to 9 families LENIN School students for December 40 repeat 40 pounds or 610 repeat 610 Swiss francs.

Total to pay 20300 repeat 20300 Swiss francs and 160 repeat 160 Gulden.
MICHAEL

4 February 1935. Nos. 82, 83
We consider movement now developing in South WALES and SCOTLAND great importance united front and extension influence Party. Recommend throw best Party forces into organisation of movement in other industrial districts organising immediately demonstration hunger marches demonstrative strike, in this way enabling more successful realisation your slogan for protest strike February 25th in industrial centres. Bring to knowledge all workers that Labour leaders turned down United Front for struggle against new bill, popularise C.P. Propose United Front to local organisation of Labour Party and trades union success of which will be best means of pressure on leaders Labour Party General Council. Direct this movement against National Government and party supporting it.
P.C.

7 February 1935. No. 7
WEST

Please inform immediately PAT, that FREDA returned safely. Soon she will leave for LONDON.
ABRAHAM

10 February 1935. No. 84
In addition to messenger for GORDON's country to organise students for school here prepare immediately one more courier for same country.

14 February 1935. No. 88
POLLIT

Wire whether messengers have brought mail or verbal message from GORDON's land. Speed up preparation next two messengers.

16 February 1935. No. 93
P.C. decided postpone final discussion your article until you come over (?) here. Could you come for few days end of February. MCILHONE arrived.
BOB

17 February 1935. Nos. 95, 96
C.P. ENGLAND
I.R.A. organises 18th February at anniversary Parisian Commune, United Front campaign against fascism particularly with ASTURIAN fighters for the right of sanctuary for release of TAELMAN, RACOSI, RUEGGS and other anti-fascist fighters. Necessary assistance of Party organisations as preparation and carrying through of campaign particularly popularisation slogans in Press and assistance of recruiting of Red aid members amongst Social Democrats and workers organised in Reformist trades unions.
Acknowledge receipt.

21 February 1935. No. 106
Could you bring with you material on CADRE question re composition Central Committee, District Local Committees, etc.
BOB

21 February 1935. Nos. 102, 103
C.P. ENGLAND
Sentence of death Socialist leaders ASTURIA, PENA and MEMENDEZ, signify another of series of death sentences also against communist leaders especially against MANZO and SIMON DIAZ. Spanish Government is very sensitive as regards International campaign.
Organise immediately mass meetings and if possible mass demonstrations and on behalf of them send protest telegrams directly to LERROUX and Spanish Parliament with demand non execution death sentences. Strengthen general solidarity campaign for Spanish revolutionaries.
P.C.

21 February 1935. No. 108
POLLIT
Could you bring with you material on CADRE question on composition Central Committee, District Local Committees, etc.
BOB

21 February 1935. No. 103
POLLIT
If you have possibility, please urgently inform South Africa they should not send delegates for Congress up to reception of new regulations.

22 February 1935. No. 105

POLLIT

Irish Party should send us a referent possibly O'NEIL. If they want send some-body else they should as our agreement.

Land Secretariat

22 February 1935. Nos. 106, 107

POLLIT

Prepare courier for GORDON's country. We shall inform you later on what he must take. Influence SAKLATVALA and HUTCHINSON to cause corres-pondence with one or another Communist or organisation of GORDON's country over head of C.C. of that place. C.C. asks for this.

DUTT MAZAMDAR in CALCUTTA affirms that on instruction of your party he organised Labour Party which he sets against C.P. INDIA with the assistance of which he leads struggle against revolutionary trades union movement. Inform us whether somebody of your place gave him such directions if so then of what kind and what would be best way to expose him.

22 February 1935. No. 109

GORDON

Beside the article 'What the Congress Socialists want' published in INPRE-CORR we sent you article 'The Problems of the Anti-Imperialist Struggle in India'. Wonder why you didn't publish this directive article.

22 February 1935. No. 109

POLLIT

Please give to GORDON on our account 75 repeat 75 pounds for publication 'Incomplete Forum' and other activities; couriers shall take along approxi-mately 200 repeat 200 pounds and not 1500.

26 February 1935. No. 110

WEST

You will receive in STOCKHOLM 4300 repeat 4300 Swiss francs. From this sum pay.

Youth ENGLAND second time advance on account.

Assistance for eight families of students LENIN School for January 590 repeat 590.

C.P. ENGLAND for Party Congress for present 2490 repeat 2490.

JONES salary for February 240 repeat 240.

Total 4300 repeat 4300 Swiss francs.

MICHAEL

28 February 1935. No. 112

Wire what news you have re two comrades who left your country for here as reported in your letter 12th February. Yours and HUTCHINSON's pamphlet not received.

GORDON

28 February 1935. No. 113

Wire immediately what was decided at LONDON District conference I.L.P. TASS reports resolution adopted favours affiliation C.I. and participation World Congress.

BOB

3 March 1935. No. 115

Anti-Imperialist League

In question Abyssinian War immediately get in touch with World Committee. In order to form an authoritative delegation for ABYSSINIA.

Political Commission

3 March 1935. Nos. 116–118

C.C.

Strengthen written and oral mobilisation against war ABYSSINIA in view of danger expansion into war of Imperialist power. Characterise it as Imperialist, Colonial predatory war from side of ITALY and as war of national independence from side of ABYSSINIA, in spite of Abyssinian relation to JAPAN, in spite of Monarchist feudalist reigning group. Expose furtherance Italian adventure through English Imperialism. Expose admission munition transports through SUEZ Canal controlled by ENGLAND as rupture of English neutrality. Find out where ENGLAND carries out orders for armanent, which English ships transport arms in order to hinder transport. Influence crews of Italian ships arriving to English ports. Expose attitude 'DAILY HERALD' which hypocritically feeds with hopes of settling things by English Imperialism. Try (?) through I.L.P. action in Parliament witty slogan 'Defeat Italy', hands off ABYSSINIA' against violation English neutrality. Popularise anti-war struggle Italian working people under leadership of C.P.

Acknowledge receipt.

P.C.

4 March 1935. No. 119

JENKINS may keep the things for her good work.

5 March 1935. No. 120

When is HARRY coming over here? Has COHEN already left for RUSSIA?

DICK

7 March 1935. No. 121

GORDON

Please reply immediately on our enquiry re article 'Problems of Anti-Imperialist Struggle in INDIA'.

Wire approximate date when first messenger will be ready to start for GORDON's country.

8 March 1935. No. 122

C.P. ENGLAND, IRELAND, South AFRICA.

On proposal representatives of C.P. CZECHOSLOVAKIA, GERMANY and FRANCE, Presidium decided to postpone Seventh World Congress to July 15th 1935 repeat July 15th 1935. This decision must not be published. Acknowledge receipt.

9 March 1935. No. 123

Please send somebody to following address:

A. SLAVENAS repeat A. SLAVENAS 149 repeat 149 Fellows Road, LONDON N.W.3.

Password: Sent from your acquaintance ANGARETES whom you went to see in LUX in MOSCOW and there you also met BERJASI repeat BERJASI.

10 March 1935. No. 127

Send O'NEILL IRELAND immediately as referent.

BOB

14 February 1935. Nos. 129, 130

You will receive in STOCKHOLM 43280 repeat 43280 Swiss francs and 290 repeat 290 Dutch gulden. Last time you received there 700 repeat 700 Swiss francs more than indicated by us so you have total 44980 repeat 44980 Swiss francs and 290 repeat 290 Dutch gulden. From this sum pay advance on account February C.P. ENGLAND C.C. 11400 repeat 11400 Swiss francs and for paper 28600 repeat 28600 Swiss francs.

C.P. IRELAND 290 repeat 290 Dutch gulden.

Anti-Imperialist League advance on account January and February 4190 repeat 4190 Swiss francs.

Salary JONES for March 230 repeat 230 Swiss francs. Assistance eight families LENIN School students for February 560 repeat 560 Swiss francs.

Total 44980 repeat 44980 francs and 290 repeat 290 Dutch gulden.

MICHAEL

15 March 1935. No. 131

Hasten reply our no. 128 concerning HEARN alias BAILEY.

17 March 1935. No. 132

Secretariat

GALLACHER must write articles on I.L.P. policy correct bad impressions created by ANDENS.

Present stage our aim win I.L.P. not make comparisons MOSLEY, GOEBBELS.

POLLIT

23 March 1935. No. 135

Portfolio received. BAILEY may remain LONDON at your disposal. School finished. SMITH arrived.

26 March 1935. No. 138

On (?) April 1st send a comrade to PARIS. He must take there a suitcase and a small thing containing something from JOHNSON, about which you know. Acknowledge receipt and forwarding.

On March 29th in STOCKHOLM there will be mail for you.

27 March 1935. No. 141

Pay to family of referent COHEN assistance for one month 9 repeat 9 pounds.

28 March 1935. No. 142

GORDON

We wired Seamen's and Harbour Workers' International whether they have to send you through HARRY connection in SINGAPORE. Spare no effort in assisting these comrades.

26 March 1935. Nos. 143–146

POLLIT

Appeal of Party of March 21st gives impression that National Government is under thumb of HITLER, while it is generally known that National Government was well informed on secret arming of GERMANY, as well as intention of GERMANY to abolish paragraph Versailles Agreement, which prohibits GERMANY to have army with General compulsory military service.

National Government supports German fascism and its military provocation against USSR. Necessary that Party considerably intensifies campaign against military policy National Government under slogan (1) 'Against league with Fascism GERMANY, (2) against war with Soviet Union, and (3) against support of JAPAN, GERMANY and POLAND who are preparing attack on Soviet union for signing East and Danube Pact, by National Government, (4) for stopping hostile action against Soviet Union by National Government'.

For this purpose necessary 'Daily' to publish material exposing role National Government as helper and instigator (?) of Fascism GERMANY, JAPAN and POLAND against USSR. Call mass workers meetings in whole country, mobilise circles sympathetic to USSR and anti-war movement for protect against anti Soviet pro HITLER Government policy.

Labour Party practically supports this Government policy. This was clearly shown at debates in Parliament on occasion SIMON's visit to BERLIN. Therefore especially necessary draw into campaign labour workers and mobilise them also against official labour policy.

P.C.

1 April 1935. No. 149

POLLIT

Old Man wants to have detailed information as regards Priests carrying through his mission in each country.

ABRAHAM

1 April 1935. No. 150
What do you know about English sailor RICHARDSON who was arrested in HAMBURG and put in concentration camp. He is charged with communist propaganda.
Wire answer.

1 April 1935. No. 151
Take from SLAVINUS material and sent it at next occasion. Wire when we can expect it.

2 April 1935. No. 155
WEST
P.C. considers not advisable invitation of I.L.P. by C.I. to 7th Congress.

4 April 1935. No. 160
WEST
Send 50 repeat 50 pounds on our account to following address:
Mr MACGOWAN, 34 Bay Street, PETONE, NEW ZEALAND. Repeat Mr. MAC-GOWAN, 34 MAY Street, PETONE, NEW ZEALAND and 36.1.6. repeat 36.1.6. to following address:
Mr W. COLLIER repeat Mr W. COLLIER, Post Office Box 42 repeat 42 repeat ARO repeat ARO, WELLINGTON, NEW ZEALAND repeat WELLINGTON NEW ZEALAND.
Wire when sent.

5 April 1935. Nos. 162, 163
Necessary extend support DUBLIN transport strike on much longer scale. Raise matter busmen Rank and File Movement, securing resolutions support of strike and protests (?) against Irish Government Intervention. Organise financial aid from busmen and other workers. Raise question sending delegate LONDON Rank and File Movement to assist strikers. Initiate work among Irish workers anti-Imperialist organisations in ENGLAND in support of strike. Strengthen treatment strike 'Daily Worker', busmen, (1 group) etc.

7 April 1935. No. 167
Have you someone to work as referent. Send particulars first.
When does O'NEAL come.
DICK

8 April 1935. No. 168
WEST
Sent you PARIS March and April M.M. INGEW TOM MANN 4,000 Swedish Crowns 34 dollars 20 cents.
Acknowledge receipt.
NORMAN

9 April 1935. Nos. 169–172

C.C. IRELAND

In view of growing discontent of workers especially strikers because of interference of Government in Tramway and Omnibus Workers Strike, and in view of the fact that Irish Republican Army, which up till now has been supporting Government openly, proposed its help to Strikers, and in view of measures taken by hands of trades union to break Strike, you must discuss question whether Party should recommend strikers to accept proposal Republican Army for support Strikers.

Perhaps this proposal could also be used for appeal on part of Party to all Worker Organisations, Civil Army and Republican Congress, and (1) call for widened joint solidarity action against interference by Government, (2) for close support of Strike up to declaration of Sympathetic Strike, and (3) for liberty of arrested workers and Republicans.

In our opinion the critical situation of Strike demands the popularisation of following slogans among the Strikers:

1. 'No secret negotiation by trades union officials behind back of Strikers'.
2. 'Not to take up work until this is decided by mass meetings of Strikers'.
3. 'To negotiate, on basis of demands concerning wages, through representations of garages, depots and Strike committees'.

Necessary to popularise, as lesson of Strike, necessity for unification Transport Unions on basis of wide internal trades-union democracy. In no case tear yourself away from mass of Reformist trades union members.

In giving appreciation of lessons of Strike, Party must popularist slogan 'Worker Farmer Republic'.

L.S.

10 April 1935. No. 178

POLLIT

P.C. appointed you member of delegation for negotiation with Second International. Get in touch with CACHIN by telephone.

P.C.

10 April 1935. No. 179

Why does not 'Daily' follow up line POLLIT's speech Trafalgar Square demonstration question war policy National Government. This grave mistake 'Daily'.

P.S

10 April 1935. No. 181

On March 27th we wired you to pay family COHEN assistance for April 9 repeat 9 pounds.

Wire if paid.

13 April 1935. No. 182

For Youth Massie

We propose to ECYCI to begin negotiations on joint struggle against Fascist militarisation. You, RAYMOND and FRIDLE are authorised to carry out negotiations. We sent letter to ECYCI and RAYMOND will telegraph answer to you. If necessary immediately leave for negotiations. Publish and spread your letter among Youth.

Sending answer to your letter.

KIM

13 April 1935. No. 183

April 13th GILES delivered two parcels. Beginning to look for deputy for FRED. Wire your opinion how long he will be able to work.

13 April 1935. No. 184

HARRY

Send SHAR and HAVERSON immediately to us for six months. They must take Polish and Finnish visas for prolonged time.

15 April 1935. No. 185

Why TOM MANN's South African Appeal not published.

Eastern Department

21 April 1935. No. 193

Our opinion monthly issue 'CHALLENGE' will make increase of circulation difficult. Necessary put question before Party and intensify campaign. We agree giving you assistance only once on condition you secure also assistance of Party and if you guarantee regular issue of paper and if it will be a weekly. Wire reply.

KIM

21 April 1935. No. 194

COHEN leaves 25th April. We remain without referent. Why don't (?) you propose new referent.

DICK

26 April 1935. No. 197

Instead of FRED we want to use temporarily our VALY. Wire your opinion. How long will FRED be sick? Perhaps he should be sent here?

ABRAHAM

28 April 1935. No. 198

ROBINSON delivered two letters and a suitcase.

28 April 1935. No. 199

Owing to (?) discussion I.L.P. question BOB will leave on (?) May 5th. What decision have you made regards threat T.U.C. to disaffiliate after May 11th Trades Councils who don't adopt Black Circular.

DICK

28 April 1935. No. 200

Change name 'Indian Forum' as you see fit. STALIN's 'Leninism' in Urdu should be printed.

(Note: This message was addressed to 'GORKIN' probably meant for 'GORDON')

29 April 1935. No. 201

How is situation RICHARDSON after intervention LANSBURY? Have you connection with his wife does she get assistance. Who is she?

8 May 1935. No. 207

Wire how much money altogether you transferred to NEW ZEALAND to both addresses.

11 May 1935. No. 214

WALLY will leave soon.

15 May 1935. No. 216

WEST

P.C. agrees your vacation starting June 10th. Prior leaving arrange continue for preparation Congress questions and settle continuous leadership during your absence.

WALLY on the way. He will come to your flat.

Acknowledge receipt.

DICK

16 May 1935. No. 217

Youth GOLLAN and MASSY

Telegraph us if POLLIT recommend or not OLIVER BELL for Colonial work.

KIM

16 May 1935. Nos. 218–220

C.C.

Conclusion French Soviet agreement and negotiations in RUSSIA, results of which were published in communiqué, serves for preservation of peace and must be considered as most important step against war intrigue of German fascist and their allies.

C.P. FRANCE will vote in Parliament in favour of this agreement. Agreement furthers interests of German workers as well as proletariat of whole world because it hinders HITLER fascism to start war. As army is in hands of Bourgeoisie, French party will vote against budget and military credits and two years military service. Declare solidarity with C.P.F. which organises struggle against reaction chauvinism and Fascism for United Front. Demand your Government to support Soviet French efforts for preservation of peace. Give answers all Social Democratic attacks against agreement.

Acknowledge receipt.

P.C.

After acquaintance with this document it must not be left in hands of addressee but personally destroyed).

(Note: This message was also sent to BASLE and STOCKHOLM)

16 May 1935. Nos. 221, 222
WEST

Draw your attention to meeting Peoples Court appointed (?) by World Committee for beginning or middle of June and organised by International committee with aim of public tribunal against HITLER (?) fascist GESTAPO murders, Abduction of people and imprisonment of TAILMAN. Consider important your and C.C. support, closets assistance and indications to corresponding English mass organisations for organising and carrying out meeting of peoples court.

Acknowledge receipt.

KUN

17 May 1935. No. 223
POLLIT

SLAVIN (? SLAVINUS) arrived.

17 May 1935. No. 225
POLLIT and PARSONS

TREASE visa sent. Enquire at Consulate in PARIS or LONDON.

KREPS

19 May 1935. No. 226
POLLIT

Herewith information you desire.

Your list contained twenty-two names including MCILHONE and DUTT. ROOKE's name was not included in your original list.

Following are additional names you want:-

Birmingham	Roberts
South Coast	Gibbons
Bradford	Selby
Tyneside	Bradshaw
Lancs	Burke
Sheffield	Dronfield

PETER

19 May 1935. No. 227
Visa for TREASE given.

21 May 1935. No. 228
Youth GOLLAN

Send information immediately re ALEX WINSTON, whether granted transfer to Y.C.L. Soviet Union and also your recommendations.

KIM

21 May 1935. No. 229

WEST

You will receive from STOCKHOLM 2600 repeat 2600 florins. Pay Youth ENGLAND to cover debt to Party publishing House 500 repeat 500 and subsidy for Youth paper 'CHALLENGE' 705 repeat 705.

C.P. ENGLAND for National Party School 1250 repeat 1250, assistance for 4 families students L. School for April 145 repeat 145.

Total 2600 repeat 2600 Dutch florins.

MICHAEL

23 May 1935. No. 230

C.C. ENGLAND, IRELAND

Congress will start at the time appointed therefore necessary that delegates arrive at that time. Illegal parties in order to avoid accidents through travelling together can send delegates (?) to Congress before this appointed.

Acknowledge receipt.

P.C.

23 May 1935. Nos. 231–233

WEST, GORDON

By all means speed up preparation and departure 2nd messenger to GORDON country, who first of all must insist that Party must at any cost send immediately 34 delegates for World Congress.

Messenger must render every possible assistance to preparation and departure of delegates, including if necessary to travel together and guide delegates to destination as well as giving necessary money for preparation and travelling expenses.

We advise that delegates should go first to East or South AFRICA and from there to FRANCE where they shall go to the editor of HUMAIN PARIS. Or delegates may go first to SHANGHAI and arriving there can go straight to Soviet steamer bound for VLADIVOSTOCK, or may come through PERSIA and cross the soviet border without any visa or permission.

Messenger must insist that all possible channels used and no energy and money spared for coming of delegates. Second task to messenger is to organise sending of students for school here.

25 May 1935. No. 238

WILSON's friends request not to forget to bring them gramophone records and needles.

Our people are not connected neither with Mrs HARDY nor with ALEX.

25 May 1935. No. 239

Youth

On basis United Front try organise sending of unemployed Youth (?) delegation with their demands to international Labour Conference League of Nations in GENEVA taking place on June 4th.

KIM

26 May 1935. No. 240

About COHEN we shall settle things with you here. We must have here first all particulars.

28 May 1935. No. 241

POLLIT

Is it possible to get for DICK with wife suitable documents for journey about which MANUILSKY spoke to you. Await urgent answer.

ABRAHAM

Political Commission agreed your vacation beginning June 10th.

DICK

29 May 1935. No. 242

Take all Party papers from KATHELIN and bring them here without fail. Couriers will probably come with you on 10th or must we expect them sooner.

29 May 1935. No. 243

Sent PARIS May June M.M. TOM MANN INGEW.

Acknowledge receipt.

PETER

8 June 1935. No. 249

BURNS

Please inform JAON BEACH PAUL (?) SCULPTOR must make necessary arrangements with his friends in LONDON.

Tell JOAN STEPNIAK correspondence being attended to will received definite message soon.

POLLIT

9 June 1935. Nos. 250, 251

Youth C.C.

Don't send people for KIM school. We shall inform you separately of date they should be sent. Choose together with the Old Man (?) one comrade whom you are sure of and who is politically developed to work with those pupils who will send in future.

Comrade will have to work as leader of your group and he must teach practice of Youth work.

Telegraph name of comrade chosen.

KIM

9 June 1935. No. 252

BOB

Inform GORDON he is invited attend 7th Congress but not to arrive until eve commencement and make suitable arrangement carry on his work, GORDON must prepare speech INDIA.

HARRY

9 June 1935. No. 253

BOB

Inform GORDON postpone indefinitely all arrangement regarding courier. Going away to organise sending of students.

POLLIT

9 June 1935. No. 254

BURNS

Inform MICHAEL break connection BOMBAY (?) for time being. Recommend MICHAEL settle DOWN's side BOMBAY and let you have address.

HARRY

10 June 1935. No. 255

BOB

Inform COHEN of ELTHAM decision will be given in six weeks. Advise him get temporary work.

HARRY

14 June 1935. No. 263

JIM and CODIST

Buy at once and send open post one copy South American handbook for 1934 and 1935.

You didn't work a few days. What is the matter? When something happens at your end you must immediately inform us.

15 June 1935. No. 264

Transfer on our account 53 repeat 53 pound to following address: Mrs LEON repeat LEON repeat SIM, HIMATANGI repeat HIMATANGI, FOXTON repeat FOXTON, NEW ZEALAND repeat NEW ZEALAND.

Wire when sent.

17 June 1935. No. 265

PAT DEVINE shall arrange to come over here in two weeks. Before leaving he should get new book for himself; PAT should call at Parisian O.M.S. and bring something for ABRAHAM.

DICK

19 June 1935. No. 266

JIM

Send MAY on next occasion a few letters addressed to RUTH informing that you must prolong your vacation. Write also something about the scenery, where you are passing your vacation. Expecting your early reply.

DOCTOR

21 June 1935. No. 269

CHARLES KEELING arrived on 'RUDSUTAK'. Until now we don't understand for what purpose he was sent.

23 June 1935. No. 272

C.C.

TAILMAN suffering from result of ill treatment in 1934 still under treatment Fascist doctors. Request urgent assistance TAILMAN Committee at sending of delegation of doctors. Also arrange sending of jurist delegation to Criminal Law Congress August 18th BERLIN. ANDRE will inform on all questions. Acknowledge receipt.

P.C.

25 June 1935. No. 273

Arrange BURNS comes 10th July. Will guarantee his return August 7th as requested.

KERRIGAN

26 June 1935. No. 273

Receive from STOCKHOLM 21000 repeat 21000 Dutch gulden. From this pay for July.

CP ENGLAND CC 5560 repeat 5560

For Paper 13800 repeat 13800

CP IRELAND 361 repeat 361

Anti-Imperialist League 1000 repeat 1000

144 repeat 144

Assistance for family ROBSON from L. School 25 repeat 25

JONES salary July 10 repeat 10

Total 21000 Dutch Gulden.

MICHAEL

26 June 1935. No. 274

CAMPBELL

Arrange with PAT MURPHY, 34 East India Dock Rd, LONDON repeat 34 East India Dock Road, LONDON meet ship SS 'GOTHIC' arriving LONDON July 2nd. Get in touch with firemen dispute over overtime payment. Legal assistance may be needed. Five members of crew belong to R.T.U.C.

TOM

29 June 1935. No. 276

'DAILY WORKER'

Indignation exists among workers against CITRINE on issue of knighthood and Party should take hold and give direction and leadership to same right up to trades union (?) and Labour Party Conference.

From July 10th send 150 'Dailies' each day.

KERRIGAN

1 July 1935. No. 278

Wire state of health FRED. Do not understand why up to now no information on him. What outlook for further work? How long will it be till he will be able to work?

7 July 1935. No. 284

Specify to what organisation in USSR invitation sent for Soviet teachers to visit OXFORD August 10th to 17th (?wire) particulars of organisations extending invitation.

12 July 1935. No. 286

11th LEVINE arrived.

12 July 1935. No. 290

C.C. YOUTH, DOLLAN and MASSIE from KIM

You have two places at the Congress of old men, of them one for a Young Communist Leaguer, who at the same time is a member of the Guild. Immediately inform us of their names for sending entrance visas to LONDON. MASSIE must come to Congress, visa already sent for him. July 23rd final date for arrival of all (?delegates).

15 July 1935. No. 292

For POLLIT

HARDY does not supersede the organiser but he goes as instructor from centre.

14 July 1935. No. 294

JIM from ABRAHAM

July 13th received letters from RUTH.

For the present JIM must still remain here, we have not yet substitute for him. Wire state of health FREDERICK. One of these days shall speak with HARRY about substitute.

14 July 1935. No. 295

YOUTH GOLLAN from KIM

GOLLAN should not leave (1 group) 20th.

16 July 1935. No. 296

STEWARD

Against DOOLEY and LONGWORTH as students but favour SELBY. BICKERTON can accept position in (1 group) your bookshop, but he should place an advertisement in such papers as HERALD or CHRONICLE for such a position to avoid being engaged through party connection.

17 July 1935. No. 297

Re SANBAG don't give any connection or information to him. He must find his own way back to his country, we cannot give him any more assistance.

DON

19 July 1935. No. 298
C.C. YOUTH

Inform South AFRICA YOUTH through Party that they have one place at Youth Congress.

Inform IRELAND they have one place. Inform us their names for sending entrance visas to LONDON. Delegates to arrive first days of September. Sending pamphlets. Pamphlets to be distributed as pointed out.

KIM

20 July 1935. No. 299
STEWARD

Essential either ABRAHAMS or SELBY leave immediately to complete our Congress Delegation. Congress opens July 25th. Send more cuttings 'Worker' during Congress.

POLLIT

20 July 1935. No. 301
C.P. IRELAND

Organise United Front protest movement against pogrom shootings, placing responsibility Northern government, showing CRAIGAVON line of raising religious antagonism as means preventing growing unity in struggle of all sections of population. Necessary institute campaign against Emergency Powers Act Unemployed Assistance Bill, directed against all sections, stressing need for Workers and Farmers unity irrespective of religious opinion. Draw Trades Council Labour Party into (1 group) protest meetings, sending protest resolutions CRAIGAVON. Strive urgently involve clergy of all denominations and liberals for widest protest indignation citizens movement. Demand conviction of all responsible for pogrom and resignation of BATES. Appeal Civil Liberties League for press statement. Raise question in Northern, Southern and British Parliaments. Issue party statement.

MURRAY

22 July 1935. No. 302
GALLACHER

Sick delegation definitely called. Impossible alter this decision. Arrangements regarding DAVIES C DONOD's visit not affected.

PETER

25 July 1935. Nos. 303, 304
GALLACHER

Political Bureau agreed in view serious situation postpone 8-page daily until October. Necessary however to immediately sound alarm in party, and mobilise all forces campaign to insure issue 8-page daily in October. We propose campaign be launched in 'Daily' immediately for increased circulation, special directives all districts and locals, representatives from circulation department to visit all distract committees. In middle August launch big appeal for donations

to enable us to get out 8-page daily by October carrying forward campaign as systematically as last year.
POLLIT

27 July 1935. No. 307
GALLACHER
Seriously alarmed that Party and Press conducts no big campaign connection August 1st. Beg you especially in 'DAILY WORKER' utilise remaining days conduct mass campaign appeal for August anti-war mass activity.
POLLIT

28 July 1935. Nos. 308, 309
GALLACHER
Advise no campaign against possible refusal by Labour Party your recent letter for 'All in' Conference to preserve peace in view important discussion now proceeding.
Utilise LANSBURY's recent speech to show workers our willingness cooperate with Labour party in common action.
LLOYD GEORGE will cause Labour Party great concern making defeat National Government more difficult.
This will have repercussions inside Labour Party and urgently emphasises need for Labour rank and file insist upon their Leaders cooperating with COM-PARTY defeat National Government.
Send no further appeals to Labour Party until JOHNNY returns.
POLLIT

28 July 1935. No. 310
GALLACHER
Strongly urge mass protest against death sentence imposed on RUDOLF KLAUS by BERLIN Court for alleged MOPR work.
Get MAXTON and BEVAN ask questions Parliament.
Protests to German Embassies and big exposure in 'DAILY'.
POLLIT

29 July 1935. No. 311
Your number 44
ORDJONNIKITZE does not know who is KNOTT. Immediately wire detailed information.

4 August 1935. No. 316
GALLACHER
Convene meeting central Committee August 16th and 17th for BURNS and CAMPBELL to report.
Convene London District Conference August 31st and Provincial District Conferences September 7th.
POLLIT

5 August 1935. No. 317
Youth
Agreed give place student delegation Congress (?) YCI. Suggest Freeman.
Visas arranged for RAVIEN, GRESSER, SETZ and GOSS. Tickets from Intourist.
GOLLAN

21 August 1935. No. 326
Send WHEN to STOCKHOLM. There he must change book

26 August 1935. No. 330
With next courier send us catalogues for paper, calico and leather for binding
of books

28 August 1935. No. 331
BOB
HARRY left already.
Absolutely do not understand why you did not receive money for July.
STOCKHOLM confirms it is your fault that only paid for August. Please wire
immediately whether you actually did not receive for July. I am worrying
about this. Who is GEORGE? His request for four months not clear. For
what purpose?
ABRAHAM

28 August 1935. No. 332
WEST
August 27th SELBY left. Wire what delivered.

29 August 1935. No. 340
C.C. Youth to GOLLAN
RAVIEN, SETZ, GOSS, GRESSER and DIGBI arrived well.
KIM

4 September 1935. No. 349
Owing to great importance of receiving direct reports from ABYSSINIA for
'Daily Worker' and whole Communist Press absolutely necessary to send
there a good English journalist. Propose for this purpose HOLMES and expect
consent of Party and Editors Office. If Party agrees then HOLMES must
urgently come to us by aeroplane to talk over details.
Secretariat

5 September 1935. No. 353
(1 group) GEORGE RENSHAW regarding T.U. information.
Am informed question was fully settled with you.
PETER

8 September 1935. No. 357
BOB WILSON here 8th September.

8 September 1935. No. 358

C.C.

Inform SHARKEY Australia if no delegate KIM Congress, send comrade immediately for discussion League situation.

Will decide question representative and finance them (?) but help Paper now. Inform GOLLAN must arrive 15th latest.

KERRIGAN, KIM

10 September 1935. No. 359

No objections husband of THOMPSON coming here if you send him.

10 September 1935. No. 360

HARRY

Urgently wire how long it will take for JIM to construct a reserve station.

I am interested in your opinion whether IRIS should come with expired passport by direct steamer from LENINGRAD to LONDON.

Wire.

Doctor

11 September 1935. No. 363

Necessary by return have from you confirmation that CC aware of facts regarding CAEREAU (South Wales), comrade and relieving officer, that exonerates him from any suspicion and fully guarantees him here.

PETER

11 September 1935. No. 364

Advisable invite on behalf of appropriate Soviet trades unions BRAMLEY, MARCH, BANKS, LAWTHER, GRIFFITHS, JAGGER, ADAMS, ELVIN, LITTLE, HALL.

Should we invite them personally or extend invitation to whole of their executives?

Advise us also to which Trade Councils should be sent invitation for October celebration.

MANUILSKY

12 September 1935. No. 368

HARRY

Pay LEO Sim alias ANDREWS 250 repeat 250 pounds on our account. He must transfer this money through a bank but in no case take it with him.

ABRAHAM

13 September 1935. No. 356

HARRY

Wire whether SHARKEY arranged with you about address for money.

13 September 1935. No. 357

Important that you understand document you get together with my letter is not final opinion of Youth delegation, Discussion still proceeding in delegation on line. My letter therefore may be misleading. Necessary you give consideration to issue raised on (1 group) report you get from ERIC. Always remembering his impressions may not reflect final opinion of delegation. JOHNNY disagrees with proposal, liquidation of League.

PETER

15 September 1935. Nos. 369, 370

C.C.

Secure good participation Parliamentary Conference particularly through Labour Party, delegates from Trades unions also through other anti-Fascist Bourgeois Parliamentarians. Use all personal connections. Try to attain as much as possible official delegation from Labour Party. Immediately transmit suitable addresses for invitation to TALEMAN conference PARIS.

Arrange wide popularisation in Labour and Left Bourgeois Press as well as communication in whole press

Second session abduction of people commission takes place October in PRAGUE. Connect this session with wider campaign against HITLER terror and against activity HITLER agents in foreign countries.

Acknowledge receipt.

Secretariat

17 September 1935. Nos. 372, 373

HARRY

Give the man who is going next few days to GORDON's country all decisions and reports 7th Congress in order to deliver these to our friends. If possible give him about ten copies of Congress resolutions and all DMITROV's speeches. TAMBE and VAN MIN speeches you will receive in near future.

Our opinion is that man who is leaving should not be given our addresses for connection in GORDON's country, as this man has not been verified by us in his work. Let him at present, serve as our man for delivery of literature and send us in suitable form regular information on Government policy tendencies and movement of masses etc.

Later we can also give him other errands. Through messenger his address can be communicated by our friends in country so that one of them could get in touch with him taking all measures of precaution.

20 September 1935. No. 378

September 20th Mr. BRANSON delivered 2 letters, books for CHARLIE and WILSON and portmanteau with clothes.

To whom belongs portmanteau with these things? Wire.

How long can husband of THOMPSON be kept here? Can we use him and for what?

21 September 1935. No. 379

Wire whether you recommend wife of STEVENS for our future school. On this will depend some of our suggestions concerning his future work.

22 September 1935. No. 377

Two German seamen should be sent to ANTWERP immediately.

I have pressed question of their maintenance during this period and representations are being made to I.S.H. PARIS with whom you should also have contact on this matter.

PETER

22 September 1935. Nos. 380–383

Line on Abyssinian situation is correct and shows boldness after some unfairness in early period.

Your stand that line of Party in ABYSSINIA is line of defence of Soviet Union, your demand for full support of FRANCO–Soviet Peace Pact and for Peace Pact between POLAND and Soviet Union, your demand to renounce German Naval Agreement and call for emergency International Conference of all working class organisations correct and campaign on this line should be further developed.

We urge also that you assist in establishing contact between French C.P. and British Labour Party both by a public campaign and personal approaches. In view strong pacifist sentiments necessary stress Party as leader in fight for peace. Show that Party line including sanctions applied by whole of League is only way to prevent war while so-called pacifist line is actually way to bring about war.

Necessary demonstrate to workers in Socialist League, ILP and Labour Party influenced by fear of being involved in support of British Imperialism and our line on ABYSSINIA is directed also against National Government's Imperialist policy towards ABYSSINIA.

Unlike Socialist League (?) and ILP our Party carries on bold United Front struggle against National Government for wage increases for miners, engineers, improvement in conditions of unemployed.

PETER, ERCOLI

27 September 1935. Nos. 390, 391

Give official who is leaving as many copies as possible of all DMITROV speeches and congress Resolutions. He can also be instructed on questions which actually are not of a conspirative character. For expedition of letters and other conspirative messages necessary speedily to prepare another person.

You will receive letter about the 15th October. Remind you necessary to prepare one more person to carry money and to organise arrival of students from GORDON's country.

28 September 1935. No. 392
Inform JIM urgently to establish reserve apparatus in safe place.
ABRAHAM

28 September 1935. No. 393
Your number 22.
Consider arrival BAKER not useful. Send her written report.

29 September 1935. No. 394
Syllabus dispatched by air mail last night.
In return send two copies of good maps of British Isles and British Empire.
Urgent.
PETER

29 September 1935. No. 395
Do you recommend MUREIL THOMSON for Travels Limited but (1 group) limited?
She is recommended by ROSE COHEN.
Your messages up to number 28 received.
ABRAHAM

30 September 1935. Nos. 396, 397
Inform Bishop 'DAILY HERALD' of 25th September published downright provocatory anti-Soviet life of Japanese adventures about Sovietisation of SINKIANG. On 26th September TASS refuted this lie in special statement. If up to present 'HERALD' didn't publish this refinement demand in name of FSU editor should do it without delay. In case of refusal publish this case in RUSSIA today or 'DAILY WORKER' and expose for 'HERALD' characteristic methods of anti-Soviet information.
TSCHERNIN

4 October 1935. No. 407
2nd October from STOCKHOLM messenger left with one portmanteau containing non-Party's new post for you.
STOCKHOLM requests you should arrange with this messenger addresses, letters and everything needed for connection STOCKHOLM LONDON
Received your messages up to No. 44.
(Note: This message is very corrupt)

5 October 1935. No. 408
PARSONS
Await invitation to DIEPPE (?) or PARIS
HENRY

7 October 1935. No. 409
ARBUS handed over a letter October 5th.

8 October 1935. No. 412

WEST

JIM must remain until substitute arrives. He can return only without agreement. Regards leaving 14th October heard about it for first time.

Doctor

10 October 1935. No. 420

HARRY

Wire about preparation students for OMS School.

ABRAHAM

10 October 1935. No. 421

While fully appreciating your difficulties we urgently request speedy action to complete your quota for School and have last of them here by first week in November.

This should not lead to any lowering of standard of selections.

MARTY, PETER

13 October 1935. No. 422

Don't understand why only now acknowledgment ANDREWS NEW ZEALAND.

16 October 1935. No. 423

POLLIT

You will receive from STOCKHOLM 9,700 repeat 9,700 Dutch florins.

Pay out this sum to C.P. GREAT BRITAIN remainder for November 8,310 repeat 8,310.

C.P. IRELAND for November 365 repeat 365.

Anti-Imperialist League for November 1,000 repeat 1,000.

Family ROBINSON relief from DICKENS 25 repeat 25.

Total 9,700 repeat 9,700 Dutch florins.

Received your telegrams (2 groups indecipherable).

MICHAEL

19 October 1935. No. 434

JESSOP handed over on 18th October three letters and things from WILSON students.

ARBUS has already realised all right one journey for us.

According to your instructions we will not utilize her any more.

Your 67 badly mutilated. Repeat.

29 October 1935. No. 434

KERRIGAN on vacation and I don't understand your telegram 51 which treats question of MULLER for radio work.

22 October 1935. No. 437
WEST
Wire whether would not be success put forward candidature HORNER in RHONDDA as he has most chances of being elected.
Secretariat

22 October 1935. No. 438
POLLIT
Your No. 67.
According to our instructions of 16th September in No. 371 relief family ROBINSON of 25 Dutch florins destined for month of July.
MICHAEL

23 October 1935. No. 440
WEST
Prepare messenger to fetch mail urgently in PARIS. We will wire later when he should leave. Do you know where to call in PARIS? If not wire where messenger will put up. Also his name and first name.
DOCTOR

24 October 1935. No. 441
Wire when JIM ready with reserve.

25 October 1935. No. 442
Urgent mail will be in PARIS October 27th.
Send same date messenger. Wire when he leaves, where he will put up and name.

26 October 1935. No. 443
WEST
Wire when courier left for PARIS to get urgent material.
We ask you to demand code which we gave WOLTON who at one time deserted from South AFRICA. Destroy this code. Wire.

26 October 1935. No. 443
'Daily Worker' still carries campaign for closing SUEZ Canal.
Our position on question of time actual beginning of war by ITALY was already made clear. We don't raise demand military sanctions and closing SUEZ Canal lead to military sanctions. We concentrate on development independent actions workers and toilers, which is also way of compelling league of capitalist governments to take serious and effective measures against fascist aggressor.
MARTY
(Note: This message was very corrupt)

28 October 1935. No. 445
Ask you for third time to inform whether messenger left for PARIS and when to fetch materials. Received your 71.

29 October 1935. No. 447

Your open telegram regarding sending greetings to you in connection elections is a mistake.

Such telegrams must be enciphered.

29 October 1935. No. 448

Friend arrived.

Why don't you wire whether you sent messenger for materials to PARIS.

31 October 1935. No. 450

WEST

You promised to put at our disposal somebody for long journey. What about Mrs. HOLMES.

Please don't forget question WILSON scholars.

When did ANDREWS sail for NEW ZEALAND?

How (?) proceeds work of JIM?

FRED arrived here too late.

Shall send soon.

DOCTOR

31 October 1935. No. 450

HARRY

Your promise firm as a rock to send soon couriers has encountered as it seems great difficulties. Otherwise it could not be believed that so far nobody has arrived, But despite all I need urgently fresh forces.

Doctor

1 November 1935. No. 452

Youth C.C. GOLLAN

Despite negative reply which we provided from OLLENHAUER it is necessary to continue with all energy campaign for proposal of World YCI Congress on United Front on question of war. Even more so because the ECYCI didn't answer the question up till now.

KIM

2 November 1935. No. 453

PARSONS

Hand over to KLEMENS DATT 30,000 repeat 30,000 French francs for you to be transmitted to BERTRAND PARIS.

DATT should have arrived there on October 24th. Please acknowledge receipt by wire, otherwise make researches at once whereabouts DATT.

Your messages up to 82 received except numbers 72 to 78. What is the matter?

BRUNO

4 November 1935. Nos. 457, 458
HARRY

In election Campaign we almost completely identify ourselves with Labour Party and abstain from criticism.

ILP utilizes this against C.P.

We fear that our campaign may confuse many sections of workers who have already critical attitude towards whole of United Front and even Bourgeois policy of L.P.

The identification with L.P. will not strengthen United Front.

'DAILY WORKER' should remember how this question was treated in DMITROV Report.

We suggest you verify this situation and if we are right in our opinion then cautiously and gradually proceed to correct it.

MARTY

5 November 1935. No. 459
WEST

During next few days WILSON student TOM ROBERTSON, school name ROTHARIGER arrives. He should take JIM's old place.

In future we will call TOM BYRON. He must know nothing about the new place. Wire when he arrives and when he begins work.

BYRON received 70 dollars from us for clothes.

ALEXANDER

10 November 1935. No. 468
Your telegram number 90 about receiving portmanteau incomprehensible. Explain more clearly.

11 November 1935. No. 469
Youth C.C. GOLLAN

Don't leave for PARIS.

Meeting of fraction will not take place.

Send answer to your decision MASSIE and GOLLAN in near future.

KIM

13 November 1935. No. 474
POLLIT

DIMITROV's telegram isn't for publication.

DMITROV isn't in MOSCOW and without his consent telegram must not be published.

MANUILSKI

17 November 1935. Nos. 475, 476
Ask KERRIGAN's return immediately as POL Bureau have first appreciation elections.

Must arrive before 26th November.

Send by post main Party (?), Labour and ILP materials.

After KERRIGAN's arrival will take care without delay question help 8-page 'DAILY WORKER'.

We ask your opinion as to immediate utilization RALPH FOX in C.I. as one of 3 political assistants in my secretariat on Dominion and Colonial questions. Urge complete without delay list 10 students.

MARTY

20 November 1935. No. 480

If you don't hear us, call again with same call. You heard us last time.

22 November 1935. Nos. 481–486

C.C. ENGLAND and IRELAND

In THAELMANN Campaign necessary to consider following view points. Actual main task consists in creating, before trial, such a feeling in masses that intention of Fascists to turn THAELMANN trial into big anti-BOLSHEVIK trial will be thwarted.

Explain political role of THAELMANN as leader connecting it with proof of his innocence from a judicial view point. Unveil whole system NAZI justice terrorist character HITLER regime and provocative character of preparation of trial.

In struggle for THAELMANN develop elementary feelings of justice in broadest masses. Put up following slogans:

Freedom of THAELMANN,

Closing of concentration camps,

Amnesty for all opponents of HITLER regime in prison,

Prevention of execution of death sentences already pronounced,

Human treatment for prisoners,

Regular law proceedings,

Right to choose own defender,

Abolition of torture methods during remand.

Link up exposure of NAZI justice with disclosure of war preparations and anti-Soviet policy.

Continue to utilise anniversary of LEIPZIG trial by publishing daily articles and documents. Point out that LEIPZIG trial has smashed all points of accusation against THAELMANN.

On this basis develop broad mass movement of United Front (1 group) Party press against terror HITLER Fascism and organise for second half of December mass demonstrations anniversary acquittal of DMITROV if THAELMANN trial is not due before.

Urge make better use of material of RUNDSCHAU and THAELMANN Committee in Press.

Secure organisation of broad THAELMANN Committee in your country.

Secretariat

23 November 1935. No. 487

Fetch as usual 19,310 D.G. repeat 19,310 D.G. of which 18,940 D.G. repeat 18,940 D.G. for C.P. GREAT BRITAIN and 370 repeat 370 D.G. for IRELAND. Wire receipt.

MICHAEL

24 November 1935. Nos. 490–493

K.C.

According to press information, in EGYPT an advance mass movement against British Imperialism and for Independence of EGYPT is being carried out.

It seems to us that in connection with the movement position of CPGB should in general be following:

To fight resolutely against policy of British Imperialism in EGYPT without weakening struggle against Italian attack.

Declare that British military forces in EGYPT don't serve cause of peace but oppress mass movement for Independence and hamper anti-war struggle of workers against ITALY.

Point out that an independent democratic EGYPT basing itself on masses would be more serious opponent against Italian attack and a sure and honest support of Abyssinian independence.

Develop broad campaign against British interference in internal EGYPT affairs,

(1) for complete independence of EGYPT,
(2) immediate recall of High Commissioner LAMPSON who is responsible for bloodshed,
(3) for immediate prohibition of utilisation of British military forces against strikes, demonstrations and other mass actions of Egyptian people.

Arrange for adoption of resolutions on this basis in anti-war meetings, in Trades Unions and other organisations.

We deem it useful to propose to I.E.Z.A. and Socialist League joint action for independence of EGYPT and thus expose falsehood of their accusation regards being left alone in (?) anti-Imperialist struggle by Communists.

Examine expediency of intervention of GALLACHER in Parliament.

Examine all questions and submit your standpoint to us.

Secretariat

23 November 1935. No. 494

PARSONS

Immediately send materials regards Congress publication concerning edition sale advertisement, Press reviews, accounts. Inform what measures taken for further increase of popularising Congress.

Received your messages up to 7.

Nine telegrams via STOCKHOLM not received.

BRUNO

23 November 1935. No. 494

Your coming not necessary. Decision will be taken if needed only after analysing position. Send back KERRIGAN immediately.

MARKET

29 November 1935. Nos. 499, 500

We urge immediate launching of campaign for independence of EGYPT (1 group) our last telegram. Also to compel EGYPT's admission League of Nations without any conditions and abolition of capitulations. Examine possibility to hasten forming of 'Committee Defence Democratic Rights and Independence Egyptian People' with participation personalities anti-Fascist and anti-imperialist, labour deputies, representatives I.L.P. and socialist League, etc. This committee should denounce contradictions between National government and Geneva declaration and its attack on EGYPT's independence. Committee should also without delay send investigating delegation on commission to EGYPT to establish contact with WAFD aiming coordinate popular movement in EGYPT with action in BRITAIN and Italian Imperialism.

2 December 1935. No. 503

POLLIT

Take all measures to see MARKET in PARIS as quickly as possible from morning of 7th.

Wire CACHEN 'HUMANITE'.

EPOCH

2 December 1935. Nos. 507–509

C.C. of G.B.

We propose to organise broad defence campaign for insurgents BRAZIL and protest campaign against white terror of VARGAS Government against National Liberation Alliance. Most distinguished Labour Party representatives, tradesunion leaders, Labour co-operative societies women leagues, well known Liberals, scientists, writers, leaders of religious sects, pacifists etc. must be drawn into this campaign.

Slogans:-

Amnesty. Re-establishment of democratic liberties. Against courts-martial.

For public proceedings with admission of foreign lawyers desirable that a delegation of best known political and society representatives must (?) go to BRAZIL (?) in order to investigate station of arrested and prisoners.

Secretariat

5 December 1935. No. 511

Youth GOLLAN

No basis of agreement of your coming to us before you left for League. We await you in near future. Telegraph when you are coming.

KIM

7 December 1935. No. 513

We expect from you end of December six to seven WILSON students. Absolutely no girls.

8 December 1935. Nos. 514, 515

POLLIT

Send monthly on our account an average of 32 repeat 32 pounds, that is once 30 repeat 30 then 35 repeat 35 etc. to address:-

Surname: PLAUMIODIS repeat PLAUMIODIS

First name: PYRRKUS repeat PYRRKUS NIKOLAS repeat NIKOLAS

VIENNA repeat VIENNA 9 repeat 9 LECHTENSTEIN STRASSE repeat LECHTENSTEIN STRASSE 92 repeat 92, 2 repeat 2 STEIGE repeat STEIGE WOHNUNG repeat WOHNUNG 27 repeat 27.

Care of Frau repeat Frau MARLE repeat MARLE.

10 December 1935. No. 529

Arrange GIBBONS leaves for MOSCOW immediately.

HARRY

11 December 1935. No. 530

BOB

FREEDMAN left for your place. Connect her with JIM. She is appointed for reserve station. She must not be connected with BYRON. Wire when intends to work in new place. In future FREEDMAN will be called SYLVIA.

16 December 1935. No. 533

STEWARD

Instruct GEORGE HARDY finish work NEWCASTLE and see POLLIT certain LONDON December 21st.

WEST

20 December 1935. Nos. 535–537

C.C. ENGLAND from Secretariat

Make all necessary measures to develop without delay mass protect against execution of CLAUS. It is not enough to take protest resolution. Organise demonstrations before NAZI embassies, consulates, travellers' bureaux, etc; obtain through bourgeois jurists collective protests against RIBBENTROP's statement in justification of execution for communist opinion. RIBBENTROP's opinion means direct threat THAELMANN and NEU-KOELIN accused. Consider concrete physical offence on the part of well known bourgeois jurists and intellectuals against NAZI representatives in foreign countries in order to turn trial into tribune against NAZI terror. Put question of public boycott of organisations which participate in NAZI Olympiad. Propose (4 groups) of well known jurists to go to GERMANY to take CLAUS's wife and four children to ENGLAND.

21 December 1935. No. 538

GOLLAN

Propose that you go to PARIS FRIEDL on your way here. Take 52 pounds repeat 52 pounds from the party which was sent for the trip of the South African delegates which is filed in your budget for the fourth quarter.

KIM

21 December 1935. No. 539

Wire why your message regarding JIM and SYLVIA ciphered December 17th was transmitted December 20th. Where was it held up three days?

22 December 1935. No. 540

GORDON

Send immediately all information re Pan-Asiatic Labour congress to be held in TOKYO April next year.

CHARLIE

22 December 1935. No. 541

C.P. from (1 group)

Urgently request English party should release ALLISON for constant work in World Committee PARIS.

22 December 1935. No. 542

When you apply for visas it is absolutely necessary to give us name, surname and nationality of passport with which (1 group) comrades are coming. Also necessary to inform us of purpose of journeys, their pseudonyms and real surnames.

22 December 1935. No. 543

POLLIT

Inform us whether our indication of December 8th was carried out regards sending PYRRKUS (1 group) 33 repeat 33 pounds monthly.

26 December 1935. No. 544

Pay Youth ENGLAND 50 repeat 50 pounds to cover expenses for participation Y.C.L. in Election. We will return 50 pounds at (2 groups) settled accounts with you.

MICHAEL

29 December 1935. No. 547

Pay out family relief LEN student DICKENS 10 pounds 10 shillings to address: ROBINSON, SHEFFIELD, 16 MILDEN ROAD, HILLSBOROUGH.

Repeat 10 pounds 10 shillings for October, November and December.

30 December 1935. No. 548

Remind you once more of necessity to hasten departure of WILSON students.

1 January 1936. No. 1

Receive in STOCKHOLM 18100 repeat 18100 Dutch florins. One of them 13800 repeat 1380 for newspaper, 4000 repeat 4000 for C.C. and 300 repeat 300 for IRELAND. These sums are advanced money for January. Wire date of receipt.

MICHAEL

2 January 1936. No. 2

Your number 29 about DEANER has been enciphered on 20th December, but transmitted only on 30th December. Such retardations are taking a systematical character. What is the matter?

2 January 1936. No. 3

C.C. Youth

We propose that you immediately liquidate all old documents, letters and resolutions which you have in your archives. Send us everything which has historic value. Keep all necessary documents in a safe place.

KIM

3 January 1936. No. 5

WEST, GORDON

Speed up preparation messenger to carry certain stuff trades-union line GORDON's country. GORDON will receive trades-union letter in PARIS 20th January.

ALEXANDER

5 January 1936. No. 6

C.P.

Inform us by telegraph simultaneously when visa application is made for persons being sent by you here name and reason. Inform reason for SMITH coming.

Your telegrams up to number 52 received.

5 January 1936. No. 7

WEST, GORDON

Speed up preparation first messenger to carry certain stuff. Wire as soon as he is ready. Second messenger carrying mail must be ready first part of February. Essential second messenger has judgment about matters over there.

8 January 1936. No. 8

Recommend publication of whole interview DISRAELI about RIBBENTROP in 'Daily Worker' and give it widest circulation.

Secretariat

8 January 1936. No. 9

Inform us whether GINA KURTIS arrived already and began work.

10 January 1936. No. 10
HARRY

Can you recommend EMMA WOOLLEY for cipher work.

13 January 1936. Nos. 13, 14
C.C.

In spite indication ECCI almost no mass action carried through against HITLER terror after execution CLAUS. Provocative letter RIBBENTROP has not been utilised. Draw your attention necessity targets polarisation DISRAELI interview. Arrange that jurists, intellectuals publicly explain their attitude towards RIBBENTROP letter. Prepare on largest basis mass meetings, demonstrations for January 30th under slogan:- 'Three years terror, for complete amnesty, for hostages of Fascism'. Acknowledge receipt.
Secretariat

14 January 1936. No. 15
Visa already given for CONWAY on 5th January. For GEORGE HARDY visa will be given on 15th January.

17 January 1936. No. 15
You will receive in STOCKHOLM 16,500 repeat 16,500 D.G. From this amount:- 100 repeat 100 Gulden for IRELAND advance for February. 2,700 repeat 2,700 advance for February for C.P. ENGLAND and 13,700 repeat 13,700 for paper. Wire date reception money.
MICHAEL

16 January 1936. No. 16
WEST

Wire when will start JIM's reserve. Long time ago you informed us that everything is ready. When does JIM intend to leave?

16 January 1936. No. 19
BRADLEY will be in PARIS 23rd and (1 group) Hotel MODERNE repeat Hotel MODERNE, Place Republic. Friend will call.

17 January 1936. No. 20
Visas ROBIN PAGE ARNOT, OLIVE ARNOT, BARBARA BEATRICE ARNOT (1 group) January 18th. Your telegrams up to No. 69 received.

17 January 1936. No. 21
Secretariat agrees to ARNOT as representative.

19 January 1936. No. 22
BRADLEY must have PALM DUTT's address.

19 January 1936. No. 24
You will receive in STOCKHOLM 700 repeat 700 Dutch florins which must be given to Youth ENGLAND as advance for first quarter.
MICHAEL

21 January 1936. No. 28

Visa for SAMSON HENRY COHEN, WINIFRED ISABELLA McKEIG and SMITH given January 21st. Visa for HARDY has already been given January 14th. SINA (? GINA) KURTIS is SARA.

21 January 1936. Nos. 29–31

Request send as soon as possible delegation to BRAZIL, to composition of which we consent. We are prepared to pay expenses delegation. Give delegation following instructions. Insurrection movement was organised not by communists but by National Liberation alliance to which adhere also strata of bourgeoisie.

(The next part of this message no. 30 is indecipherable)

At present time provocations against USSR and CI continue by using false captures and accusation of type of affair REICHSTAG. Task of delegation to stir public opinion all countries especially USA and ENGLAND.

MONROE and WATERLOO

26 January 1936. No. 34

POLLIT

Repeating telegram. Agree to composition of delegation to BRAZIL. Expenses will be paid. Immediately wire when you receive our 29, 30 and 31 re our agreement to composition of delegation to BRAZIL and when handed over to POLLIT.

MONROE

27 January 1936. No. 38

Visa for MASSY given January 27th.

29 January 1936. Nos. 40, 41

Today we wire STOCKHOLM to pay you according to your bill for different expenses 612 pounds 15 shillings repeat 612 pounds 15 shillings. Further 50 percentage fares for delegates 142 repeat 142 pounds. And according to list of L school 297 pounds 17 shillings repeat 297 pounds 17 shillings. Total 1052 repeat 1052 pounds 12 repeat 12 shillings or 7640 repeat 7640 gulden.

31 January 1936. No. 42

Please send with CLARA DIENER three metres blue or brown smooth material of best quality for a lady's coat. Your number 94 arrived, admitted to school.

1 February 1936. No. 43

POLLIT

According to your wire send HARDY here as quickly as possible.

MARKET

1 February 1936. No. 44

Please make it clear about FREEMAN. We can find no request for such a person.

MARKET

2 February 1936. No. 45

Your number 74.

As comrade who spoke with KERRIGAN is one here at present, please explain question concerning MILLER.

2 February 1936. No. 46

Your No. 97

Begin utilising new cuttings for ciphering when old stock finished.

Your 105.

Repeat addresses. Mutilated.

2 February 1936. Nos. 47, 48

You will receive in Stockholm 682 repeat 682 Dutch florins. Of this sum send C.P. NEW ZEALAND reminder of budget last year 480 repeat 480 florins and for family ANDREWS for August, September and October last year 130 repeat 130 florins. Pay KERRIGAN fee for paragraph in periodical C.I. on elections 14 August 14 florins. POLLIT fee for article number 21 C.I. 29 repeat 29 florins. Send PALM DUTT fee for article in number 21 of C.I. 29 repeat 29 florins. Total 682 repeat 682 florins.

MICHAEL

3 February 1936. No. 49

Consent to candidate MARY TAYLOR. Sending WADON her name. When (? She) comes give her small post for is. Visa for HARDY given January 14th.

4 February 1936. Nos. 51–55

C.C.

Brazilian (? Reactionary) rages against participants National Liberation Movement, it acts in capacity of principal supplier of anti-C.I. anti-Soviet falsifications and lies for Fascist Press whole world. Last days in centre this campaign stands question arrest of a certain BERGER EWERT whom they tried to expose as 'Comintern agent' and 'Organiser' of November insurrection. Sentence of death threatens him. Urgently necessary development energetic campaign for victim White Terror BRAZIL. Instruct Press necessity wide explanation last events BRAZIL as struggle for international liberation and for democratic rights people. Use material published in League of Nations speeches, LITVINOV and all other material in order to attack BRAZIL Government, against terror, suppression of rights and betrayal of interests BRAZIL people condemning it before world publicity and (?) same time show that this and the policy was cause of People's revolt. Demand liberation participants insurrection, expose Fascist false documents especially in connection with arrest EWERT. As it is well known EWERT was prominent Reichstag deputy and for some time engaged himself in studying Colonial problems, as anti-Fascist emigrant he went to place where there are better possibilities for studying problems that interest him.

Demand his immediate (?) release (?) and failing this expulsion to EUROPE except GERMANY where HITLER Fascism endangers his life.
Secretary

4 February 1936. Nos. 57, 58
Your number 97
Sums must be allocated as follows. For November: LEAGUE 1000 repeat 1000 florins, IRELAND 365 repeat 365, ENGLAND 8310 repeat 8310, DICKENS 25 repeat 25, YOUTH ENGLAND 182 repeat 182, for Elections 7240 repeat 7240, Assistance for families August 25 repeat 25, YOUTH ENGAND 853 repeat 853, Total 18,000 repeat 18,000 florins.
For December 18940 repeat 18940 ENGLAND and 370 repeat 370 IRELAND. Total 19310 repeat 19310 florins.
MICHAEL

7 February 1936. Nos. 65–67
C.C.
TROTZKI transferred campaign of lies against Soviet Union and STALIN into HEARST Press. January 19th TROTZKI started a series of articles in 'New York American', he accuses Soviet Government of imprisonment and tortures of 'innocent' TROTZKISTS and affirms STALIN and COMINL have helped HITLER to come to power. You must use this fact of block TROTZKI with worst anti-Sovietmongers, supporters of HITLER and point of concentration American fascism HEARST for further exposure of counter revolutionary role TROTZKI and also his role as helper of fascism in struggle against proletarian revolution and Soviet Union. Some time ago through this accelerate separation of all honest elements from TROTZKIST groups. Before this who still believe in TROTZKI put direct question of condemnation block TROTZKI with HEARTS.
Secretariat

6 February 1936. No. 68
POLLIT
'HERALD' from February 3rd contains announcement appearing series CITRINE articles on Labour in Soviet Union. Recommend sharp campaign in Press trade unions exposing CITRINE's slander. Use material on CITRINE tour which we send you.
MARKET

10 February 1936. Nos. 69–71
POLLIT
Information from ARNOT received.
Inform PALM DUTT of our indication and your conversation with Professor in order that PALM DUTT meet him would have knowledge whole matter. Practically this moment most important to attain following:
   1. Assistance of Professor for admission into Congress trades-Unions in which our friends are (?) working.

2. His consent to put up as Congress candidates some legal Socialist and Trades-Union workers who actually are our followers.

3. To win over Professor in general for benevolent neutrality as regards our friends in country and for benevolent attitude towards their tendency to participate in work of Congress.

DISRAELI

11 February 1936. No. 75
POLLIT

Cipher material has been send via STOCKHOLM on 7th February. Acknowledge receipt.

15 February 1936. No. 77
Did CLARA DIENER leave and when? Your numbers up to 118 received.

20 February 1936. No. 81
Send us detailed datas on LEE Frank, BROWN Isabella, MACKEYWOR Beatrice, necessary for visas.

21 February 1936. No. 82
POLLIT

In next days begins in BUCAREST before court martial trial ANNA PAUKER, and comrades. Trial of great political importance because directed against whole Party of ROMANIA. Necessary publication (9 groups indecipherable) terror and civil justice and supporting accused PAUKER and others. Use materials of RUNAG.

KIN (? KIM)

(Note: Nearly all the groups in the latter part of this message were corrupt)

22 February 1936. Nos. 83–87
POLLIT

Draw your attention to two absolutely inadmissible actions of 'DAILY WORKER' editorial board: In February 15th issue, to a communication of RUNAG regarding anti-Japanese Association of National Freedom in North CHINA, Editorial Board in an arbitrary manner added that this association 'was created on initiative of C.P. INDIA on basis of decisions 7th Congress C.I.' This is actually direct support of Fascist anti C.I. campaign thus giving them possibility of referring to C.C. (?) organ, one of the most important sections of C.I.

February 19th Editorial board enquired in MOSCOW by open telegram about insurrection in PARAGUAY.

Is it possible that Editor does not understand that in MOSCOW there can be no other information on such questions besides communications from Associated Press or other American Agencies who also have their offices in LONDON, and is it possible that he does not understand especially now after recent anti-Soviet campaign in connection with events in BRAZIL and in breaking of diplomatic relations between URUGUAY and USSR, that the fact alone of a Communist paper wiring such a request to MOSCOW represents, under the best circumstances, an objective proviso?

Investigate who is completely responsible and reason this has been possible. Take measures to prevent similar things happening in the future. Notify us about result of investigation. We advise you to charge SHIELDS and COS thoroughly to look through whole paper and above all Foreign Rubric before publishing paper.

Secretariat

23 February 1936. No. 88

Tell ANDREW 'TRTD' impossible but other means will be sought letter from MARKET. On basis first reading programme of action recommend you delay for short time its publication as basis for discussion until you get our observations.

ARNOT

23 February 1936. No. 89

DOUGHY must speak October Club February 28th instead of me. RUTIAM ill. Discuss with COHEN.

GOLLAN

23 February 1936. No. 90

Two NEW ZEALAND students (1 group) WILLIAMS and FRANK LEE waiting in LONDON for visas. Speak with them to get their characterisation such as social origin, party standing and position reliability and send us with your opinion by wire or other quickest way. As soon as we receive this we will decide about sending visas.

MARKET

23 February 1936. No. 91

Why no information about SARAH. Did she commence work.

25 February 1936. No. 92

Communicate us exactly who are the five person for whom (?) you request visas, stating character of work of each. We repeat again, that without exact dates, without stating purpose of journey and passport name and Christian besides Party pseudonyms we will not give any visas.

26 February 1936. No. 93

POLLIT

In addition to our telegram No. 83–87 draw your attention to BISHOP's review and inscription to photograph of STALIN in 'DAILY WORKER' of 2nd February. This most irresponsible fact once more confirms the necessity to observe closely what is going on in Editorial Board. Awaiting answer concerning measures taken.

Secretariat

28 February 1936. No. 95

POLLIT

Wire immediately characterisation your four students also two from NEW ZEALAND. Wire characterisation mission and who personally met GALVIN (1 group).

29 February 1936. No. 96

POLLIT

We need two typists. Request send immediately five to six biographies and characterisations of typists recommended by P.B. for work in C.I. Inform possibility of sending (? SAMWELL) to work as typist here.

ROBIN

29 February 1936. No. 97

PARSONS

Publish pamphlet on IRELAND, to be ready beginning of April, of Tom MANN's pamphlet for his anniversary. Also prepare new drive for old pamphlet MARX ENGELS 'LENIN on IRELAND'.

BRUNO

3 March 1936. No. 89

POLLIT

Sending visas for New Zealanders and British. Due to factional struggle in Orient request to cable all possible details of South Africans, what capacity in Party, who personally sent him, etc.

ROBIN

4 March 1936. No. 102

COHEN and wife arrived 3rd. Brought one letter.

6 March 1936. No. 104

HARRY

CANADA asks if leading comrades can speak TORONTO May Day. They promise pay all expenses.

ARNOT

7 March 1936. Nos. 105–107

POLLIT

According to newspapers PRESTES arrested in BRAZIL. Is manacled (? and in) direct danger of being killed. Necessary bring wide public to its feet in order to save PRESTES. Endeavour get prominent Labourists and other public figures come out with this demand. Put questions in Parliament, intervene with Brazilian Ambassador, and telegrams Brazilian Government, etc. Must endeavour get publicity campaign in bourgeois press by means information articles letters. Popularise PRESTES in press raise alarm that he (? is) threatened with vengeance and must stay hand (? or) be murdered. Get into contact British delegation in BRAZIL in order it endeavour obtain meeting with PRESTES and investigation (?) his situation. By the way inform us whereabouts delegation its route and composition. We emphasise great point (?) all importance emergency campaign.

DISRAELI

7 March 1936. No. 108
Visa sent ANN GRAY.

8 March 1936. No. 109
Urge you to nominate comrade (?) who knows well Political and Party question who can travel absolutely legal to BRAZIL. Necessary that he examines and investigates actual situation of Brazilian Party after the crushing (?) of insurrection and makes us his proposals.

9 March 1936. No. 110
POLLIT

Regard your proposal sending four comrades. Our opinion after consultation with GREY it would be inconvenient in view the fact that present course (?) half finished. However difficult find teachers for them. Therefore consider better not send them for this course.

MONROE and MARKET

9 March 1936. Nos. 111, 112
In your country exist official and private radio schools. Desirable that you find 5 to 7 tried and reliable members (especially from Youth) with respective technical knowledge and to send them to these schools and finish complete course. Expenses of course in our account. If taking part in school is connected with giving up professional work then we will pay whole salary for such candidates. Communicate us your practical proposals on this point as soon as possible.

10 March 1936. No. 127
At present critical moment of war it seems to us inexpedient to recall HOLMES from ABYSSINIA. Perhaps temporary another comrade could be used as editor of foreign section.

11 March 1936. No. 128
Regarding ISADORE GALVIN answer will be given in eight days. Wire details (?) VICKERS.

ROBIN

11 March 1936. No. 129
POLLIT

Widest publicity needed on Lady HASTINGS etc arrest and treatment so as to arouse indignation against Brazilian authorities. Try 'GUARDIAN' and other bourgeois papers on HASTINGS also on arrest and peril PRESTES. This connection expose alleged suicide American ALLAN BARON. Campaign also in 'DAILY WORKER'.

Secretariat

14 March 1936. No. 133

Necessary that POLLIT and if possible GALLACHER come here not later than March 20th. Next days Americans and French will also arrive here. Urgently wire when leaving.

DISRAELI

16 March 1936. No. 137

From STOCKHOLM you will receive 101600 repeat 101600 French francs. From this credit advance on account April CC CPGB 19780 repeat 19780. For Newspaper 71220 repeat 71220 FF. CP IRELAND 6100 repeat 1600 FF. Total 101600 repeat 101600 FF.

MICHAEL

16 March 1936. No. 139

Visa sent for PURDY

Hard factional struggle in South AFRICA makes impossible grant visa to GALVIN who should return to South AFRICA.

MARKET

23 March 1936. No. 145

POLLIT

Visa for URQUHART was sent on 17th March.

KIM

2 April 1936. No. 147

JIM

Time 1430 G.M.T. does not suit us. Instructions as regards time you will receive in a few days.

3 April 1936. No. 149

Please ask POLLIT where is (? engineer) BEYLY at present time, how is his attitude. As we are informed he was Party member and two years ago left Party.

8 April 1936. No. 165

Render all possible help to Irish comrades (? to) understand as from you their present tasks in the struggle for peace. Also give practical help in carrying on this broad united May-day (?).

ARNOT

10 April 1936. No. 168

From April 11th we are working for JIM every day at 2000 repeat 2000 G.M.T. Calls and answers as arranged.

10 April 1936. No. 169

Received suitcase ANNE GREY. Books promised not enclosed.

13 April 1936. No. 170
POLLIT
Can you send NICKNANIZO.
ARNOT

14 April 1936. No. 171
POLLIT
How much do Irish want each week?
ARNOT

15 April 1936. No. 176
New station which has been arranged by JIM must be considered as reserve. We shall call this station every day and even perhaps we shall transmit something, but station must answer only in case that we specially request such answer. Inform if understood.

22 April 1936. No. 183
You will receive in STOCKHOLM 9700 French francs. From this sum pay Youth ENGLAND advance on account (?) second quarter 7500 repeat 7500 French francs and POLLIT 2200 repeat 2200 French francs for covering 30 pounds paid to HANS EISLER. Total 9700 French francs.
MICHAEL

23 April 1936. No. 184
POLLIT
Decision BICK does not come here but (? goes) to convalescent resort either in BRITAIN or preferably FRANCE. All expenses paid (?) (1 group) communicate when and where.
ARNOT

23 April 1936. No. 185
POLLIT
(2 groups) tries to get interested LLOYD GEORGE and other English politicians for THAELMAN. Try through your connections with Labourites to support this.
DISRAELI

23 April 1936. No. 188
POLLIT
Arrange that GALLACHER, other members of House of Commons, in name of 10 deputies (?) who signed TAELMAN protest, put question to Government demanding information why HITLER Government didn't receive deputation of two representatives of House of Commons on question TAELMAN. Demand protest of Government against disregard of English public opinion on part of HITLER.
EPOCH

27 April 1936. No. 190
POLLIT
Question GIBBONS favourably settled.
Your action re South African confirmed.
ARNOT

27 April 1936. No. 191
Tell us when BIC can come to PARIS to give information.
OKANN

30 April 1936. No. 195
ENGLAND IRELAND GADR Party
According to decision Secretariat we urge you not to choose to send any
(? more) students for International School here but organise instead central
school in country self.
Secretariat
(Note: This message was also sent to SPAIN)

5 May 1936. Nos. 197, 198
BICKERTON will come around 17th May to PARIS, Hotel PONT ROYAL
repeat PONT ROYAL, Rue MONTALAMBERT 7 repeat 7. Comrade will ask
there for Mr. BICKERTON and tell him parole: 'How is GEORGES now?'
BICKERTON answers: 'He is better'. He must bring all information for
OKANO. If he cannot come himself send courier to bring explained Japanese
contacts. (If ?) you must send them by courier (?) name of courier, hotel and
parole remain the same.
OKANO

14 May 1936. No. 204
Visas for JANE MEAD and GOLLAN JOHN sent to LONDON.

14 May 1936. No. 205
POLLIT
Considering impossible delay arrival GOLLAN till Autumn for cure (?) because
of his state of health secretariat (?) YCI considers necessary immediate arrival
GOLLAN here if Head consents. Visa sent LONDON.
KIM

15 May 1936. No. 206
MASON
Don't know SIDNEY. Were LAPEFF and CAMERON known in AUSTRALIA
under name of DOBROWSKY living at GIRRAWEN. What credentials have
either of them from Australian Party.

17 May 1936. No. 209

Will you characterise and recommend MAGMAKIN (SHIELDS knows her) and JACOB MILLER SHEFFIELD graduate known by us for work in publishing house? Urge (1 group) other visas of each will not be extended.

ARNOT

(Note: This message very corrupt)

17 May 1936. No. 210

GIBBONS and Robert BURNS finally settle later leaves earliest possible (?)

ARNOT

17 May 1936. Nos. 211, 212

Send Y soon as possible following maps:

1. Phillips commercial map of CHINA on linen.
2. Separate maps of Chinese provinces: JHEHOL, CHAHAR, SUIYUAN, SHEN-SI, SHAN-SI.
3. Full atlas of Chinese provinces.
4. Detailed map of MANCHUKUO.
5. Detailed map of Chinese railroads, navigation (?) and river traffic.

19 May 1936. No. 214

POLLIT

YOUNG, Esther, you can send.

DISRAELI

25 May 1936. No. 217

WEST

Permit to use temporary reserve station. We shall also work on this station.

25 May 1936. No. 218

Telegram sent by us to MOBO was returned by post office with remark that addressee left and whereabouts unknown. What does this mean?

BRUNO

25 May 1936. No. 219

PARSONS LONDON

I would not agree to leave magazine without a comrade specially in charge. There must be a suitable comrade in charge she will be well paid.

26 May 1936. No. 220

POLLIT

Maps of CHINA, MANCHURIA and MONGOLIA, we asked for, you may get by Y.P. PORTER, 145 Minories, LONDON E.C.3, Admiralty agent for charts and publisher nautical books. These maps are issued there by British Admiralty and British War Office. Send immediately.

28 May 1936. Nos. 222, 223

POLLIT

Editorial 'DAILY WORKER' committed a mistake in printing only first part of Disraeli article, in addition excluding two important paragraphs, one of which paragraphs re doctrine -ians in peoples workers party.

Reference in Imprecorr absolutely insufficient. Mass of D.W. readers don't read magazine. Necessary to publish article fully in paper with special edition or in two parts in two ordinary numbers with note that article was written before May 1st. This article finding an echo everywhere must also be brought to notice of wide working masses in ENGLAND.

Secretariat

29 May 1936. No. 229

Send us immediately Chinese Year Book all (1 corrupt group) – 1936, SHANGHAI, with separate special map of CHINA. Published by Chinese Year Book Publishing Company 1935.

1 June 1936. No. 231

Impossible to help DOBROVSKYS. They need to return to Australia or settle in London. Absolutely no chance of getting visa from this end. Explain him situation.

MASON

2 June 1936. Nos. 232–241

C.C.

June 8th in GENEVA takes place plenary session initiative committee World Peace Congress. Campaign enters decisive stage and must stand in the centre (?) of timely (?) anti-war campaign of (? Mass) organisations and party (1 group) during next months. Up to now our press didn't attach sufficient attention to popularisation preparation Peace Congress. Popularising appeals and proclamations of Peace Congress, our press must explain non-party and non-Communist character of Peace Conference. Simultaneously explaining our line in spirit of editorials in CI on this question.

Party must publicly give positive aid to initiative of calling Congress. It must emphasise that Communists will give most active assistance to every real peace initiative. Simultaneously begin in our press to popularise systemically line of ECCI Presidium and May article 'GUARDIAN' on problem of struggle for preservation of peace. Within this compass carry on (2 groups) and discussion with bourgeois pacifist conceptions. On one hand struggle against pro-Hitlerian conceptions of certain pacifist strata and on other hand against sectarian conceptions on question preservation of peace. Make greatest effort to develop propaganda Peace Congress is Social Democratic, Trades Union, Co-operative, women's and social political press. Therefore, use workers May delegation returning (from ?) USSR. Emphasise necessity mass participation of delegates of all political opinions of working class movement, in first line mass participation of Trades-Unions. Simultaneously arrange delegations for factories, co-operatives, culture and sport organisations, women's, youth, Christian leagues, as well as by peace forces. Middle class, intellectual and bourgeois pacifists. Centre of gravity of our work must be placed on formation of non-party peace committee and of already existing war, anti-fascist Youth Women's and other committees. After good preparation to begin already beginning of June in some Trades Unions factories to elect delegates on basis of widest united front. On adoption of decisions of welcoming peace appeal of initiative committee put forward our line in non-party form. Consider possibility convocation (1 group) conferences of elected delegates and existing peace committees.

Elected delegates and new created committees must immediately establish contact with national initiative committee. Propose Political Bureau to work out concrete plan Congress campaign. Entrust well-known member C.C. to be exclusively responsible for Congress work and to establish close contact with our fraction of World Committee Paris. Request to send us twice a month detailed written reports regards campaign and work carried on.

Acknowledge receipt and transmission.

Secretariat

(Note: This message was also sent to AMSTERDAM, Basle, Copenhagen, Prague, Spain and USA)

3 June 1936. No. 242

POLLIT

We need experienced well-qualified translator for German and French into English, desirable as well knowledge of Russian. Request (1 group) do all possible to find such (?collaborator) and to send us first his credentials (1 group) also your opinion about him.

DISRAELI

3 June 1936. Nos. 243, 249

C.C.

Papers received today telegraphically declaration Soviet citizen MATVEIEV, witness ANTIKAINEN trial, on his terrorisation in FINLAND. By air mail sent newspapers translation protocol (? Interrogation) MATVEIEV by representative Finnish Ministry of Justice in presence of Soviet Ambassador. Most essential of this unprecedented scandal consists in that Finnish Fascism anxious to receive by all means material for charge against ANTIKAINEN tried to terrorise MATVEIEV who appeared in Court. Although, Finnish Government had plainly guaranteed full immunity to invited witness, attempts were made immediately to (1 group) him by threats, extorting falsely dictated statements against ANTIKAINEN; after that MATVEIEV was led away from Court, arrested and not allowed to go to Soviet Embassy. Only next day through a trick MATVEIEV succeeded to escape from violators. He came to Soviet Embassy declared that (1 group) false statements given by him in court.

(Note: The next two parts are translated from the German as they were not received by 'LONDON')

Statements which the Finnish policy extorted from him through threats and force and begged to be allowed to travel as soon as possible to the Soviet Union. On the grounds of scandalous provocation ANTIKAINEN was convicted of a murder he did not commit.

This campaign will certainly be seized on by the Fascist Press in other countries. It is necessary to publish immediately all the material of the protocol to the trial of MATVEIEV and relying on this, to develop a great protest campaign against the unheard of provocations with which Finnish Fascists, following the example of their German leaders, attack their opponents. Organise in connection with this campaign for the defence of ANTIKAINEN. Send protests, deputies of various circles, especially jurist associations and to Finnish Embassies and Government (1 group) of prominent intellectuals, large liberal Press (1 group), abolition sentence, liberation ANTIKAINEN of this case must be utilised too (2 groups) in order to show whole civilised world how fascism does not even recoil from dirtiest methods, that there exists no law for it, that only mighty voice of whole (?cultured) humanity as it was in the days of LEIPZIG trial, can stop sword of executioner which moves over heads of TALEMAN, PRESTES, ANTIKAINEN, and other anti-Fascist fighters. Inform us on measures taken.

Acknowledge receipt.

Secretariat

(Note: This message was sent also to Amsterdam and Copenhagen)

4 June 1936. No. 250

POLLIT

TOM MANN's pension will continue. CAMPBELL not necessary now. On draft programme ME and Irish question. Will inform you later.

MARKET

4 June 1936. No. 251

POLLIT

Our estimation English May workers delegation to Soviet Union, as well, representative and authoritative. They accepted declaration for unity and Soviet peace policy. Important establish and keep personal contact in centre and districts with member of delegation such as FOWCET (? And) LARSTOW, POPE) and give full help to carry reporting campaign and publish report as they intended to do.

MARKET

5 June 1936. Nos. 253–255

POLLIT

It is possible that EWERT, his wife, and wife of PRESTES, OLGA BENARIO, will be sent to Germany on one of the German steamers, which will call at VIGO,

CORUNA, BOULOGNE-SUR-MER, SOUTHAMPTON. Necessary, by all means, to hinder that these comrades be transported as far as Germany.

Organise that well-known persons address themselves to Government with request that Government demands for EWERT, his wife, and OLGA BENARIO to be permitted to go ashore in SPAIN, FRANCE, or in ENGLAND. Arrange that well-known personalities lawyers address themselves to port's authorities. Send authoritative delegations on steamer. Organise in ports mass demonstrations as far as hinder departure of steamer in case of refusal or liberation.

Secretariat

(Note: This message was also sent to SPAIN and UNITED STATES)

5 June 1936. No. 256

POLLIT

Urgently request send your opinion whether would be of use to organise this year International Anti-War day on August 1st or would it be better instead of International Anti-War Day to leave it to parties to organise anti-war demonstrations on different dates in August in connection with World Peace Congress.

Secretariat

5 June 1936. No. 252

Youth C.C. MASSIE and GOLLAN

Develop broad campaign for freedom of PRESTES, attempt to involve in it all anti-Fascist Youth Organisations, especially Socialist, Republican, Democratic. Pay special attention to student organisations. Send protest telegrams and delegations to Embassy and VARGAS. Utilise INPRECOR material for campaign in Youth Press.

KIM

(Note: This message was also sent to SPAIN)

7 June 1936. No. 257

Send by air mail to Australian friends pages of INPRECORR number 23 with article DISRAELI.

MARKET

7 June 1936. No. 258

My introduction to FRANCE in future was sent to LAWRENCE from PARIS May 29th.

MARKET

11 June 1936. No. 260

Leaving LENINGRAD boat 13th mentally sick delegate (?) MARSH in care of THOMAS both AUSTRALIAN. Meet give assistance including financial if necessary we will reimburse.

MARKET

15 June 1936. No. 261

Send immediately name address organisation to whom request for war veteran delegation for 1st August LENINGRAD should be sent. (1 group) delegates fares return re LENINGRAD to be paid from ENGLAND all else including (3 groups) by war veterans S.U. Answer urgent.

MARKET

15 June 1936. Nos. 262, 263

C.P.

Despite reactionary Zionist character (1 group) consider necessary partici-pation representatives unprofitable as Jewish toilers World Congress Jews Geneva. (1 group) campaign and Congress for mobilisation broad masses against anti-semitism, race hatred and above all against HITLER fascism. Try during campaign and on Congress put in foreground fight against HITLER fascism. Show up necessity incorporation Jewish tolerates movement peoples front respective countries and combat attempts reactionary Zionist elements to soften anti-HITLER movement in order obtain concessions from HITLER.

Secretariat

15 June 1936. No. 266

We don't know name German ship on which EWERT repeat EWERT being transported. Make all efforts to (1 group) on all German ships coming from RIO going HAMBURG.

EPOCH

15 June 1936. No. 267

POLLIT

MARSH in care of THOMAS on s.s. 'SIBERIA'. Inform us after departure for AUSTRALIA date name of s.s.

MARTY

17 June 1936. No. 286

Youth MASSY

ANTONE BROWN will be in PARIS on the evening of 18th June in Hotel MONT-JOLI, rue FROMENTIN (?) 8.

BROWN has an AUSTRALIAN passport in the name of ANTONE URBAN. We ask that a tour be organised to PARIS for MAGGIE JORDAN, who will buy two week-end train tickets to PARIS and return for BROWN.

KIM

19 June 1936. No. 287

BRADLEY must come here immediately with all material concerning his country.

KUUSINEN

20 June 1936. No. 288

Harry

Your letter received. As I must undergo cure end of July it would be best you come to us middle of July. Eventually you could spend your vacation in SOVIET UNION. (Last three groups undecipherable)

DISRAELI

22 June 1936. No. 294

KATHLEEN arrived 21st delivered material and books, Received sending from BROWN.

22 June 1936. No. 295

POLLIT

We do not oppose DEVINE going back to English work and recall MURRAY. Prepare for near future exact information on whole question.

Secretariat

22 June 1936. No. 296

Ask you come here July 19th with GALLACHER and one or two other friends for discussing problems of Party such as Trades-union and Parliamentary work 'DAILY WORKER' activity toward coming Labour Party and Trades-union Congresses.

Secretariat

22 June 1936. No. 297

Knowing Irish paper is closing down please advise what you intend to do for its reappearance.

MARKET

23 June 1936. No. 298

C.P. CANADA entirely legal since 21st. Send and publish greetings for mass work that permitted such victory.

27 June 1936. No. 302

POLLIT

Am awaiting you and GALLACHER on 20th July and maybe also somebody from P.B.

DISRAELI

28 June 1936. No. 303

28th June received things for FRED also letter will be remitted 30th.

2 July 1936. No. 310

Youth MASSIE

You mailed us one legal letter absolutely incorrect. Write only the number of the post box without any additions as to whom it belongs.

KIM

7 July 1936. No. 314
POLLIT

Report accident MARGARET sent to MOPR. Necessary steps already done through MOPR. All material sent by MAURICE BROWN received. Many thanks.

9 July 1936. No. 318
POLLIT

According news received week ago in LONDON arrested on landing Brazilian citizen PRADORAFAEL coming from MOSCOW via Danish port ESBERG. Arrest probably due lack of British visa. Is Italian comrade who should have gone to DUNKERQUE and took by mistake boat to LONDON. Enquire through well-known lawyer about his fate and give him assistance to free him for departure to FRANCE.

10 July 1936. No. 321
POLLIT

Brazilian comrade safely (? arrived) PARIS.

11 July 1936. No. 326
POLLIT

In connection with death sentence ANDRE move at International Trades-union Congress through French, English and Spanish delegates immediate protest for non execution (?) death sentence (1 group) sending (?) of delegation embassy LONDON and BERLIN. Arrange through GALLACHER immediate intervention members House of Commons. Organise mass protest, above all in ports through trades-unions. Acknowledge receipt.

Secretariat

11 July 1936. No. 327
POLLIT

Agree your arrival 20th, SHIELDS one or two days before.

MARKET

13 July 1936. No. 328
POLLIT

Bring Congress Socialist file from Percy's office also my new documents.

DON

16 July 1936. No. 332
POLLIT

Please arrange to meet negro comrade WINIFRED PALMER arriving LONDON Soviet boat 17th give assistance in sending her back to SOUTH AFRICA.

MARKET

16 July 1936. No. 333
POLLIT

Actual situation makes travel FOX in AUSTRALIA impossible. Send biography of WALTER KNOX PAGE. Received your telegrams up to No. 283.

MARKET

20 July 1936. No. 334
Political Bureau

Mobilise masses and public opinion against counter revolutionary Fascist putsch in SPAIN for solidarity with Popular Front. Organise meetings utilise for this purpose all other meetings taking place. Put the question broadly in Press.

(DISRAELI ?)

23 July 1936. No. 338

As impossible to send negress HENDERSON from English port find out about next possibility to send her from French or Italian (?) port. Give her necessary additional money and give her all necessary assistance. Wire.

2 August 1936. Nos. 376, 377
Parsons

Participate actively in support democratic republic in SPAIN. Publish through WISHART possibly together with GOLLANCZ and 'Left' book good report.

If necessary send well-known journalist to SPAIN. Furthermore order by wire small topical book (? letters) or pamphlets directed to democratic public opinion by leading 'Left' republican personalities as well as socialists such as BONDLERO and communists such as DIAZ Pay (1 group).

HENRY

5 August 1936. No. 379
HARRY

MOORE can only get visa if you ask for it to be given.

ARNOT

7 August 1936. No. 382
POLLIT

Pay from your funds 65 repeat 65 pounds advance to representative KIM MASSY for trip to GENEVA and salary from August 11th to September 11th and TOM MANN for July, August, September 84 repeat 84 pounds. Total 149 repeat 149 pounds. This sum will be refunded to you next possibility.

MICHAEL

9 August 1936. No. 389
Youth MASSY

You are member of YCI delegation to Geneva Congress. Be in Geneva August 28th. Funds sent.

RAYMOND

11 August 1936. No. 390

You receive from STOCKHOLM 23750 Dutch guilders. From these pay for September C.C. 5146. Newspaper 13370. C.P. IRELAND 267. POLLIT 1097 as refunding of 180 or 149 pounds expended by him according to our order 382. For work in INDIA 2524, and for sending of couriers 1346. Total 2370 Dutch guilders. Notify us.

MICHAEL

14 August 1936. No. 292

Concerning the comrade who is going to Far East as representative of a company we want to know his identity in that country; don't give him any (?) task now. Ask him to study on the spot possibilities of his help for us.

14 August 1936. No. 293

POLLIT

Got informed that ENGLAND is sending aeroplanes for insurgents. Absolutely imperative to take all measures to prevent this crime. Necessary (? at) same time to organise purchase of all necessary materials for struggling Spanish people, utilising for instance Mexican Consulate as juridical (?) person. Necessary also secure by the Labourite substantial help through their connections.

Secretariat

17 August 1936. No. 397

We gave order to STOCKHOLM to hand over to you 1109 repeat 1109 florins equivalent of 150 pounds from MOPR for Indian work.

19 August 1936. Nos. 298–402

POLLIT

Supply of arms and aeroplanes to insurgents by GERMANY and ITALY, criminal policy of sanctions applied to lawful Spanish Government by FRANCE and ENGLAND have for result that last days insurgents get ascendancy, subject workers in BADAJOS to mass extermination, increase number of victims of best sons of Spanish people. Don't let (1 group) be accomplished greatest crime of struggling Spanish republic (1 group) hands of German and Italian fascists with toleration of English Conservative Government. Conduct of English Government has decisive significance, would be sufficient for English Government to speak with fascist instigators of war in a firm way that they should retreat. Mobilise all forces of working class, its Trades-union Labour Party, all Left bourgeois public men, all honest people in order to obtain from English Government decisive intervention in favour of (1 group) Spanish Government and against support Spanish insurgents by ITALY and GERMANY, cessation of PONYIUS PILATUS which (1 group) leads to defeat of Spanish democracy. Necessary send delegation well-known politicians to BALDWIN, EDEN and other members of Government, necessary organise mass demonstrations (?) to address to Government protest (1 group) necessary intervention left public men of workmen's movement and local trades-unions with letter to

General Council and leadership of Labour Party, that they should put ultimatum to Government that if Government does not change its course toward smash of democracy, triumph of fascist and outburst of war, General Council and Labour Party will call workmen masses to political strike. Acknowledge receipt.

Secretariat

20 August 1936. No. 421
BRADLEY
Up to new indication don't send courier.

23 August 1936. No. 422
HARRY
Send us urgently 5 repeat 5 comrades for messenger service.
ABRAHAM

15 October 1936. No. 8
Visa for CLARK DEANER given to LONDON. Awaiting arrival. Repeat your 1 and first name of 2.

23 October 1936. No. 20
POLLIT, PARSONS
Arrange with PRITT and GOLLANCZ for publication of pamphlet ZINOVIEV trial in French, German (?) Czech, Spanish, Dutch, Scandinavian languages. All our publishers are informed. Arrange for suitable honorarium. Send copies to our publishers. If publication of pamphlet not yet arranged for in USA let it have it (?)
BRUNO

23 October 1936. No. 26
Secretary
Send BRADLEY here. Forwarding visa.

27 October 1936. No. 36
Re your station I agree that she starts work when you will find a new location. Inform us when work starts. Book for this station Treasure Island.

2 November 1936. No. 41
POLLIT
Invitation ADAMS from here impossible (?) but you can instruct our people in F.S.U. to (one group) him immediately.
ARNOT

9 November 1936. No. 42
NELLY (?) and BEN FRANCES arrived. Received everything.

28 November 1936. Nos. 57, 58

Police International Settlement in SHANGHAI handed over 4 leaders Chinese Association of National Emancipation to Chinese authorities for anti-Japanese activity on territory of Settlement. Necessary begin campaign for their release. Desirable that prominent labourist and bourgeois public men firstly make interpolation in Parliament demanding that arrested be returned to Settlement, secondly approach NANKING Government with demand to release arrested because of their activity directed not against CHINA but against enemies Chinese nation and general peace (1 group) Japanese imperialism.

Secretariat

29 November 1936. No. 60

POLLIT

Bring light material for coat colour dark grey, three meters of best quality and lining. (1 group) is for (?) the chief.

8 December 1936. No. 76

NELLY

Send as many as possible copies of DICKENS.

RICHARD

15 December 1936. No. 70

Inform me how many copies Dickens and pamphlets sent up to date.

RICHARD

18 December 1936. No. 71

POLLIT

Send to SPAIN at disposal of ANDRE 10 repeat 10 surgeons.

MANU

17 January 1937. No. 1

HARRY

Trial PRESTES – GHIOLDI begun. Danger murder PRESTES during trial under pretext of attempt to flight. By means of press, meetings, mass demonstrations personalities protests to Brazilian Embassies A.S.O. Mobilise public opinion for liberation of PRESTES and other accused.

Secretariat

5

KRIVITSKY'S DEFECTION

MASK necessarily ceased as a source when Olga Gray was revealed as an MI5 agent, even though her true name was never disclosed at the Old Bailey trial of Percy Glading and his co-conspirators. Referred to only as 'Miss X', she appeared as a witness with the most damning testimony of her participation in what was clearly a very extensive espionage network. Afterwards she was paid off with £500 by MI5 and got married to a Canadian airman with whom she went to live in Ontario. It was not until the arrival in London in January 1940 of Walter Krivitsky that MI5 learned of the extent of the spy-ring, and realised how close they had come to seizing some of Moscow's key players. Indeed, looking at Krivitsky's material today one can only gasp at the amount of knowledge MI5 accumulated in 1940, but never fully investigated or exploited. As MI5's declassified files reveal, it had within them all the pieces of the jigsaw to construct a very full picture of Soviet intelligence operations in England, and the long-suspected overlap between the CPGB and Moscow's espionage apparatus.

Born Samuel Ginsberg, Walter Krivitsky for years had been a key figure in the GRU's illegal military intelligence apparatus in western Europe. Posing as an antiquarian book-dealer named Dr Martin Lessner, and eventually based in The Hague, he had been responsible for supervising networks in Germany, France, Holland and Austria, and was personally close to all the leadership in Moscow. His decision to defect had been prompted by the purges, and his recall to Moscow in September 1937, following the murder of his friend Ignace Reiss in Lausanne, was correctly interpreted by him as a death warrant. Instead of following instructions he fled to Paris, obtained a passage to Canada, and negotiated the translation of his memoirs by Isaac Don Levine, a well-known New York journalist of Russian origin.

When Krivistsky finally reached London in January 1940, at the height of the 'phoney war' and travelling under his new identity, Walter Thomas, he was accommodated in a suite in the Langham Hotel and interviewed there by Jane Archer, an experienced MI5 officer who had practised at the bar in London before she had been invited to join the organisation. While Krivitsky claimed to know little about the CPGB, he knew immeasurably more than the

Security Service about the relationship between the Party, its underground membership and Moscow's spy-rings. In particular, he could fill in many of the gaps in MI5's understanding of certain recent cases of espionage, and MI5 concentrated on three about which it had accumulated much material. The really current case was that of John King, the Foreign Office cipher clerk who had been arrested once he had been identified by Krivitsky, and had confessed. Krivitsky also provided details of another Foreign Office spy, Ernest Oldham, who had committed suicide seven years earlier, but had been handled by some of the recurring Soviet intelligence personalities, among them Henri Pieck and Theodore Mally. Finally, he had supplied vital information about the Woolwich Arsenal case, which had resulted in the imprisonment in 1938 of the CPGB's former National Organiser, Percy Glading.

Unlike most of the others named by Krivitsky, Pieck survived the purges and the war, and in 1950 was in The Hague, anxious to travel to England to participate in an exhibition sponsored by the Board of Trade. Knowing that his knowledge of prewar Soviet intelligence operations might still be of some value, Pieck had contacted the Dutch Security Service and offered to be interviewed by MI5. The officer who conducted the interview, in London in April 1950, was Michael Hanley, a future Director-General, and he took down a lengthy statement from the former Soviet illegal. Pieck recalled that he had joined the Dutch Communist Party in 1923 following a visit to Hungary during Bela Kun's regime. Six years later he had visited the Soviet Union, and he had made another trip in1930. His recruitment had taken place in 1932, and his first posting, in 1933, had been to Geneva where he had learned the art of recruiting and running agents. In 1933 he began to visit England, and was John King's principal contact between1935 and 1937.

Pieck's career as a Soviet spy had come to an abrupt end in 1936 when a friend, John Hooper, warned him that the British authorities were taking an interest in him. Hooper knew because until recently he had been employed by SIS, but had been dismissed in that year, following the suicide of Captain Hugh Dalton, the SIS head of station in The Hague who had been implicated in the embezzlement of visa funds. 'Pincher' Hooper's tip had forced Pieck to abandon King, but he remained on friendly terms with the former SIS man and even helped him out financially.

In his statement Pieck described his encounters with Mally and Krivitsky and, talented artist that he was, sketched them for MI5. He had also known Ignace Reiss, who had directed the GRU's operations in England from Amsterdam between 1928 and 1929, and the latter's murder had been another incentive to distance himself from the Soviets. Although he had been active in the Communist resistance to the Nazi occupation, Pieck insisted he had never engaged in espionage again, and had spent the war years, from April 1942 in Buchenwald concentration camp.

While it is fruitless to exercise perfect hindsight and emphasise the many opportunities missed by MI5, it is clear from the summary of Soviet agents compiled by Jane Archer (see Appendix III) that some of the key players, who were later to make extremely important contributions to the Soviet espionage network in Britain, had been correctly identified by their true names. For example, Kitty Harris had been Donald Maclean's Soviet controller in 1938, and is listed as having spent considerable time in London during the crucial period she had not only run him, but had been his lover. In his book Krivitsky described her as one of a 'number of graduates of our secret schools' (Krivitsky 1940: 279). She was 'exceptionally reliable' and 'had been connected with our secret service for some years' according to Krivitsky, who had despatched her on a clandestine mission to Europe at the end of April 1937. Harris had held meetings with her lover in a basement flat in Oakley Street, Chelsea, and then had followed him to Paris in October 1938. Altogether, Kitty handled Maclean for four years, but after their last hurried rendezvous in Paris in June 1940, when the Wehrmacht were less than fifty miles from the city, they never saw each other again.

Similarly, Edith Tudor-Hart, née Suschitzky, whose name and address had been found in a notebook belonging to Percy Glading, had introduced Kim Philby to Dr Arnold Deutsch, the illegal who had recruited him. Of a notoriously nervous disposition, Edith was an Austrian Jewess from Vienna, and a close friend of Philby's first wife, Litzi Friedman. It was Litzi who introduced Philby to Edith, and it was to be Edith who, at the end of May 1934, invited Philby to meet her friend 'Otto' on a bench in Regent's Park, thus beginning his induction into the service of the Soviets. Edith was also a talented photographer who was to achieve world-wide recognition, but she had come to London as the wife of a Welsh doctor from the Rhondda Valley, Alex Tudor Hart, who had been recruited by the NKVD *rezident* in Barcelona, Alexander Orlov, during the Spanish Civil War, where the Communist zealot had been working as a surgeon in a field hospital. Among her espionage tasks had been the purchase of a Leica camera used by Glading at his safe-house in Holland Road and traced to her studio in Acre Lane, Brixton by Special Branch detectives, but this clue was never pursued.

Originally a kindergarten teacher, and the daughter of a bookshop owner in Vienna, Edith had separated from her husband after his return from Spain, and had devoted herself to her handicapped son, her child portraits and the Workers Camera Club. Later she was to work as a photographer for the Ministry of Education, but in 1940 she acted as an intermediary for Anthony Blunt and Bob Stewart, when the *rezidentura* at the embassy suspended its operations. This curious episode occurred in February 1940 when the *rezident*, Anatoli Gorsky, was ordered home because Moscow Centre mistakenly believed that the London *rezidentura* had been penetrated. In retrospect it is easy to understand how the NKVD came to this conclusion, for in recent years it had suffered two defections, of Alexander Orlov and Walter Krivitsky. Whereas the Barcelona *rezident* Orlov had declared that he would remain loyal to Stalin for as long as his family was safe, it was clear from the disclosures in the *Saturday Evening Post* in New York that Krivitsky had sold out, and the proof, if any more was needed, was the (unannounced) arrest, conviction and imprisonment of John King. In addition, the NKVD had experienced the loss of the Woolwich Arsenal network, and both Theodore Mally and Mikhail Borovoy, having been recalled for interrogation had confessed before their inevitable executions to have acted as spies for the capitalists.

This was, of course, sheer paranoia on the part of the NKVD's depleted senior management, and Gorsky was back to resume his activities in December, but in the meantime, and in the absence of any contact with illegals, Burgess, Maclean, Philby and Litzi communicated to Moscow via Edith and Stewart. The isolation of the Cambridge ring, once Deutsch, Mally and Orlov had withdrawn, must have been extremely frustrating for its membership, and the conduit represented by Edith and Stewart was certainly a hazardous one, as all must have recognised. Moscow Centre was nervous about the ease and speed with which Georg Hansen had been arrested, and the way in which the Woolwich Arsenal spy-ring had been penetrated by Olga Gray, and doubtless had speculated about the extent to which the rest of the Party apparatus had been compromised. Considering that Krivitsky had specifically named Orlov-Nicolsky and Kitty Harris in his book as NKVD illegals, this must have been reasonable grounds for suspecting that the British authorities were on to them and maybe their sources too. Certainly Kitty Harris was considered compromised, and when Paris fell she moved into the Soviet embassy, travelling on 19 July to Moscow via Berlin, carrying a passport identifying her as the wife of a Soviet diplomat.

This understandable anxiety is evident from the fact that, as we now know from the KGB's declassified files, Blunt was disbelieved when he reported to Moscow that MI5 did not maintain a permanent watch on all Soviet diplomats in London. From the point of view of the Cambridge Five, Cairncross was supplying first class material from the very heart of the government, Maclean was leaking vast quantities of Foreign Office circulars in Paris to Kitty Harris, Burgess was on the fringes of the secret world, working for SIS's Section D, while Blunt was of lesser interest, as an Intelligence Corps officer attached to the Field Security Police in France, and Philby was a war correspondent, also in France, until he joined Special Operations Executive in July 1940. Thus, after Kitty's withdrawal, three spies had information to pass on but had not the means to do so, while the other two were probably in need of guidance about their future plans. In these circumstances it must have been entirely natural for Philby to re-establish contact with Edith in the hope of being put in touch with the Soviets again. Deutsch and Mally, of course, had long since departed, so Edith had been forced to rely on Stewart, a wise choice.

Burgess, Blunt and Philby, as the most exposed members of the network, were acutely aware of their vulnerability, and when Blunt discovered the existence of TABLE and KASPAR he expressed his anxiety to his Soviet contact about the possibility of an indiscreet word from Stewart being picked up by one of the microphones. Naturally the NKVD had taken the appropriate steps to warn Stewart, but although Blunt knew of Edith's role, he never met her. Had he done so, and realised her highly-strung temperament, he would have had good cause for serious concern, but in the event MI5 never pursued her, and the only incriminating evidence linking her to Philby, a portrait taken by her in Vienna, she destroyed after receiving an anonymous telephone call in 1951, when he had fallen under suspicion following the defection of Burgess and Maclean.

Dr Deutsch, who had fled London in 1937, had been named as an illegal with a wide circle of friends, especially in university circles, by Krivitsky who recalled him as having supervised an important 'naval and military agent operating in the United Kingdom'. This was presumed by MI5 in 1940 to be a reference to the spy-ring that had penetrated the Woolwich Arsenal, which had been penetrated and wound up two years earlier, in January 1938. In that case, although Glading and some of his fellow conspirators had been arrested, their Soviet controllers had escaped because they had been tipped off by the clumsy enquiries made about them. MI5 had maintained a watch on one suspect, 'Willy Brandes', but he and his wife had fled the country after the porter at their block of flats in the Edgware Road had told him he was under surveillance. Brandes invariably had tipped the porter the handsome sum of ten shillings, and by that means had bought his loyalty. MI5 had acquired a large file on 'Brandes', and had failed to arrest him, but had never suspected the involvement of Arnold Deutsch in the same spy-ring. According to Krivitsky, Deutsch had been subordinate to the legal *rezident* at the Soviet Embassy, Anton Schuster, and then Theodore Mally, alias Paul Hardt, his illegal counterpart in London between 1936 and June 1937.

Deutsch had arrived in England in February 1934 on a genuine Austrian passport, as a legitimate academic, studying post-graduate psychology at London University, and in 1935 was joined by his wife, his radio operator, who was to give birth to their child in London, and worked as a volunteer with the Quakers, helping Jewish refugees to find accommodation in London. Deutsch lived in Lawn Road flats in the fashionable district of Hampstead, worked under his own name and attracted absolutely no attention, even though his chosen field of specialisation was considered very avant-garde, the study of human sexuality. Undoubtedly a skilled psychologist who well understood how to inspire his recruits, Deutsch compiled impressively accurate profiles on them, a technique that was intended to help Moscow Centre understand the motivation of these willing volunteers. His KGB file credits him with accomplishing an unprecedented twenty successful recruitments, among them James Klugmann, codenamed MER, who acted as a talent-spotter, recommending other suitable candidates from his acquaintances, such as John Cairncross. Always an overt CPGB member, Klugmann was later to serve during the war in SOE's Middle East headquarters in Cairo, and eventually was selected to write the CPGB's official history, although he died before he could embark on the second volume.

Although not much is known about Deutsch, and there has been some obfuscation about many of his personal details, perhaps for what were seen as valid operational reasons, he seems to have enjoyed a wide circle of friends, among them his next-door neighbour in Hampstead, Gertrude Sirnis. Her husband, Alexander Sirnis, was a Latvian émigré who had been a pacifist since his arrival in England as a refugee in 1907. Sirnis had acted as translator for Leo Tolstoy's literary executor, Vladimir Chertkov, and Gertrude was also a friend of another neighbour in one of the thirty-two flats in the Lawn Road complex, Jurgen Kuczynski, an economist, a senior figure in the KPD, and later a leader of the German opposition to the Nazis in England. After his arrival in England Sirnis had adopted Marxism and was to become closely associated with Maxim Litvinov, Lenin's unofficial ambassador in England until his expulsion in 1918. Litvinov was to be detained at Brixton prison while (Sir) Robert Bruce Lockhart was under arrest in Moscow, and when he left the country he was escorted to King's Cross station by Sirnis.

Alexander Sirnis died when his children, Gerty and Melita, were very young, and they were brought up by Gertrude, a formidable woman with close connections to revolutionary circles in England. For a time they had lived at Tuckton House, Chertkov's sanctuary near Bournemouth for revolutionaries and others who had been exiled from Russia, and Gertrude became acquainted with Andrew Rothstein, the man who recruited her older daughter, Melita, then aged twenty-one, for the NKVD in 1934. In that same year Melita had joined the British Non-Ferrous Metals Research Association, a trade organisation funded mainly by the industry with 40 per cent of the costs met by the British government, to conduct experiments concerning corrosion and temperature that would assist British engineering. None of this work was classified, and the results were published among BN-FMRA's subscribers. She was to remain at BN-FRMRA's headquarters near Euston Station, as secretary to the chief liaison officer Leo Bailey, until 1943, by which time the office had been evacuated to the Cooper Institute at Berkhamsted in Hertfordshire. She then took a year's maternity leave, and returned in 1944. Melita's husband Hilary Nussbaum, a science teacher whom she had married in 1932, was also a CPGB member whose Polish émigré parents had been ardent socialists and, knowing her mother well, had given Melita accommodation in their house in Hendon when she had come up to London. Soon after their marriage, in an attempt to help Hilary find work, the newly-weds had decided to Anglicise their surname to Norwood.

In 1934, while working as a volunteer for Medical Aid for Spain with her mother and sister, a student at the London School of Economics, the family's involvement in the clandestine *apparat* became known to MI5 when Gertrude's address, 173 Hendon Way, appeared in MASK traffic as a suitable letter-drop for Moscow's correspondence with the CPGB. Doubtless they had also been logged as members of the Friends of the Soviet Union, and both Hilary and Melita sold copies of the *Daily Worker* on Saturday mornings outside Golders Green tube station.

Deutsch's decision to rent a flat in Lawn Road is curious, for as well as having Jurgen Kuczynski at No. 6 and Gertrude Sirnis as neighbours, others living in the same block included Simon Kremer, the GRU *rezident* at the Soviet embassy, and Eva Collett Reckitt, the founder of the famous left-wing book-shop in the Charing Cross Road.

Andrew Rothstein was a key figure in the NKVD's *apparat* in England, as had been his father, Theodore, another revolutionary forced to flee his native Lithuania by the Tsar's feared *Okhrana*. Initially Theodore had lived in Germany, but later had moved to Hull before settling in Leeds where there was an extensive Russian Jewish émigré community. An enthusiastic supporter of Lenin, he translated and published his *State and Revolution* and effectively acted as his personal representative in England, as well as the London corre-spondent of *Pravda*. The recipient of secret funds from Moscow, he was very active in the Labour Party, and came to prominence in the trade union move-ment at the turn of the century, but returned to Moscow in 1920 having played a key role in the Unity conference which transformed the British Socialist Party into the CPGB. When he attempted to return to England in August 1920, Rothstein was refused entry. He was also closely associated with Gertrude Sirnis' brother, Thomas Stedman, and they campaigned together on many political issues. For example, in 1910 Rothstein had published *Egypt's Ruin*, and he had served on the executive committee of the Britain–Egypt Associa-tion with Stedman, and both opposed British imperialism and the occupation of Egypt. A practising solicitor and supporter of the trade unions, Melita's uncle had encouraged her to join the Association of Women Clerks and Secretaries, and acted as another link to the Rothsteins.

When Theodore Rothstein was refused re-entry to Britain he took up a senior post in the Foreign Ministry, while his son Andrew, a journalist and graduate of Balliol College, Cambridge, remained in London as editor of the *Sunday Worker*, was elected to the CPGB's Central Committee, wrote for the *Communist Review* as 'C.M. Roebuck' and was on the editorial board of *Labour Monthly*.

Among those overlapping the covert networks of the early Socialist move-ment and Soviet intelligence were David Ramsay, James Messer and Tom Bell, the Glaswegian Communist whose wife Nancy Harris was an experienced spy, like her sister Kitty.

Thus, in defiance of all the well-established rules of *konspiratsia*, there were strong social links between the members of a clandestine organisation that one might have expected to have been compartmentalised into separate, self-contained independent cells. Curiously, in this case, there was a considerable overlap with close social and geographic links between the Kuczynski family, the Sirnis family and Deutsch. The fact that Melita Sirnis remained an active and undetected spy for another two decades may help explain the reticence of the various component parts of the organisation, such as Jurgen and Ursula Kuczynski who both published their memoirs, to be entirely candid about their past activities.

Like Deutsch, neither Schuster nor Mally had previously come under MI5's scrutiny, and were entirely unknown to them, although the role of Soviet legal and illegal *rezidents* was by then well understood. Krivitsky, as an officer of the Red Army's military intelligence service, later known as the GRU, explained at length the relationship between his agency, the *Razvedupr*, and the OGPU, which was later to be renamed as the NKVD, and demonstrated that although they were parallel organisations, there was a cross-fertilisation of agents and handlers. If the OGPU had not the resources to service a particular agent, it could call upon the GRU to help out, and vice versa. Thus Krivitsky had been pulled in from Holland to assist with running Captain John King, and another GRU illegal had been sent to Rome to support the OGPU's spy in the British embassy.

As Ernest Oldham was dead when his covert career as a Soviet spy was revealed by Krivitsky, MI5 could only undertake a forensic investigation to assess the extent of his treachery, but learned that he had been controlled by another illegal, Dmitri Bystrolyotov, alias Hans Galleni, who travelled on a Greek passport. At that time the OGPU illegal *rezident*'s principal assistant in England had been a man named Nicolski who had worked under an American business cover, and later had been sent to Spain. When Oldham had descended into chronic alcoholism, he had been pressed for the names of some other suitable sources of information, and he had recommended another colleague in the Cipher Department, John King, who had been cultivated and recruited by another illegal, Henri Pieck.

A decorator and talented artist, Pieck had played a key role in running King in London between 1935 and 1937, but he was withdrawn from England when Krivitsky became suspicious of Jack Hooper, a former SIS officer in The Hague with whom Pieck had become acquainted. Pieck claimed that Hooper had been indiscreet and had supplied him with some useful information about the local British Passport Control Office, SIS's semi-transparent cover. However, when Krivitsky had investigated Hooper he had suspected the SIS officer had been playing a double game, and decided it was too dangerous to allow Pieck to continue operating in London if he had been compromised. Accordingly, Pieck had been reassigned to Germany in November 1937. Meanwhile Hooper had concealed his illicit contacts and MI5 had made use of his linguistic skills during the war as an interpreter and interrogator.

Krivitsky's account of Pieck's handling of King was extremely detailed and identified his co-conspirators as a decorator named Parlanti, whose offices in Buckingham Gate were used to transact their business, and an elderly German photographer, Wolf Levit, who ran a studio where King's documents were copied. The entire operation had been supervised by Theodore Mally who posed as a Dutch banker, 'Mr Petersen', and persuaded King that he was using his information for commercial advantage, a classic 'false-flag' recruitment. Mally's principal courier was Brian Goold-Verschoyle, the young Irish CPGB zealot whom Krivitsky insisted believed that he was engaged on purely political work, and had been carrying pamphlets and other literature. He recalled that Goold-Verschoyle had been shocked when a package he was handling had come open and he had seen that it contained Foreign Office secret documents. At the time he was associating with a Jewish refugee from Germany, Margarete Moos, whom Krivitsky also thought had been an OGPU agent.

In the spring of 1936, through Krivitsky's intervention, Goold-Verschoyle had realised his ambition of visiting Russia and had been a student at Abramoff's radio school in Moscow. The following year he had been sent as a radio operator to Spain, as described by Krivistsky in his memoirs, *I Was Stalin's Agent*, calling him by what was actually his codename, FRIEND. Nothing was heard of him again but his brother, Hamilton Neil Goold-Verschoyle, returned to England from Moscow, where he had been living with a Russian wife. On 15 April 1939 the New York *Saturday Evening Post* gave an account of Goold-Verschoyle's mysterious disappearance in Spain, after which Margarete Moos returned to London, and Brian's mother, Sybil, contacted Krivitsky from her home in Oxford, hoping for more news of her son. According to Krivitsky, Brian had been suspected of Trotskyite tendencies in Spain and had been lured aboard a Soviet ship in Barcelona, bound for Odessa, on the pretext of repairing a radio transmitter, and had been abducted. Once back in Russia, Brian had disappeared into the Gulag, never to be seen again.

MI5 must have taken some comfort from the disruption it had caused to the Soviets by its penetration of the Woolwich Arsenal spy-ring, and according to Krivitsky the illegal *resident*, Theodore Mally, had been replaced temporarily by a man on the CPGB's Central Executive whose name had begun with the letter 'B'. Undoubtedly this had been Brian Stewart, the dour Scot who had long been suspected by MI5 of having acted as a link between the Party and the underground organisation. As we shall see, Stewart turned out to have been a key figure in Soviet espionage in England over very many years.

Krivitsky's reference to an illegal operating in London under the alias Nicolski appears to have been filed away and forgotten by MI5, but it was to be highly significant. Nicolski, as Krivitsky had revealed in his book, was a veteran OGPU officer who had been sent to Spain to run the organisation in the areas held by the loyalists, and was 'alias Schwed, alias Lyova, alias Orlov'. Unfortunately MI5 failed to connect 'Nicolski' with General Alexander Orlov who disappeared in Spain in July 1938 and only emerged publicly fourteen years later in the United States, much to the embarrassment of the FBI which had never suspected his presence. Codenamed SCHWED, meaning 'Swede' in Russian, Orlov omitted to tell his FBI and CIA debriefers that he had spent fifteen months in London before the war as the illegal *rezident*, and had remained silent about his knowledge of the ring of spies he had run at Cambridge University and elsewhere. Incredibly, although Krivitsky had told Jane Sissmore in February 1940 that 'Nicolski' had been in England before the war as an important illegal using an American business cover, neither she nor anyone else at the Security Service tried to question him when he eventually surfaced in the United States in early 1953 when he began serialising his memoirs in *Life* magazine. In contrast, the French DST (Security Service) continued to submit questionnaires to his CIA debriefers as late as July 1965.

The information of greatest concern to MI5 in 1940 would have been Krivitsky's disclosure that in 1936 Mally had acquired a source with access to the printed reports of the Committee of Imperial Defence (CID), the Cabinet sub-committee which deliberated on the most sensitive foreign policy issues. This was not only a hideous breach of security, involving the loss of naval, military, air and political secrets, but had served to compromise a British source in Moscow. Krivitsky revealed that when he had last visited the OGPU's headquarters in Moscow, in May 1937, he had been shown a document by Abram Sloutski which included a reference to a report of a Politburo meeting attended by the Soviet Foreign Minister, Maxim Litvinov. Based on this single item, the OGPU realised that the British had been running a well-placed spy in Moscow, although it would be a further year before the culprit was identified.

When cross-examined by MI5 on the likely source of the CID leak, Krivitsky claimed he was certain that Mally's agent was a young man, driven by ideological motives 'almost certainly educated at Eton and Oxford' who was 'the secretary or son of one of the chiefs of the Foreign Office'. According to Guy Liddell's diary for 27 September 1939, the task of finding the mole had been taken up by MI5's Director of Counter-Espionage, Brigadier Jasper Harker, and he had consulted Sir Horace Wilson, the head of the Civil Service, in a vain effort to narrow the search. It would be more than a decade before MI5 took a fresh look at Krivitsky's tip and realised that the source had been John Cairncross, the Foreign Office official seconded to the Cabinet Office as secretary to Lord Hankey. Cairncross had been educated at neither Eton nor Oxford, and certainly was no aristocrat, as suggested originally by Krivitsky but, as he later acknowledged, he believed that only the sons of nobility went to Eton. A French scholar and a graduate of the Sorbonne, Cairncross, of course, had been to Cambridge, and had obtained his post with Lord Hankey through his friendship with his son. During the period he had worked for Lord Hankey he had enjoyed access to all the CID's most secret papers, including some assessments made by Sir Nevile Henderson, the British ambassador in Berlin, which Krivitsky had seen for himself in Moscow.

At the time of Krivitsky's disclosures the Security Service had not suspected a spy in either the Cabinet Office or the Foreign Office, and as well as pointing to Cairncross, he made a single reference to 'a young Englishman, a journalist of good family, an idealist and fanatical anti-Nazi' who had been sent to Spain to assassinate Franco. The only person who fitted this description was Kim

Philby, the *Times* correspondent in Spain during the Spanish Civil War. While it could be argued that he was not of a particularly good family (his eccentric father, the Arabist St John Philby, would be detained in 1940 under the Emergency Regulations as a Nazi sympathiser) Philby did have left-wing credentials and was well-established as a journalist, one of a limited number who had been to Spain prior to 1937.

While his correct identification in February 1940 might have proved extremely useful, and maybe prevented his future employment later the same year by Special Operations Executive as a lecturer in propaganda techniques, and by the Secret Intelligence Service as an expert on Spain, Philby was not then engaged in espionage against Britain, and thus far had not committed any criminal offence in the UK.

MI5's apparent inaction, which allowed both Cairncross and Donald Maclean to haemorrhage British secrets from the heart of Whitehall, may be connected with Krivitsky's assertion that in 1936 he had actually vetoed the recruitment of another source in the Foreign Office so as to protect King and the source of the CID documents. Apparently a Soviet agent in Holland, who previously had worked for *The Times* in Budapest, reported that he had been contacted by a Briton with access to Foreign Office information on Japan. Krivitsky attempted to check on this offer but was unable to verify that the source was employed by the Foreign Office, so he turned it down, remarking that he had 'forbade the engaging of another agent in the Foreign Office as there were two there already and a third might be prejudicial to the other two'. On this basis MI5 might have concluded that with the arrest of King in September 1939, there was only a single leak left to trace. In fact, of course, Donald Maclean was active in February 1940, operating at the British embassy in Paris, and over the next few months Guy Burgess would penetrate SIS's Section D, and Kim Philby would join SOE and then SIS. During the course of MI5's investigation into King, it transpired that he may not have acted alone, and that a Major Grange may have been involved, although MI5 concluded that a 'Mr Oake' probably was not. As Guy Liddell confided to his diary on 27 September 1939, there was no question of prosecuting the other pair.

Another spy Krivitsky knew of was an OGPU source inside the British embassy in Rome for whom he had acted as an intermediary when it had been judged too risky to use the OGPU's legal *rezident* in Rome. Although he only knew the source by his codename DUNCAN, Krivitsky believed that he was an Englishman who had still been active in 1937, but in fact this was a Chancery servant, Francesco Constantini, who was later revealed to have been selling British diplomatic papers and codes to the Italians too. In addition, Krivitsky claimed that up until 1936 or 1937 there had been a Soviet spy in the British embassy in Constantinople. He had no further details, apart from the fact that he had been run by the local OGPU legal *rezident*, a man who used the alias Tann and was in fact Wolf Levit's son.

MI5's analysis of Krivitsky's revelations continued for many years, and over the decades was found to contain more tantalising clues, not just to Bob Stewart, but to another potential counter-intelligence breakthrough. Krivitsky had mentioned an illegal *rezident* in London named Nicolsky, and had described him as having worked under a commercial cover as an American businessman. But who was he really? It would be many years before Alexander Orlov revealed himself, in the United States, as a former senior NKVD officer who had vanished from Barcelona in July 1938, together with his wife and daughter. Orlov was a career Chekist, but a telegram summoning him to a meeting on a Soviet steamer in Antwerp indicated to him that he was likely to be the next victim of Stalin's purges, lured onto a ship and then abducted like so many others. Orlov's reaction had been to go into hiding in France with his family, and promise Stalin by letter that he would keep his secrets as long as his family in the Soviet Union remained free. The bargain was a good one for the NKVD, for Orlov knew plenty, and had worked in Paris under Trade Delegation cover between 1926 and 1928, and in Berlin from January 1928 until April 1931. Thereafter, Orlov admitted to US immigration officials in 1954 that he had arrived in Madrid in September 1936, but he was vague concerning his whereabouts in the meantime. In fact, during this period Orlov had been engaged in some of the most sensitive intelligence operations of his career, so delicate that he did not even refer to them in his secret diaries, *The March of Time*, which were only declassified twenty years after his death.

After his recall from Berlin Orlov did not remain in Moscow, as he claimed later to the CIA, but had undertaken two important assignments. The first, in September 1932, was to New York where he enrolled as a language student at Columbia University, but his true purpose seems to have been the acquisition of an authentic American passport in the name of William Goldin, which was issued two months later, and was used extensively by Orlov to travel through Europe over the next two years, until July 1934 when he had been appointed the illegal *rezident* in London.

The position of legal *rezident* in London had lapsed in 1927 when Jakob Kirchenstein had been forced to flee as his office in the Arcos building demonstrated his vulnerability, and his replacement had been Yevgenny P. Mitskevich who had not arrived until 1931, having previously served as an illegal in Hamburg and Italy. Mitskevich had been formally appointed *rezident* in 1932 and had reported on the two major Soviet espionage networks then in existence, recommending to Moscow in early 1933 that the Woolwich Arsenal spy-ring was vulnerable because it was 'led by a prominent member of the local Communist Party'. Although this has been taken to be a reference to Percy Glading, it is more likely that he was really talking about Albert Williams, to whom Glading deferred, even if he held a higher overt position in the CPGB. Mitskevich's solution had been the estabishment of an illegal *rezidentura*, and this suggestion was acted upon later the same year when Ignaty Reif and Arnold Deutsch were despatched to London. Of Polish extraction, Reif finally arrived in London from Paris in April 1934, without his wife, on a fraudulently obtained Austrian passport identifying him as Max Wolisch, supposedly a businessman engaged in trade in Scandinavia, and living at 17 Talbot Square in Bayswater. His communications to Moscow appear to have been by secret writing, and were routed to Copenhagen to conform to his commercial cover. However, less than a year later Reif had been summoned to the Home Office to discuss his status as an alien, and had been served with an order requiring him to leave the country by 15 March 1935. Anxious that his false passport might land him in trouble, Reif had complied with the order, leaving the illegal *rezidentura* in the hands of Alexander Orlov and Arnold Deutsch.

Orlov had arrived in England at Harwich in July 1934 from Stockholm, carying an American passport with an entry visa stamped in Sweden a few days earlier. He was under commercial cover, establishing premises for the American Refridgerator Company Limited at a large office block in Regent Street. Thus prepared, Orlov had brought over his wife Maria and their daughter Veronika, who lived together in a separate flat in Bayswater. They were not publicly identified as his family and travelled on false Austrian passports, but Maria was herself a trained illegal and a radio operator whose task was to assist her husband in managing the illegal *rezidentura* and running its four principal agents, PROFESSOR, BEAR, ATTILA and SUCCESSOR. By December 1934 he had been introduced by Deutsch to Kim Philby, and thereafter met him ten or twelve times, almost always in Regents Park over the next nine months. Although Philby was then merely a struggling journalist, contributing to the *Review of Reviews*, a periodical owned by a friend of his father, Philby's KGB file shows that in July 1935 he achieved a considerable coup by giving Orlov a restricted War Office directory listing the various branches of military intelligence and their personnel, which he had acquired from an old university friend, Tom Wylie, a homosexual civil servant working in the private office of Sir Robert Cready, the Permananet Under-Secretary. Having overseen the successful recruitment of Philby, Orlov had met, on Philby's recommendation, Donald Maclean, and encouraged him to cram for his Foreign Office examination.

Orlov's tenure as the illegal *rezident* in London ended prematurely in October 1935 when he accidentally encountered an academic in the house where he had rented rooms who had known him in Vienna in 1931 and had given him English lessons. At that time Orlov had been living openly as a Soviet citizen, 'Leo Nikolaiev', and his teacher therefore knew very well that he was not an American named 'William Goldin'. Orlov had moved instantly into a hotel nearby and conveyed the bad news to Moscow, which had insisted on his immediate withdrawal before he contaminated any of his agents, leaving their supervision to Reif, as Deutsch at that moment happened to be away on home leave. Although Orlov had only been in England for fifteen months, he had helped lay the foundations for an extensive network of young graduates destined for careers as moles, and his relationship with Kim Philby would be renewed in Narbonne when they met again during the Spanish Civil War.

Reif's principal task while in England was supposed to have been the management of the Woolwich Arsenal spy-ring, and he certainly handled one of its members, codenamed ATTILA, who had been introduced to Deutsch by Percy Glading and accidentally recruited his son, HEIR. According to a report on this incident from Deutsch, Reif's English was so bad that when ATTILA had asked if he could bring his son to the next rendezvous, he had misunderstood's Reif's reply; Reif had been horrified by the son's appearance, but he turned out to be so enthusiastic and useful that he was enrolled onto the Soviet books as HEIR. Although neither has been formally identified, it is likely that HEIR was Charles Munday, a twenty-two-year-old assistant chemist employed at the Arsenal who was one of the four defendants at the trial, and the only one to be acquitted. The evidence against him really had been limited to a single meeting with Glading, observed by Special Branch detectives at Charing Cross station, at which Glading had handed him plans that had been photographed, for return to the Arsenal.

The Moscow archives also show Reif's indirect supervision of Kim Philby, through Deutsch and his direct contact with Donald Maclean whom he met for the first time in October 1934. Reif had ensured that Maclean had discarded his contacts with the CPGB and encouraged him to join the Foreign Office and prepare for the Civil Service Examination which he was to sit in August 1935. Penetration of the Foreign Office, of course, was a key target for the Soviets, and in February 1935 Reif reported that he was cultivating a woman, codenamed BRIDE, for access to her boyfriend, apparently another potential recruit in the diplomatic service. Finally, Reif returned to Moscow and subsequently headed the NKVD's British section before disappearing in the purges to serve eight years of hard labour in Siberia.

Because none of the Woolwich Arsenal defendants cooperated with their MI5 interrogators the Security Service never came close to identifying Ignace Reif as the illegal *rezident*, and certainly never connected him to Max Wolisch. Indeed, even when Walter Krivitsky mentioned 'Reiff' during the interviews conducted with him by Jane Sissmore in February 1940 there was no record of him. Similarly, MI5 had no knowledge of Arnold Deutsch until Krivitsky named him, and even less of his wife Josefine, the radio operator who had been taught her wireless technique at the Comintern's school in Moscow.

After his sudden withdrawal from London, Orlov had remained in Moscow acting as a desk officer for Reif and Deutsch until September 1936 when he was posted to Madrid as the NKVD *rezident* with the miliary rank of major-general, and accredited to the embassy as a politcial attaché. Orlov later moved his headquarters to Valencia, and established a guerrilla training camp just outside the town at Benimamet, which was duplicated at Bilbao, Argen, Barcelona and in Madrid itself. Eventually, in the middle of September 1937,

Orlov crossed the French border to rendezvous at Biarritz with Philby, who had arrived in Spain in June, and had been working as a freelance war correspondent, reporting from the nationalist front at Salamanca for *The Times*. Thereafter Orlov met Philby every fortnight in Narbonne, until his decision to disappear in July 1938.

Even then, Philby was not told the truth, and was informed that, once again, it had been necessary to withdraw Orlov without any advance notice. This left Philby in direct contact with the *resident* in Paris, to whom he continued to send his reports, but it left him incommunicado when he finally returned to London on Friday, 21 June, on one of the last ships to leave Brest before the French surrender. He had no means of communicating with his Soviet contact in Paris, now under enemy occupation, and eventually he was forced to re-establish his link with the Soviets via the London acting-*resident*, Anatoli Gorsky, through Bob Stewart and the CPGB. This he achieved by approaching Donald Maclean, whom he had met only once, some years earlier, and asking for his help. The young diplomat, just back from Paris and unaware that Philby had been recruited long before him, had been suitably cautious, and reported Philby's plea. Then, at a second meeting with Philby, Maclean had put him in touch with Bob Stewart. Similarly, in early 1941 when Anthony Blunt had wanted to make contact with the Soviets, he too had resorted to passing a message through Philby. He had known of Philby's role, but had lost his link to the Soviets when he had been posted to Boulogne by the Field Security Police in December 1939. As MI5's Peter Wright later observed, 'we had missed the greatest CPGB secret of all' (Wright 1987: 228). According to Blunt, the Cambridge spies had been run through 'a complex series of couriers: from Litzi Friedman messages passed to her close friend and fellow Comintern agent, Edith Tudor Hart, and thence to Bob Stewart, the CPGB official responsible for liaison with the Russian embassy, and thence on to Moscow. Until Blunt confessed we were entirely unaware of this chain, and it had enormous implications' (ibid.).

Philby would continue his espionage career uninterrupted, first in Special Operations Executive and then in SIS, until November 1951 when he was sacked because of suspicions that he had tipped off Donald Maclean to plans for his imminent arrest in May that year. Nevertheless, Philby remained in contact with SIS until his eventual defection in January 1963, apparently confident that Orlov would not compromise him. Certainly he knew that any danger from Krivitsky had been eliminated by his death, supposedly by a self-inflicted gunshot, in his Washington DC hotel room in February 1941.

6

BOB STEWART

The three volumes of Bob Stewart's MI5 file open in September 1920 with a report from SIS that identified him as a Communist and 'a secret agent for England on behalf of the Third International'. Born in February 1877 in Eassie, in Angus, Stewart was trained as a ship's carpenter, but never went to sea to practise his trade. Instead he took up politics, became a member of the Dundee Town Council and achieved some considerable notoriety locally until he moved to London in 1929. Even then he did not sever all his connections with Dundee, and stood for the city as the Communist Party candidate in the June 1929 general election, when he polled 6,160 votes, and again in 1931 when his vote increased to 10,261, although he was in September that year sentenced to thirty days' imprisonment for obstructing the local police.

Stewart had been a founder member of the Party when it was created in 1921, and the following year had been appointed the CPGB's Scottish Organiser. He remained a member of the Executive Committee until 1936, when he became secretary of the Control Commission, the Party's hardline, disciplinary body, and between1925 and 1926 he had served as acting General Secretary. In 1924 he had been appointed the British representative on the Comintern's Executive Committee, and had visited Moscow often, to attend the 4th Congress of the Third International, and to be elected to the Praesidium of the 5th Congress. All of this political activity was a matter of public record, and even *The Times* reported, in June 1924, that Stewart had taken charge of the Party's propaganda section.

It was Stewart's move to London that appears to have marked his participation in the underground cells, and in March 1930 he made a visit to Germany which may have been significant because thereafter Moscow's financial support for the Party was channelled through him exclusively. Within a month of his return to England he was in Ireland to organise the Party there, and by August he was writing articles in *Pravda*, under his own name, supposedly as a specialist in military affairs. This new role coincided with MI5 noting that he had approached a member of the Party, who lived in Crayford and worked at Vickers, for information about new weapon designs. Almost simultaneously, the Dublin Garda reported to MI5 the existence of 'a prominent Soviet agent' living at Stewart's north London address.

By June 1932 Stewart had been elected to the CPGB's Central Committee, and it was in this capacity that his name had become known to Krivitsky. Meanwhile, Special Branch detectives were filing reports on his many visits to Ireland, to meet Communists and members of the Irish Republican Army, and over the following year the number of his trips abroad escalated considerably, with a departure logged in October 1932 to Berlin, where he was seen staying at the Bavaria Hotel; to Paris in January 1933 where he stayed at the New Hotel in the rue St Quentin, and to Zurich in March. In April he stayed in Brussels with Joseph Arent, and in June he was seen visiting the home of another senior CPGB figure, Rajani Palme Dutt. In addition Stewart undertook other trips to Esjberg, Copenhagen and Amsterdam and on each occasion either SIS was alerted to monitor his movements, or the local police kept him under surveillance. His MI5 file contains a memorandum, dated 20 December 1934, from a Special Branch detective in Folkestone who reported his departure for Boulogne to Major Valentine Vivian, then SIS's Director of Counter-Espionage. However, when he went to Moscow in June 1936 no such facilities were available, and he was able to confer with his Soviet intelligence controllers in relative freedom. On this trip Stewart may have been submitting a progress report on Percy Glading, with whom he had been in contact in May and June, immediately prior to his departure.

In contrast, Stewart's activities were watched extremely closely in London, and a microphone, codenamed TABLE, picked up all his office conversations in King Street. Another, codenamed KASPAR, recorded sound from another CPGB building in Great Newport Street, but both sources were to be betrayed by Anthony Blunt in 1940 when he gained access to the relevant MI5 files. Instead of ripping out the wiring, and maybe demonstrating the fact that the Party had discovered the covert equipment, Stewart pretended he was unaware that his office contained a bug, and carried on his business as normal. This allowed MI5 to spend fruitless hours making transcripts of his exchanges with another Scottish Communist, Jimmy Shields, a former Able Seaman on HMS *Norfolk* and an Invergordon mutineer, the long-serving head of the CPGB's International Department, who held that post until his death in 1949. Shields was responsible for supervising Moscow's financial support for the Party, and much of what was heard over the microphones consisted of Shields counting thousands of US dollar bills, donated by the Soviets. In addition, Stewart's home telephone was tapped and all his mail was intercepted, photographed and tested for secret writing. However, significantly, Stewart dropped from sight soon after the outbreak of war. Whereas he had made countless short trips to the Continent during 1938 and early 1939, and had been seen to play an active role as a member of the CPGB's Executive Committee, frequently attending speaking engagements in Scotland, he simply disappeared during most of 1940, and was thought to have been working from home. MI5 noted that callers for him at King Street were informed 'it was no good enquiring for him' and that he was not at the headquarters, 'nor likely to be'.

There are two explanations for Stewart's apparent disappearance from the CPGB's overt activities. One is that during this period he was fully preoccupied with running the Party's underground cadres, and in particular was acting as the Soviet illegal *rezident* in London. The evidence for this explanation comes from Walter Krivitsky who recalled in 1940 that when Paul Hardt had fled the country in 1937, when he realised he had come under Special Branch surveillance, he had been replaced by a member of the CPGB's Executive Committee whose name, so he thought, began with a 'B'. Most likely, this was a reference to BOB. The second explanation is that at about this time Stewart himself may have become aware, from a tip from within the Security Service, that MI5's technical surveillance on King Street, the source codenamed TABLE, had identified him as a prime target. Anthony Blunt, who did not join MI5 until May 1940, later acknowledged that, motivated by self-preservation, he had warned his Soviet contacts that Stewart's conversations were being monitored and could incriminate his contacts. It is also possible that the CPGB's other mole inside MI5, Celia Luke, may have passed on a warning too. However, whatever Stewart was doing in 1940, it is known that the legal *rezident*, Anatoli Gorsky, did not return to London to take up his duties until December 1940. When he did so, he was probably aware that he was venturing into a very dangerous environment which had seen the withdrawal in recent years of all the illegal *rezidents* sent from Moscow, and into a territory where the local security apparatus may have had the benefit of briefings from two authoritative sources, Krivitsky and Orlov, both of whom could be expected to have acquired an extensive knowledge of Soviet operations in England. But had they imparted this to MI5? Anthony Blunt definitely provided a copy of Krivitsky's debriefing to Moscow, but the NKVD must been reassured to learn that Orlov apparently had maintained his silence.

Stewart did not reappear in the Party life again until September 1941 when he was placed in charge of the CPGB's National School for Political Organisers, and once again took up speaking engagements. He was also responsible for giving classes for what were termed 'Shock Brigades', but in the latter part of 1942 his health failed him and he again dropped from MI5's sight until July 1943 when he was active on the Control Commission and resumed his travels across the country to give instruction to other militants. In September he attended all the meetings of the Party's Secret Legal Group which had been formed to consider the implications of Douglas Springhall's arrest and imprisonment. Although the Party's public response was Springhall's expulsion, it is more likely that Stewart's group was one component of a damage limitation exercise, designed to identify any leaks from within King Street, improve security and assess the implications of the scandal.

By the end of the war Stewart's overt role within the Party had changed from 'watchdog' to that of 'elder statesman', but he retained considerable authority, probably because of his covert links with Moscow, and because of the influence of his wife Margaret Stewart, his daughter Annie Stewart and his assistant Agnes Aitken.

7

DAVE SPRINGHALL

Dave Springhall came to prominence as a youthful activist in 1923 when he was co-opted, as one of the younger CPGB members, to join the YCL's National Council, but by then he had been dismissed from the Royal Navy for causing dissent. In 1924 he had been a delegate at the Communist International in Moscow, and during the 1926 General Strike had been convicted of possession of seditious material. A year later he had been in Moscow, attending a course at the Lenin School.

During the Spanish Civil War Springhall was to act as Political Commissar to the XIth (British) International Brigade between January and March 1937, and play a key role in the campaign, acting as a link between the British base in Albacete and King Street. The main CPGB figures in Spain were Peter Kerrigan, a tough Glaswegian and formerly the CPGB's Scottish District Secretary, and Bill Rust of the *Daily Worker*. The battalion's first commander was Wilfred Macartney, recently released from Parkhurst prison after serving ten years for espionage, who was to be wounded in the elbow in a shooting accident when Kerrigan accidentally discharged his pistol. On the night before he was due to return temporarily to England, to register in London as part of his conditions of release, he had swopped sidearms with Kerrigan, but had passed his weapon without the safety catch on. This incident served to highlight the inexperience of the battalion's nearly two thousand volunteers, and the leadership they required, and received, from Springhall, who was later to show great courage and be wounded during the battle of Jarama.

In February 1937 Springhall had helped lead a disastrous attack by four hundred men of the Abraham Lincoln Battalion in which all but twenty-five were killed or wounded. He and the American commander, Robert Merriman, were wounded, but the British joint commander, George Wattis, was court-martialled for his role in the debacle, by a panel on which Fred Copeman acted as the military adviser. Wattis was convicted and later was seen running the staff mess, whereas Springhall emerged as something of a hero, returning to England to address the CPGB's Fourteenth Congress at the end of May. Later he was to be appointed by the CPGB to the Comintern's headquarters, where he worked under the codename GIBBONS.

In September 1939 Springhall was the CPGB's representative who returned to London from Moscow to provide the Comintern's explanation for an extraordinary reversal of policy following the Molotov–Ribbentrop pact. At a meeting of the Central Committee on 25 September, to which he had first been elected in 1932, Springhall had conveyed the news imparted to him by the Comintern's General-Secretary, Georgi Dmitrov, that the CPGB should declare its opposition to what was now termed 'an imperialist and unjust war for which the bourgeoisie of all the belligerent states bear equal responsibility' (Hyde 1950: 68) against Nazi Germany. Moscow had directed that 'in no country can the working class or the Communist Party support the war . . . The Communist Parties which acted contrary to these tactics must now immediately correct their policy' (ibid.). Hitherto the CPGB had lined up against the Fascists in Rome and Berlin, but now the Party was under instructions to take the diametrically opposite position. This reversal baffled Harry Pollitt and J.R. Campbell, who had already commited the Party to opposing the Nazis, announcing that the Party

> voices what is in the heart and mind of every worker, of every sincere friend of democracy in this country, when it declares that in taking part in this war Britain must have no hidden aims, no imperialist designs of its own, and no secret understanding with the facist forces. The Government of Britain must at once issue a solemn declaration that the aim of the anti-Hitler alliance is not only to restore the independence of Poland, but also to restore the independence of a democratic Austria and Czechoslovakia.
>
> (Hyde 1950)

In contrast, Bill Rust and Rajani Palme Dutt accepted the new Party line directed by Moscow, as of course did Springhall. All this was to change again in June 1941, with the unexpected Nazi attack on the Soviet Union, by which time Springhall had become the CPGB's National Organiser, and Pollitt had recanted.

In practical terms the CPGB's opposition to the 'imperialists' war' led to a certain amount of industrial agitation, but in fact only one member, John Mason, was detained in July 1940 having fomented discontent and organised strikes at the English Steel Corporation plant at Sheffield, where he had worked since 1938. He was eventually released in June 1941, following the intervention of Willie Gallacher MP with the Home Secretary, and MI5's COMPLAN, a coordinated scheme to arrest thirty-six leading CPGB figures and thereby paralyse the Party, was never required to be implemented. COMPLAN had been devised in acknowledgment of the CPGB's penetration and control of various key trade unions in the engineering and aircraft industries which, for the first twenty-two months of the war, had advocated obstructionism in the workplace to undermine Britain's ability to fight the

Nazis. The *Daily Worker* had been banned in January 1941, amid widespread concern that the CPGB exercised quite disproportionate influence over the labour force. COMPLAN, devised by MI5's David Clarke, calculated that although the Party was well organised, its power was concentrated at King Street, and the elimination of the leadership would lead to the evaporation of support from less ardent adherents. Isolating the revolutionary core was a strategy intended to neutralise the sympathisers, and Clarke's tactics included the release of embarrassing material, including selected extracts from the Central Committee's minutes which had been discovered in Guildford during a police raid.

Although COMPLAN proved unnecessary, MI5 remained concerned about Springhall who was known from October 1939 to be recruiting a clandestine network in the armed forces. He had set up a special interviewing room at his flat at 11 King Street, close to the Party's headquarters at number 16, where he and two subordinates met men who had been called up into the services. Ostensibly the purpose for these meetings was to maintain contact with CPGB members or sympathisers who had been called up so that they could participate in local discussion groups, but clearly Springhall and his trusted associate, Robert Robson, a member of the CPGB's feared Control Commission, were developing a comprehensive cell-like structure which was based on covert means of communication, and often relied on word of mouth, committing nothing to paper. Robson had been the CPGB's London District Organiser from 1927 to 1933, and during the Spanish Civil War had been a key recruiter at King Street for volunteers to join Springhall in the British Battalion of the International Brigade.

The Commission was the CPGB's internal security unit and monitored political deviation as well as other threats to the Party's commitment to the class war. Douglas Hyde, then the news editor of the *Daily Worker*, recalled that in May 1935 Stalin had made a speech calling for the creation of cadres, which had been defined as people 'specially trained for providing the framework for the communist battalions in their fight for communism. In communist jargon to be a *cadre* meant to be someone trained and ready to do anything, anywhere, for communism' (Hyde 1950). However, this development had

> led to the Cadres Departments acquiring a responsibility for the doc-
> trinal purity of the Party's propaganda and, in particular, for ensuring
> the theoretical soundness and Marxist "purity" of all members. They
> had therefore, a direct interest in and responsibility for all purges; in
> capitalist countries one aspect of their work was to become a sort of
> NKVD within the Party organisation itself. The Cadres Department
> became almost a separate party within the Party, with over-riding
> authority when it came to keeping the Party free of deviations and
> deviationists.

Moscow's willingness to exploit the CPGB was apparent even before the war was declared, when Mihel Kaptelsev, an engineer at the Soviet Trade Delegation, approached Robinson Walker of Vickers Armstrong for information. In a slightly risky operation Walker had been supplied with worthless information which he had passed to Kaptelsev, and in September 1938 he was charged with breaches of the Official Secrets Act and imprisoned for three years. Kaptelsev would also have been detained, but he had left the country as soon as Walker had been caught, only to be replaced in March the following year by Aleksei Doschenko.[1]

Also an engineer assigned to the Trade Delegation in Hatton Garden, Doschenko had embarked upon a tour of Britain's munitions factories and shipyards, and his requests for access to particular sites were reported to the Security Service which took little interest in him until a manager at Rollston's aircraft factory at Croydon Airport revealed that one of his more patriotic employees, Tom Hannry, had been approached by Doschenko for information. According to Hannry's very detailed account, he had attended a couple of local CPGB meetings and then had been accompanied by Rajani Palme Dutt up to the Soviet travel office at Bush House to meet Doschenko who had dictated a list of military topics he wanted to learn more about. John Archer, the MI5 officer responsible for air security, had intended to allow the case to develop until he learned that his principal witness, Tom Hannry, had a string of criminal convictions and in November 1927 had been confined in an insane asylum near Chester. There he had been regarded as a dangerous lunatic who had pretended to be an IRA terrorist named Francis O'Beirne, and claimed to have been sentenced to death in Ireland with Erskine Childers.

Embarrassed by Hannry's unstable personality, Archer had arranged for Special Branch to detain Doschenko, and he was arrested in the street at Chancery Lane tube station. When searched at his home in Hampstead, Doschenko had tried to destroy a slip of paper concealed in his wallet bearing notes of naval catapult equipment. He was then interrogated by John Maude and Major Sinclair at Brixton prison, where he denied all knowledge of the incriminating note. The Admiralty declared the notes to be highly classified, and the Soviet engineer was kept in custody until the end of January 1940 when he was deported from Folkestone, despite the muted protests of the ambassador, Ivan Maisky.

The cases of Kaptelsev and Doschenko illustrated the vulnerability of Britain's defence plants, and proved a link between the CPGB and Soviet espionage, although Palme Dutt's role was never revealed because of MI5's reluctance to risk placing Hannry in the witness box for the prosecution. Indeed, when his employer learned the details of his past he was given the sack, prompting him to try and sell his story to the *Sunday Pictorial*. Wartime censorship ensured the episode went unreported, but MI5 became increasingly conscious of the close relationship between Moscow's espionage apparatus and some senior figures in the CPGB.

Certainly Douglas Springhall did not have to look very far for information to pass on to the Soviets, and the volume of material delivered to King Street escalated dramatically after the Nazis turned on Stalin in 1941, as Hyde witnessed:

> The spying which had gone on during the 'imperialist war' phase was nothing to that which followed. The information came from factories and the Forces, from civil servants and scientists. And the significant thing to recognise is that those who did it were not professional spies, they took big risks in most cases, received no payment whatever and, this is doubly important, did not see themselves as spies and still less traitors. As Party members they would have felt that they were being untrue to themselves and untrustworthy of the names of communist if they had not done it.
>
> (Hyde 1950)

The existence of such a clandestine organisation was revealed in 1942 when an Edgware Road printer, Oliver Green, had been arrested on a charge of counterfeiting petrol coupons. During a search of his premises the police had uncovered a collection of photocopied classified War Office documents, and this discovery had led to his interrogation in prison by MI5's Hugh Shillito. A veteran of the International Brigade who had fought at Jarama, Green admitted that he had been recruited by the Soviets in Spain, and had been controlled by two men MI5 identified as members of the Soviet trade delegation in London. He confessed to having recruited an informant in the army, an ex-member of the RAF, a merchant navy sailor, a fitter in an aircraft factory, a civil servant and a source with access to aircraft production figures. Green also claimed that several wireless operators, who had been trained during the Spanish Civil War, transmitted the information to its ultimate destination, and that they were sufficiently experienced to take precautions to avoid interception. They switched wavelengths, broadcast early in the morning or late at night when their signals would be less likely to be detected, and employed a sophisticated high-speed punch-tape machine to compress the traffic, thereby reducing the danger of interception.

Green was so helpful to Shillito that he was never charged with any offences relating to his espionage, but his information generated several other investigations, and ended with Springhall's imprisonment. His arrest had come as a consequence of a tip in October 1942 from a woman who shared a flat with Olive Sheehan, a Customs and Excise clerk who had been seconded to the Air Ministry. Although she was not a CPGB member, her husband, then serving on an RAF station, was, and he had also fought in Spain. Sheehan had been passing information to Springhall but when, on one occasion, she had fallen ill, she had entrusted an envelope to her flatmate to give to a certain 'Peter' who would call for it. Suspicious of Sheehan, whom she had overheard discussing the passes used by the secret services, the woman had shown the envelope to an RAF officer who had steamed it open and then alerted MI5 to its contents, a detailed description of WINDOW, an ingenious method of deceiving enemy radar, and a reference to an underground cell in the Air Ministry. Under interrogation Mrs Sheehan admitted having compromised files concerning the development of the jet engine and she was charged with offences under the Official Secrets Act. She was sentenced to three months' imprisonment and also agreed to appear as a prosecution witness against Springhall, who was arrested by Special Branch detectives at his flat in King Street on the morning on 17 June 1943.

MI5's investigation of Springhall included scrutiny of his diary which revealed references to Ormond Uren of SOE, and Ray Milne of SIS. Captain Uren, commissioned into the Highland Light Infantry, was a member of SOE's Hungarian Section and had been selected by his commanding officer, Harold Perkins, for a mission to drop blind into Hungary. Fluent in Hungarian, Uren had first passed classified information about SOE's activities in the Balkans to Springhall at a meeting in the Charing Cross Road on 9 April 1943, and did so again on four more occasions. He worked at Norgeby House, SOE's headquarters in Baker Street, and had lived in an SOE safe-house in nearby Dorset Square since May 1942. As well as revealing British policy in Yugoslavia, Poland and Czechoslovakia, Uren had provided a floor plan of Norgeby House. He was arrested in September 1943, court-martialled at the Duke of York's Headquarters in Chelsea the following month and sentenced to be cashiered and imprisoned for seven years. Springhall was tried at the Old Bailey and also sentenced to seven years. When he was convicted he was expelled from the CPGB, and his wife lost her job on the *Daily Worker*.

The other person incriminated by Springhall's diary was Ray Milne, an extremely well-regarded and hard-working secretary employed by SIS's Section V where she handled the very highest categories of top secret intercept material, including ISOS, the Abwehr's hand ciphers which were read on a daily basis at Bletchley Park. Her friend Ann Gresson, also a CPGB member, had introduced her to Springhall who had asked Milne to let her know if she came across anything that might be of interest to the Party. Ann Gresson was well known to MI5 but Ray Milne had slipped through SIS's primitive vetting procedures even though she had been active in the Peace Pledge Union before the war. The daughter of a Post Office official, she had been interviewed by MI5's Roger Hollis and the head of SIS Section V, Felix Cowgill, and her candour had placed them in a dilemma. She readily acknowledged having split loyalties, but insisted that she had not given Springhall any information apart from mentioning the confidential nature of her job, she had insisted that she would have reported Springhall if she thought he had been working for the Nazis. Worried by the possibility of a fatal leak about ISOS, it was decided to remove Milne from her access, but not prosecute her. However, according to

Uren, whom she had also known, she had freely admitted that she had been employed in the indexing of personalities in the German intelligence service.

The problem of dealing with such awkward cases, where CPGB members had burrowed their way, not just into the armed services, but into sensitive posts where they had access to very delicate information, was highlighted when a mole was discovered in MI5. The woman was Carola Luke, a CPGB member working as a clerk in the Registry where she handled extremely secret material which, under interrogation by MI5's Edward Cussen, she admitted she had supplied to her Soviet contacts. Among the items she admitted having compromised was the identity of M-8, Max Knight's source inside King Street. M-8 was Tom Driberg who could not understand how his covert role had been revealed to Harry Pollitt, who had summarily expelled him from the Party, accusing him of working for MI5 as a spy codenamed 'M-8'. Although this had meant nothing to Driberg, it was considered proof by the master agent-runner and recruiter Max Knight that MI5 had been penetrated. Carola Luke had taken the blame for the leak, thereby allowing the true culprit, Anthony Blunt, the freedom to continue his espionage undiscovered for another two decades.

Not all MI5 officers were convinced that Carola Luke alone had been responsible for betraying M-8, and Max Knight remained convinced that the organisation continued to be penetrated, and wrote a memorandum, 'The Comintern Is Not Dead', articulating his fears about the danger posed by the NKVD. This view, of course, was unpopular, but those counter-espionage experts who had studied the Springhall case remarked that he had been caught largely through his own amateurishness and his failure to exercise even the rudimentary precautions that might have been expected from a Soviet spy-ring. A pattern had emerged prewar of the highly professional use of dead-drops and intermediaries as 'cut-outs' to insulate the key players from potential contamination, yet none of these characteristics had been in evidence during the investigation of Springhall who had even left incriminating notes in his diary. One explanation for this strange behaviour was that Springhall had been a self-inspired spy whom the Soviets had been happy to exploit, but had not been indoctrinated into the principles of *konspiratsia*, Moscow's rigid security procedures. While it was known that two Soviet diplomats had been withdrawn from the embassy soon after his arrest, there had been nothing to link him to any wider espionage, and the collective MI5 opinion was that the case was an isolated one, based on Springhall's own development of 'discussion groups' within the services that had given him access to conscious and unconscious sources which he had cultivated on his own initiative, apparently unconnected with the Party's more sinister underground cells.

With the benefit of hidsight, some of these cells look remarkably obvious, and some of their members made no effort whatever to conceal their political allegiance. This strange paradox was described by Douglas Hyde as the 'opportunity to use many of our crypto-communists on public activity', and he cited the deep shelter campaign as a good example. The CPGB had seized on the failure of Neville Chamberlain's government to build sufficient shelters to protect London's population from enemy air-raids of the kind that Professor J.B.S. Haldane had witnessed first-hand in Madrid during the Spanish Civil War. An eloquent and often inflammatory public speaker, Haldane addressed meetings across the country claiming that the government had refused to build shelters because the Home Office believed that once inside the working population would refuse to leave them. In fact the government was embarrassed that only a few key buildings in London had been strengthened to resist Nazi bombs, but the situation had been defused by opening the capital's tube stations for Londoners to sleep in during the Blitz.

Haldane lent his support, as one of the country's leading scientists, to the call for an emergency shelter construction programme and a CPGB-sponsored campaign headed by a Cambridge physicist, Dr Allan Nunn May. In 1946 Dr May would be imprisoned as a spy who had betrayed atomic secrets to the NKVD, and Professor Haldane identified by MI5 as a GRU source codenamed INTELLIGENSIA, a member of a spy-ring known as the X-GROUP which also included the *Daily Worker*'s war correspondent, the Hon. Ivor Montagu. Thus, while secretly engaged in espionage, May, Haldane and Montagu were publicly associating themselves with a headline-seeking political campaign intended to embarrass the government and undermine public confidence in Chamberlain's administration.

As well as the spies 'hidden in plain sight', the cadres supervised by Springhall and the secret cells supervised by Bob Stewart, there was a further CPGB organisation, shrouded in secrecy, which coordinated with other émigré Communist Parties in exile, among the most significant being the French and German. Douglas Hyde called this 'a hush-hush body in London which came near to being a little communist International in itself' noting that 'its administration was the responsibility of an old and trusted one-time political bureau member, Tommy Bell, who kept me informed of all that was going on in various foreign parties. Had MI5 kept itself sufficiently aware of their activities too it is probable that the Fuchs case would never have occurred' (Hyde 1950). This barbed comment, of course, was a reference to the fact that the KPD's leader in London, Jurgen Kuczynski, had been approached by Klaus Fuchs for help in contacting a Soviet intelligence officer. The irony is all the greater when one considers, as Hyde could not have known in 1950, that the GRU officer selected to handle Fuchs had been Kuczynski's own sister Ursula, codenamed SONIA.

It was not until March 1947, and the defection of Allan Foote, that MI5 received confirmation that Springhall had played a vital role in passing Foote, a fellow International Brigade veteran, on to the GRU. Foote recalled that he had been approached by Springhall in September 1938 to work overseas for the cause, and had been given the address of a contact in St John's Wood. MI5 later established that this had been Birgette Kuczynski, who had given

Foote instructions on how to meet his next contact, at Geneva's main railway station in October. This rendezvous had been attended by another woman, who later turned out to be Ursula Kuczynski, Birgette's sister, and an important GRU officer. In other words, Springhall had not only been an important spy in his own right, but he had also been a significant cog in a much greater organisation.

8

THE ROBINSON PAPERS

Although the source codenamed MASK came to an end in 1937, the British intercept operators maintained their vigilance and in 1940 they were rewarded with access to a new source, codenamed ISCOT. This traffic continued, unread, until the end of 1942, but initially MI5 had no clue as to who was handling the messages in London. The first clue materialised in February 1943 when James Shields, a member of the CPGB's feared Control Commission, was seen meeting Jean Jefferson, a graduate of the Wilson School whom he tried to recruit to run a wireless from her home in Wimbledon. From conversations picked up between the two, MI5 ascertained that the CPGB had recently lost radio contact with Moscow, and was unable to read much of the traffic being broadcast, some of which Shields believed should be relayed to the United States. The third person involved in this effort to re-establish contact with Moscow was Bob Stewart, and MI5 monitored a meeting he held with two other Wilson School graduates, Sam Cohen and his wife, who had previously worked as CPGB wireless operators. When none of these efforts appeared to have borne fruit, and Stewart seemed to spend more time on overt Party activities, MI5's concentration on the CPGB faltered, but a discovery by the 21st Army Group in Belgium in 1945 offered a considerable breakthrough.

One of the first buildings to be occupied after the liberation of Brussels in September 1944 was 453 avenue Louise, the local Gestapo headquarters which was found to contain a large archive documenting the German counter-espionage activities throughout the Nazi occupation. Of particular interest was a group of files, later known as the Robinson Papers, which had been generated during a lengthy investigation of a Soviet network that had been rounded up in December 1942, and had been headed by Henri Baumann, alias Henri Robinson, a KPD youth member and a leader of the Comintern's youth movement. Together, this collection represented the most extensive study of Soviet espionage ever gathered together in one place, and covered separate but co-ordinated enquiries conducted in France, Belgium, Germany and The Netherlands by a special *Sonderkommando* headed initially by *Kriminalkommissar* Karl Giering, who died in August 1943 of cancer, and then by *Haupsturmfuhrer*

Heinz Pannwitz, with Baumann being the common thread linking the various tentacles of an immensely complex organisation.

A German Jew born in 1897 in Frankfurt-am-Main to a Polish mother and a wealthy Russian merchant, Baumann had read law at Zurich University and together with Willi Münzenburg and the Swiss Communist Jules Humbert-Droz had created the Communist Youth League which, in 1920, formed the Communist Youth International (KIM). However, of greatest interest to MI5 had been his espionage career which had begun in 1924 as a technical chief in a GRU *apparat* covering central and eastern Europe. Then, four years later, he had been appointed assistant to 'General Muraille', the senior intelligence officer in charge of administration in France, an old Bolshevik who would be arrested for espionage in April 1931 and imprisoned until 1934. Based in Paris, and in close contact with the Soviet military attaché, Baumann had been promoted in 1930 to the head of OMS bureau in Paris, liaising with other Soviet agencies in France, Switzerland and Great Britain. Thereafter, until his arrest by the Nazis in 1942, Baumann had supervised various spy-rings in England, only one of which had been known to MI5.

Ironically, although MI5 had been aware of the case, at the time it had not been considered one of espionage, but rather one of carelessness. According to the prosecution, Major Wilfred Vernon, a CPGB member, had returned to his home in Farnham in Surrey in August 1937 to discover that during his absence on holiday he had been burgled. The break-in had been reported to the police who had promptly traced the vehicle carrying the four burglars back to London and arrested them. They also searched the property and discovered a cache of classified information from the Royal Aircraft Establishment at Farnborough, where he had worked as a technical officer since 1925. Also implicated was another Air Ministry employee, a Dubliner named Frederick Meredith; both men were dismissed, and Vernon was later convicted of the relatively trivial offence of the unauthorised possession of official documents. Although both defendants had been logged as CPGB sympathisers, but not actual card-carrying members, they had been part of a group of eight RAE employees who had visited the Soviet Union as tourists in May 1932. Evidently the burglars, all members of Mosley's Blackshirts, were politically inspired, and one of them had worked at Farnborough and had objected to the 'study group' organised by Vernon, at which left-wing politics had been propagated. According to one of those convicted, J.C. Preen, he had been directed to Vernon's home by a senior BUF official, whom he named as P.G. Taylor, not realising that 'Taylor' was an alias adopted by James McGuirk Hughes, one of MI5's longest-serving informants.

There the matter had ended, except that according to the Robinson Papers, which were misplaced and not properly studied until 1947, both Meredith and Vernon were Soviet spies who had been haemorrhaging aviation secrets to their controller, Ernest D. Weiss, since at least 1936. Of this trio, Vernon was of particular significance as he had collaborated closely with Tom Wintringham to train the Home Guard during the Second World War, had worked as a lecturer for the Workers Educational Association in the Bournemouth and Portsmouth area, and in July 1945 he had been elected the Member of Parliament for Dulwich with the narrow majority of 211. Thus a CPGB member and spy, whom MI5 had failed to recognise, was in the Commons when his principal contact, Ernest Weiss, was traced to an address in London, 164 Gloucester Terrace, and interviewed in February 1948 by MI5's Jim Skarden and Michael Serpell.

Weiss, a concert pianist and self-styled 'transport economist', turned out to be quite cooperative (or so it had been thought at the time), had adopted the name Walter Locke and become a naturalised British subject. His story was quite astonishing, and proved to be yet another piece of the jigsaw of Soviet intelligence operations in Britain before and during the war. Originally from Breslau, and a graduate of Breslau University, Weiss had joined the KPD and had been recruited in Cologne in 1931 by a university contemporary, Hans Demetz, for work overseas, which had brought him to Paris where he had been introduced to HARRY I (also referred to as FRANK) in January 1932. Within five months he was in London, supposedly to undertake 'industrial research' but actually working with two seamen who acted as his couriers. According to MI5's indices, Hans Demez had been identified by Walter Krivitsky as a fellow GRU officer from Breslau.

Under interrogation Weiss claimed that he had not really realised that he was involved in espionage until December 1933 when he read in the newspapers that Robert Switz, to whom HARRY I had introduced him three months earlier, had been arrested in Paris. Immediately afterwards, in early 1934, Weiss had been called to an emergency meeting in Switzerland, together with another subsidiary source, Ilse Steinfeld, and both had been warned to lie low for a while. This had been wise advice for Switz, an American of Russian extraction caught in an espionage case in Paris, had been implicated in another one in the United States, and had been obliged to flee the country. Under interrogation by the French, Switz had compromised more than two hundred OGPU personalities across Europe, and evidently had forced Moscow to suspend operations while Switz's leads were being followed up by the *Deuxième Bureau*.

Following that episode Weiss did not make contact with his controller until the autumn of 1935 when he was summoned to Enge, Switzerland, to meet a new handler, HARRY II, who was known to him as André. In December the following year, while he had been handling material passed to him by Frederick Meredith and Wilfred Vernon, to whom he had been introduced by HARRY II in May, Weiss had been asked to establish contact with Sam Baron, a journalist on *Socialist Call*, then at the London School of Economics. Baron had been the newspaper's correspondent in Spain, and had been a member of a CPUSA front, the North American Committee to Aid Democracy in Spain. In 1938 Baron went to the United States, and in 1941 worked at the British Embassy in Washington DC. During this period, Weiss claimed, Baron's local contact in America had been Lauchlin Currie, an economic adviser at the White House, and a Soviet spy.

This was Weiss's most active period, or so he had told MI5, and HARRY II had provided him with a car so he could keep a regular schedule of meetings with Meredith and Vernon. When he received their documents he had photographed them and then passed the unprocessed film to a courier he knew as PAULINE.

Weiss emerged during his interviews as a key figure in Soviet espionage, and named numerous others as his contacts, although he occasionally appeared to feign a memory lapse when pressed for specific details. While he admitted that he had maintained contact with HARRY I through a pair of couriers whom he identified, under pressure, as Franz and Germaine Schneider of Brussels, he was vague about HARRY II, who apparently had dropped out of the scene in 1937 and had been replaced by Baumann, whom he met for the first time at a rendezvous in Jersey in September 1937. MI5 was able to check the exact date because a forged passport in the name of 'Otto Wehrli' had been recovered from his apartment at the time of his arrest. Weiss claimed that Baumann had other sources in England about whom he knew nothing, but meetings with some of these individuals had been recorded in the Robinson Papers, and his passport showed that he had visited England in February and June 1936. Finally, Weiss claimed that he had seen Baumann in Rouen in August 1938, while on a motoring holiday with friends in France, and had met him for the last time in Paris in July 1939, and had been inactive ever since. A check on the Schneiders revealed that both were known Comintern couriers and managers of safe-houses. Franz's official job, as a Unilever employee, required him to travel constantly across Europe, and this had given him excellent cover to conceal his clandestine work for the GRU.

MI5 was sceptical about Weiss's assertion of having broken with Baumann a few weeks before war had broken out, but it was understandable that the pianist should have been anxious to distance himself from any charges of espionage during hostilities. Whatever the truth, the Robinson Papers disclosed the existence in England of a spy codenamed JEAN who had collected information from BOB, ELLEN, PROFESSOR, and his wife SHEILLA. According to the files, JEAN, whom Weiss denied ever having known, communicated in code by mail and by courier to Baumann, and because he was not in direct radio contact with Moscow he had passed the material to LUX who delivered it to the Soviet embassy in Vichy. When the embassy was withdrawn in June 1941 he had relied on an illicit French Communist Party wireless located at Le Raincy, and when the Germans traced this in June 1943, and another at Choisy le Roi, they found evidence that they had been exchanging signals with a transmitter in England. This claim was to baffle MI5 because, according its official post-mortem of the Robinson Papers, 'there is no evidence of a

Party wireless transmitter operating from Great Britain during the war. There is indeed marked evidence to the contrary.'

Not much seemed to be known about JEAN, but in a letter he wrote in a plain language code to Baumann, dated 22 January 1940, he complained about lack of contact since September 1939, and mentioned that BOB had recently acquired an important position. This news had prompted Baumann to signal Moscow that JEAN had become more valuable 'since BOB got his step up'. JEAN appears to have been sufficiently important to justify, in January 1941, the despatch of an agent from Moscow to deal with him direct in England. Evidently Baumann had arranged for this agent to reach England somehow, and this journey had been accomplished successfully, thereby cutting Baumann out of JEAN's traffic to Moscow. In 1949, when reviewing this episode, MI5 speculated that this agent might have crossed the Channel as a member of the resistance, but there is an easier explanation. Although MI5 was unaware of her true role as an important GRU officer in 1949, we now know that Ursula Kuczynski reached England in January 1941, acting on instructions from Moscow. Hitherto she had been living in Switzerland, but she had made her way to Lisbon for a sea passage to Liverpool via Gibraltar. The coincidence of two Soviet agents reaching England, in the middle of the war, in the same month, seems too improbable, especially since Kuczynski has acknowledged that one of her tasks in England had been to supervise the atom spy Klaus Fuchs. In these circumstances it is possible that the agent code-named BOB who had recently received a promotion may have been Fuchs who had been invited to join the British atomic research project. When the Security Service first scrutinised Kuczynski, it had concluded that 'there is no good evidence of intelligence interests in her movements between 1941 and 1949', one of the more spectacular miscalculations of the era. Again, with the benefit of hindsight, there is a strong chance that Weiss himself was JEAN, but could not bring himself to admit it because the letter from JEAN in January 1940 contradicted his assertion that he had lost touch with Baumann four months earlier.

Further evidence concerning JEAN was to emerge from the postwar VENONA project which recovered a single message, from the GRU's *rezident* in London, Colonel Ivan Sklyarov, to his Director in Moscow dated 5 June 1941. Almost entirely fragmented, the text read

DUBOIS [65 groups unrecovered] Therefore JEAN could not go across from [65 groups unrecovered] [72 groups unrecoverable]

Although DUBOIS and JEAN were unidentified, the cable served to prove at least that the GRU *rezidentura* in London, based at the Soviet embassy, was aware of the existence of an agent codenamed JEAN whose name had been spelled out in the Roman alphabet, which in turn suggested that the codename JEAN had not been chosen by a Russian who, judging by past performance, would probably have selected an easier name to encode. From this it can be deduced that JEAN was active in London in June 1941 (when Weiss had insisted he had been dormant) and although now handled by a case officer attached to the embassy, had been run originally through some other means. Hardly a conclusive argument, but sufficiently convincing to suggest that Weiss probably was JEAN, and had been much more active in the war than he had led his MI5 interrogators to believe, for entirely understandable reasons. Clearly MI5 had accepted his tale because he had been allowed to remain in England, despite having entered the country illegally, and having remained for so long. According to MI5's records, his address in 1948 was recorded as 88 Church Street, Kensington.

Another piece of the puzzle fell into place in August 1947 when a CPGB member, and veteran of the International Brigade, Allan Foote, defected from the Soviets in Berlin while preparing for an undercover mission to the United States, and gave his MI5 interrogator, Courtney Young, an astonishing story. Although he was carrying papers identifying him as a repatriated German PoW named Albert Mueller, he was really from Kirkdale, Liverpool, and until his arrest in Lausanne in November 1943 by the Swiss Bundespolizei, had worked as a GRU agent, managing a Soviet spy-ring for much of the war.

According to Foote, he had been persuaded initially to avoid formal membership of the CPGB by his friend George Brown (a Party organiser in Manchester later killed in Spain during the Brunete campaign), on the grounds that he could be of greater use as an outsider. In December 1936 he had joined the British battalion of the International Brigade at Madriguerras, then headed by Wilfred Macartney, and had met Douglas Springhall, the Political Commissar. Appointed the battalion's transport officer, Foote had been sent back to England in December 1938 to attend the CPGB's Congress in Birmingham, with the intention that he should return, ostensibly as a Red Cross ambulance driver, but actually as a CPGB courier. However, while on a visit to King Street, he had been recruited by Fred Copeman, one of the Invergordon mutineers and later commander of the British battalion of the International Brigade, for a very dangerous assignment abroad. Copeman was, said Foote, 'merely acting as the mouthpiece for Springhall. Though the latter remained in the background, his role as a talent-spotter and recruiter was clear.' Foote had regarded him 'as the contact man for the Red Army in the British Communist Party. Gossip in Spain went so far as to state that he had held Red Army rank in his time' (Foote 1949: 20).

Copeman had sent him to a woman at a flat in St John's Wood, and MI5 later established that this had been Birgette Kuczynski, who had directed him to go to Geneva where he had met her sister, Ursula, who had indoctrinated him into the GRU. Over the following five years he had worked for her spy-ring in Switzerland, fulfilling the role of accountant, wireless operator and cipher clerk, spending up to ten hours a day enciphering and transmitting messages to Moscow. He also recalled that he had acted as a radio instructor, teaching others wireless techniques, among them another volunteer from King Street, Len Beurton, a friend and veteran of the Spanish Civil War whom he had recommended as a reliable courier. Beurton was given a mission to Frankfurt but was recalled to Switzerland just before the outbreak of war. Thereafter he remained in Lausanne, and married Ursula so she could obtain a British passport and travel to England at the end of 1940, with him following in July 1942.

Foote's first assignment, given to him by Ursula upon his arrival in Switzerland, had been to establish himself in Munich and report on local political and economic conditions, keeping in contact with her and attending a regular rendezvous in Lausanne. Of interest to MI5 had been his recollection that when he had found lodgings in Munich, Foote had been instructed to convey his address to London by using secret writing in a book and mailing it to England. This proved, if further proof was necessary, that the CPGB's underground cells had spread right across Europe.

When Allan Foote disclosed the scale of the Soviet spy-ring that had operated in Switzerland, MI5 began to pursue his leads and found that several led back to Britain, and to the CPGB. Although Foote had been persuaded to change Len Beurton's name in his autobiography, *Handbook For Spies*, to 'Bill Philips', MI5 traced him to Oxfordshire where he was a member of the CPGB's local branch in Chipping Norton. Both he and his wife, Ursula, had run Soviet spies in Britain since their arrival during the war. Both were interviewed by MI5 in September 1947, based on Foote's information, but they denied having actively engaged in espionage in England. To be on the safe side, Ursula left the country in February 1950 and moved to East Germany while Klaus Fuchs, who had been one of her sources, had been arrested and was under interrogation by the Security Service. Delayed by Len's motorcycle accident, which had left him with a broken arm and a broken leg, she finally made her departure on the eve of Fuchs' Old Bailey trial.

Although they learned of Vernon's espionage from Weiss, MI5 decided not to interview him while he was a Member of Parliament, although the Prime Minister was informed in 1948 that he had been a spy. However, by the time Vernon lost his seat in October 1951, MI5 had interrogated Weiss and Meredith, now a chief designer at Smith's Instruments, the aircraft equipment manufacturer where he had worked since leaving Farnborough. Meredith had been seen by Skardon in January 1949 and had implicated Vernon, allowing the interrogator to prepare carefully for his confrontation with the ex-MP who had since been elected to the London County Council. When Vernon realised that MI5 had talked to Meredith and Weiss, and knew that Weiss had passed him £50 from the Soviets after his conviction, he was crestfallen, but reluctant to implicate others. He confirmed everything that MI5 knew, such as Vernon's two trips to the Soviet Union, once in June 1935, to Leningrad aboard the *Smolny*, and back the following month on the *Cooperatsia*, and then again in August 1936. Vernon admitted only that on his second trip he had carried an introduction to Reginald Bishop, and insisted that his espionage had been prewar, and ideologically motivated. Skardon omitted to mention one piece of evidence, from a TABLE transcript, in which Emil Burns had been heard to refer to Vernon's activities, implying that he had been aware of his involvement with the Soviets.

The reinvestigation of Vernon threw up two interesting facts. Among the documents found at his home at the time of the original burglary was his personal address book which was found to contain many names well-known to MI5 as CPGB activists. Among these was also the name and address of Andrew Rothstein, now known to have been a Soviet intelligence recruiter. The other discovery, from Meredith, concerned Vernon's defence counsel, D.N. Pritt QC MP, himself long known as a Stalinist and Communist sympathiser, and suspected of having been a Soviet spy. According to Meredith, Vernon had explained his espionage role to his lawyer, who had then insisted in court, when Vernon was prosecuted, that there was an entirely innocent explanation for his client's possession of classified documents, and on no account should the court place a sinister interpretation on his retention of them. In other words, Pritt had completely betrayed his profession's ethics by deploying a defence he actually *knew*, by the defendant's own admission, to be completely false. As far as MI5 was concerned, this behaviour amounted to proof of Pritt's own complicity in Soviet espionage.

In all Skardon conducted two interviews with Vernon in 1951 and, while concluding that he was no longer engaged in espionage, thought he had been evasive. There MI5 let the matter rest, contemplating only to take further action if Vernon returned to active politics and risked embarrassing the Labour Party.

Gradually the evidence emerged from the Robinson Papers, and from the captured files of the German investigation into what they had termed the 'Rote Kapelle', that the network of which Foote, Beurton and Kuczynski had been members, had in fact been part of a much larger GRU organisation that had been based in Brussels, but had operated in Britain before the war to a much greater extent than had been suspected hitherto. Although Ernest Weiss had known about his part in the ring headed by Henri Baumann that had included Wilfred Vernon and Frederick Meredith, he apparently had been unaware of visits to Britain made by other senior figures, such as Leopold Trepper and Alexander Rado.

Leopold Trepper, a Polish Jew known as 'Le Grand Chef', had been appointed the GRU's director of operations in western Europe in 1936, having been recruited in Paris four years earlier, spending three years in the interim in the Soviet Union undergoing training at Kums University. The precise details of his true background are largely unknown because the only information about him in the west comes from the interrogation reports compiled after his arrest in December 1942, and during the nine months of his captivity, so it is impossible to know what he chose to conceal, and what the Nazis had no great interest in. The Germans believed that Trepper had switched sides, willingly betraying members of his network, and was fully co-operative, but there is plenty of other evidence to suggest that Trepper played a very shrewd double-bluff and only identified people whose arrest he judged to be inevitable. Either way, the German dossier on Trepper remains the best source of information about him, and reveals that upon his arrival in Paris from Moscow in December 1936 he had concentrated on developing a spy-ring in France and Britain, working under a variety of commercial covers and carrying a Canadian passport in the name of an industrialist and Polish immigrant, 'Adam Mikler', issued in July 1937 in Ottawa. Research in Canada showed that Mikler's passport had been issued originally to Michael Dzumaga, a volunteer who had used it to travel to Spain and fight with the International Brigade. He had surrendered it upon arrival in Spain, and this was the document, altered in Moscow, that had been given to Trepper.

MI5 was able to corroborate some of Trepper's earlier movements because of his criminal record in Tel Aviv, where he had been a leading figure in the Communist Party of Palestine's Central Committee. He had served fifteen days' imprisonment for attending an illegal meeting of International Red Aid and upon his release had been expelled. MI5 later speculated that Trepper may have been recruited from the Polish Communist Party, and that his work for the GRU had predated his first arrival in Palestine in 1925. In either event, he was a senior GRU officer when he first visited England in 1937, and he returned again the following year. But what exactly had he been doing on those two occasions? His German interrogators, uninterested in this aspect of Trepper's clandestine activities, had failed to pursue the matter, leaving MI5 to conclude that this dynamic professional had been managing a network as yet undiscovered.

After his escape from the Nazis in September 1943, Trepper spent much of the war in hiding, emerging in January 1945 to fly back to Moscow, coincidentally on the same flight as Allan Foote. Whereas Foote was trained for another assignment, Trepper had been imprisoned, only to be released in May 1954, following the death of Stalin. Upon his release he went to live in his native Poland, where he remained until 1973 when he emigrated to Israel. Curiously, in his memoirs published in 1975, he never mentioned his prewar visits to London.

Similarly, Sandor Rado, a distinguished Hungarian cartographer and Soviet spy, had also visited Britain for three days in November 1937. Rado had joined the Hungarian Communist Party in 1919 and had moved to Moscow where he had found work in the Comintern's secretariat. A graduate of the University of Jena, he had been appointed a geographer with the *Almanac de Gotha*, a job he retained until March 1933 when he fled the Nazis, settling in Paris in June 1933 where he was a co-founder of Inpress, an independent news agency. Although it employed Arthur Koestler, Maximilian Scheer and Vladimir Posner as editors, Inpress was probably a business cover for Soviet espionage, but commercially it was not a success and three years later he set up Servico Geopress, a distributor of maps, in Geneva. According to Allan Foote, who transmitted much of their wireless traffic, both Rado and his Russian wife Helene were Soviet agents 'of long standing' and their maps were much in demand, but he was later to accuse Rado of losing his nerve and unnecessarily endangering the entire network in Switzerland.

Rado's spy-ring remained active until the Swiss Bundespolizei began to round up his organisation, forcing him to go into hiding in August 1943, from which he emerged only in September 1944 when he and his wife, who had worked in Moscow as Lenin's secretary, escaped to Paris. Finally, in January 1945, he joined Foote and Trepper for a flight to Moscow, but when the plane stopped overnight in Cairo to be refuelled he disappeared, apparently as a consequence of a conversation he had held on board with Trepper, whom he had sat next to among the dozen other passengers. He certainly attempted suicide in Cairo, but was persuaded to continue his journey, accompanied by a Soviet official, at the end of July 1945. This particular episode remains shrouded in mystery, and Foote recalled that Rado had been apprehensive about his repatriation and feared his likely reception in Moscow. Somewhat unsympathetically, Foote had remarked that 'he only had himself to blame', which had only served to plunge him into an even deeper depression. Trepper was later to claim that in Cairo Rado had begged the British authorities for help, but they had refused his appeal and helped the NKVD trace him.

Once in Moscow Rado was arrested and convicted of treason, and remained in prison until 1955 when he was released to be appointed Professor of Cartography in Budapest. His memoirs were published in Hungary in 1971, but made no mention of his mysterious visit to London from 7 to 10 November 1937, supposedly on Geopress business.

Until his death in April 1958 Allan Foote remained MI5's principal source of information about the Soviet espionage network he had helped run in Switzerland, having incriminated Fred Copeman, Birgette Lewis (née Kuczynski), Ursula and Len Beurton, and one final participant, Rachel Dübendorfer, of the International Labour Office.

According to Foote, Dübendorfer had been a 'cut-out' for Sandor Rado, acting as an intermediary between him and Karl Hofmaier, the leader of the Swiss Communist Party. Codenamed SISSY, she also ran numerous sub-sources for Rado, one being Christian Schneider, a translator at the ILO's headquarters in Geneva. Another named by Foote was Alexander Abramson, an ILO official originally from Lithuania, and a third he described as a relation by marriage who had provided material from the League of Nations, and (incorrectly) as having been codenamed BRANT. In fact this was her son-in-law, Jean-Pierre Vigier, who had been codenamed BRAUT and whose father, Henri Vigier, worked for the United Nations. Most important of all Dübendorfer's contacts had been Rudolf Rössler, a former German soldier who had lived in Lucerne since 1935 and ran his own small publishing business while working for Swiss intelligence. According to the analysis conducted by the Bundespolizei after he and Dübendorfer had been arrested in June 1944, her best information had come from him, the implication being that he had acquired it from his own separate contacts inside the Swiss military intelligence service.

Although Rössler had been charged with espionage by the Swiss, he had been acquitted at his trial in October 1945, but almost all the others named by Foote were of interest to MI5. Indeed, his identification of Abramson was to prove of special interest because his name had come up in the investigations prompted in September 1945 by the defection of a GRU code clerk, Igor Gouzenko, from the Soviet embassy in Ottawa. When Gouzenko had walked out of the building for the last time he had removed 109 documents purloined from the GRU's *referentura*, and among them was one linking Abramson and Dübendorfer to the GRU.

Foote's relationship with the official Communist Party in Switzerland had never developed because although he had been instructed by Moscow in 1941 to contact the Party's president, the former priest Jules Humbert-Droz, and encourage him to build his own underground network, he had been unable to do so because of his arrest on charges of attempting to re-establish the local Party, which was then the subject of a ban. Instead of creating a secret network, Humbert-Droz, who was an old Comintern hand, and formerly the editor of *Communist International,* spent six months in prison, and was anyway expelled from the Party in 1942. The willingness of Humbert-Droz to meet Foote, exchange recognition codewords with him, and then plan the development of an underground cell was eloquent testimony to the overlap between the Comintern and the Party's covert cadres. Indeed, Foote's initial introduction to Humbert-Droz was a personal message from Georgi Dmitrov. With that recommendation, and satisfied that Foote was his communications channel to Moscow, Humbert-Droz had appointed an apparently respectable Zurich bookshop owner, Selma Gessner-Bührer, to be their cut-out.

Following the invasion of the Soviet Union in June 1941 Foote had been instructed by Moscow to make contact with two experienced agents, Charles and Elsa Martin, who had lost touch with 'the Centre' but were living comfortably at Chailly, above Lausanne, in a villa that contained a well-equipped photographic laboratory. Armed with their personal details, and the knowledge that Martin had worked under cover in the Far East as an engineer in China and Japan, Foote was able to reactivate them, but was reluctant to do so because he came to believe that either they, or their mysterious sub-sources in Germany codenamed BARRAS and LAMBERT, were probably under Nazi control. Foote suspected both, though pretending to be Swiss, were really Russian, but they were not pulled in for questioning by the Swiss until 1955. The following year they were both convicted of espionage, sentenced to three years' imprisonment and then deported to the Soviet Union.

As well as his two German sources, Martin hinted that he was receiving information from a French *Deuxième Bureau* officer, and also named Marius Mouttet, a former minister in the French government, and a postwar member of the French senate, who had fled to Montreux when France was occupied. Mouttet's recruitment by Martin had been undertaken under a false flag, with Martin pretending to work for British intelligence, apparently having been informed by the GRU in London that Mouttet had let it be known he was available to assist the Allies.

Foote had been right to be suspicious of the Martins, for when he reached Moscow in 1945 he was told that the couple had sold out to the Abwehr years earlier, and proof of their duplicity had been found in captured German documents. According to their Abwehr dossier, they had made repeated attempts to identify Foote and, despite his precautions, had succeeded in doing so, and in tracing his apartment. Foote eventually had been arrested early in the morning of 20 November 1943 while he was transmitting to Moscow, and the rest of the network was scooped up simultaneously.

With Foote and Rado in the hands of the police, and short of money, Rachel Dübendorfer was anxious to contact Moscow, and the only channel she knew of was through another ILO colleague, Hermina Rabinovitch, who had moved to Montreal with the ILO's headquarters in September 1940. A former employee of the Soviet trade delegation in Berlin, Rabinovitch was a Lithuanian who had previously acted as a cut-out for her in Geneva, so Dübendorfer sent her a lightly coded message through the ILO's internal mail system asking her to contact the local embassy and arrange for $10,000 to be sent to her urgently. An ingenious route, using a New York watchmaker was found for the transfer to Alexander Abramson, but the full details of Dübendorfer's desperate plea, and Rabinovitch's visit to the embassy, were contained in five of the 109 documents removed from the embassy by Igor Gouzenko in September 1945. When the documents were examined by the Royal Commission set up to investigate Gouzenko's material Rabinovitch was called as a witness and underwent a very painful cross-examination to authenticate their content. Hopelessly incriminated, Rabinovitch had been forced to resign by the ILO, refused a visa to re-enter the United States, and so made her way to Paris. Once Foote had exposed Dübendorfer as a key Soviet agent who had been active in Switzerland throughout the war, the French DST interviewed Rabinovitch and she was deported to Israel in September 1950.

Meanwhile Abramson, equally compromised, lost his job with the ILO and in 1947 found work as an assistant to a French trade union leader, Leon Jouhaux, who in 1950, as president of the French Economic Council, intervened unsuccessfully on behalf of Rabinovitch to prevent her deportation.

Allan Foote's odyssey, from transport officer in the Spanish Civil War, through secret agent in Munich, to a line-crosser to the British in Berlin exacerbated the damage to Soviet intelligence operations inflicted by Igor

Gouzenko, whose defection is often referred to as marking the opening salvo of the Cold War. His extraordinary experience began in King Street, when he was accepted as a volunteer for the International Brigade, and had taken a significant turn when Fred Copeman had offered him dangerous work overseas. Certainly neither Copeman nor Dave Springhall could have anticipated the ultimate disruption caused by Foote's acceptance into the GRU's underground network.

Foote's first-hand evidence of the GRU's exploitation of national Communist Parties served to confirm what had become evident in Canada through the testimony of Gouzenko and close scrutiny of the papers he had removed from the Soviet embassy. Without exception, those implicated in the defector's documents and identified had been either Party members, or had been closely associated with Communist-sponsored 'discussion groups'. The spy-ring exposed by Gouzenko had been headed by a Communist Party MP, Fred Rose, with Sam Carr, the Party secretary, a graduate of the Lenin School and editor of the Party's newspaper, *The Call*, assisting him, and several of their agents, among them Dr Allan Nunn May, Norman Veall and Kay Willsher, had been CPGB or YCL members before they had moved to Canada.

Although there was no proof that either Veall, a young chemist, or Willsher, who was employed by the British High Commission in Ottawa, had engaged in espionage in England, Dr May most certainly had been in contact with Soviet intelligence officers prior to his arrival in Montreal in January 1943. Although he never admitted exactly when he had been recruited, the graduate of Trinity Hall, Cambridge had visited Leningrad in September 1936 and would have been of interest to the GRU as soon as he had been engaged in April 1942 as a research physicist working on the Tube Alloys project at the Cavendish Laboratory in Cambridge.

The picture that emerged from Ottawa, as Gouzenko appeared before a Royal Commission into his disclosures, conformed with the pattern established by Foote and scrutiny of the Robinson Papers. Coincidentally, further confirmation would reach MI5 from the unlikely source of Japan where the American occupation authorities had stumbled across a lengthy confession extracted from a Soviet spy, Richard Sorge, prior to his execution in Tokyo's Sugamo prison, in November 1944.

A former German soldier and well-known as a *Frankfurter Zeitung* journalist and expert on the Far East, Sorge had been arrested in Japan in October 1941 with more than thirty members of his spy-ring while working as a press attaché at the German embassy and masquerading as a Nazi. Under interrogation he revealed that he and his radio operator, Max Klausen, had been KPD activists who had worked for the Comintern and the GRU for years. Most of his network had either been members of Japan's banned Comunist Party, or were closely associated with its underground cells. However, of particular interest to MI5 was Sorge's admission that in 1929 he had travelled to London, apparently on a clandestine mission that had been abruptly terminated in

May, after just ten weeks, by the unexpected appearance of a Special Branch detective who had interviewed him and placed him on the Aliens' Register. Acknowledged as a master spy, who incidentally had recruited Ursula Kuczynski when they had been in Shanghai together in 1930, Sorge and his wife Christiane had visited Moscow for the first time in October 1924 to work on the Comintern's journal *Inprecorr*. There, he admitted, he had been sponsored by Ossip Piatnitsky and Dmitri Manuilsky of the Comintern, and Solomon Losovsky, the Deputy Minister for Foreign Affairs. Later Christiane would return alone to Germany, subsequently living in England and the United States, leaving Sorge to undertake several secret assignments in Europe before his arrival in China, ostensibly as a newspaperman and Nazi.

When he had visited Britain Sorge had been thirty-three years old and, according to his very detailed, lengthy confession, had already undertaken missions for the Comintern to Denmark, Sweden, Norway and Germany.

> It had long been a practice to send special emissaries from the Organization division of the comintern headquarters to assist local parties with organisational problems, and it was decided such functions would have to be expanded to include intelligence work. I was sent to the Scandinavian countries in 1927 to engage in intelligence activities concerning their Communist parties, their economic and political problems, and any important military issues which might arise.
>
> (Willoughby 1952: 149)

Whereas he had told his interrogators that he had been engaged on secret work while on these assignments, he had been vague about the purpose of his visit to London, saying only that he had been directed while in Scandinavia 'to go to England to collection information' and to

> study the labour movements, the status of the Communist Party and political and economic conditions in Britain in 1929. My instructions to remain strictly aloof from internal party disputes fitted in perfectly with my personal inclinations and enabled me to devote more attention to political and economic intelligence work than had been possible in Scandinavia.
>
> (ibid.)

While the Japanese may have been willing to accept this version, and they had not pressed Sorge on the issue, MI5 was naturally interested in the precise nature of his activities in England. When (Sir) William Deakin studied Sorge's case, with help from David Footman, formerly the head of SIS's Political Section, he concluded that Sorge had come 'on a separate intelligence assignment' (Deakin and Storry 1956: 50) and had 'never contacted the members of the Politbureau of the British Communist Party while he was on his English mission, nor did he come as a Comintern emissary. The relevant official who maintained liaison between Moscow and London at this time was a Russian named Petrovsky, known in England as "Bennet" or "Brown"' (ibid.).

A. David Petrovsky, alias A.J. Bennett, was a mysterious figure who had acted as the Comintern's liaison with the CPGB between 1924 and 1929. Shortly before his return to Moscow in 1929 he had married Rose Cohen, then working at the Labour Research Department, who later edited the English language *Moscow Daily News*. Both were arrested in April 1938, charged with being counter-revolutionaries, and disappeared into Stalin's *gulag*. However, in January 1952 MI5's Dick Thistlethwaite reactivated his file on the rumour from one of his sources, a Mrs Degras, that Petrovsky had 'survived as a very important Comintern agent until fairly recently' (Petrovsky, personal file).

MI5 had pursued the subject of Sorge's mission to England in an interview with Elizabeth Poretsky whose husband, Ignace Reiss, had controlled the GRU's operations in England at that time from Amsterdam where he had maintained a commercial cover, posing as a wholesale stationer. According to Poretsky, he had taken over the GRU *rezidentura* from Max Unschlicht with instructions to collect information in England, safely distant from the reach of the feared British intelligence service. She recalled that 'Britain was greatly respected and envied in those days, especially for its intelligence service; and as one of the foremost capitalist powers, it was considered the most dangerous enemy of the Soviet Union' (Poretsky 1969: 73). Unschlicht, a close friend of Walter Krivitsky, had been dragged from his room in the Savoy Hotel in Moscow by the OGPU in the purge of March 1937, so in 1966, when these leads were followed up by MI5, almost the only surviving witness to Sorge's mission in 1929 appeared to have been Reiss's widow. Although she remained bitter at the murder of her husband, she was still a believer, living with her memories in Paris, and only willing to confirm that her husband had run an important spy in England in 1929 who had been a British intelligence officer, and that Sorge's mission to meet him had been a dangerous one. This had been startling news for hitherto there had never been any suggestion that British intelligence had been penetrated prior to the recruitment of Kim Philby into SOE eleven years later, in 1940. Who could have been Sorge's spy? Henri Pieck's widow also acknowledged that such a spy had existed in England, so an interview was arranged with Christiane Sorge, then living in an upstate New York convent, and it was conducted by Stephen de Mowbray, then SIS's head of station in Washington DC. No longer a Communist, Christiane recalled having accompanied her husband to London, and having also kept a watch on the street in London while he had met his contact and received military information, an event that might have earned them twelve years' imprisonment if he had been caught. Unfortunately, she could remember little else, and certainly not the spy's identity, but the episode proved that even three decades later there lingered a chilling significance to Sorge's mission, perhaps suggesting the existence of an undiscovered spy in some branch of British intelligence.[2]

9

CONCLUSION

Although the MASK traffic ended, as far as GC&CS was concerned, in January 1937, further Comintern messages were intercepted during the Second World War and were designated ISCOT. Naturally, as Stalin by then had joined the Allies, the cryptographic work undertaken on the top floors of Aldford House, overlooking Park Lane, was considered highly secret, and the small team of codebreakers, led by the Cambridge mathematician Dr Bernard Scott (later Professor of Mathematics at Sussex University), were isolated even from GCHQ's Diplomatic Section, which was also located in Mayfair, above Madame Eleda's couturier in Berkeley Street. Actually, 'Madame Eleda' was Adèle Croft, the mistress of a member of the Baring banking family, himself working as an intelligence officer.

The fact that a source codenamed ISCOT[1] existed was disseminated sparingly throughout the relevant branches of MI5 and SIS, and a detailed analysis of the traffic was completed by Jane Sissmore on behalf of Section IX. Kim Philby, confident that ISCOT contained nothing incriminating in respect of himself or the CPGB, had assigned the task to her, 'to keep Jane busy' and preoccupied with a topic where she could do him no harm. Not surprisingly, given Philby's interest in ISCOT, in early 1945 the Diplomatic Section was 'suddenly unable to break into any of the transmissions over the comintern network' (Philby 1968: 130). As one of the younger cryptographers, John Croft, recalled, 'the agents had gone over to one-time pads now that their operations were relatively secure behind Russian lines in the east, while the volume of traffic – never very extensive – in the west began to peter out.'[2]

Precisely what happened in the meantime, between the loss of MASK and the appearance of ISCOT, is unclear but there is some evidence that NKVD channels to the Soviet embassy were utilised by the CPGB, and the Central Committee archives in Moscow show that in September 1942 Harry Pollitt was in direct communication with General Pavel Fitin, the chief of the NKVD's foreign intelligence directorate, and relied upon him as an intermediary for correspondence with Georgi Dmitrov. In a memorandum dated 10 July 1942, from an NKVD laision officer named Mozorov and addressed to Dmitrov, it was suggested that messages for London be sent 'to Comrade Fitin for resending through his channels to our comrades in London'. On 30 September 1942 Pollitt complained through 'Comrade Fitin's apparat' that his wireless operator had been listening for transmissions from Moscow, but none had been received.

Appendix 1

MASK Traffic

This analysis shows the number of intercepted messages on a monthly basis

1934	Moscow–London	London–Moscow
February	18	16
March	13	11
April	5	7
May	9	8
June	12	19
July	1	14
August	12	9
September	19	28
October	40	17
November	22	27
December	27	26
1935		
January	39	15
February	42	7
March	30	19
April	29	13
May	26	14
June	27	7
July	31	20
August	10	12
September	39	39
October	19	34
November	24	25
December	45	21

1936	Moscow–London	London–Moscow
January	31	28
February	43	41
March	44	27
April	50	22
May	25	24
June	69	20
July	55	15
August	57	26
September		
October	16	12
November	6	5
December	3	6

Appendix 2

INFORMATION OBTAINED FROM GENERAL KRIVITSKY DURING HIS VISIT TO THIS COUNTRY

January–February 1940

CONTENTS

INTRODUCTION

MI5 have recently been able to arrange a number of private interviews with Samuel Ginsberg a.k.a. General Krivitsky, the author of *I Was Stalin's Agent* published simultaneously in New York and London in December 1939.

In order to appreciate the value of the views expressed by Krivitsky and the information he has given, it is necessary to state briefly the main facts as regards the man himself, and the circumstances which led to the series of interviews recorded here.

Krivitsky's real name is Samuel Ginsberg. He is probably of Jewish extraction having been born in South Russia, the son of a Polish émigré from Posen and a Slav mother. He is a keenly intelligent, widely read and cultured man of 43 years of age; trained as an engineer, he seems to have joined the Red Army in November 1917. Ginsberg adopted whole-heartedly the cause of the Bolshevik revolution, and became a staff officer of the Red Army early in his career. He joined the Fourth Department of the Military Intelligence about 1919, and from that time became known as Krivitsky.

The Fourth Department of the Red Army Military Intelligence dealt with the active acquisition of military and naval intelligence from abroad. Krivitsky was a specialist on German military espionage and was responsible for many years for that work. From 1935 to 1937 however he was given a wider commission embodying responsibility for Soviet secret operations in all Western European countries.

In the autumn of 1937 Krivitsky was operating in Paris. At that time Stalin's purge of the Red Army was at its height. General Tukhachevsky, seven other generals and innumerable Red Army officers had been executed in Moscow, as well as a number of Krivitsky's colleagues of the Fourth Department. In August Krivitsky received his recall. Aware that the time for his 'liquidation' at the hands of the OGPU had arrived, he temporised for some months and eventually refused to return. Under the protection of the French Government he remained in France with his wife and child until at the end of 1938 he emigrated with them to the United States of America.

In April 1939 a series of articles by Krivitsky began to appear in the New York *Saturday Evening Post*. The articles dealt with Stalin's policy in Spain, intrigues with Hitler, and secret activities of the Military Intelligence and OGPU operations abroad. These articles aroused great general interest as well as a storm of abuse from communist circles in the U.S.A. As well as material found to be wholly corroborated by MI5 records, the articles contained a great deal of information of additional interest.

In the autumn of 1939 Krivitsky was preparing the book *I Was Stalin's Agent* in collaboration with a translator, one Isaac Levine. Almost simultaneously MI5 were reopening investigations into the activities in this country of a known Soviet agent, a Dutchman living at The Hague. These investigations had progressed so far that it appeared that in 1936 this Dutchman was closely associated with certain Foreign Office officials from whom he was receiving secret documents from which he made photographic copies for transmission to Moscow.

On the 4th September 1939 a telegram was received in London from the British Ambassador in Washington stating that Levine, Krivitsky's translator, had informed the British Embassy that the Soviet espionage service had an agent named King in the Cipher Department of the British Foreign Office. Levine had obtained this information from Krivitsky. A few days intensive investigation into the affairs of John Henry King of the Cipher Department of the Foreign Office proved conclusively that he had been closely associated with and received large sums of money from the Dutchman whose activities on behalf of the Soviets had long engaged the attention of MI5. King was arrested on 25th September 1939. He confessed his guilt and was subsequently sentenced to ten years imprisonment.

This incident, and certain other information supplied by Levine together with further investigations into the case of King, indicated that Krivitsky was in possession of a great deal of information, some of which must be of acute interest to the Security Service.

He was accordingly invited to visit the United Kingdom in order to place his information at the disposal of the Security Service.

He arrived in London on the 19th January 1940. It seemed at first that little was to be gained from the visit. Krivitsky repudiated any suggestion that he had knowledge of, or was in any way responsible for Soviet secret activities in this country, and appeared quite unable to remember the names of any of his assistants or friends who had operated in or against the United Kingdom. It was evident that OGPU methods of investigation and the Moscow reign of terror during the purge had made such a deep impression on his mind as temporarily to obliterate his fairly comprehensive knowledge of British criminal procedure. He obviously feared lest any admission from him of participation in Soviet espionage activities against the United Kingdom would lead to a 'full examination' as understood by citizens of the U.S.S.R.

In regard to his assistants and friends, Krivitsky was actuated by a genuine sense of loyalty; it was only in the last few interviews that he gained sufficient confidence to talk more freely of them, and that after much time had been spent in explaining that British procedure would not admit of arrests on the uncorroborated word of a single informant. Even so he has definitely 'stalled' as regards one or two of his more personal friends, explaining that he did not intend to copy Stalin in destroying those who had served him best.

With these reservations, in spite of the difficulties of language, the Russian temperament, and the lapse of time since his break with the Soviet Government, Krivitsky has undoubtedly supplied the Security Service with most valuable information on which to base the work of combating Russo-German espionage in this country.

Krivitsky's motive in accepting the invitation of the British Government was apparently passionate hatred of Stalin, based on the murder of personal friends, relations and colleagues, and not less on the personal injustice he himself has suffered. There is no doubt that Krivitsky had devoted his whole life and energy to the work of the Soviet Military Intelligence, and that in spite of growing misgivings, he worked conscientiously and loyally for the Soviet Regime up to the time of his recall in August 1937.

More than this Krivitsky has a burning conviction that if any freedom is to continue to exist in Europe, and the Russian people freed from endless tyranny, Stalin must be overthrown. He feels it his duty to humanity and the Russian people to fight against Stalin by any means in his power.

Krivitsky has been a member of the Russian Communist Party for 18 years. He was now no longer a communist in any of the accepted meanings of the word. He himself said that there are now no longer Trotskyists, Leninists, Stalinists – all that has been thrown overboard. Stalin is now out purely for military aggression in order to stabilise his own position.

No attempt has been made in any way to edit Krivitsky's information, nor to amplify or compare it with official records. The facts and views expressed are put down as nearly as possible as told by him. The work represents an attempt to sort out and put into a coherent form a mass of information gleaned from Krivitsky at odd moments in the course of lengthy and diffuse conversations extending over three or four weeks. It is presupposed that these chapters will be read in conjunction with Krivitsky's published book *I Was Stalin's Agent*, and matters fully dealt with there are not included, neither was Krivitsky encouraged to enlarge on the activities of Soviet agents whose identity and activities are already known to MI5.

The information contained in these chapters relates to Soviet Intelligence organisations as they existed up to 1937. It is doubtful whether in 1940 there is any distinct line of demarcation between the espionage activities of the OGPU and those of the Russian Military Intelligence Department.

Of greater importance to the counter-espionage service is the probability that the line of demarcation between the Soviet and German Intelligence Services has become equally indistinct. In view of the close co-operation which existed between Soviet and German Intelligence personnel less than a decade ago, it is only to be expected that there is now a resumption of that co-operation and that the German espionage service is taking full advantage of the existing Soviet intelligence organisation in this country.

CHAPTER ONE
THE SOVIET MILITARY INTELLIGENCE
DEPARTMENT

Section 1. General organisation

The Soviet Military Intelligence Department or Razvedupr is in Soviet Military circles known as the Fourth Department. Its function is to acquire, collate and distribute every kind of information both from within and without the Soviet Union which might be of use to the General Staff of the Russian Army in war. Apparently the Fourth Department was not charged with counter-espionage matters, or at any rate Krivitsky had no knowledge of it.

The Department is divided into a number of sections.

Certain sections deal with Intelligence organisations attached to the various command head-quarters of the Red Army.

Command headquarters in 1937 were located as follows:-

Leningrad:	For the Finnish front and part of the Soviet frontiers with the Baltic States.
Minsk:	For the Polish frontier and the remainder of the Baltic States frontiers.
Kiev:	For the South Polish frontier down to the Black Sea and along the River Dniester.
Tiflis:	For the Caucasian Military District.
Khabarovsk:	For the Far Eastern Front.

The Fourth Department trains the Frontier Guards in espionage. These Frontier Guards wear green caps. On the Russian western front each frontier guard has about fifty miles of front on which to operate for espionage purposes. Their reports do not go direct to the Fourth Department, but to their Command Headquarters. These guards deal only with military matters. They act on definite instructions and are not allowed to deal with political questions or matters affecting civil OGPUs on the frontiers. Members of this corps who are to be employed on the South Eastern frontiers are sent to Ashkhabad where a special intelligence school is provided for them. The Department has a very important centre at the terminus of the railway at Kutchki on the Afghan frontier – naturally also they have a number of men at Mishet.

The sections of the Fourth Department which are of primary importance as regards the British Empire are the second and third sections. The second section deals with the results of the activities of the third section. It collates the information obtained, and distributes it to the correct departments. The third section deals with all matters concerning the acquisition of military information from countries outside the U.S.S.R.

Third section agents are charged to obtain not only the fullest possible information about a foreign Army, Navy or Air Force, but all political and economic information which, when collated, might influence the General Staff and the Politburo in matters of foreign policy. At one time an attempt was made to draw a distinction between military and political and economic intelligence, but it was found impossible to divorce political and economic questions from those of pure military intelligence. A special sub-section of the third section deals solely with the study of British colonial problems particularly in the Near and Far East.

The third section is also charged with the work of 'decomposition', that is the creation in countries with which the Soviet Government might eventually find itself at war, of internal situations which would be of value to the Russian Army if, and when, an active military situation should arise. Subversive activities in the military forces of foreign countries is an important part of the work.

Intimately connected with the third section is a special section which was for many years, and possibly still is, in charge of two brothers called Lazowski. The men are expert forgers who have a number of experts under them who prepare spurious documents, such as passports, credentials, signatures, and in fact any false documents required by the Fourth Department. The section employs an Armenian aged 24–30 who is so expert in the forging of handwriting that he can memorise it and make a perfect reproduction. During the Spanish war he spent his whole time forging passports and shipping documents.

Another section of the Fourth Department dealt with relations with foreign powers. Military Attachés take a course in this section before they are appointed. Military Attachés are not therefore third section men fully trained in underground espionage matters although their secretaries invariably are. The head of the department for relations with foreign powers was up to 1937, and may still be, a man called Heckert.

In the earlier years after the Bolshevik revolution and in fact until the period of Stalin's attacks on the Red Army from 1935–1937, the Military Intelligence Department ranked highest in importance among the departments of the Russian military machine. The headquarters of the organisation and all the senior posts were staffed by officers of the Russian army picked for their outstanding ability as well as for their political integrity. It was understood that any officer of the Red Army who displayed unusual brilliance should at once be transferred, or at least offered to the Fourth Department. Foreigners were never employed in the military departments of the Red Army with the exception of a small number who have grown up in the organisation of the Soviet Union.

The Staff Officers were not themselves highly paid but were never refused expenses however great for the acquisition of important information. General Berzin, head of the Military Intelligence Department for the greater part of Krivitsky's career always insisted that valuable agents should receive handsome remuneration. His rule was that eighty percent of the expenses of obtaining valuable information must be handed as clear profit to the agents concerned. Staff officers who did particularly well were not rewarded with a cash bonus, but with decorations such as the red banner, or as a signal sign of favour, with the grant of an apartment in Leningrad or Moscow. This meant that the recipient of such an apartment held it in perpetuity. He could leave it to his wife and family or pass it on to his friends.

Officers of the Military Department retired on a small pension and with a number of privileges. If they were obliged to stop work owing to ill health they were similarly provided for. In 1936 a special meeting of the General Staff was held to consider the serious wastage of intelligence officers on account of ill health. It was found that the average age limit for work in the third section of the Fourth Department was 33–34, and that this was almost invariably due to overwork. Krivitsky himself and most of his assistants worked from ten o'clock in the morning until eleven or twelve at night. At the age of 43, Krivitsky, after three years release from the service, has the appearance of a man of 55.

As regards subordinate agents they are given a careful training either abroad or in Moscow before they are permitted to start work. In 1923 the Fourth Department started their own schools for agents in Moscow. These schools train agents for work abroad and they usually take a three months course. The schools have no connection with the OGPU or with the Lenin school, and the pupils though drawn from the Communist Party are forbidden to make Party contacts when sent on their missions. This precaution is to prevent the hampering of an agent's activities and a safeguard against detection and arrest.

So strictly was the general rule observed that Fourth Department men operating abroad were to have no connection with official Soviet or Communist circles, that Krivitsky himself had the greatest difficulty in obtaining permission for his wife to travel abroad with him. She had during 1926 worked officially in the USSR Embassy in Vienna, and it was feared that this might become known and Krivitsky compromised.

Agents trained by the Fourth Department in Moscow were usually Russian born or had acquired Soviet citizenship. Stalin himself made a rule in 1936 that persons of foreign origin were never to be used for work in any department with such foreigners' country of birth.

Security of agents and documents

The Military Intelligence had a number of most stringent rules for the safeguarding of documents and the identity of agents. It was a practice in the Fourth Department that from time to time commissions made up from a number of sections should unexpectedly visit another section with full powers to check up their security arrangements. These commissions had full powers to check up documents, and see that they were all available and properly safeguarded.

As regards safeguarding the identity of agents the rule was that utmost precautions must be taken in rewording reports and so dealing with other material that nothing went out of the Fourth Department in such a form that it could possibly give a clue to the source from which it had been obtained.

Krivitsky had two valuable agents who, in Germany in 1933, secured from a factory there the complete plans of a new aero engine. Through carelessness these plans were sent to a Soviet aero engine factory in their original form. The German espionage service had an agent in this Soviet factory who saw the plans and by examining them was able to report to the German service when they had been obtained. Krivitsky's two agents in Germany were arrested and the officers in Moscow responsible for the blunder were shot.

Section 2. Organisation of military espionage abroad

Krivitsky emphasised at every opportunity that up till 1935 he had been concerned solely with the organisation of military espionage against Germany and that after that date, although he was charged with the general supervision of the activities of the third section in Western Europe, he had only a general knowledge of matters affecting those countries other than Germany, and left English affairs largely to his assistant, Parparoff.

Nevertheless the general principles on which the third section operates are the same in all western countries, and he is confident from his personal knowledge and from his general experience that, allowing for variants which occur in all intelligence services, the activities of the Fourth Department in the United Kingdom are organised on the lines which he describes.

Agents

Agents of the third section of the Fourth Department employed abroad are divided into two main classes – legal and illegal *rezident*s.

Legal rezidents

Legal *rezident*s are members of the Fourth Department not necessarily senior staff officers but always members of the third section. Places are found for these men on the staffs of Soviet Embassies or Legations. They are here as officials of the Soviet Government and their Embassy status provides a social standing which enables them to make official contacts. The secretaries of the Military and Air Attachés are almost invariably third section men.

The duties of the legal *rezident*s are to collect all possible military information which can be obtained through contacts made by him or by the military attaché and to assist the illegal *rezident* by every means in his power. He acts as a postbox for the illegal *rezident* and arranges for the ciphering and deciphering of urgent messages for him. Mail is usually received and dispatched for the illegal *rezident* twice a month. The legal or official *rezident* sometimes makes contacts or hears of likely contacts whom he hands over entirely to the illegal *rezident*.

He can and does call for assistance upon the Communist Party of the country to which he is accredited, but as the Embassy must on no account be compromised, his communist connections are most carefully concealed. He must never have direct contact with known members of the Communist Party, or with the illegal *rezident*. His woman secretary is usually used as a runner to take messages which she passes onto a woman employed in a similar capacity by the illegal *rezident* or by the Communist Party member with whom the legal *rezident* is working. His woman secretary is usually entrusted with the ciphering and deciphering of messages for him and for the illegal *rezident*.

Simon Kremer, the present secretary of the military attaché, is a Fourth Department man. Krivitsky knows him well. He was originally a pupil in a military school dealing with the mechanisation of the army, and afterwards worked at the intelligence centre of the Kiev command. Before he came to this country he took a course in the section under Heckert dealing with relations with foreign powers. He is not a senior officer nor likely to become one, but is of considerably more importance than the Military Attaché.

Although he does not know him Krivitsky thinks that Boris Dicki, the secretary to the Air Attaché – Cherny – is a Fourth Department man and of considerable importance.

Sub-agents, both of the legal and illegal *rezident*s, are of course recruited locally. Agents are sought first amongst the ranks of the Communist Party and its sympathisers, and secondly amongst Irishmen, the latter merely because they have an anti-British bias which makes their recruitment comparatively easy.

Illegal **rezidents**

The third section of the Fourth Department employ three types of regular illegal agents for work abroad. Head agents in control of organisation are always staff officers of the same type as Krivitsky himself. Then there are *rezident* agents holding responsible permanent posts, or acting as principal assistants to the senior agent or *rezident*. These men have almost invariably been staff officers of the Fourth Department but, having failed to procure promotion, have worked abroad so long and out of personal contact with Moscow that they have lost standing there. Sometimes they have even lost their membership in the Russian Communist Party, since, for this to remain valid has to be periodically renewed from within the Soviet Union.

The third class of agent is called the 'speculant' class. These 'speculants' – mainly Austrian, Czechs, Hungarians or Romanians, are usually people who have become outlaws from their own countries on account of their communist activities. They have nothing to lose by employment in the Fourth Department and hope to gain a good deal. Krivitsky while acknowledging the necessity of employing this type both as regular and casual agents, regards them as a danger in that if bribed by a promise of permanent domicile in a foreign country and the means to live they might in many cases be prepared to betray their service. Krivitsky emphasised the horror which which this class of agent and sometimes also the second class view the possibility of a recall to Moscow and the necessity of living in the Soviet Union.

The question of agents for the United Kingdom was always a difficult one. In the early years after the Bolshevik revolution there were a number of *rezident* Russians here, refugees from the Tsarist regime. These men made excellent agents, a number of them had a sound political background and a special knowledge of the United Kingdom. Theodore Rothstein, father of Andrew Rothstein of the Tass Agency, belonged to this class and was a successful agent of the Fourth Department for many years.

Later it became very difficult for the Fourth Department to place head agents here. The *rezident* head agent had to be a staff officer of the Fourth Department and there were few who knew the language sufficiently well and enough about this country to make it possible for them to work.

One man who was earmarked to act as head agent here was Krivitsky's assistant Max Unschlicht. The proposal to use him in this capacity was cancelled in November 1927 after the arrest and imprisonment in the United Kingdom of the young German Communist Georg Hansen. Hansen was employed by the Fourth Department. His association with Macartney, with whom he was arrested, was only incidental to his visit. His main purpose was to ascertain the best means of establishing Unschlicht in the United Kingdom, and if possible, to prepare the ground for his residence here. Krivitsky stated as a definite fact that from 1935 until 1937 the Fourth Department had no *rezident* senior staff officer of the first grade in the United Kingdom, but as long visits as possible were paid by Fourth Department agents from the Continent, with instructions to 'stay as long as you can and photograph all you can'. This was partly due to the difficulty of getting Army staff men with a knowledge of English who could get permission for permanent residence, and partly to the fact that after 1935 the OGPU, on Stalin's orders, began to work on military information and build up a military espionage organisation in this country. The chief objective of Stalin's espionage during these years was details regarding the mechanisation of the Army.

Passports for illegal rezident or visiting agents

Although the Fourth Department in Moscow were able to produce perfectly forged passports of any country it was much preferred that espionage agents should travel on genuine passports procured, if necessary, by means of forged documents of identity.

Up to 1928 or 1929 Soviet agents usually travelled on Austrian, German or Danish passports. At one time genuine Austrian passports were easily obtainable in Austria. To obtain the issue of a legal Austrian passport a certificate of domicile was more important than a birth certificate. At one time the Fourth Department had as their agent the head of the local council of a small town in Austria. This man issued false certificates of domicile whenever required. A confederate in a nearby town issued false birth certificates if these were necessary. Sometime before 1934 both these men were arrested and the Department was obliged to use Moscow-made Austrian passports for the time being.

A foreign passport obtained by a Soviet agent never bears any indication that he has been in Russia. If for instance the agent is to come to the United Kingdom posing as an Austrian with an Austrian passport he will travel from Russia to Vienna on his Soviet passport and pick up his new passport in Vienna. He will then leave his Soviet passport at the Soviet Embassy or Legation for use on a return journey to Russia at a future date, or else give instructions that it shall be returned to Moscow until he indicates where he wishes it to be sent for his return journey.

About 1928–1929 it was discovered how easily American and Canadian passports could be obtained, and they came into very frequent use both for Foreign Department and OGPU agents. Krivitsky explained that anyone could pass as a citizen of the USA who could speak a little English, and the same applied to French Canadian passports so long as the agent in question could speak French.

Krivitsky states most emphatically that he had never known a Soviet agent to travel on a passport of the United Kingdom, nor did the Fourth Department ever ask for a United Kingdom passport to be forged in Moscow. None of the officers of the Fourth Department knew English sufficiently, or enough about this country to use an English passport without incurring enquiries or suspicion.

Cover for illegal rezident agents

It sometimes happened that a senior staff officer or an officer of the second class of agent might be an expert in some matters outside his military capacity, or have, such as Krivitsky at The Hague, an opportunity to pose as such. In these cases permission for residence in the United Kingdom could be obtained on these grounds.

Most frequently some form of business cover would have to be arranged. Sometimes a firm was actually created for a particular purpose and sometimes it was possible to arrange through an intermediary that the intended agent should come to this country as the representative of some genuine and important Continental firm. In these latter cases the firm would probably be quite unaware of the true character of their representative.

A highly important firm called Wostwag or the Eastern Trading Company, was created by the Fourth Department in Berlin in 1922. It provided a genuine business cover for a large number of Fourth Department agents. The principal business of the firm was the sale of Russian produce in Germany. The business was passed to them through the Soviet Trade Delegation in Berlin. In one year the firm made over a million roubles profit. As Krivitsky points out this profit was merely the putting of money from one Soviet pocket to another. Nevertheless the proceeds of Wostwag trading were retained by the Fourth Department to augment their espionage and internal disruption grants.

Two junior staff officers of the Fourth Department, the brothers Abraham and Aaron Ehrenlieb, were put in charge of the organisation and espionage side of the firm. They were of Polish origin naturalised Austrians. The business side of Wostwag, and later its various branches was in the hands of an old Bolshevik – a Latvian – a personal friend of General Berzin. He travelled a good deal with a speculant agent – Leo Katz – a Romanian. Leo Katz visited this country at some time in connection with the affairs of the firm. (He must not be confused with a Hungarian, an OGPU agent, of the same name.)

About 1925 or 1926 the Fourth Department suspected that the activities of the firm had become known to the German police. They decided to withdraw the Ehrenlieb brothers and other members of the Russian General Staff and let the firm continue purely commercial activities under a speculant agent called Zloczower. A man called Stuchka also worked in connection with Wostwag and its affiliated companies.

After their recall from Berlin the brothers Ehrenlieb worked for a time in the Fourth Department. Both men were first class accountants and managed the accounts of the Fourth Department in the second section. After a time Abraham Ehrenlieb was sent to Tientsin where he founded and built up a very important firm – the Far Eastern Trading Co. The profits were retained for their work in China by the Fourth Department, and were a useful source of foreign currency. Incidentally Abraham managed to inspire sufficient confidence in Tietsin to be appointed president of the Austrian Chamber of Commerce there. Later Adam Purpis, a Lett, who travelled on a Honduras passport became head of the Tientsin firm. He passed through London in 1937 or 1938, but probably only in transit to Russia from some other Western European country. Soviet ships sailed regularly to Leningrad from Hay's Wharf, London, and the Fourth Department frequently used this means of returning agents to Moscow.

The other brother Aaron was sent to Urga, the Soviet colony in Outer Mongolia. In 1935 he was recalled to Moscow with the idea that he should go to the American branch of Wostwag. The firm in the USA became very active and a lot of material can be obtained from the American authorities. This plan fell through owing to the difficulty of obtaining an American visa. It was decided, in 1936, to send him to London where an affiliated company of Wostwag, known as the Far Eastern Fur Trading Company was formed in February 1936.

The Far Eastern Fur Trading Company is properly registered in the United Kingdom and is staffed by commercial men carrying on legitimate business. Certain members of the staff however devote a proportion of their time to

Fourth Department work. Zloczower was in London working for a time with Ehrenlieb and during the Spanish war Krivitsky sent a man called Samuel Hockstedt or Hochstedt to meet Ehrenlieb in London and the two worked together in the export of arms from Sweden to Spain. Stutchka, at that time in Paris, was also involved in these deals. Samuel Hochstedt is now in the USA.

Incidentally, Krivitsky is of the opinion that both Zloczower and Katz could be bullied or cajoled into acting as double-cross agents for the British. He always considered Katz more trustworthy than Zloczower but neither of these men have any strong political beliefs and money counts for a great deal with them. A threat to make it impossible for them to live in any Western European country and thus force them to return to the Soviet Union would, he thinks, make either of them disclose all he knew.

Krivitsky does not know Rubin Clucksmann, the present chief of the Far Eastern Fur Trading Company in London, but is certain he is a Fourth Department man. He believes that he is not an Austrian and that his passport is Moscow made. Krivitsky regards it as highly important that a thorough investigation should be made into the whole personnel of the Far Eastern Fur Trading Company, although it is possible that Clucksmann himself is actually still under training and held in reserve for more active work at a later stage. This is the usual procedure for newly appointed heads of companies established by the Fourth Department.

In regard to the creation of the firm, Krivitsky feels sure that the solicitor – Herbert Oppenheimer – would not have been used accidentally for the legal formalities. Something must already have been known about him in the Fourth Department. Krivitsky believes that he actually met him in Paris in connection with arms deals for Spain.

A firm established by the Fourth Department in Paris was a firm for the Importation of Legumes Secs in the Rue de Neuilly. The firm was founded by a Fourth Department man called Eisenberg who in 1928 was working in a private firm in Danzig. A most important senior staff officer of the Fourth Department who had a false American passport in the name of Kleges or Klages subsequently became head of the firm. His real name can probably be ascertained as he was acting as Second Consul in the Soviet Legation in Prague in 1927/28. The firm is still operating although the entire staff was changed in 1938.

Methods of work

When a legal or illegal *rezident* agent merely goes to a country to take over from a predecessor his task is comparatively easy, but when he has to create an organisation, the position becomes much more complicated. In such cases when the agent has been chosen and a suitable cover or place at the Embassy arranged, it is still necessary that he should become personally known or receive a special introduction to a senior official of the Communist Party of the country in which he is to work.

During Krivitsky's service this was usually arranged personally between General Berzin, head of the Fourth Department, and Piatnitsky, head of the OMS (*Otdyel Mezhdunarodnoi Svyazi*), the Foreign Liaison Department of the Comintern. As regards the United Kingdom an opportunity was usually taken to introduce prospective agents to senior members of the Executive Committee of the Communist Party of Great Britain who might be visiting the Soviet Union. Harry Pollitt and Willie Gallacher were frequently used in this way. It would always be arranged that each chief Fourth Department agent should have a specially tried and trusted member of the Communist Party put at his disposal. The *rezident* embassy agent has probably only a man earmarked whom he can use when necessary, but he has his own special man, and not a Party member already working for the OGPU legal *rezident*. The OGPU Embassy agent is always a thorn in the side of the Fourth Department legal *rezident*. There is sharp friction between the two. Material and visitors to the Embassy are frequently withheld from the Fourth Department agent in favour of the OGPU *rezident*. The position has become still more difficult since the GUGB began to control the *Razvedupr* in 1935.

When a chief illegal agent of the third section of the Fourth Department starts work in the United Kingdom, a picked member of the Communist Party is put entirely at his disposal. He is usually not a manual labourer, but a man of the clerical type. It sometimes happens that the best man that can be obtained is already an important Communist Party organiser, but any objections to his release are always overruled on the grounds that intelligence work takes precedence over purely Party matters. The selected Communist Party member drops all his political work and is gradually trained by the Fourth Department agent. The period of training lasts six months or more, during which time the man is instructed to make contacts wherever possible but on no account to attempt to obtain any secret information. In order to keep him fully occupied during his period of training he is sent to public libraries to obtain information on industrial and economic questions. He looks up trade directories and visits industrial districts to gain information as to the numbers of factories turning out military material and if possible full details about them.

The Fourth Department illegal *rezident* invariably employs a woman through whom he maintains contact with his colleague in the Embassy. This woman is often a German or Austrian here in the guise of a student and it is her sole work to act as intermediary between him and the woman 'runner' for the Fourth Department agent in the Embassy.

After about six months when the illegal *rezident* has thoroughly established himself in this country and trained his assistants, he begins to work. He meets people useful for his purpose in different walks of life and gains their confidence. For instance, as the Soviet Government are always particularly interested to receive confidential maps, the illegal *resident* tries to cultivate a man in a map-making establishment. He finds out his private circumstances, gives him presents and subsequently money, and eventually recruits him as a sub-agent. Russian made maps are very bad and always have been. The best maps in the possession of the Mobilisation Department of the Soviet Army are British. Krivitsky could not remember the name of department, but he said that about 1930 the Fourth Department had an agent in a department or institute which made military maps, and from this source the Soviet obtained a large number of maps made from aerial photographs.

Through his Communist Party assistant the Fourth Department agent gradu-ally recruits as agents workmen and technicians in important factories. Details regarding these workmen and technicians are checked up by the Communist Party. Later plans are brought out of the works and photographed. Plans are never stolen; the originals are always replaced. The Fourth Department would have a photographic studio installed either at the back of a small shop or in a house. Material from a distance is brought up over a weekend, or if this is not possible, a Leica camera is used on the spot.

The Fourth Department agent is himself always an expert photographer. Someone carefully trained by him would be sent to a distant town with a small suitcase containing everything he could want for photographing documents. This portable suitcase was frequently used and after several failures had been experienced with small makes, always a Leica camera.

Although as a general rule the Fourth Department agent arranged for his own photography, there were occasions when the plan or document was taken to the Soviet Embassy to be photographed. Krivitsky recalls an instance when he was at The Hague and managed to obtain for a very short time a large and highly important plan of a French submarine. He could only retain the plan for a short time, not long enough to make trial photographs on his own apparatus. He therefore took it to the Soviet Legation who had a much larger and permanently erected apparatus and where moreover there could be no risk of molestation.

Methods of communication: Communications to and from Moscow

1. Soviet embassies and legations

The normal method of communication on illegal matters between foreign countries and Moscow is through the Soviet Embassy or Legation of the country in which the illegal work is in progress.

All documents and plans obtained by illegal means are photographed and the negatives sent to the Fourth Department Embassy agent in a sealed packet for transmission unopened to the third section of the Fourth Department in Moscow. No important Soviet espionage agent ever leaves the United King-dom carrying the fruits of his espionage activities or reports on his organisation.

Krivitsky wrote his reports by hand, photographed them and forwarded them to Moscow through the Soviet Embassy in Paris. He says that, although they are not used in peace time, the Soviets have attaché cases and containers for the transport of films which are fitted with an igniting arrangement so that if the container is opened in ignorance of the correct method, it catches fire and the contents are destroyed. Containers can also be arranged for self-destruction by acid if inexpertly opened.

2. Secret inks

Secret inks are never used by the *Razvedupr* except in countries where there is no Soviet Embassy or Legation, or where an agent is in a district too remote from the Soviet diplomatic representative to make use of his services. When, much earlier in his career, Krivitsky was stationed in Vienna for the purpose of running a military espionage organisation in Romania, he relied very largely on secret inks. There was no Soviet Legation in Romania at that time and it was the only safe method of communication. The secret inks he sent to his agents were usually in the form of powders, but he himself received what he called recipes from Moscow, bought the ingredients from local pharmacies and made up the powders according to the recipes. A large number of different recipes were always available in the Fourth Department.

3. Ships' crews

In 1920 the Military Intelligence began to organise a courier system through members of ships' companies in order to ensure a method of communication with countries which might be at war with the Soviet Union and consequently no longer have a Soviet Embassy or Legation. A specialist was sent from Moscow to Hamburg to work out a courier system between a variety of countries. A man was also sent to each important European port to recruit suitable personnel. In the early stages of this work valuable help was obtained from Edo Fimmen at that time in charge of the Seamen and Transport Workers Union in Hamburg.

During the years 1926–1937 the Fourth Department recruited about two hundred agents on ships plying between a number of European and American ports. Agents were established at each of these ports to deal with the reception and despatch of material. Krivitsky thinks that some of the Fourth Department agents who visited the United Kingdom between 1935 and 1937 may have used one or two of these agents to transmit material but he is more inclined to think that the system had not been put into actual operation at any rate up to the outbreak of the present war. The period from 1926 was spent in testing the system and personnel. Dummy packages of newspapers and other unimportant documents were constantly despatched from port to port to test the reliability and resource of recruited personnel. The work of the bearers of these packages was carefully watched and recorded. Out of the two hundred originally recruited Krivitsky says that some twenty or thirty were found to be sufficiently reliable to be used as couriers in case of need. Of these a fair proportion were capable of use as general agents as well as couriers. He has no doubt that some of these men will now be allocated to ships plying to and from the United Kingdom.

4. Wireless

The Fourth Department have never been satisfied with their wireless apparatus although their gear was considerably better than that of the OGPU, who were severely reprimanded in 1937 for the poorness of their equipment. Military Intelligence stations existed in various countries of South Eastern Europe as well as in Switzerland and Germany. In Vienna a group of Soviet officers were arrested with a wireless transmitter. The department has good gear which was used with much success in the Chinese war, but the apparatus is cumbersome and inconvenient for use in built up areas. Sometime before 1937 some preparatory work was done to set up a radio station for the Fourth Department in the United Kingdom but Krivitsky does not think it ever functioned for practical purposes.

In 1937 Krivitsky was provided with a small portable set of a type which could be built into a car. The set worked well if an aerial of about twenty yards in length was thrown over a branch of a tree, but was never satisfactory if the aerial was wound round the car. Krivitsky experimented with the set round Paris but never used it for practical purposes. He mentioned that in wireless messages transmitted by the Fourth Department to their stations abroad he was referred to as 'Valentine'.

Communications between agents working within a foreign country

As has already been mentioned communication between 'illegal' military espionage agents and their 'legal' colleague in the Embassy is almost invariably maintained through a woman agent working for the illegal *rezident* and the woman secretary or wife of the legal *rezident*. There might even be a third or fourth intermediary between the two women. Illegal agents themselves never visit the Embassy and only in cases of greatest necessity do they have any contact with the legal *rezident*.

The illegal *rezident* maintains contact with his sub-agents through a system of messages left at reliable addresses where safes are usually installed. Each principal sub-agent has a different address at which he, or more probably his wife or a woman friend, leaves messages or material for his chief. The illegal *rezident* never visits these addresses himself but employs one or more women to collect material from the addresses at regular intervals. Only in the most urgent cases is a sub-agent allowed to communicate by telephone with his chief. Most Fourth

Department men arrange with each of their principal sub-agents a definite time and place where they can be found if serious need arises.

Communications through the post are always discouraged but sometimes inevitable. Letters are always written in accordance with a prearranged code. Meeting places are settled in advance and never mentioned. Times of meetings are most carefully disguised. For instance if a correspondent says he bought a book in the morning for 10/6, this would read as 10.30 a.m. but there is always a previous arrangement to subtract or add a number of hours to the time stated.

Krivitsky says that Fourth Department agents are so well trained in the technique of throwing off possible watchers that it is extremely difficult if not impossible to link up an organisation by observation methods. In Paris he always instructed agents to take taxis wherever possible. However, he added that when an important sub-agent is first recruited then satisfactory results may be obtained by keeping him under observation. For instance, a young man, new to espionage and nervous is not given full directions for evading observation in the first month or so that he is working. The greatest care is taken not to impress upon a new recruit the danger of his position. As time goes on and the recruit becomes more hardened he is given the fullest instructions.

Instructions to agents

Instructions as to the material to be collected by Razvedupr agents abroad are forwarded by the Fourth Department through the Soviet Embassy or Legation in the country in which he is working. Instructions take the form of questionnaires which are always compiled in the third section of the Fourth Department. Questionnaires are always regarded as highly secret and are only sent to senior staff officers who memorise them and hand them through an intermediary to the Soviet Embassy where the Fourth Department agents – legal and illegal – each have their own safe.

When a senior staff officer is first appointed to his post he is sent a general questionnaires which usually covers work for a year ahead. After six months this is elaborated and followed up three months later in greater detail and with a number of special instructions concerning current work.

Payment of agents

Money for the payment of Soviet Intelligence organizations abroad is sent in bundles of Bank of England notes direct from Moscow to the Embassy of the country in which the agents are working. As Krivitsky was frequently in Paris his money was usually sent to the Soviet Embassy there whence, if necessary, it was sent by courier to Holland.

The counteracting of Soviet espionage in the United Kingdom

In Krivitsky's opinion there are only two methods effectually to counteract the work of Soviet espionage agents.

The first method is the one adopted by the British Intelligence Service in the case of the girl who betrayed Percy Glading's organisation: that is, 'to grow up agents from the inside'. This method had a great disadvantage in that results might not be obtained for a number of years, but it was regularly used by Soviet intelligence services abroad. Krivitsky mentioned that the Fourth Department was prepared in some instances to wait for ten or fifteen years for results and in some cases paid the expenses of a university education for promising young men in the hope that they might eventually obtain diplomatic posts or other key positions in the service of the country of which they were nationals.

The second method is by bribery of known Soviet agents. This is a much easier method at present than it has been in the past when the political ideals of servants of the Soviet Union amounted to a fierce fanaticism. Since 1937 it can be assumed that all those who held the old Bolshevik faith will have been eliminated from important positions in the Soviet Intelligence Services and Embassies abroad. New people will occupy the posts and will have no strong political faith. The method of approach must be most carefully thought out in each individual case but there is one basis which will appeal to all. Every Russian, day and night, is beset by the ever-present idea of fear. The only way to approach a Russian working for the Soviet Government is to present him with a plan to eliminate this fear. Such a plan would necessarily involve providing him with protection and a means to live outside Soviet Russia.

Section 3. Colonial work of the Fourth Department

The Soviet Politburo and General Staff have always been intensely anxious to keep abreast of the colonial problems of Great Britain. Stalin has a complete misconception of the British Empire, and regards the full measure of self-government accorded to the Dominions as a sign of weakness. He is convinced that the Achilles Heel of Great Britain is in the Near East and India, and takes a profound personal interest in all records dealing therewith.

A special sub-section of the third section of the Fourth Department is charged with the function of studying the colonial question. Stalin himself appointed a man called Schipoff to this section to collate colonial reports for his consideration. Schipoff was succeeded by one Marcovitch whose work was regarded of much importance.

The colonial section concentrates on the Near and Far East. The most detailed summaries are made of all information necessary for the General Staff in studying these countries from a military point of view, particularly in connection with British vulnerability in the Near East. Everything appears in these summaries; movements of troops, conditions of natives, religious questions and economic questions. Krivitsky remembers seeing about 1929 when there were Arab uprisings, a most detailed summary of the situation in Arabia prepared for the Russian General Staff. This summary and indeed all the Near East summaries presented a very pessimistic picture of the situation from the point of view of Great Britain.

Other reports of a like pessimistic nature regarding the British position in the Near East reached Stalin through Nikonov. Nikonov was an expert on the Near East, knew Arabic and other eastern languages and was head of the VNO, the Military Scientific Society. This Society though not part of the Fourth Department worked closely with it. Many of the summaries compiled by the third section were submitted to Nikonov for his consideration and frequent debates and meetings with members of the Fourth Department were based thereon.

The third section of the Fourth Department receive first class information as regards Palestine, Egypt and the Near East. The Suez Canal is regarded by Stalin as a most vulnerable area for Great Britain and there are always Fourth Department as well as OGPU agents concentrated there.

They had their own special schools for the training of agents for colonial work. Pupils took a three or four months' course. There was a special course for Armenian, Georgian and Turkist agents. Russians who could speak Persian were largely employed, as also Rumanians, Greeks and Cypriots – in fact all those nationals who could live and have legitimate business in the Near East.

From 1921 to 1923 a large number of agents employed in the Near East were Italians, refugees from Fascist Italy. They were found eminently suitable for the work and produced excellent reports. About 1936–1937 however ninety percent of Italians *rezident* in Russia were 'purged' so that it is hardly likely that Italians are still employed. Krivitsky thinks that Rumanians are now largely employed and that since the Spanish war a number of Spaniards will have been trained for work in the Near East.

Correspondents of French left wing and other papers are used to provide Near East information. A Fourth Department man posing as a newspaper correspondent approaches, for instance, in Athens a genuine newspaper correspondent who would like to go to Arabia, but has not the necessary funds. Money is provided by the Fourth Department man who sometimes persuades the man to work as a regular Fourth Department agent.

Most of the information from the Near East is obtained from agents on the spot, but at one time a good deal was obtained by tapping a British source in Constantinople. At one time also much of the material in regard to the Near East consisted of Colonial Office instructions to their officers abroad, and Krivitsky thinks that those may have been obtained from Colonial Office contacts in London.

Sometime between 1921 and 1929 the third section had what they considered a most valuable agent for British Colonial matters who was a member of the staff of the Japanese Embassy in Berlin. His name was Petroff – agent No. 401 – a White Russian. No. 401 was much relied upon as a source of information on British colonial problems. He not only had access to Japanese sources but himself wrote reports on the subject. He would never disclose his source. After some time Krivitsky, who regularly read translations of articles by 'Augur' in the Times began to notice similarities not of wording but in the matter contained in the reports. Krivitsky informed General Berzin of his suspicions that No. 401 was either in touch with 'Augur', or rewriting his articles for Soviet consumption. General Berzin ordered Krivitsky to speak to No. 401 on the subject: this was done. Petroff denied any association whatever with 'Augur' or reliance upon his articles, but confidence in No. 401 was thereafter badly shaken.

When the news of the death of Lawrence of Arabia reached Moscow, it was treated sceptically, and considered as a manoeuvre connected with contemporary events in the Near East. Krivitsky himself was convinced that Lawrence was still alive and wrote an article on the subject in Pravda entitled 'Lawrence died and was resurrected'. While on this subject Krivitsky mentioned that he had at one time hoped that the young man whom he had transferred to the OGPU for work in Rome (see section below on 'The British Embassy Source in Rome') would become Lawrence of the Fourth Department. He was a genuine archaeologist, spoke Arabic well and had a life long ambition to work in Arabia. Krivitsky thought his time in Rome would give him additional opportunities to study archaeology which would be valuable if it was later found possible to employ him for work in Arabia.

India

The work of the Military Intelligence agents in India is regarded as one of the failures of the Fourth Department. The third section tried very hard between 1926 and 1928 to form an efficient organisation but never achieved any good results from agents inside India, chiefly because they could not penetrate official circles there. They were obliged therefore to fall back on native informants whom they recruited from a number of Indians who had been students in Berlin. The third section had no professors of their own capable of training these men and were obliged to enlist outside aid for the purpose. Few of the students proved of any value. A number of natives associated with Roy were Fourth Department agents as also for a time Chattopadhaya. Krivitsky himself interviewed Chattopadhaya and had great hopes of him, but after a time he was suspected of employment in the German service and was dropped. Roy's wife Louisa Scheller was at one time an informant of Krivitsky's, but Roy parted with her and subsequently married Ellen Gottschalk.

The Fourth Department have not sent Russians to India for the last seventeen years. German communists were sometimes enlisted and occasionally produced useful material.

Unlike the OGPU agents, however, local Fourth Department men were on the whole of little use. On the other hand excellent information was obtained from London, Singapore and Shanghai. Moreover the Moscow headquarters of the OGPU passed on to the Fourth Department a good deal of useful information collected by local Comintern agents.

Shanghai was a regular meeting place for Fourth Department agents in the Far East. Agnes Smedley made her headquarters there and although she was strictly an OGPU agent, she was also closely in touch with the Fourth Department agent there and considered a very useful source. She was not paid for her work.

In 1935 the Fourth Department compiled a book on India for the use of the Russian General Staff. The Department was immensely proud of this book and claimed that it contained everything about India that it was necessary for the commander of a military campaign against India to know. Most of the information was obtained from the libraries and books of reference in London, but a large proportion was secret material including details of the Singapore naval base. The secret material was obtained from Shanghai.

Incidentally Krivitsky mentioned that the Politburo were always particularly anxious to win Gandhi over to the Soviet point of view. For this purpose Radek sent picked men from the *Narkomindel* (Foreign Office) to see what they could do. They failed entirely to enlist his sympathy. Later when Gandhi was in Europe another attempt was made through a French intellectual communist – Krivitsky believes it was Henri Barbusse – but again the attempt failed.

The Dominions

The Fourth Department are not really interested in the Dominions. They are too remote to be of interest from a military point of view. In 1932 the Fourth Department had a man in Sydney, Australia, but he was there as part of the Shanghai organisation. Apart from economic questions the Fourth Department were only interested as regards Australia in collating material which would tend to show whether or not Australia would make a move for complete independence from the British Empire.

Canada was regarded more or less as part of the United States. The Fourth Department had a man there but purely for technical reasons such as the obtaining of false Canadian passports.

Ireland

Ireland, like the Dominions, has up to the time of the present war appeared too remote from a possible military situation affecting the Soviet Union to have been the subject of special attention. Krivitsky believes that from 1927 or 1928 up to the time of his break with the Soviet Intelligence Service in 1937 neither the Military Intelligence Department nor the OGPU had any connection whatever with the IRA as a political body, although individual members may have been recruited as intelligence agents for special purposes.

Sometime about 1926 the IRA sent representatives to Moscow to ask for Soviet support for their organisation. Krivitsky recalls meeting them there and the mirth caused by the military titles they assumed. The Politburo refused assistance because of their anxiety not to offend the British Government as well as the impossibility of supporting the nationalistic aspirations of the IRA at the same time as the international activities of the Irish Communist Party.

Later, Krivitsky met three officers of the IRA in Holland. He cannot remember their names but thinks the date was early in 1927. He departed from his usual practice of handing over agents other than those who were to work in Germany to his assistant Max Unschlicht and dealt with them himself. He worked them purely as intelligence agents and for a time got quite useful information out of them, at the same time experiencing difficulty in evading attempts to interest him in the terrorist activities of their organisation. After a short time the Politburo temporarily forbade any dealings with the Irish in order to avoid possible prejudice to their attempts to obtain credits in London. When the ban was lifted Krivitsky got into touch with his IRA contacts again but after a while they made definite suggestions for collaboration in a terrorist plan. Krivitsky then decided to sacrifice their information rather than risk political repercussions from associating himself with activities in which he was not interested.

Since then he believes that up to the present time there has been no connection whatever between the Soviet Union and the Irish as a political body. Irishmen have been and will continue to be recruited as individuals when occasion arises. If the OGPU or Military Intelligence find it necessary to recruit an agent in a particular place, their first recruiting ground is the Communist Party: if that fails they invariably try and seek out an Irishman who would make a good agent. This practice is based purely on the hypothesis that an Irishman would probably be anti-British and can more easily be persuaded to work for a foreign power than an Englishman.

Section 4. Decomposition work of the Military Intelligence Department

By decomposition work of the Military Intelligence Department is meant the creation of situations and organisations in foreign countries to provide favourable military factors for the Soviet Union in case of need.

This was mainly the work of the third section and tackled most seriously in countries bordering on the Soviet Union or with which there was some probability that a state of war with Russia might at some time exist.

Krivitsky was for many years in charge of decomposition work as well as military espionage directed against Germany. He was convinced that in a state of war between the Soviet Union and Germany a good sabotage system would be of infinitely more value than a vast network of subordinate espionage agents. He explained that it was obviously of more value to an invading or retreating army to destroy the munition depots of the enemy by sabotage than to obtain details of their location, contents and personnel for the Military Intelligence Department. He seems to have organised his work so that a proportion of agents used for espionage in time of peace could be utilised for acts of sabotage in time of war. As he maintained the closest personal contact with his organisation in Germany he is quite sure that since his break with Stalin in 1937 the whole of his organisation in Germany will have been liquidated. He thinks it probable that the OGPU will have taken charge of any work that is being carried on there now.

As regards Poland, the Soviet Government had always maintained decomposition work at a very high level and had utilised both the Fourth Department and the OGPU for this purpose. Everything possible had been done before the outbreak of the present war to prepare organised assistance from within for an invading Russian army. Both Fourth Department and OGPU had agents working in key positions in Government departments. Over a period of years large numbers of Polish communists had been drafted into the Polish Army to prepare for just the eventuality which ultimately arose. Poland was not specifically mentioned but Krivitsky stated that it was the duty of the Fourth Department, in countries bordering on Soviet Russia, to organise groups of communists to act under the orders of specially trained Russian Army parachutists who, in the event of war, might be dropped behind the enemy lines to act in accordance with a prearranged plan.

In August 1936 during the Spanish War Krivitsky was ordered to arrange for the rapid supply of munitions of war to Government Spain. The work had to be done with the utmost despatch and secrecy, and he was supplied with large numbers of additional staff both by the Fourth Department and the OGPU. The methods by which he carried out his orders and the personnel he employed are already recorded in his book and will not be repeated here.

An important agent recruited for this particular purpose by the OGPU was one Weissblatt of Aero Marine Engines Ltd. Weissblatt was employed by the Fourth Department to obtain the necessary export licences for arms for Spain, particularly from the French Government. He had personal friends at the head of most French Government Departments. A man like Weissblatt, however, would only rank as a speculant agent and would be dropped by the Fourth Department as soon as he had served his purpose. He might of course be used from time to time by the OGPU who know of his arms deals and would not hesitate to bring pressure to bear upon him.

When Krivitsky received orders from the Fourth Department to concentrate on the shipment of arms to Spain he employed a number of his own Fourth Department agents on this work although he knew that they would probably become known to Foreign Governments and therefore be useless for further work in Western Europe. He thought the sacrifice well worth while in view of the large number of new contacts they would make in the course of their work. These contacts who pocketed a lot of easy money at that time might prove useful to the Soviet Intelligence Services at a later stage when they had spent the money but still had the guilty knowledge that they had done something 'which was not quite all right'.

As regards the United Kingdom, so far as could be ascertained decomposition work appears to have been confined chiefly to attempts at penetration of the British Armed Forces and the probable organisation of a system of sabotage to meet the eventuality of a war with the Soviet Union. (See sections below on 'Sabotage' and 'Decomposition Work in the Army'.) In this connection Krivitsky was asked his views on the erection in [blank] of a chain of R.O.P. oil storage depots throughout the United Kingdom. He said he believed that the R.O.P. depots in the United Kingdom were built for the sole purpose of procuring foreign currency to finance the purchase of machinery and equipment required for the industrialization of Russia. Neither oil nor any other commodity exported from Russia was handled on normal business lines. Because a business such as Russian Oil Products was run at a loss it could not be said that it necessarily existed for some purpose other than the sale of oil. On the other hand when such an organisation as R.O.P. was set up in a foreign country the GUGB and Military Intelligence Department would both be informed as a matter of routine in order that, if they wished, they might take advantage of its personnel, sales organisation or depots.

In the event of war with the Soviet Union it is quite possible that R.O.P. storage depots might form part of a scheme for setting fire to adjacent oil supplies, railway sidings, docks and waterways.

CHAPTER TWO
THE GUGB AND OGPU

Section 1. General organisation

'The Secret Service will save the Government'. Those were Stalin's words in the Spring of 1937. They expressed his long rooted conviction that on the shoulders of the Security Service rests the safety of the Soviet State.

This is the explanation of the undoubted fact that the whole machinery of government in the USSR is designed to give the servants of the Security Service the maximum of assistance and authority.

The headquarters organisation of the Security Service in Moscow is known as the G.U.G.B. – that is the Department of State Security of the Home Office. The Russian title of the Home Office is NKVD (*Narodny Kommissariat Vnutrennich Dell*).

The staff of the GUGB is known as the OGPU. The operations department of the G.U.G.B. is known as the Operod. It is divided into three sections; the INO, or foreign department; the Osobiotdel, the department for counter-espionage within the USSR; and the dreaded Spetsotdel which deals with espionage and disciplinary matters directed against Soviet officials and Party members. Each of these sections had its own chief, but in May 1937 when Krivitsky was in Moscow, there was a plan on foot to amalgamate the departments under one chief.

The new department was to be known as the KRO or counter-intelligence department. Up to that time a case taken up by the Osobiotdel or Spetsotdel which had ramifications extending beyond the Soviet frontiers, had to be transferred for further investigation to the INO, a totally different department. This practice led to friction and delay. It was felt that a combination of the three departments under one chief would lead to greater secrecy and efficiency. Krivitsky does not know whether the new plan has been adopted but if it has he thinks that there will be a *rezident* representative of the KRO as well as the INO in foreign countries. The INO is the department which sends OGPU agents abroad. Up to 1937 the OGPU representatives collected information concerning the country to which they were sent and also reported on Soviet officials and Party members in those countries. If the departments have been amalgamated as proposed in 1937 then the latter duties will fall upon the KRO representative.

The head of the INO of the GUGB subdivides his work among his head assistants each of whom has under him a section dealing with a particular foreign country. Unlike the Fourth Department each section not only gives instructions to its agents abroad and receives the results of their work, but digests all its own material and makes its own summaries. The head of each section has under his care its organisation, the signing of material, the remitting of necessary funds and is generally responsible to the departmental chief. Each section trains its own representatives before they are sent abroad. The representative works and studies in the section for periods which may vary from fourteen days to six months. The head of the INO of the GUGB in 1934 was A.C. Artusov.

While Krivitsky was still in the service the head of the British section of the INO was a man called Reiff who had been the representative of the OGPU in England from 1931 to 1934. The chief of the German section was a Hungarian called Silly. He was arrested in May 1937.

The first section of the GUGB or Security Service was the passport section. The section did not deal with the issue of passports or forged passports, but the passport of every Soviet citizen who was given permission to leave Russia was scrutinised by this section before he went. This practice enabled the OGPU to make enquiries as to all Soviet citizens visiting foreign countries and to select those suitable to act as OGPU agents while they were abroad.

The OGPU were always particularly interested in the personnel of Soviet Government purchasing commissions visiting foreign countries. From 1923 to 1925 visiting commissions were chosen exclusively by the OGPU. Later some difficulty was experienced in explaining the numbers of members composing such commissions. Visiting trade delegations and purchasing commissions are always used for intelligence purposes, but latterly the delegates themselves have not been chosen by the OGPU. The OGPU have to choose their agents from among the delegation or commission already appointed. The chosen members take a short course of instruction on the particular work they are to carry out during their visit.

There exists a working arrangement between this section and the Fourth Department that any engineers, technicians or personnel visiting the United Kingdom for the purchase of military or naval equipment should be handed over to the Fourth Department for a course of training in Military Intelligence before they leave. There is always friction because the Fourth Department complain that the OGPU do not hand over all the technicians that they should, but themselves train and use persons whose qualifications should according to the agreement have made them Military Intelligence agents. The OGPU insisted on retaining for instance engineers attached to Russian Trade Delegations abroad. These men are eminently suitable for the collection of military information, but the Fourth Department are given no opportunity to train them themselves before leaving Russia. They have to fall back upon the unsatisfactory method of sending them instructions through the legal *rezident* Fourth Department representative in the Soviet Embassy in the country of their destination.

There is never any argument about persons buying purely military or naval equipment. These are all trained by the Fourth Department before they leave and are most valuable, particularly the inspecting personnel attached to armament firms fulfilling orders for the Soviet Government. In addition to their instructions to gain a complete knowledge of the factories to which they have access, these inspectors are invariably instructed to find contacts in those factories through whom the Soviets can continue to obtain information after the inspectors themselves have left.

While Yagoda was head of the GUGB of OGPU, quite apart from the regular branches of the OGPU, there was a separate and very secret organisation responsible direct to Yagoda. Its exact ramifications and personnel were unknown to the members of the usual OGPU and Military Intelligence Services. From time to time men were withdrawn from their normal Security Service activities or official organisations and not seen again. It was presumed that these men were appointed to Yagoda's personal service. It is not known whether this special service exists under Yezhov, the present head of OGPU.

Section 2. Organisation of OGPU activities abroad

The framework of the OGPU organisation is much the same as that of the Razvedupr or Fourth Department. Up to 1934 OGPU representatives in the United Kingdom and other Western European countries were mainly concerned with the acquisition of political, economic and commercial information; the supervision of Soviet and local Communist Party organisations and personnel, and the penetration of anti-Soviet and White Russian societies. Military and naval information was obtained whenever opportunity offered, but up to 1934 it was not a primary objective. After 1934 the OGPU began to usurp the functions of the Fourth Department and on the direct order of Stalin deliberately created organisations for the illegal acquisition of military, naval and air force information. Material thus collected is not passed to Fourth Department representatives abroad but despatched direct to the I.N.O. (Foreign Department) of the OGPU in Moscow where friction promptly ensues with the Military and Naval authorities.

A typical instance occurred in May 1937. The Military Intelligence Department had been informed by I.N.O. of the OGPU that certain naval material of the utmost importance had been obtained from England. Orlov, head of the Russian Navy, must see it immediately. The material would be sent over to the Fourth Department for Orlov to see. Orlov duly arrived and waited for a long time but the naval information was not sent. It was an unheard of thing to keep Orlov waiting, and still more insulting when the OGPU finally refused to entrust the material to the Fourth Department and Orlov was obliged to go to the OGPU building and examine it there. This particular material was in the hands of Reiff, head of the English section of the INO of the OGPU. It had been obtained by Dr. Arnold Deutsch at that time a highly successful OGPU military and naval espionage agent operating in the United Kingdom.

Agents

Exactly in the same way as in the Fourth Department the directing personnel of OGPU activities abroad are divided into legal and illegal *rezidents*, but they are termed official and unofficial or underground representatives.

These representative are appointed by the head of the INO of the GUGB (State Security Service) in Moscow in conjunction with the head of that section of the INO which deals with the country concerned.

The official representative

The official representative has full diplomatic privileges and is a member of the official Embassy staff. The position he holds gives him sufficient status to make the necessary outside contacts and is arranged by agreement between the INO of the GUGB and the *Narkomindel* (Soviet Foreign Office). Frequently it is the

Second Secretary who is the OGPU *rezident*. While Krivitsky was still in the Soviet Service the OGPU *rezident* in the Soviet Embassy in London was Anton Schuster. He is inclined to think the present man might be Ivan Popoff.

His duties

The OGPU official representative seldom does any ordinary Embassy work. His first duty is to organise a miniature OGPU within the Embassy and arrange that he has informants in all its sections to report in detail on every member of the Embassy staff.

His second duty is to supervise the personal and official lives of members of the Soviet Trade Delegation working in the country to which he is accredited. He has therefore to arrange, through an assistant in the Trade Delegation, an OGPU Service within the Delegation. He also arranges to have agents in Soviet trading firms and any large concerns employing Russian personnel.

Russian Trade Delegations are important centres for OGPU activity. Persons who visit Delegations for the purpose of obtaining contracts with the Soviets are considered primarily in the light of potential agents for the collection of information. Each of such visitors is required to complete a questionnaire which is handed to the OGPU representative for his perusal. It is generally a sine qua non of a contract that the merchant or inventor or expert does something to assist the Soviets; often he is an unconscious agent, but bribery of businessmen is not infrequent. Krivitsky stated that he estimated that eight out of every ten fur merchants who deal with Russian Trade Delegations are conscious OGPU agents. Every British engineer or technician who visits Russia is the subject of special OGPU attention, and it can be taken as certain that four-fifths of these men eventually do some kind of work for the OGPU as the result of pressure of all kinds which is put upon them so soon as they reach the Soviet Union. Only in the last resort is blackmail used, more often they are got at through women or money.

Thirdly, the official representative must assist the underground representative in every possible way, but must not have direct contact with him. The contact procedure is approximately the same as that for the Fourth Department. He must arrange for the receipt and despatch of mail for his unofficial colleague; the ciphering and deciphering of his telegrams, and the provision of a separate safe where he can keep his instructions and questionnaires from Moscow. A thoroughly efficient photographic studio must be provided, which can be available for immediate use by the underground representative. Most of the work in connection with the underground representative is done through women employed in the Embassy. Krivitsky stated that each of the Attachés and men secretaries of the Attachés had women secretaries and clerks, and it was essential that they should be carefully watched. The secretaries, typists and cashiers have not diplomatic, but service passports, which are something between a diplomatic and an ordinary passport. The names and photographs of all persons of this type coming to the United Kingdom from Moscow can of course be obtained from the British Consul there.

The official representative is also responsible for the submission of detailed reports on the activities and personnel of White Russian organisations. For this purpose he employs a number of White Russian agents. Both he and the underground representative indulge freely in blackmail to recruit these men who are often unpaid but reimbursed for out-of-pocket expenses. White Russians abroad who have relations or friends in Soviet Russia know that OGPU agents hold influential positions in all Government departments in Moscow, and have unlimited powers over *rezidents* in the Soviet Union. Threats against relations and friends there can and will be carried out with the maximum severity. White Russians recruited by these blackmailing methods are never employed in key positions where a betrayal of trust could have serious consequences.

Lastly the official representative must maintain close but indirct contact with the local Communist Party. He has a special Communist Party assistant but is not allowed to have any dealings with him for several months after his arrival for fear of compromising the Embassy.

At one time all members of the Soviet Embassy were encouraged to collect information and indulge in any illegal or subversive activities useful to the Soviet Union. It was soon found that such activities were incompatible with their normal functions, and in 1922 they were drastically curtailed. However inter-departmental and diplomatic disputes continued to occur as the result of the free use of Soviet Embassies for the passing of money and documents connected with intelligence matters. Further curtailments took place in 1935 when this class of work was centred in the OGPU official representative.

The unofficial or underground representative

The OGPU unofficial representative functions in much the same way as the illegal Fourth Department *rezident*. He has his own complete organisation and does not in any way depend upon that of the Fourth Department *rezident*. In Western European countries he has a great deal more power than Fourth Department representatives ever had and employs a larger number of agents.

White Russian agents

Owing to the immense powers wielded by the OGPU in Soviet Russia the underground representative has always been in a position to compel White Russians to work for his organisation. Krivitsky is certain that now Stalin has openly embarked on a nationalist policy of military aggrandisement such compulsion of White Russians to work for the Soviet Union will no longer be necessary. The Russian nationalist spirit is strong and White Russians will work as military intelligence agents now that the Soviet Union is engaged on a policy of military conquest. Stalin's domination of the Baltic States will appeal to every Russian whatever his political faith may have been. During one of his latter visits to Moscow Krivitsky was discussing with the OGPU chief, Yezhov, purges that had already taken place amongst Soviet underground agents abroad, and the question of replacements. Yezhov said quite seriously that the Soviets would always have a large reserve of good agents all over the world because they could now begin to utilise White Russians who after all were Russians.

In the late summer of 1937 an incident occurred in Paris which seemed to show that the policy of co-operation with White Russians abroad was already in course of preparation. Spiegelglass, assistant chief of the INO of the OGPU was in Paris, and took immense trouble to bring about a quiet meeting in a Paris café between the OGPU *rezident* in the Soviet Embassy, then Count Ignatiev, the head of the White Russian Club in Paris, and the head of the Russian Young Fascist organisation there. Krivitsky remarked that a meeting between Count Ignatiev and the head of the Russian Young Fascist organisation was not significant in that the latter was in any case an OGPU agent, but the presence of the head of the White Russian Club was extremely significant, particularly as although the facts leaked out and were exposed in the Russian Monarchist paper in Paris, he was not obliged to resign from the Presidency of the Club.

Spiegelglass could not help boasting to Krivitsky that he had arranged the meeting, but as the two men were on bad terms at the time Krivitsky could not question him on its purpose or results.

Cover for underground OGPU agents

Certain important OGPU agents such as Henri Christian Pieck were able to visit this country freely using their professional or artistic reputations as a genuine cover. Pieck who paid regular visits to London from The Hague from January 1935 to November 1937, was a decorative artist and cartoonist; he was a cultured man well known in artistic and literary circles, and had no difficulty in explaining his frequent presence here. The OGPU have much less difficulty in finding suitable agents for the United Kingdom as, unlike the Fourth Department, they are not confined to a particular caste to fill their most responsible posts. Nevertheless in many cases it is essential that a business cover should be provided. For this purpose the OGPU create firms to carry on genuine business in exactly the same way as the Fourth Department.

A firm so created was that of GADA in April 1933 in Amsterdam. At this time the *rezident* OGPU agent in the Soviet Embassy in London had an uncle in Poland – Bernard DAWIDOWICZ – who had some knowledge of the Polish import trade in rags and waste paper. DAWIDOWICZ was sent by the OGPU in Amsterdam to found the firm of GADA which would appoint representatives to work in London in connection with the export of rags to Poland.

The sole purpose of this manoeuvre was to provide a genuine business cover for an OGPU agent in London, who was here charged with the sole mission of 'looking after' a clerk in the cipher department of the Foreign Office who had for a long time been supplying the Soviets with political information of considerable value but showed signs of losing his nerve. In October 1933 the Foreign Office clerk committed suicide and his OGPU 'guardian' left the country. In OGPU circles this OGPU representative of GADA was known as 'Hans'. Krivitsky believes him to have been here on a Greek passport in the name of Galleni or Galeni.

The firm of GADA continued in Amsterdam and provided the necessary business cover for Theodore Mally, alias Paul Hardt, the chief OGPU illegal *rezident* for the United Kingdom during 1936 and 1937.

Since 1928 or 1929 several illegal *rezident* agents have operated in the United Kingdom posing as American business men. This was the cover used by Nicolski, Hardt's predecessor in London. Nicolski was later sent to Spain to help with the organisation of the OGPU there. Nicolski is this man's real name, not the name under which he obtained his American passport and operated in the United Kingdom.

Methods of communication

The normal method of communication between the OGPU agents operating abroad and Moscow is through the OGPU representative in the Soviet Embassy and the same technique is used as by Fourth Department agents.

Secret inks are rarely used but on occasion this method is employed even in countries where a Soviet Embassy or Legation is at the disposal of the OGPU representatives. Mally alias Hardt is known to have written a report to Moscow on a matter of particular importance in secret ink. It is not known whether after doing so he sent the document through the Soviet Embassy in the usual way.

Wireless. There was no OGPU radio station operating from the United Kingdom prior to 1937. It is not known whether one is in existence at present. OGPU radio arrangements were always very poor.

Foreign embassies and legations

In the event of a war between the United Kingdom and the Soviet Union Krivitsky stated categorically that communication between Moscow and the OGPU agents in this country would be maintained through the Embassies or Legations of neutral powers. There is an OGPU agent on the staff of the Legation of each Baltic State. There is, or was in 1937, an OGPU agent on the staff of the American Embassy in London. The OGPU has striven for years to penetrate the diplomatic services of all foreign powers. Promising young men have been specially educated at the expense of the OGPU in the hope that they might be successful in entering the diplomatic service of their respective countries and successful approaches have been made to existing personnel. Pressed on the point Krivitsky insisted that, unknown of course to their Ambassadors or Ministers, the majority of foreign embassies in this and other countries have a man on their staff working or awaiting instructions to work for the OGPU in case of emergency.

Information of the first importance, first political and later relating to military and aviation matters, was supplied to the OGPU from a source in the French Foreign Office. The source was recruited through a Hungarian journalist in Paris possibly called Gutmann. In 1934 this journalist was responsible for a newspaper connected with the Paris source. His OGPU chief was a Lettish Jew who lived at Passy with his wife. The pair had Lettish passports and disappeared after the assassination of Ignace Reiss. They are known to the French police.

Instances of OGPU interference with the staff of the British Foreign Office and diplomatic service are the subject of a separate memorandum.

The illegal rezident *since 1937*

As Theodore Mally alias Paul Hardt was recalled to Moscow only a short time before Krivitsky's own downfall the name of the present OGPU chief underground representative is unknown to him. Hardt left London hurriedly in June 1937 and a member of the Executive Committee of the Communist Party of Great Britain took his place temporarily as the OGPU representative. He is sure that this man's name began with the letter 'B' and that he had been one of Hardt's most important recruiting agents through the Communist Party. This can, however, have been only an emergency arrangement for a short period as Hardt had no authority to hand over his duties to anyone without the express sanction of the I.N.O. of the OGPU in Moscow. Owing to drastic purging of OGPU personnel and technical difficulties Krivitsky doubts whether it has yet been possible for the OGPU to replace Hardt with a man of equal calibre. His functions will probably be divided up, and men with Canadian, French or U.S.A. passports will be doing his work.

If a Yugoslav called Kral is still in the OGPU service he will undoubtedly be used for operations in the United Kingdom. Kral speaks good English and German. He has friends in most of the Yugoslav Consulates and could no doubt get to the United Kingdom with their assistance. Failing that he could always pass as a sailor. Kral was staying at the Carlton Hotel, Amsterdam, in June 1937 on a four days visa obtained through a friend in a Yugoslav Consulate in Belgium. He is an expert lock breaker. He is 46–49 years of age; tall, very dark and thin; in looks very like King Alphonso of Spain. Krivitsky thinks his name was originally Ivanovitch, but on entering the service of the OGPU he became Kral which is his Party and service name. Kral was known to

Hardt and was always at Krivitsky's disposal for the making of keys or breaking of locks.

APPENDIX TO CHAPTER 2
OGPU AGENTS IN THE BRITISH FOREIGN
OFFICE AND DIPLOMATIC SERVICE

E.H. Oldham: cipher department of the Foreign Office

At some date which Krivitsky cannot remember but believes was about 1930 or 1931, a man called Oldham, employed in the Cipher Department of the British Foreign Office, called at the Soviet Embassy in Paris offering to sell British diplomatic ciphers and other secret material to which he had access.

At that time Valovitch, Deputy Chief of the Operod (Operations Department) of the GUGB (Headquarters Staff of the OGPU) was in Paris working at the Embassy under the name of Yanovitch. Yanovitch at first refused to see Oldham, believing him to be an agent-provocateur. A month later Oldham called again bringing specimens of material to which he had access. On this, though still suspicious of Oldham, Yanovitch arranged with him for further supplies of Foreign Office material in return for substantial money payments. He gave Oldham the 'service' name of ARNO.

For some time Oldham was allowed no contact with OGPU agents in London and was obliged to take his material to Paris himself, although Yanovitch realised the importance of his information. As soon as the OGPU were satisfied that Oldham was not a British double-cross agent it was arranged that a man should be sent to London specially to handle his material and obviate the risks and delays caused by frequent journeys to Paris. Oldham was of a highly nervous disposition and a heavy drinker. Yanovitch accordingly decided that the agent despatched to London to handle his material should have the close supervision of Oldham as his sole responsibility.

Oldham's OGPU guardian arrived in London on a Greek passport. Krivitsky cannot remember his name but recollects certain details of his earlier career. He was at one time an Intelligence Officer in General Wrangel's Army. As a Soviet secret agent he did important work in Bulgaria in 1920 when a White Russian force was in process of formation there. During the Stamboullist period he managed to steal three ships lying at Varna and despatch them to Odessa, thereby causing considerable trouble as the ships happened to be French owned.

During the period of this man's role as 'guardian' Oldham was dismissed from the Foreign Office for drink. Completely in the hands of the OGPU and in dire straits for money he continued to obtain Foreign Office material by making use of his previous position there. Krivitsky described how immense was his own astonishment when he heard that in spite of his dismissal Oldham was still allowed free access to the Foreign Office to visit his friends. During one of these visits Oldham took an impression of one of the important keys and thereafter was able to bring away material from time to time. The key in question was made from the impression by the Fourth Department and that is how Krivitsky first came to hear the story.

About this time Oldham's 'guardian' was relieved by a second OGPU agent also the holder of a Greek passport. This man's service name was 'Hans'. He was here as representative of the Amsterdam firm of GADA, which firm was specially created by the OGPU to give him the necessary business cover. The surname adopted by 'Hans' is believed to have been Galleni or Galeni. Galleni was a cultured and good-looking man. On one occasion while travelling from London to the Continent he was in the same carriage with a British King's Messenger, who actually asked him to look after his bags while he left the carriage. Galleni did not try to take the opportunity of tampering with the bags as he could not believe that a diplomatic courier would make such a request to a stranger in good faith!

Galleni had a very difficult time. Oldham had become a confirmed drunkard and drug addict. He was so nervous that only by threats of exposure and the cutting off of financial supplies could he be persuaded to continue his visits to the Foreign Office. Galleni was constantly at his side. He took him abroad for a holiday and in London stayed with him either at hotels or in his own house. His nerves were in such a condition that on one occasion he created a scene in a cinema because Galleni momentarily forgot to rise for 'God Save the King'. About this time also Galleni was considerably worried as he had some reason to think that a British Secret Service agent had got into touch with Oldham who had somehow aroused suspicion.

As it appeared that Oldham would shortly break down completely Galleni concentrated his efforts in trying to obtain from him sufficient details of the private lives of his colleagues to guide the OGPU in their attempts to obtain a future source for the same material. Oldham at first refused to supply the requisite information but after considerable pressure had been brought to bear both on him and his wife, he gave Galleni five or six names. One of these names was that of J.H. King also employed in the Foreign Office Cipher Department.

Shortly afterwards Oldham committed suicide and Galleni left the country. Later, during November and December 1936 Galleni is known to have been living at a hotel in the Rue Cambon, Paris. There are only one or two hotels in the Rue Cambon which is a very short street.

J.H. King: cipher department of the Foreign Office

Some little time after Oldham had supplied the OGPU with details of his colleagues in the Foreign Office several of these men were sent to Geneva as cipher clerks to the British Delegation there. The OGPU promptly ordered two agents to Geneva to cultivate their acquaintance. Henri Christian Pieck, a Dutchman, and a Russian, an ex-sailor, who had lived in the United States, were the two OGPU agents chosen for the work.

Pieck was an intelligent and cultured man of great charm. He had a genuine reputation as a decorative artist and cartoonist, and with the assistance of the OGPU lived with his wife in considerable comfort at The Hague. He had little difficulty in meeting Captain Harvey, the officer in charge of the British cipher clerks. He paid much attention to Harvey's daughter. By dint of adding lavish hospitality to his natural charm, he became a popular figure not only with Harvey's circle, but generally with British journalists and officials. The Russian ex-sailor was a stupid man whose knowledge of English was his sole qualification for this particular work. The standard of ability of the two men can well be judged by repeating Krivitsky's statement that a British agent in Geneva confided to Pieck that the Russian ex-sailor was a Soviet spy!

Pieck's expenses in Geneva ran into thousands of pounds. He achieved his object and henceforth could count on five or six Foreign Office employees as his personal friends. Even so he proceeded with the utmost caution. He did nothing more at Geneva. Later he invited two or three of his Foreign Office friends to stay with him at The Hague from time to time. Here he lavished hospitality upon them, gave them handsome presents and lent them money. By this time he knew all the circumstances of King's private life and that he had a mistress living in London. On him the choice finally fell. In the summer of 1937 Pieck came to London. He made a direct approach to King telling him that he knew a banker in The Hague through whom they could both make a great deal of money if King would supply advance information from the Foreign Office on international affairs. King agreed. In the meantime in order to have a ready excuse for his presence in London and to have some room where he could count upon being undisturbed, Pieck went into partnership with a British subject called Parlanti in a genuine decorative art business, and the partners leased premises in Buckingham Gate. Parlanti was unaware of the true purpose of Pieck's constant presence in London. He never did any work for the OGPU although at one time he was a Communist Party sympathiser.

King passed regularly to Pieck carbon copies of deciphered telegrams passing between the Foreign Office and British Embassies abroad. When Pieck was in Holland the two men communicated through King's mistress whose acquaintance both Pieck and his wife had assiduously cultivated.

By this time King was regarded as an important agent. Early in 1936 the OGPU decided that continued association with Pieck might endanger King. King was accordingly introduced to Theodore Mally alias Paul Hardt under the guise of 'Mr Petersen', the representative of a Dutch bank.

'Mr Petersen' rented a house in London. King deposited the Foreign Office material in a safe in this house or in Pieck's old office in Buckingham Gate on his way home. For some time the material was fetched from there and taken to 'Mr Petersen' by a young Englishman, Brian Goold-Verschoyle. If the material contained matter of urgent importance Hardt telegraphed its contents to Moscow through the Soviet Embassy. If not, he sent it by Brian Goold-Verschoyle, or by another courier to Wolf Levit to be photographed.

Wolf Levit was an elderly man, an ex-Fourth Department agent in Paris. At Hardt's request Krivitsky transferred him to the OGPU as photographer for the London organisation.

King continued regularly to supply Foreign Office material up to June 1937 when Hardt left London. Krivitsky has no knowledge of King's activities subsequent to that date.

Unknown source of 'Imperial Council' information

In 1936, while Theodore Mally alias Paul Hardt was the illegal OGPU *rezident* for the United Kingdom, the I.N.O. of the OGPU began to receive what Krivitsky called 'Imperial Council' information of high Naval, Military, Air Force and political importance. From his description of photographic prints of documents he saw in Moscow on two or three occasions in 1936 and 1937 there is no doubt that printed reports of the proceedings of the Committee of Imperial Defence and other highly confidential reports available to the same source were regularly made available to and photographed by OGPU agents in London. Krivitsky recalls that one of the latest of such reports dealt with defence measures and an appreciation of the situation in Germany by the British Ambassador in Berlin.

Reports supplied by the 'Imperial Council' source were especially dealt with in Moscow. The printed report, which ran into a very large number of pages, was translated literally into Russian. When the translator was not sure of the Russian translation the English word was put in brackets after it. Extracts were made of the more important passages and bound up in the form of a book, typewritten on pale green paper. Only five copies of this book were made – one each for [Chief of Defense] [Klement] Voroshilov, [Assistant Chief of Defense] [Vladimir] Orlov, [Chief of NKVD] [Nikolai] Yezhov, [Chief of NKVD Foreign Department] [Abram] Sloutski and [General Secretary of the Communist Party] [Josef] Stalin. Photographic prints of the original report and the full Russian translation were always attached to Stalin's copy.

In the last days of April, or in the beginning of May 1937, when Krivitsky was in Moscow for the last time, he called on Sloutski, head of the Foreign Department of the OGPU. Sloutski was Krivitsky's friend as well as chief of the OGPU
[Line missing]
. . . side of the commission with which he had been entrusted in 1935. Sloutski handed him the latest book of extracts of information from the 'Imperial Council' source and asked him particularly to read a report bound up with it which dealt with a special meeting of the Politburo at which [Foreign Minister] [Maxim] Litvinoff was present. From this report Sloutski deduced that the

British Intelligence must have a source in the Narkomindel (Soviet Foreign Office). The man in the English section of the INO who actually received the material made the same comment. This report although bound up with extracts from the usual printed 'Imperial Council' report was additional to and not part of the report.

At that time Sloutski was not at all certain of his own position and he wanted Krivitsky to think over the report with a view to making any possible suggestions as to where the leakage in the Narkomindel could be. Sloutski felt that if he could discover this it might save his own position. Krivitsky says that he could not give his attention to the report although he skimmed through it. At that time he was only anxious to get out of Moscow. He told Sloutski he would return and go into the matter thoroughly but in fact he never did.

As regards the source of the 'Imperial Council' information, Krivitsky has little definite knowledge.

He is certain that the source was a young man, probably under thirty, an agent of Theodore Mally, that he was recruited as a Soviet agent purely on ideological grounds, and that he took no money for the information he obtained. He was almost certainly educated at Eton and Oxford. Krivitsky cannot get it out of his head that the source is a 'young aristocrat', but agrees that he may have arrived at this conclusion because he thought it was only young men of the nobility who were educated at Eton. He believes the source to have been the secretary or son of one of the chiefs of the Foreign Office.

Krivitsky reported the following incident in support of his recollection that the young man in question obtained his information from the Foreign Office.

Krivitsky had as his agent at The Hague an old Dutchman and Social Democrat. He cannot recollect his name but says he was sent by *The Times* to act as their correspondent in Hungary during Bela Kun's time there.

In 1936 this old man reported that he had had meetings with an employee of the British Foreign Office who was offering to supply Japanese information. Krivitsky sent a message to Hardt to have the man looked up in the Foreign Office List and is sure that in reporting that he was unable to find any record of him, Hardt said he had consulted his other agent (not King) in the Foreign Office regarding the proposed new recruit. Krivitsky recalls that in connection with this incident he forbade the engaging of another agent in the Foreign Office as there were two there already and third might be prejudicial to the other two.

Krivitsky cannot say whether since the disappearance of Mally (alias Hardt) this young man is still working. He is quite certain that although they would almost certainly drop the remainder of Hardt's organisation in London, the OGPU would not willingly give up the 'Imperial Council' source because his information was of vital importance. He thinks it more likely that since the Stalin–Hitler alliance the young man will have tried 'to stop work' for he was an idealist and recruited on the basis that the only man who would fight Hitler was Stalin: that his feelings had been worked onto such an extent that he believed that in helping Russia he would be helping this country and the cause of democracy generally. Whether if he has wanted 'to stop work' he is a type with sufficient moral courage to withstand the inevitable OGPU blackmail and threats of exposure Krivitsky cannot say.

The British Embassy source in Rome

About 1933 Artusov, at that time head of the INO of the OGPU, asked Krivitsky to let him have one of his agents to 'look after' and to act as intermediary for a valuable source of information from the British Embassy in Rome. Artusov said that up to then the British Embassy source had dealt direct with the OGPU *rezident* in the Soviet Embassy. This practice was considered too dangerous to be allowed to continue. Krivitsky had no authority to transfer an agent of the *Razvedupr* – the Military Intelligence – without the permission of General Berzin, head of the Military Intelligence Department. He discussed the matter with Berzin who said that the information was of such importance that Artusov must, if necessary, be lent an agent of the Fourth Department.

Krivitsky accordingly arranged to send one of his best agents to Rome. He chose a young Russian Jew, a student of archaeology. Krivitsky had originally hoped that this young man would be the Fourth Department's 'Lawrence of Arabia'. He was a genuine archaeologist; spoke Arabic well and had a consuming ambition to work in Arabia. Krivitsky thought that his time in Rome would give him additional opportunities to study archaeology and would not be time wasted if he could eventually get him back and send him to Arabia. It took three or four months to make the necessary arrangements to transfer this young man to Rome. He was finally despatched with an Austrian or German passport in the guise of a young professor of archaeology. Krivitsky thinks he must have already started work early in 1934 because he remembers that a number of Fourth Department agents were arrested in Rome in that year, and Artusov enquired whether these arrests would in any way jeopardise Krivitsky's late agent.

In 1937 he was still working in Rome and had made quite a big name for himself in archaeological circles there. The Englishman was still working up to 1937. Krivitsky himself read some of the material from Rome in the winter of 1933–1934. He says it could only have emanated from the British Embassy, but he could not say for certain whether the Englishman who was obtaining it for the OGPU was himself actually working there.

Incidentally Krivitsky mentioned that in the G.U.G.B. (Headquarters Staff of the OGPU) it was the work of one special man to edit the material obtained from King, the 'Imperial Council' source, the British Embassy in Rome, and from the high official in the French Foreign Office, to whom previous reference has been made.

British Embassy in Constantinople

Between 1933 and 1934 a man called Levit who was probably then using the name Tann was the OGPU legal *resident* in the Soviet Embassy in Constantinople. He had great success in obtaining information from a source in the British Embassy there. Krivitsky says the British source has probably been liquidated, for in 1936 or 1937 Levit alias Tann was transferred to the Fourth Department and sent to the USA to get an American passport before his despatch to Poland for Fourth Department work.

This man is the son of Wolf Levit who acted as the expert OGPU photographer in London during the period of Mally alias Hardt's activities here.

CHAPTER THREE
RELATIONS BETWEEN THE OGPU AND THE
FOURTH DEPARTMENT

The history of the relations between the OGPU GUGB and the Fourth Department of *Razvedupr* is one of the continual struggle by the OGPU to control both organisations. The feud between the two departments dates back as far as 1921, but nevertheless the Fourth Department managed to retain complete independence until 1934. There were certain definite rules for co-operation in Moscow such as for instance that military information obtained by the OGPU must be passed on to the General Staff, but there was continual official friction between the two departments. Such little real co-operation as existed was the fortuitous result of friendships which might exist between OGPU and Fourth Department chiefs. Abroad the greatest jealousy existed between the OGPU and the Fourth Department, neither availed itself of the organisation of the other nor was personnel interchangeable without express approval from the heads of the respective departments in Moscow. As a general rule there was no contact between Fourth Department and OGPU illegal *rezident*s in foreign countries. Communist Party assistants were forbidden to meet in any circumstances although in practice it was found almost impossible to enforce this rule.

Even before 1934 the OGPU with the might of the all-powerful GUGB behind them were in a far stronger position abroad than the *Razvedupr* man and were able to maintain a tighter hold over their agents. Many White Russians and Soviet citizens abroad were recruited and forced to work for the OGPU through fear of retaliation on their relations and frien[ds in] Russia. The OGPU because of their influence on the Comintern were able to demand much unpaid service both from Soviet officials and local Communist Party members. They could thus afford to have a far greater number of agents than the Fourth Department. The frequent and successful use of threats against persons living in the Soviet Union was such a potent source [of] service and information to the OGPU that the technique for retention of every kind of agents by means of blackmail gradually became highly developed and was regularly used.

Krivitsky denied categorically that the Fourth Department ever had recourse to such methods. It is true that many Fourth Department agents started work from idealistic and Party motives and without pay, but when these agents became more closely connected with the organisation they had to be put on the pay roll to ensure their dependence on the Fourth Department. Up to 1932 in Germany and elsewhere Krivitsky recruited the majority of his agents through Communist Parties, but subsequently tapped the wider field created by the anti-fascist organisations. Up to 1933 eighty per cent of OGPU men were recruited through Communist Parties, but with the United Front and anti-Hitler movements the figures gradually decreased until in 1937 only about fifty per cent were recruited through their Party and affiliated organisations.

The percentage of *Razvedupr* to OGPU agents varied with the countries in which they worked. In the United Kingdom there were about thirty regular OGPU agents to each *Razvedupr* man but in countries such as Romania, Hungary and Poland where an acute military situation with the USSR might exist at any time, there would be perhaps twenty *Razvedupr* to each OGPU agent.

It is quite clear from Krivitsky's explanations that the Fourth Department, particularly as it applied to the Western countries, was a specialised department employing few but carefully chosen and highly trained agents. The OGPU having a multitude of agents and the whole force of the State behind them could afford to take great risks, sacrifice agents where necessary, and cover a much wider field. Although Krivitsky fought against OGPU influence in the Fourth Department and disliked their methods, he admits they had 'very great success' in the United Kingdom.

In 1934 on direct orders from Stalin, the OGPU were empowered to place their own men in control of the second section of the Fourth Department. Artusov, head of the INO of the GUGB was appointed head of the second section, and General Berzin, former head of the second and third sections, was sent to the Far East, and in 1935 [sic] to Spain. Berzin's place at the head of the third section was nominally filled by Uritzky, a young and inexperienced man. The second section was the most important in the Fourth Department. It therefore followed, that the OGPU gained the real control of the whole of the *Razvedupr*.

In 1935 again on Stalin's direct order, the OGPU formed military as well as political espionage organisations, particularly in the Western European countries. Nevertheless the organisation of military espionage services abroad though not the personnel appears to have been left in the hands of the Fourth Department.

Thus it came about that in 1935 Krivitsky, still enjoying the confidence of both OGPU and *Razvedupr*, left Moscow with a commission to visit every head of the Fourth Department and OGPU *rezident* and illegal agent and advise on his organisation. At that time Stalin still feared a war with Germany and consequently Krivitsky was given the right to transfer Fourth Department agents to the OGPU organisations and to earmark any suitably qualified OGPU agents for work in Germany.

One of the agents so transferred was Wolf Levit from the Fourth Department in Paris for work in London under the OGPU agent Paul Hardt. It was through this commission given to him in 1935 that Krivitsky gained his knowledge of the efficient military and political espionage organisation operating in the United Kingdom under Theodor Mally – Paul Hardt. Hardt was not directly under Krivitsky's orders, but Krivitsky had the right to know what he was doing and advise him on his work. It was also under this commission that Krivitsky sent his own assistant, Parparoff, to interview the ex-Passport Control employee Hooper in order to satisfy himself that Hooper was not a British double-cross agent. On Parparoff's report Krivitsky was not entirely satisfied. He warned Pieck against Hooper and withdrew Pieck himself for work in Germany.

In the summer of 1937 when the purges took hold of Soviet life, particularly the Red Army and the OGPU, Yezhov took the further opportunity to undertake a reorganisation of the OGPU and the Fourth Department culminating in the virtual co-ordination of the work of the two departments. Krivitsky is however convinced that the Fourth Department cannot be entirely eliminated and must continue to have some form of existence as an entity of its own.

CHAPTER FOUR
THE COMMUNIST PARTY

Section 1. The Comintern

The Comintern was founded in Moscow in 1919. It was to be the instrument of World Revolution and the guarantor of the continued existence of the Socialist State in Russia.

The Comintern, once all-powerful in Soviet Russia and wielding immeasurable influence through the civilised world is now merely the personal weapon of Stalin and the servant of his totalitarian dictatorship.

Nevertheless although Krivitsky says that Stalin no longer thinks in terms of world revolution or socialist theory it is important for him to maintain Communist Parties abroad as propaganda agencies for the Soviet Union and to implement his present policy of military aggression. The present head of the Comintern is Dmitroff with Manuilski as his assistant.

Two organisations maintained by the Comintern enable that body to control the political education and activities of Communist Parties abroad. They are the Lenin School for the training of political propagandists and the O.M.S. (*Otdyel Mezhdunarodnoi Svyazi*), the International Liaison Section or Foreign Relations Department.

The Lenin School

The Lenin School was founded in 1926 to train foreign communists politically and practically in the work of revolution and at the same time to produce a body of propagandists from foreign countries to organise and educate Communist Parties abroad.

The School curriculum provides for political and military education. The building was originally in Moscow where the Hotel Lux was used as a hostel for the students, but after 1935 it was moved to Sparrow Hills in the suburbs. The head of the School was and still may be the wife of Yaroslavski, head of the Russian 'League of the Godless'. Assistant teachers and professors may be either Russian or foreign communists.

At first pupils for the school were drawn chiefly from Central Europe, but as it expanded classes were arranged for students from the United Kingdom and America. There were few English compared with representatives of other Western European countries, but after a while British students came in batches of about ten at a time, and by now a considerable number have passed through the school. A few natives of India have also passed through the school.

The Lenin School is intended solely for the working class and intellectuals are always discouraged.

On their arrival students are given a sound grounding in history, geography and mathematics in order to enable them to take the fullest advantage of their political education.

After they have attended the school for three or six months the best of each batch of students qualify for the military course. The military course is controlled by the army and lasts for two or three months during the summer. A number of experts from the Military Intelligence Department assist at the course. Krivitsky mentioned that one of these men was the son-in-law of the now notorious Finnish communist, Kuusinen. During their time with the army the students live exactly like soldiers; they are drilled, taught to shoot, and given a practical knowledge of the technique of street fighting. At the end of the course they are expected to have enough knowledge to enable them to act as military leaders of a revolution if and when opportunity arises.

At the end of the military course a limited number of the ablest students are selected by the Fourth Department for an intelligence course. The intelligence course lasts for at least six months and is directed entirely by the Fourth Department. The students are taught radio work, the use of secret inks and the technique of obtaining false passports. They also take a sabotage course where they acquire a knowledge of chemicals and explosives, how to cut water supplies, wreck machinery and disconnect telephone wires. When they graduate from this course the students are expected to know everything necessary for a first class intelligence or sabotage agent working on his own. A man called Kleber was one of the most brilliant military specialists attached by the Fourth Department to this course. He was subsequently sent to the Far East and eventually became leader of the International Brigade in Spain. He disappeared during the purge of the Red Army.

Krivitsky himself made a short visit of inspection to the intelligence course in 1934 and again in 1935. He is quite sure he could not recognise any of the English who were there, but he says he is certain that there were not more than three or four Englishmen who took the intelligence and sabotage courses in these years. He cannot remember any Indian taking the course but says that by now a few may have been trained. In 1934 and 1935 the Comintern was concentrating almost entirely on Central Europeans.

It is quite clear that the duration of the stay of a pupil in Russia is no guide as to what courses he has attended. During the preliminary course a factory worker from England might show outstanding ability in grasping industrial or social educative problems. Such a man might be sent for six months or even a year to work and study in a variety of factories throughout the U.S.S.R. He might be away from his own country for two years without having attended the military or intelligence courses. OGPU agents operate amongst every batch of students. They might pick on a man as having particularly useful connections in the country of his origin and after a short preliminary training send him back almost immediately as an OGPU agent. In the main however it can be assumed that a student will not have completed the intelligence course unless he has been in Russia for two or three years.

On one of the later occasions when Krivitsky was in Moscow before his break with the Soviets he heard a discussion as to whether it would not be a good thing to have a branch of the Lenin School in Stockholm. It was thought that European events were moving so quickly that Moscow was too remote for rapid instruction. He believes that for the last few years some sort of centre has existed in Stockholm where there was probably only one instructor to meet urgent cases. He feels sure that since the outbreak of war there will certainly be a branch of the Lenin School in Stockholm in order to give rapid instruction on the ever-changing Party line to communist representatives from Western European countries. The school must necessarily be on a small scale. Owing to the present difficulty of aliens residing in Stockholm for any length of time he thinks the courses would be purely political and last for about a fortnight – certainly not more than two months. He regards it as quite impossible that the whole Lenin School should move to Stockholm or that it should operate on a large scale there.

The OMS

The Department of International Relations or, as it is also called, the Foreign Liaison Section of the Comintern, is of vital importance and is the soul or centre of the Comintern. Up to 1937 the executive head of the organisation was Piatnitsky who has now been succeeded by Trelisser. Trelisser has been head of the Foreign Relations Department of the OGPU and subsequently a member of the Control Commission of the Comintern, a most important body responsible for the discipline of the highest Communist Party officials.

The OMS is the organisation through which the Comintern finances, disciplines and maintains contact with the Communist Parties abroad.

Although like every other body in Soviet Russia it is honeycombed with OGPU agents, it is not an OGPU organisation nor connected with the Military Intelligence Department. It has its own secret courier system and its own representative on the Executive Committee of each Communist Party abroad. These representatives report to Moscow fullest details of the political views, activities and personal affairs of the senior executive officials of the Communist Party they represent.

A striking instance of the work of the OMS representatives abroad was provided in April 1939 when Harry Pollitt, Leader of the Communist Party of Great Britain, objected to the Party line in support of conscription in the United Kingdom. Pollitt's views were duly reported by the OMS representative. Thereupon the Comintern ordered a number of prominent French communists to visit London and convince Pollitt of the correctness of the Party line. They were instructed as to the arguments they should use by Rajani Palme Dutt. Krivitsky is certain that if Rajani Palme Dutt is on the Executive Committee of the Communist Party of Great Britain he will be the OMS Representative. He says that Dutt is undoubtedly 'Piatnitsky's man' during his previous residence in Brussels.

As regards the United Kingdom the OMS organisation was of great importance up to 1925 while the Comintern still believed it possible to provoke a working class revolution here. Since the Stalin–Hitler rapprochement it is of vital importance for it is through the O.M.S. that Stalin will be making preparations for the time when a state of war may exist between this country and Soviet Russia.

Abramoff's organisation

Abramoff was chief assistant to Piatnitsky in the OMS and in charge of communications with foreign Communist Parties. He was removed by Stalin in 1936 and shot during the great purge of 1937.

Quite independently of the OGPU or the Fourth Department Abramoff started in 1925 a secret radio school in the Moscow suburb of Metischev. He trained there a number of young men and women of all nationalities to act as radio operators abroad. These students were kept very much isolated and were only allowed to visit Moscow once a week.

Abramoff had a secret wireless system through which he communicated with Communist Parties abroad. He had no portable apparatus for this purpose and his wireless apparatus abroad was cumbersome and constructed by amateur collaborators or pupils who had been through the school.

Krivitsky stated categorically that neither the Fourth Department nor the OGPU ever made use of or trusted Abramoff's organisation. He was obviously unaware that Abramoff's organisation had a wireless system operating to and from this country from 1934–1936.

Section 2. The Communist Party of Great Britain

Krivitsky knows little about the details of Communist Party organisation in the United Kingdom, but he has a good general knowledge as to its strength and its potentialities as a military factor in the event of an open rupture between this country and the U.S.S.R.

Communist movements abroad are regularly discussed in the Party cell of the Fourth Department. Reports of foreign Communist Parties on conditions in their respective countries are forwarded by the Comintern to the Military Intelligence Department who extract anything of interest which might affect the army in the event of war.

Krivitsky has heard many discussions on the subject of the British Communist Party which as regards numbers is admittedly a disappointment in Moscow. He cannot, however, emphasise too strongly that since 1935 Stalin has regarded the Soviets as in 'a war position', and from that date Communist Parties and the Intelligence Services have been functioning as in preparation for war. Since 1935 during their visits to Moscow senior communists officials such as Pollitt and Gallacher have been interviewed by officers of the Military Intelligence Department. Their views have been obtained on the political situation in Britain, on the British General Staff, conditions in the British Army and any other subjects of possible interest from a military point of view. Records of these interviews together with relevant extracts from information received from the Comintern are passed on to the Mobilisation Department where a report is prepared giving the most complete picture possible of conditions prevailing in the United Kingdom.

Stalin no longer considers the subject of world revolution and although he still fears war on any large scale, Krivitsky is convinced that he is so determined on the destruction of the British Empire that he will go to any lengths in collaboration with Hitler to obtain his object.

With British diplomatic relations with the Soviet Union strained as they are at present Krivitsky is genuinely astonished that he cannot in our press, or periodicals, or in the speeches of ministers, find any indication that the British people realise the gravity of the existence of such an organisation as the

Communist Party of Great Britain in time of war. He agrees that in time of peace the British Government are right in thinking that a healthy democracy will eventually cast off, or at any rate, keep in a state of impotence, undesirable elements in left wing movements, but in time of war, particularly when there is a danger of war with the Soviet Union, he is most emphatic that the existence of the Communist Party organisation is a very real danger.

Krivitsky is most anxious not to convey the impression that he advocates the eradication of any spontaneous British Left Wing movement, however revolutionary it may be. His point is that the Comintern has no longer any genuine interest in the needs of the British working class and that the Communist Party organisation is merely a Russian agency superimposed upon extreme left wing opinion in order that it may be used as a weapon to assist Stalin in his aggressive military policy. He is genuinely convinced that, in the event of war between Russia and this country, immediate steps should be taken to sterilise the activities of the Central Committee and all the paid officers and organisers of the Communist Party of Great Britain on the grounds that they are purely an agency of the Soviet–German war machine. He remarked that if Daladier was able to suppress the Communist Party, the British Government should be able to do so, at least as well.

The character of the struggle carried on by the Communist Party organisation and the means it uses must change with the requirements of the Stalin–Hitler war against the British Empire. There is now no question of a long range policy but tactics and action are and will be laid down from moment to moment.

Sabotage

Krivitsky spoke at great length on the subject of sabotage which in his view is certain on a wide scale in the event of an open rupture with the Soviet Union. The British communist will then have the same responsibility as the Russian communist; he must fight for Stalin by undermining and awakening Great Britain by every means in his power. All workers in factories will be given orders for sabotage and every Communist Party member will automatically become a sabotage unit.

At this juncture Krivitsky was reminded that he himself had remarked on the small numbers of British communists who had taken the sabotage continuation course from the Lenin School and was asked to explain exactly what he meant by sabotage. He said that to a Russian sabotage means not only destruction but obstruction in every sense of the word. Sabotage can be divided into three categories:

Firstly there is the skilled destructive sabotage of the trained saboteur. This is where the services of the few Moscow trained British communists will be utilised. Krivitsky himself created a sabotage organisation in Germany and is certain that an officer in the Fourth Department will now be in this country occupying himself with such an organisation. He will be trying to arrange the correct distribution of reliable communists in all vital military, naval and air force centres, in factories, arsenals and above all in utility companies. Until the moment for action arrives, these men will be given instructions to keep quiet and retain their jobs in 'key' factories. The men are described as 'shock units', instructed in their duties by a specialist in the Red Army. Their work is termed 'diverse sabotage' in the rear of the military front. Not more than one or possibly two members of the Central Committee of the Communist Party will be likely to know of this underground organisation, but it is probable that payments to prospective saboteurs will be made through one such member of the Central Committee entrusted with special funds for this purpose.

Secondly, there is the sabotage which can be carried on by all factory workers, including women, without preliminary training. As regards the women, the Soviets has always believed in using women for effective anti-war demonstrations. Both men and women workers will be expected to slow up production by causing as much trouble as possible and putting out faulty products.

Thirdly, there is the 'mass sabotage' of the rank and file who will receive general instructions to take part in such work of obstruction and destruction as may be possible in the course of their daily life and ordinary work. Every member of the Communist Party must discharge his revolutionary duty of sabotaging the war wherever he may be.

Krivitsky does not suggest that the whole of the membership of the Communist Party will perform acts of sabotage, and agrees that at the last stage the majority of communists may leave the Party. He insists, however, that there will remain sufficient stalwart and trusted members to cause serious damage and possibly loss of life on the home front. Communists are not anarchists and will be unlikely to commit pointless outrages. It can therefore be expected that any acts of sabotage committed by members of the Communist Party will be part of a prearranged plan, and performed in accordance with a prepared time table.

Krivitsky believes that the French authorities have a good deal of material about Soviet sabotage activities which would be of value in studying this subject.

Decomposition work in the Army

Krivitsky, who was of course quite unaware of the measures that are and have for many years been taken in this country to frustrate communist activities in the Forces, insisted that the work of decomposition in the Army should be carefully watched. By the work of decomposition he means Soviet penetration of the Army. He explained that although decomposition work was ideological in character in its initial stages, it was directed by the Fourth Department and not by the OGPU or the Comintern.

He knows that between 1926 and 1930 there was an agent of the Fourth Department in the United Kingdom directing anti-militarist work and that the London District Committee of the Communist Party had groups specially trained with the object of spreading communist propaganda within the British Fighting Forces. He recalls that at first this work was very badly done, that material was put out for the troops and thrown over barrack walls which had no appeal to the ordinary soldier. Later, however, a military man was attached to the Fourth Department specialist, and wrote leaflets to be distributed through communist cells in various military units. Gradually the propaganda was much improved, but at no time within his knowledge did this work meet with the same amount of success as in France. The greatest and most spectacular successes were achieved in Poland and other Eastern European countries.

Krivitsky is certain that at the present time work amongst the Fighting Forces in Great Britain must be an important side of the Soviet Government programme. He emphasises that the work was never purely ideological. Members of the Forces who come favourably to notice in the course of anti-militarist work, and especially non-commissioned officers, form a pool from which the Fourth Department recruits trusted agents for espionage and sabotage.

In later years many young Polish communists were sent to join the Polish Army with the instructions 'You must be very good soldiers, for the higher rank you obtain the more useful you will be to your cause'. He believes the same policy is being carried out in the British Army and that there are undoubtedly officers wearing the British uniform who are awaiting the opportunity to assist the Soviet Union in the event of war.

Conclusion

Krivitsky is astonished and perturbed that Stalin's rapprochement with Germany and invasion of Finland have not had a catastrophic effect on the Communist Party of Great Britain, nor seriously diminished its membership.

He believes this is due to lack of force in our political propaganda and is very insistent that every effort should be made to find somebody in this country who has the necessary knowledge and experience to create an organisation to counter Soviet activities in the United Kingdom. He thinks such propaganda should emanate from a source which cannot be attributed to the Government.

Propaganda should emphasise that Bolshevism, Leninism and socialism are dead in the Soviet Union, and that no genuine attempt is now being made to carry out the teachings of Karl Marx. That the Soviet Union has become a rigid dictatorship maintained by a system of wholesale purges, and Stalin is attempting to maintain his unstable position by a policy of military aggression.

Krivitsky now honestly believes that the Russian revolution was inevitable and that the Bolsheviks took charge only because Lenin was the most capable man available at the time when the revolution took place. He says that pure Bolshevism in the Soviet Union existed only up to the end of 1921. Trotsky is the only man who knows the real facts of Lenin's death. Krivitsky believes Lenin finally committed suicide and knows as a fact he died a very unhappy man, realising the impracticability of the Bolshevik theory. He believes that if Lenin had lived some form of modified capitalism would have been reintroduced in Russia.

Propaganda in America

Krivitsky has very definite views as to the necessity for better and more forceful British propaganda in America. He says that both Soviet and German propaganda are making great headway there, and practically nothing is produced to present the British point of view. He says that the American public is surprisingly ignorant on the subject of the British Empire, and the average American has not the slightest idea of what the British Empire is, or the means by which it remains a single entity though composed of self-governing dominions.

He is emphatic that now is the time to publish a good popular book in America which would describe the British Commonwealth of Nations as a league of nations. The book should be written in popular language and should explain what Britain has done for her colonies, and why she cannot give India self-government at the moment. The book should be short and very simply written with good illustrations. Krivitsky is convinced that it would be widely read if written on these lines, and would pay for itself.

CHAPTER FIVE
RELATIONS BETWEEN THE GERMAN AND SOVIET MILITARY INTELLIGENCE SERVICES

Although Krivitsky has a wide general knowledge of Soviet Military Intelligence methods and personnel he was primarily a specialist on German affairs. Most of his career was devoted to a study of conditions in Germany and the organisation of the Soviet military espionage system there.

In the course of conversation regarding Soviet espionage activities in the United Kingdom he stated quite definitely that since the Stalin–Hitler alliance there could be no possible doubt that the German and Soviet Intelligence organisations would be working in close collaboration here. It could be taken as certain that the Soviet Diplomatic bag, always used for Soviet espionage material, was now used for the despatch to Berlin and elsewhere of the fruits of German espionage.

There has always since the Treaty of Versailles been a special relationship between the organisation and personnel of the Soviet and German military intelligence services.

In the first years after the Great War the Soviets had only one ally – Germany. General von Seeckt the reorganiser of the German Army was a firm believer in co-operation with the Soviet Union and counted on her support for the eventual liquidation of the Versailles Treaty. His opinion of the Russian Army was poor and he always felt he should have been entrusted with its re-organisation. Failing in this objective he did all he could for the improvement of the Russian Army through the interchange of expert military personnel. As recently as 1935 there were some fifteen or twenty Soviet officers at a military school in Germany.

As regards intelligence material, co-operation was close and interchange free until 1934.

It is common knowledge that until the firm establishment of the Hitler regime in Germany, Putna, then Soviet military attaché in Berlin, directed from there Soviet espionage activities against England with the full cognisance of the German authorities and exchanged with them the intelligence material he obtained. Berlin was, in fact, a clearing centre for intelligence reports of common interest to the Soviet and German Military Intelligence Departments.

At this time the Soviet Intelligence frequently made use of the German Embassies in Poland and Rumania. In 1923–1924 Krivitsky was in Breslau running a military espionage service into Poland. Through his assistant he was in daily communication with the German military authorities. On one occasion some of his officers got into difficulties in Poland. Krivitsky could do nothing for them but their escape was arranged through the good offices of the German Consul in Katowitz through Krivitsky's German colleagues.

Krivitsky related the following story as illustrative of how the Soviet Intelligence could obtain any information in Berlin in the early nineteen thirties.

On one occasion while Krivitsky was in Berlin he was approached by a Count Nelidoff, a White Russian, who said he had worked as a British agent in Constantinople. Nelidoff's approach coincided with a meeting of British representatives from all the Baltic provinces which was in progress at the British Legation in Berlin. The day after the meeting Nelidoff brought Krivitsky a cipher telegram which he said had been despatched by the British Legation the day before.

He did not of course know that Krivitsky had at this time an arrangement whereby he was supplied with a copy of every telegram sent by any Embassy or Legation in Berlin. Krivitsky was therefore able to inform Nelidoff by the following evening that the alleged cipher telegram was a forgery and had never been sent. The same night he received information through a German intelligence agent that Nelidoff had offered to work for the Germans, together with Nelidoff's account of his previous interview with Krivitsky!

Krivitsky subsequently ascertained that Nelidoff had originally been employed by the British but had been sacked.

Many years later Nelidoff became a purveyor of forged documents. On one occasion he sold a document to the German Intelligence for £3,000. When confronted with the fact that it was a forgery, he said he would refund the money. He did – with forged money, and was prosecuted by the German police.

Although up to 1933 or 1934 reports were freely exchanged there was no actual interchange of intelligence agents. But it occasionally happened that by mutual consent responsible Soviet and German Intelligence Officers employed the same agents. This led to a very awkward situation about 1931 when a group of Soviet Military Intelligence Officers were arrested in Vienna. The senior of the group, in order to protect the Soviet Government, referred the Austrian police to General Bredow. General Berzin, head of the Soviet Military Intelligence Service was horrified at what had happened, fearing that the Austrian police would obtain proof of Soviet connections and the fact of the German–Soviet intelligence collaboration in Austria would become known and an international scandal ensue. Krivitsky was sent immediately to Vienna to try and find out exactly what had happened. Officers sent by General von Bredow had already arrived to try and effect the release of the prisoner. Krivitsky refused their assistance and instructed the Soviet military attaché in Vienna that he was to have nothing whatever to do with them. He also managed to convey instructions to the prisoner through a lawyer who was permitted to visit him. Incidentally Krivitsky mentioned that when he bribed a senior Austrian police official to let him have for a short while the dossier of the Soviet agent in question it could not be produced because it had already been lent to the British Intelligence Service!

Excellent information from Czechoslovakia and Poland was supplied to Moscow from Berlin in 1929 and 1930. Up to 1933 Krivitsky received through official German channels intelligence reports regarding Danzig and Poland and through friends in the German Intelligence Service obtained their official summaries as late as 1935.

It follows that in spite of the purges and executions which have taken place in Russia and Germany since the advent of the Hitler regime there are still friendships existing between Russian and German Intelligence officers which can be revived in the common cause. General von Bredow is dead but it is obviously through his late friendship with him that Krivitsky is aware of the activities of a German agent – Egon Hessling or Haslinger – a Captain in the German Army who was at one time assistant to Protze a member of von Bredow's staff. Hessler was sent to Copenhagen in 1934 as a Gestapo agent in the guise of a German refugee.

Krivitsky says that in later years the German espionage service into Soviet Russia has been very cleverly run and that the German Intelligence in Czechoslovakia, Poland and the Balkans has been fully posted with first class information. There is also a network of excellent German agents in the Low Countries, especially Belgium. The German espionage service in the United Kingdom, however, is not so satisfactory and that is another reason why he is certain that at the present juncture Germany will make full use of facilities provided by the Soviet espionage organisation here.

Collaboration between the German and Soviet intelligence services has undoubtedly been extended in the Comintern.

The *Daily Herald* of the 10 February 1940 published a report on the return to Prague of two prominent communists who fled from Czechoslovakia at the time of the German occupation. These two men – K. Gottwald and B. Smeral – were friends of Eduard Benes. They are journalists and assisted in the initiation of the Czechoslovak pact with the USSR. They could only have been allowed to return to Czechoslovakia by agreement between Hitler and Stalin – presumably for the purpose of propagating the doctrine that Czechoslovakia should co-operate with Hitler and not hinder the destruction of France and Great Britain, the instigators of the present war.

As regards the present activities of the German espionage service operating in the United Kingdom, Krivitsky has little definite knowledge. He made, however, the following statement which he knows to be true:

(1) The Hungarian intelligence service has for a long time worked very closely with the Germans and he believes that German agents are at present employed in the Hungarian Legation in London.

(2) The German Nazi Party in the United Kingdom did a lot of intelligence work but on the whole the intelligence organisation here was weak, at any rate up to 1937.

(3) The Germans employ freely Irish agents in the United Kingdom and co-operate closely with the Irish as individuals and with the IRA and other underground organisations.

(4) German espionage against the United Kingdom is operated from Holland, but more especially from Belgium which since the rise of the Rexist Party has been highly organised for German espionage activities. A number of transport firms have been created or taken over recently there for the sole purpose of assisting German espionage.

(5) German agents steal documents – a practice forbidden to Soviet agents.

(6) A firm selling calculating machines is used as a cover for German espionage in the United Kingdom.

(7) The *Auslands Deutsche Dienst* or *Auslands Deutschtum* an organisation with headquarters in Stuttgart is a very important centre for German espionage. Before the Hitler regime it existed as an ordinary organisation for the holding together of Germans abroad but has now been taken over entirely for espionage purposes. Krivitsky says he regarded it as so important that he planted an agent there who was subsequently discovered and shot.

The head of the organisation was one Bohle who was subsequently transferred to the German Foreign Office during the process of Nazification of that department. He explained that the German Foreign Office was slow to become Nazified and that until this took place Rosenberg ran his own office for Foreign Policy in a building on the other side of the road.

(8) A man who may be in the United Kingdom and if he is will certainly be working for the Nazi Intelligence Service and the OGPU, is an Austrian who was Head Commissar of Police of the 15th District in Vienna in 1935. In that year as a German agent he was arrested by Schuschnigg's police. He was also an OGPU agent having been recruited at a time while he was connected with some swindle in Vienna. While he was in the Police Service he provided the OGPU with very valuable material. His arrest took place in the winter of 1934–35 and his name was in the Press. He may be in this country ostensibly as a refugee. He will do anything for money and might be useful to the British Intelligence. This man joined the OGPU in 1932, but also did work for the Fourth Department.

Appendix 3

SOVIET SECRET AGENTS MENTIONED BY WALTER KRIVITSKY

Name	Service	Remarks
ARNO	OGPU	Codename of Ernest Oldham, Foreign Office clerk, committed suicide October 1933.
'B'	OGPU	Member CPGB Central Committee in 1936. Recruiter for Theodore Mally.
BASSOFF, Serge	OGPU	Now living at Bronx, New York. Ex-Russian Black Sea Fleet. Still working for the OGPU. A courier for Krivitsky who recently met him in New York and learned that Theodore Mally might still be alive.
BELETSKI, V.S.	OGPU	OGPU agent who used to work in Paris.
BIBRING, David	OGPU	An agent of the 4th Dept. in 1934 but later employed by the OGPU in Austria. The OGPU asked Krivitsky for his opinion of him in 1936.
BORODIN alias GRUSENBERG	OGPU	OGPU agent working abroad.
BRANDES, Willy	OGPU	Subordinate agent of Mally. Krivitsky met him in Moscow but does not know him personally or his real name.
BROWDER, Earl	OGPU	Now in prison in USA. Brother of Jean Montgomery. Former husband of Katherine Harrison.
BRUSSE, Hans	4th Dept.	Dutch, born in Rotterdam. Age 25–26, looks about 35. Height about 5'7". Travels on a legal passport in his own name.

Was originally a Social Democrat. One of Krivitsky's best agents. Has worked in Holland, Germany, Poland, Norway and Sweden. Is probably still in Soviet employ. Speaks very good English and might well be sent to the UK. He was in the USA in 1937 but back in Paris on his way to Moscow in May of that year. At the end of 1937 he was one of the people sent to Marseilles to assassinate Krivitsky when he was leaving France for America. Krivitsky is sure that he did not realise what his mission was in Marseilles as he was devoted to him and would not voluntarily have harmed him. Brusse was an expert in opening safes. He personally designed and constructed a camera to photograph the inside of key-holes. He was a keen mathematician and could usually arrive at the proper combination for opening safes. He always wanted to be sent to the Far East and if still in Soviet employ may well be there. Brusse loved his work and did not work purely for money. A most able agent under a good chief. Krivitsky believes he would like to get out of OGPU service and would work for the British if he was properly approached.

BRUSSE, Nora née JONGERT	4th Dept.	Wife of Hans Brusse. Collaborated with him in all his work. Dutch-born. About the same age as Hans. Good-looking; tall and thin. Speaks good English.
CHATTO-PADHAYA	4th Dept.	Anti-British Indian. Remained in Germany during the Great War. Recruited by Krivitsky for work in India but dismissed when it was found that he was also a German agent.
DAVIDOWICZ, Bernard	OGPU	Pole. Chief of firm of GADA in Amsterdam.
DEMETZ, Hans	4th Dept.	German: age 33–34, born at Breslau. Volkswirt. Recruited in 1925 and is probably still working.

DEUTSCH, Arnold,	OGPU	Codename STEFAN. Austrian. Doctor of science. Arrived in the UK on a genuine passport in his own name in 1933–34. He was still sending important information on naval matters to Moscow in April 1937. Highly successful agent for naval and RAF material. He first came to the United Kingdom with his other chief, Reiff. His wife followed him in 1934 and also worked for the OGPU. She had a child during their stay here. Mrs Deutsch was a radio operator trained in Abramoff's school. Subsequently Deutsch brought his mother-in-law to London. He obtained permission to come to the UK through an influential relative. He had a large circle of acquaintances here, particularly in university circles, and visited various parts of the country. He worked under Anton Schuster, the OGPU legal *rezident* in the Soviet Embassy in London, and subsequently under Mally who complained he was difficult and bumptious. In June 1937 he went abroad to report to Krivitsky that a woman OGPU agent in London had lost her diary and it was feared the whole organisation might be compromised. Krivitsky cannot remember anything about the woman except that her hair was always untidy and she was apt to get very agitated and nervous. If this description fits Edith Tudor-Hart he thought it might be she.
DUNCAN	4th Dept.	A very important 4th Department man. Krivitsky thinks he was in the UK about 1936 or 1937, and seems to connect him with the source of information from the British Embassy in Rome. DUNCAN may be his pseudonym, his surname, his Christian name, or part of either.
DUTT, Rajani Palme	OMS	Employed as informer on the CPGB. He was an agent of Piatnitsky, head of the OMS during his previous residence in Brussels.

303

EHRENLIEB, Abraham	4th Dept.	Naturalised Austrian of Polish origin. Member of firm of Ostwag in Berlin. Later founder of Far Eastern Trading Co. in Tientsin.
EHRENLIEB, Aaron	4th Dept.	Naturalised Austrian of Polish origin. Started work in 4th Department 1921. Founder of Far Eastern Fur Trading Co. in London.
EISENBERG	4th Dept.	Founder of the Paris firm 'Pour l'Importation de Legumes Secs'. Assistant to Klages.
FEWERABEND	OGPU	An OGPU and not a 4th Department agent. Krivitsky has seen but does not actually know him.
FRASER Bros.	OGPU	Newspaper correspondent stationed in Vienna 1932–33.
FRIEND	OGPU	Alias of Brian Goold-Verschoyle.
GALLENI, Hans	OGPU	Greek passport. Representative of GADA in United Kingdom. Agent in charge of Ernest Oldham.
GIBARTI	OGPU	Red haired Hungarian. Journalist. Worked with Willi Munzenburg, 1932–33. Speaks good English and French. May be in the UK, USA or France.
GIPSY	OGPU	Codename of Katherine Harrison.
GLADING, Percy	OGPU	Krivitsky never saw the results from Glading's organisation. They were sent by Mally direct to Moscow. Glading took his orders from Mally, but passed material to him through a third party. Krivitsky thinks Glading must know a great deal about Hardt's organisation. He thinks that Hardt, who was worried at the latter part of his stay here regarding his own position and had become careless, may have allowed Glading to hear or know of his important agent in the Foreign Office. To obtain any information from Glading it would be necessary to approach him on ideological grounds.
GLUCKSMAN, Rubin	4th Dept.	At present in London on a forged Austrian passport. Runs the Far Eastern Fur Trading Co. here.

GOOLD-VERSCHOYLE, Brian alias FRIEND	OGPU	Born in Ireland in 1912, a youth of the public school type, was from an early age a student of Karl Marx. On leaving school he became an electrical engineer and joined the CPGB. He had a brother – Hamilton Neil Goold-Verschoyle – living in Moscow and married to a Russian woman there in the service of the OGPU. Brian became a member of the underground OGPU organisation in London. He was used as an intermediary by Mally to handle King's Foreign Office documents.
GRUSENBERG	OGPU	Alias of Borodin.
GUTMANN	4th Dept.	Hungarian journalist in Paris.
HAMMERSTEIN	4th Dept.	Ex-Commander-in-Chief of the German Army. Both his daughters are 4th Department agents.
HANSEN, Georg	4th Dept.	German. Arrested in London in November 1927 for espionage.
HARDT, Paul	OGPU	Alias of Theodore Mally.
HARRISON, Katherine	OGPU	Aged about 40, was in London in 1936 for a long time and again in 1937. Former wife of Earl Browder. She was used as a courier and messenger by Mally.
HERMANN, Leo	OGPU	Active in OGPU since 1933. Has been *Paris Soir* correspondent in Vienna. He accompanied the French Premier, M. Laval, on his visit to Moscow.
HERTFIELD, John	OGPU	German origin. An artist, he came to the UK some years ago. Had some difficulty at the port but managed to convince the Immigration Officer that he was a genuine artist, as indeed he was. Originally a 4th Department man. Probably identical with the John Hertfield who wrote an article for the February issue of *Inside Germany*. May be connected with George Hollering.
HOCHSTEDT, Samuel	4th Dept.	Mentioned by Krivitsky in connection with Zloczower and The Far Eastern Fur Trading Co.
HÖLLERING, George	? OGPU	A Soviet agent whom Krivitsky believed to have some connection with John Hertfield. He can remember no further details.

HORNER, Arthur   4th Dept.   British. A miners' leader in South Wales. Recruiting agent for the 4th Department in the UK. Some years ago worked in the Profintern in Moscow.

IGNATIEV, Count   OGPU   OGPU *rezident* in Soviet Embassy in Paris in summer of 1937.

IVANOFF   OGPU   Codename of a Russian Orthodox priest recruited by the OGPU in Vienna. Went to a Russian church in France – probably Paris.

IVANOVICH   See KRAL.

JAHNKE, Kurt   4th Dept.   In 1927 during the period of close economic co-operation between Russia and Germany Stresemann did not consider that Kristinski, the Soviet Ambassador in Berlin, had sufficient authority and decided to visit Stalin in Moscow. Secret preparations were made for the journey. Jahnke obtained the information in advance from Niedermeyer, a member of the Prussian Diet, and sent the information to Moscow. As a result the visit did not take place.

KASSVEN   4th Dept.   A Lett who travels on a false Canadian passport and was living in Paris in 1929.

KATZ, Leo   OGPU   Hungarian journalist.

KATZ, Leo or Leib   4th Dept.   Roumanian, born in the Buchovina. Speculant agent. In London for some time in connection with the affairs of the Far Eastern Trading Company.

KING, John Henry   OGPU   British. Clerk in the Foreign Office's cipher department.

KLAGES or KLEGES   4th Dept.   Founder of 4th Department firm in Paris of importation of 'Legumes Secs'. Holds a false US passport.

KRAL alias IVANOVITCH   OGPU / 4th Dept.   Yugoslav, aged 46–49. Speaks good English. Likely agent for the UK.

KREMER, Simon   4th Dept.   4th Department legal *rezident* in Soviet Embassy in London, cover as Secretary to the military attaché.

LEVIT alias TANN   OGPU / 4th Dept.   OGPU legal *rezident* in Soviet Embassy in Constantinople probably under the name of Tann. Sent to USA in 1936 or 1937 to

		obtain an US passport for purpose of going to Poland to do 4th Department work. Son of Wolf Levit.
LEVIT, Wolf	OGPU	German, aged about 64. 4th Dept. Recommended to Soviets by his son Levit. Kept a chemist's shop in Germany till 1933 and married a German woman. Left Germany when Hitler came into power and started a photographic studio in Paris where he worked for the 4th Department. Later he was transferred to London to work for Mally and it was at his studio that material supplied by King was copied.
LIEBERMAN, Katherine	OGPU	See Harrison, Katherine.
MAGIDSOHN	4th Dept.	Latvian Jew, aged 33–34. A lawyer, he has worked for 4th Department since 1930 and is probably still working.
MALLY, Theodore alias HARDT, Paul, alias PETERS	OGPU	Codenamed MANN. Mally was the OGPU *resident* in the UK from January 1936–June 1937. He and his wife came here on Austrian passports in the names of Paul and Lydia Hardt. 'Paul Hardt' posed as the representative of the Amsterdam firm of GADA. Mally was originally a monk. During the Great War he was taken prisoner by the Russians while acting as chaplain to an Austrian regiment. Later he became a communist, and took an active part in the Bolshevik Revolution. Mally was responsible for the activities of Henri Christian Pieck up till 1936 and for the military espionage organisation of Percy Glading. Arnold Deutsch was another of his agents in London and it was Mally who obtained highly important information concerning the Committee of Imperial Defence. Brandes was one of his subordinates, and also the old photographic expert, Wolf Levit. Mally was not a subordinate of Krivitsky, but the two men were personal friends. Under the commission given to him in 1935

Krivitsky had the right to enquire into Mally's organisation and in certain cases to give him orders. Mally's codename was MANN and it was in this name that his instructions and money were sent to him at the Soviet Embassy. Early in 1937 the OGPU received orders from Stalin to arrange the assassination of General Franco. Hardt was instructed by the OGPU chief, Yezhov, to recruit an Englishman for the purpose. He did in fact contact and sent to Spain a young Englishman, a journalist of good family, an idealist and fanatical anti-Nazi. Before the plan matured, Mally himself was recalled to Moscow and disappeared. Hardt left Paris for Moscow on 2 July 1937. Krivitsky did his best to dissuade him. He knew that all Mally's colleagues and collaborators in Moscow had been arrested and regarded Mally's recall as a preliminary to his final liquidation. Hardt himself was worried and uncertain of his position but believed that Yezhov, then head of the OGPU, would give him his support. Mally had been in Moscow in August 1936. He had received the highest praise from Yezhov, who told him that his excellent services had been specially brought to the notice of Stalin. Moreover Mally would be rewarded by a personal interview with Stalin before he left Moscow. This interview never materialised. Krivitsky tried in vain to make Mally realise the atmosphere in Moscow as he had experienced it in May 1937 and told him that no reliance could be placed on Yezhov's previous attitude. It was all in vain. Hardt felt that he had no choice but to return. Some weeks later Krivitsky had a letter from Mally written from a sanatorium in the Caucasus, since when nothing has been heard from him. For a long time Krivitsky believed that

		Mally had been shot and that he was sent to the Caucasus while the OGPU were deciding his fate. But in New York Krivitsky met Serge Bassoff and a remark he let slip in the course of conversation led him to believe that Mally was still alive.
MANN	OGPU	See Mally, Theodore.
MINK, George	4th Dept.	A member of the Max Unschlicht organisation in Copenhagen. Arrested by the Danish police.
MONTGOMERY, Jean	4th Dept.	School teacher. Sister of Earl Browder and worked for Krivitsky in Germany from 1936–1937. Krivitsky considered her careless and feared that she would endanger his organisation there. He therefore transferred her to Switzerland and sent a girl from Switzerland to take her place in Germany. Krivitsky thinks that she has now been recalled to Russia.
MOOS, Margarete Charlotte	OGPU	German Jewess, married to a German Jewish refugee in England. A close friend of Brian Goold-Verschoyle. On this pretext she called on Krivitsky in New York after his publication of Brian Goold-Verschoyle's story in the New York *Saturday Evening Post* on 15 April 1939. She then stated she was shortly returning to the UK. Krivitsky is convinced she is an OGPU agent.
NIKOLSKI	OGPU	Predecessor of Mally as OGPU illegal *rezident* in the United Kingdom. Nikolski was his real name; he was in England under another name posing as a businessman and holding a US passport. He was subsequently sent to Spain to organise an OGPU organisation there.
OLDHAM, Ernest	OGPU	Codenamed ARNO, Oldham was a clerk in Cipher Department of the Foreign Office. He committed suicide October 1933.
'P'	4th Dept.	An American woman whose name sounded like the English equivalent of the French 'paysanne' was used in the UK.

		She can be identified because in the winter of 1936 she stayed at the Hotel Castille, Rue Cambon, Paris.
PARPAROFF or PAPAROFF	4th Dept.	Travels on a Uruguayan passport. Head assistant to Krivitsky in 1937. Was staying at the Carlton Hotel, Amsterdam, in June 1937 at the same time as Kral. Description: black hair, small nose, black eyes, height about 5′8″, slightly built, appearance of Frenchman.
'PERCY'	OGPU	Krivitsky cannot dissociate the name of 'PERCY' with the source of leakage of the CID material.
PIECK, Henri	OGPU 4th Dept.	Dutch, resident in The Hague. He was the OGPU agent who recruited Ernest King and ran him until 1936. Krivitsky does not know whether Pieck is still in the service of the Soviets. He thinks that if Mally is still alive he will certainly have kept in touch with Pieck as the two men were great friends, and Hardt had great confidence in him. Since the arrest of King, however, Mally would in any case allow Pieck to live in penury for some time in order to deceive the British Intelligence Service. It should be borne in mind that Pieck and his wife are friends of Madeleine Werker who may also be living in The Hague.
POPOFF, Ivan	OGPU	Second Secretary of the Soviet Embassy in London. Krivitsky thinks he may be the present OGPU legal *rezident*. The Second Secretary is usually the OGPU representative.
PRITT, Denis KC MP	OGPU	Pritt is one of the chief recruiting agents for Soviet underground organisations in the UK. Krivitsky is quite definite that Pritt will do everything possible to assist the Soviet Union in the event of war with Britain. His personal staff, contacts and activities should be thoroughly investigated. Pritt spent some time in Moscow and worked with Viskinsky

preparing the material for the Zinoviev–Bucharin trial. His mission was to write up the trial in such a way that it would be accepted by Western European countries. This book will keep Pritt bound to the Soviets. Even if at a later stage Pritt should desire to change his views and cease to work for Stalin, he will not be permitted to do so. At present Pritt approves Stalin's methods and writes in the interests of the Soviet without pressure, but should he hesitate he will be made to do what he is told.

PURPIS, Adam	4th Dept.	A Lett, he travels on a Honduras passport.
REIFF	OGPU	The OGPU illegal *rezident* in the UK 1931–1934, during which time Arnold Deutsch was his assistant. Recalled to Moscow to the OGPU's headquarters staff.
SCHOELLER, Louise	4th Dept.	Ex-wife of M.M. Roy, she was a personal friend of Krivitsky and probably therefore a 4th Department agent during the time when she was living with Roy.
SCHUSTER, Anton	OGPU	The OGPU legal *rezident* in the Soviet Embassy in London in 1936 and 1937. Had dealings with Deutsch whom he called by his codename of STEFAN.
SMEDLEY, Agnes	OGPU	British. Worked in Shanghai. 4th Dept.
SMITH	4th Dept.	Austrian origin. An agent of Krivitsky who passed through London on an American passport in the name of Smith in the summer of 1937. He was then returning to Russia on one of the Soviet boats. In 1927–28 Smith worked for the 4th Department in the UK under another name and on a different passport.
SPIEGELGLASS, Anton	OGPU	In 1937 was assistant to the chief of the Foreign Department of the OGPU. He worked for a long time in Paris, the Far East and the USA, but never in the UK.
STEFAN	OGPU	See Deutsch, Arnold.
STUTCHKA	4th Dept.	Used for work in connection with the 4th Department companies – Ostwag, Far Eastern Fur Trading Co. etc. Was in

		Paris during the Spanish war in connection with the export of arms to Spain.
TANN	OGPU	See Levit a.k.a. Tann.
THALER, Dr	OGPU	In about 1930 Thaler was 4th Dept. working in Vienna as an agent of the Reichswehr. He was secretary to Stahlberg, a member of the Schuschnigg Cabinet. He became an agent of the OGPU in 1932 and in 1934 he went to Germany and worked in Vorsching's department. Although he was an OGPU agent he worked also on behalf of the 4th Department. Good agents for Germany were scarce at this time and THALER did good work for the 4th Department.
URBAN	4th Dept.	A man of this name was active 4th Department agent in the UK.
VALENTINE	4th Dept.	Codename of Krivitsky.
VALOVITCH alias YANOVITCH	OGPU	Deputy Chief of the Operod of the GUGB. Attached to the Soviet Embassy in Paris at the time when Oldham offered his services to the Soviets.
WEISSBLATT	OGPU 4th Dept.	Used by the 4th Department as a speculant agent in connection with the obtaining of export licences for arms for Spain.
WERKER, Madeleine	4th Dept.	Dutch. Private secretary to Krivitsky until 1937 and worked for him in Holland and France and on one or two occasions he sent her to England with money. Comes of a good family who live at 12 Prince Maurice Place, The Hague. Krivitsky thinks her sister is married to Prof. Snellen at The Hague, and if so, she may still be working for the 4th Department. Her associates may repay investigation. She was a friend of the Hardts, the Piecks and the Levits. Aged about 56, a tall blonde, blue eyes, well educated, speaks English, German and French.
YANOVITCH	OGPU	See VALOVITCH.
ZLOCZOWER	4th Dept.	Speculant agent. At one time head of 4th Department firm of Ostwag in Berlin. Then in London in connections with the Far Eastern Fur Trading Co.

Appendix 4

SOVIET ILLEGALS IN LONDON

Name	Alias	Codename	Period of Operation
Reiff, Ignaty	Wolisch, Max	MARR	1931–1934
Deutsch, Dr Arnold		STEFAN	1934–1935
Orlov, Alexander	Nicolski	SCHWED	1934–1935
Harris, Kitty	Suschitzky	GYPSY	1935–1939
Brandes, Willy	Stevens		1935–1937
Bystrolyotov, Dmitri	Galleni, Hans	HANS	1930–1933
Pieck, Henri		COOPER	1935–1937
Mally, Theodore	Hardt, Paul Dr Peters	MANN	1936–1937
Rado, Alexander			1938
Sorge, Richard			1929
Trepper, Leopold	Mikler, Adam		1937–1938
Tudor Hart, Edith		EDITH STRELA	

SOVIET INTELLIGENCE ORGANISATIONS

Cheka	1917–1922
GPU	1922–1923
OGPU	1923–1934
NKVD	1934–1941
NKGB	1941–1946
MGB	1946–1954
KGB	1954–1999

NOTES

CHAPTER 1

1 US House of Representatives, Committee on Un-American Activities, *The Shameful Years: Thirty Years of Soviet Espionage in the United States*, 30 December 1951, pp. 6–7, 9, 20, 26.

2 The Denniston memorandum, *The Government Code and Cypher School Between the Wars*, 2 December 1944, reproduced in *Intelligence and National Security*, Vol. 1, No. 1, pp. 48–70.

3 The MI5 investigation of the Federated Press of America is contained in KV2/1099-101. See also Rose Cohen KV2/1395-7.

CHAPTER 7

1 Doschenko's MI5 file (KV-2/834) reveals his deportation was dealt with in the Home Office by Jenifer Williams, herself an underground member of the CPGB. Later, as Jenifer Hart, she wrote *Ask Me No More* (Peter Halban, 1998).

CHAPTER 8

1 See William Deakin's account in *The Case of Richard Sorge*, p. 50.

2 Sorge's unknown spy was believed to have been C.H. (Dick) Ellis, an SIS officer who later admitted having sold secrets to the Nazis.

CONCLUSION

1 ISCOT has been described by John Croft in Reminiscences of GCHQ and GCB 1942–45, *Intelligence and National Security*, Vol. 13. No. 4, pp. 133–143.

2 See *My Silent War*, p. 130.

3 During the four years Arthur Ewart was in China he is alleged to have befriended Roger Hollis who, in 1938, was recruited into the Security Service and became MI5's expert on the CPGB.

4 In 1955 HCUA testimony, Mildred Blauvelt, an NYPD undercover member of the CPUSA, identified Baron as speaking to the 9th Assembly District Club (a known Communist front) twice in May 1943, the second time following Earl Browder by two days and adhering closely to his line. Baron also gave evidence to the Martin Dies Committee.

BIBLIOGRAPHY

Primary sources
The full MASK decrypts are available in the National Archive, Kew, in the HW17 series of declassified GCHQ files. The individual files, numbered from 1 to 37, are in the alphabetical order of the countries intercepted, and consist of:

1–2	Austria
3	China
4–8	Prague
9–11	Copenhagen
12–18	Paris
19–22	London
23–24	United States

HW17/38 consists of correspondence from Commander Alistair Denniston with the Air Ministry intercept station at RAF Waddington.

The Security Service personal files on suspected Soviet spies in the CPGB are to be found in the KV2 series, with the following piece numbers: Tom Bell 1537–9; Reg Bishop 1599–1602; Willy Brandes 1004–7; John Campbell 1186–9; Enest Cant 1051–3; Jack Cohen 1059–61; Rose Cohen 1395–7; Walter Dale 997–9; Patrick Devine 1573–4; William Ewer 1016; Allan Foote 1611–16; Percy Glading 1020–3; George Hardy 1017; Paul Hardt 1008–9; Alice Holland 589–590; Walter Holmes 1000–2; Albert Inkpen 1532–7; Peter Kerrigan 1030–2; Nicolas Klishco 1411–6; Robert Koling 806; Richard Krebs 1102–4; Arthur Laker 989; Tom Mercer 1024; Sean Murray 1185; David Petrovsky 1433; Henri Pieck 1388; Denis Pritt 1062–5; Eve Reckitt 1369–75; Robert Robson 1176–9; Fred Rose 1015; Andrew Rothstein 1575–84; Bill Rust 1048–50; Christian Schneider 1406; Douglas Springhall 1594–8; Bob Stewart 1180–3; Alexander Tudor Hart 1603–4; Edith Tudor Hart 1012–4; Wilfred Vernon 992–6; Charles Whomack 1136–8; Albert Williams 1003.

Secondary sources
Agabekov, G., *OGPU: The Secret Russian Terror*, New York: Brentano's, 1931.
Banac, Ivo, *The Diary of Georgi Dmitrov*, New Haven, CT: Yale University Press, 2003.
Braun, Otto, *A Comintern Agent in China 1932–1939*, Stanford, CA: Stanford University Press, 1982.

Belloten, Burnett, *The Spanish Civil War*, Chapel Hill, NC: University of North Carolina Press, 1991.

Braunthal, Julius, *History of the International 1914–1943*, Westport, CT: Frederick Praeger, 1967.

Brook-Shepherd, Gordon, *The Storm Petrels*, William Collins, 1977.

Carr, E.H., *Twilight of the Comintern*, New York: Pantheon, 1982.

—— *The Comintern and the Spanish Civil War*, New York: Pantheon, 1984.

Chase, William, *Enemies Within the Gates*, New Haven, CT: Yale University Press, 2001.

Clark, Ronald, *J.B.S. The Life and Work of J.B.S. Haldane*, Quality Book Club, 1968.

Costello, John, and Oleg Trasev, *Deadly Illusions*, Century, 1993.

Dallin, Alexander, and F.I. Firsov, *Dmitrov & Stalin*, New Haven, CT: Yale University Press, 2000.

Dallin, David, *Soviet Espionage*, Oxford: Oxford University Press, 1955.

Damaskin, Igor, *Kitty Harris: The Spy with Seventeen Names*, St Ermin's Press, 2001.

Deakin, F.W., and G R. Storry, *The Case of Richard Sorge*, London: Chatto & Windus, 1956.

Drachovitch, Milorad, *The Comintern – Historical Highlights*, Hoover Institution, 1966.

Duff, William, *A Time for Spies*, Vanderbilt University Press, 1999.

Foote, Alexander, *Handbook for Spies*, London: Museum Press, 1949.

Footman, David, *International Communism*, London: Chatto & Windus, 1960.

Gannon, Francis, *Biographical Dictionary of the Left*, Western Islands Press, 1969.

Haldane, Charlotte, *Truth Will Out*, Vanguard Press, 1950.

Hallas, Duncan, *The Comintern*, Bookmarks, 1985.

Hart, Jenifer, *Ask Me No More*, London: Peter Halban, 1998

Hulse, James Warren, *The Forming of the Communist International*, Stanford, CA: Stanford University Press, 1964.

Hyde, Douglas, *I Believed*, London: William Heinemann, 1950.

Kern, Gary, *A Death in Washington*, New York: Enigma, 2003.

Krivitsky, Walter, *I Was Stalin's Agent*, Right Book Club, 1940.

Luzikh, Branko, *Lenin and the Comintern*, Hoover Institution, 1972.

—— *Biographical Dictionary of the Comintern*, Hoover Institution, 1986.

McDermott, Kevin, and Jeremy Agnew, *The Comintern*, London: St Martin's Press, 1997.

McMeekin, Sean, *The Red Millionaire*, New Haven, CT: Yale University Press, 2003.

Masters, Anthony, *The Man Who Was M*, London: Basil Blackwell, 1984.

Morais, Fernando, Olga: *The Gift to Hitler*, London: Peter Halban, 1990.

Nollau, Gunther, *International Communism and World Revolution*, Hollis & Carter, 1961.

Orlov, Alexander, *The Secret History of Stalin's Crimes*, Random House, 1953.

Perrault, Gilles, *A Man Apart*, London: Zed Books, 1987.

Philby, Kim, *My Silent War*, London: McGibbon & Kee, 1968.

Poretsky, Elisabeth, *Our Own People*, Oxford: Oxford University Press, 1969.

Pratt, Don, *The Rote Kapelle*, University Publications of America, 1979.

Rado, Sandor, *Codename Dora*, Abelard, 1977.

Romerstein, Herbert, *Heroic Victims*, Council for the Defence of Freedom, 1994.

Romerstein, Herbert, and Eric Breindel, *The Venona Secrets*, Regnery, 2000.

Scott, Michael, *A Time To Speak*, London: Faber & Faber, 1958.

Swerakowski, Witold, *The Communist Internationaland its Front Organisations*, Hoover Institution, 1965.

Valtin, Jan, *Out of the Night*, Alliance Book Corporation, 1941.

Willoughby, Charles, *Shanghai Conspiracy*, E.P. Dutton, 1952.

Wright, Peter, *Spycatcher*, Australia Heinemann, 1987.

INDEX